GLOBE FEARON
LITERATURE

■ *Gold Level* ■

Upper Saddle River, New Jersey
www.globefearon.com

PROGRAM REVIEWERS

Kathy Babigian, Coordinator, Tioga Literacy Center, Fresno, California

Pat Bartholomew, M.A., Reading Specialist, Milton, Ohio

Jennifer Dilks-Mundt, English Teacher, Brant Rock, Massachusetts

Ann Fitzgerald, M.A., Education Director, Southshire Community School, North Bennington, Vermont

Pat Miller, M.A., Reading/English/Language Arts Supervisor, Prince Georges County Public Schools, Maryland

Artie P. Norton, English Teacher, Suffern, New York

Timothy Rasinski, Professor of Curriculum and Instruction, Kent State University, Kent, Ohio

Cynthia Saska, M.A., Professor of English, University of Texas, San Antonio, Texas

Margaret-Mary Sulentic, Ph.D., Assistant Professor of Literacy, Department of Curriculum and Instruction, University of Southern Mississippi, Hattiesburg, Mississippi

Dr. Helen W. Taylor, Director of Programs K-12 Curriculum and Instruction, Portsmouth City Public Schools, Virginia

CONSULTANTS

Dr. Virginia Bryg; Josephine Gemake, Ph.D.; Alfred Schifini, Ph.D.; Deborah Walker; Robert Wandberg, Ph.D.

Supervising Editor/Team Leader: Karen McCollum
Editors: Ayanna Taylor, Amy Greenberg, Theresa McCarthy
Editorial Developer: Pearson Education Development Group
Marketing Assistant: Kate Krimsky
Production Editor: Travis Bailey
Associate Production Editors: Amy Benefiel, Alia Lesser
Senior Designer: Angel Weyant
Manufacturing Buyer: Mark Cirillo
Cover and Interior Design/Production: Pearson Education Development Group
Photo Research: Pearson Education Development Group

ABOUT THE COVER

Fireworks and Illuminations at his grace the Duke of Richmond's at Whitehall on the River Thames, 1749 by English School. Private Collection/Bridgeman Art Library. The artist of this painting is anonymous; English School refers to any artist from England who remains unknown. The painting depicts a fireworks display held in 1749 in the Privy Garden of the Second Duke of Richmond's mansion in Whitehall. The display marks the 1748 treaty which ended the war over the Austrian Succession. What does this painting tell you about British society in the 1700s?

ISBN 0-130-23585-7

Printed in the United States of America
1 2 3 4 5 6 7 8 9 10   04 03 02 01 00

Globe Fearon

1-800-848-9500
www.globefearon.com

Preview

HOW TO USE THIS BOOK

UNIT 1 *Early Voices in British Literature*

UNIT 2 Writers of the English Renaissance

Writing • Vocabulary • Grammar, Usage, and Mechanics
Speaking and Listening • Critical Thinking • Effective Studying
• Test Preparation

UNIT 3 *The Rise of the Romantics*

UNIT 4 Expressions of the Victorian Era

UNIT 5 *The Modern View*

Writing • Vocabulary • Grammar, Usage, and Mechanics
Speaking and Listening • Critical Thinking • Effective Studying
• Test Preparation

UNIT 6 *The Contemporary Perspective*

References

HOW TO USE THIS BOOK ▬▬▬

Welcome to *Globe Fearon Literature*. As you read this textbook, you will learn about many new worlds. By reading literature you can experience the past and the future, and you can learn about people—how they feel and how they think.

To get the most out of this book, you will need to become an active reader. Active readers think about reading materials before they begin, during, and after they read.

TIPS FOR IMPROVING YOUR READING

Before You Read

- Think about the title of the selection. What does it tell you about the topic? What do you already know about the topic?
- Determine the genre of the selection. For example—if the selection is a poem, ask yourself, "How will this be different from reading an essay or short story?"
- Set a purpose for reading. What do you think you will learn by reading this selection?

As You Read

- Predict what you think will happen next. Then pause occasionally and ask yourself if your predictions were correct.
- Form questions about what you are reading. For example, ask yourself, "What idea is the author trying to convey?"
- When you encounter a word you are unfamiliar with, use the help that Globe Fearon Literature gives you. Difficult words are defined at the bottom of the page they appear on.

After You Read

Consider the following questions:

- Did the selection end the way you anticipated?
- What did you learn from reading this selection?
- How does this selection relate to others you have read?

THE BOOK IS ORGANIZED TO HELP YOU

Your literature book has been organized into units. Each unit is introduced with a piece of fine art and a quote. Look at these pages. What do you think this unit will be about?

The next two pages of the unit give you a preview of what to expect. These two pages will help you set the stage for reading and understanding the selections. You may want to refer back to these pages as you read through the unit.

The "Focus On" feature gives you some tips to help you understand specific genres of literature, such as fiction or poetry. You will notice that each Model selection has blue notes in the margin. These are study hints to help you read actively. The notes relate back to the "Focus On" feature. The notes will help you identify key elements of the genre. Later, you can look for similar elements in other selections as you read independently.

Before each selection, you will be introduced to a reading skill, a literary skill, and a writing activity. The reading skill will help you understand what you are reading. The literary skill will call your attention to elements of literature. The writing activity will help you relate the literature to your own life.

There are review questions at the end of each selection. These questions help you think about what you have just read. They will also help you relate this selection to others that you may have read.

Globe Fearon Literature was created for you. Reading literature can be one of the most rewarding experiences you can ever have. There are new worlds to explore and exciting people to meet. It's all here. So, let's begin. . .

Early Voices in British Literature

Light was first
Through the Lord's word
Named day:
Beauteous, bright creation!
—Caedmon

April: Engagement Scene, Très Riches Heures du Duc de Berry, Anonymous.
Muśee Condé, Chantilly. Giraudon/Art Resource

658–680 Caedmon's "Hymn," the oldest preserved English poem, is written.

750 Surviving version of *Beowulf* is composed.

890 *Anglo-Saxon Chronicles,* a record of current events, begin.

500	550	600	650	700	750	800	850	900	950	1000	1050

597 St. Augustine converts Anglo-Saxons to Christianity.

1034 Duncan I inherits Scottish throne.

1040 Macbeth murders Duncan I.

Early Voices in British Literature

Do you enjoy reading about King Arthur and his Knights of the Round Table or Robin Hood? These tales are classics of British literature that have been handed down from generation to generation in the form of poetry, ballads, and stories. Isn't it surprising that the time in which they originated is known as the Dark Ages of British history?

■ LIFE IN EARLY BRITAIN: WAR AND CONQUEST

For the first 700 years of its recorded history, the island of Britain was a virtual battlefield. Led by war chiefs, small bands of fighters struggled to establish their authority, only to be defeated in turn by other warriors. In 500 B.C., a people called the Celts occupied the whole of Britain. Over 400 years later, in 55 B.C., the Romans invaded the island and drove the Celts to the west and the north. During their long occupation, the Romans built roads, walls, towns, and forts. Some still exist today.

When their empire fell, the Romans left Britain, and the Celts took over again—but not for long. Around 500 A.D., seafaring Germanic tribes called Angles and Saxons invaded and defeated Celtic war chiefs, including the famous King Arthur. They organized the country, by now called AngleLand, into seven powerful kingdoms. From 800 to 900 A.D., the seven kingdoms turned back ferocious Viking raiders from Denmark.

In 1066, French warriors called Normans crossed the English Channel and defeated the Anglo-Saxons at the Battle of Hastings. They seized Anglo-Saxon lands and property, including the holdings of Robert Fitz Ooth, who may have been the person commonly known as Robin Hood. The Norman invasion united England under one king and led to the establishment of Parliament, a democratic assembly.

■ EARLY LITERATURE: POETRY

Do you like to listen to people tell stories? The ancient Britons did. The Celts had a special class of poets, called bards, who composed and

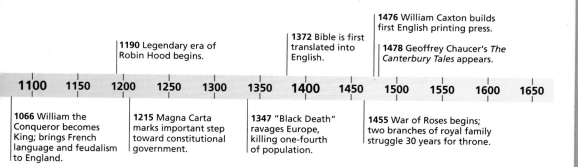

1190 Legendary era of Robin Hood begins.

1372 Bible is first translated into English.

1476 William Caxton builds first English printing press.

1478 Geoffrey Chaucer's *The Canterbury Tales* appears.

| 1100 | 1150 | 1200 | 1250 | 1300 | 1350 | 1400 | 1450 | 1500 | 1550 | 1600 | 1650 |

1066 William the Conqueror becomes King; brings French language and feudalism to England.

1215 Magna Carta marks important step toward constitutional government.

1347 "Black Death" ravages Europe, killing one-fourth of population.

1455 War of Roses begins; two branches of royal family struggle 30 years for throne.

recited verses about the tribe. The poems were not written down, so the bards became living libraries of knowledge. The bards were trained by Druids, Celtic priests who worshipped nature.

The Anglo-Saxons liked poetry, too. They composed and sang narrative verses or poems called **epics.** Epics told about the gallant deeds of their folk heroes. The greatest of all Anglo-Saxon epics was *Beowulf.*

■ KNIGHTS, PRINCESSES, AND COMMONERS

British literature changed after the Norman invasion. Do you prefer tales of adventure or love stories? The Normans combined both in their romances, which tell of the adventures of knights as they try to earn their ladies' love. The stories celebrate chivalry, the knight's code of moral conduct. But, knights and princesses were not the only subjects for literature. In ballads and stories like *The Canterbury Tales*, writers began to explore the everyday lives of common people.

■ ONE LAND, ONE LANGUAGE

The selections you will read in this unit are translations, as though they had been written in a foreign language. That is because before the fifteenth century, the English language was a confusing mixture of words and dialects. Anglo-Saxons spoke Old English, a Germanic language. The Norman nobility spoke and wrote in Norman French, but the common people of each region of Norman England had a different way of representing the word sounds of the language now known as Middle English. It was not until 1476, when the printing press was introduced in England, that rules for spelling and pronunciation became standardized, leading to the development of modern English.

As you read the selections in this unit, think about what life must have been like in England long ago.

CHARACTER

Characters are the representations in words of people and animals. In early British literature, characters can also be monsters or kind-hearted wizards.

Sometimes a writer will tell you precisely what a particular character is like, and how it looks. More often, however, the writer will give you hints that you must first detect, then evaluate.

Imagine, for example, that you are trying to decide if your best friend is a loyal person. You listen to your friend and observe his or her actions. By doing these things you get clues. By evaluating the clues, you can determine whether or not your friend is loyal.

Good writers constantly ask you to make these kinds of decisions about the imaginary characters they create.

As you read "Grendel," ask yourself:
1. What kind of creature is Grendel?
2. What actions, thoughts, or events, help you determine his character?

WRITING CONNECTION

Write a paragraph that explains how a hero or villain usually acts. Include specific character traits that determine his or her behavior.

READING FOCUS

Recognize Sensory Details Authors use figurative language to create images that appeal to the senses—sight, touch, smell, hearing, taste. As you read, watch for sensory details and note your reaction to them.

GRENDEL
from
BEOWULF

ADAPTED   **translated by Burton Raffel**

Plot Summary

One of the oldest written poems in English literature, Beowulf is a classic story of good winning over evil. When Beowulf hears of Grendel's attacks on Hrothgar's hall, Beowulf goes to help. He fights Grendel barehanded and wounds the monster badly. Grendel crawls back to his swamp to die. Grendel's mother then comes seeking revenge against Beowulf. Beowulf goes under water to fight her.

Beowulf wins again and eventually becomes king. He rules well for many years until someone disturbs the local dragon. Although Beowulf is old now, he feels he must fight the dragon himself. He triumphs but is badly wounded. The story ends with Beowulf being given a hero's burial. Beowulf is buried with all the treasures he has earned from his victories.

     A powerful monster, living down
In the darkness, growled in pain, impatient
As day after day the music rang
Loud in that hall. The harp's rejoicing
5   Call and the poet's clear songs, sung
Of the ancient beginnings of us all, recalling:
The Almighty making the earth, shaping
These beautiful plains marked off by oceans,
Then proudly setting the sun and moon
10 To glow across the land and light it.
The corners of the earth were made lovely with trees
And leaves made quick with life with each
Of the nations who now move on its face. And then,
As now, warriors sang of their pleasure.

15   So Hrothgar¹ and his men lived happy in his hall
Till the monster stirred. That demon, that fiend,
Grendel, who haunted the moors, the wild
Marshes, and made his home in a hell,
Not hell but earth. He was spawned in that slime.
20   Conceived by a pair of those monsters born
Of Cain². Murderous creatures banished
By God, punished forever for the crime
Of Abel's death. The Almighty drove
Those demons out, and their exile was bitter,
25   Shut away from men; they split
Into a thousand forms of evil—spirits
And fiends, goblins, monsters, giants,
A brood forever opposing the Lord's
Will, and again and again defeated

30   Then, when darkness had dropped, Grendel
Went up to Herot³, wondering what the warriors
Would do in that hall when their drinking was done.
He found them sprawled in sleep, suspecting
Nothing, their dreams undisturbed. The monster's
35   Thoughts were as quick as his greed or his claws:
He slipped through the door and there in the silence
Snatched up thirty men, smashed them
Unknowing in their beds and ran out with their bodies,
The blood dripping behind him, back
40   To his lair, delighted with his night's slaughter.

       At daybreak, with the sun's first light, they saw
How well he had worked, and in that gray morning
Broke their long feast with tears and laments
For the dead. Hrothgar, their lord, sat joyless
45   In Herot, a mighty prince mourning

---

moors (MOORZ) an area of open, rolling wasteland
spawned (SPAWND) born or produced
¹**Hrothgar:** King of the Danes
²**Cain:** the son of Adam and Eve. In the Bible story (Genesis 4), Cain killed Abel,
  his brother, and was cursed by God.
brood (BROOD) a group of a particular kind of people
³**Herot:** a great hall where the King and his warriors lived

The Dragon for the High Kings, George Sharp

The fate of his lost friends and companions,
Knowing by its tracks that some demon had torn
His followers apart. He wept, fearing
The beginning might not be the end. And that night
50　Grendel came again, so set
On murder that no crime could ever be enough,
No savage assault quenched his lust
For evil. Then each warrior tried
To escape him, searched for rest in different
55　Beds, as far from Herot as they could find,

Seeing how Grendel hunted when they slept.
Distance was safety; the only survivors
Were those who fled him. Hate had triumphed.

So Grendel ruled, fought with the righteous,
60 One against many, and won; so Herot
Stood empty, and stayed deserted for years,
Twelve winters of grief for Hrothgar, king
Of the Danes, sorrow heaped at his door
By hell-forged hands. His misery leaped
65 The seas, was told and sung in all
Men's ears: how Grendel's hatred began,
How the monster relished his savage war
On the Danes, keeping the bloody feud
Alive, seeking no peace, offering
70 No truce, accepting no settlement, no price
In gold or land, and paying the living
For one crime only with another. No one
Waited for reparation from his plundering claws:
That shadow of death hunted in the darkness,
75 Stalked Hrothgar's warriors, old
And young, lying in waiting, hidden
In mist, invisibly following them from the edge
Of the marsh, always there, unseen.

So mankind's enemy continued his crimes,
80 Killing as often as he could, coming
Alone, bloodthirsty and horrible. Though he lived
In Herot, when the night hid him, he never
Dared to touch king Hrothgar's glorious
Throne, protected by God—God,
85 Whose love Grendel could not know. But Hrothgar's
Heart was bent. The best and most noble
Of his council debated remedies, sat
In secret sessions, talking of terror
And wondering what the gravest of warriors could do.
90 And sometimes they sacrificed to the old stone gods,
Made heathen vows, hoping for Hell's
Support, the Devil's guidance in driving

Their affliction off. That was their way,
And the heathen's only hope, Hell

95 Always in their hearts, knowing neither God
Nor His passing as He walks through our world, the Lord
Of Heaven and earth; their ears could not hear
His praise nor know His glory. Let them
Beware, those who are thrust into danger,

100 Clutched at by trouble, yet can carry no solace
In their hearts, cannot hope to be better! Hail
To those who will rise to God, drop off
Their dead bodies and seek our Father's peace!

So the living sorrow of Healfdane's son

105 Simmered, bitter and fresh, and no wisdom
Or strength could break it: that agony hung
On king and people alike, harsh
And unending, violent and cruel, and evil.

In his far-off home Beowulf, Higlac's[4]

110 Follower and the strongest of the Geats—greater
And stronger than anyone anywhere in this world—
Heard how Grendel filled nights with horror
And quickly commanded a boat fitted out,
Proclaiming that he'd go to that famous king,

115 Would sail across the sea to Hrothgar,
Now when help was needed. None
Of the wise ones regretted his going, much
As he was loved by the Geats: the omens were good,
And they urged the adventure on. So Beowulf

120 Chose the mightiest men he could find,
The bravest and best of the Geats, fourteen
In all, and led them down to their boat;
He knew the sea, would point the prow
Straight to that distant Danish shore.

---

affliction (uh FLIK shun) something that causes great pain or distress
heathen (HEE *th*un) a person who didn't worship the God of the Bible
prow (PROU) the forward part of a ship or boat; bow
4Higlac: king of the Geats, a people who lived in southern Sweden

Review the Selection

UNDERSTAND THE SELECTION

Recall

1. How is Grendel described?

2. After two nights of Grendel's assaults, what do Hrothgar's warriors do to escape from him?

3. When Beowulf goes off to do battle with Grendel, he takes the bravest and the best men of his land with him. How many does he take?

Infer

4. Why do the Danes conclude that the murderer is not a man?

5. Who is Healfdane?

6. What does "His misery leaped the seas, was told and sung in all men's ears" mean?

7. Who is "mankind's enemy," referred to in line 79?

Apply

8. Retell the story in your own words.

9. What religious conflict can you identify from the narrator's tone?

10. What idea or concept do you think that Grendel symbolizes?

Respond to Literature

How is Grendel typical of other monsters you have read about or have seen in movies? How is he different?

WRITE ABOUT THE SELECTION

Throughout this section of *Beowulf,* Grendel has demonstrated his vicious temper and extraordinary strength. No human being seems competent to defeat the monster. The section concludes, however, with Beowulf's decision to battle Grendel. Can you visualize Beowulf as an ancient superhero? Write an episode that depicts the first encounter between Beowulf and Grendel.

Prewriting   Think about the character traits of both Grendel and Beowulf. Ask yourself: How does each prefer to settle disputes? How would they confront each other? Would they fight or talk? Would they be evenly matched in a battle? Freewrite your responses.

Writing   Use your freewriting to describe the first encounter between Beowulf and Grendel. In it, use sensory words to describe the most likely outcome of this meeting.

Revising   When you revise your episode, make sure that the characters' actions and dialogue reflect what they would really say and do. Ask yourself whether an audience would find your episode exciting and believable.

Proofreading   When you proofread, check to see that quotation marks surround any dialogue you have written. Be sure that your commas, periods, question marks, and exclamation points are enclosed within the quotation marks.

THINK ABOUT CHARACTER

A character's personality is composed of permanent qualities, or traits. A character's emotions, however, are not permanent. They are temporary feelings about, and responses to, a specific event or situation. Emotions often influence or motivate a character's behavior, but they cannot alter his or her personality. For example, a courageous warrior may feel nervous about an upcoming battle. His inner bravery, which is part of his personality, allows him to conquer these temporary feelings of fear or anxiety.

1. What does Grendel think about the Danes?

2. Which of Grendel's actions tell you this?

3. Although the narrator doesn't give a complete description of Grendel, the monster is still very believable. Describe briefly what you think Grendel looks like.

4. What kind of a character is Beowulf?

READING FOCUS

Recognize Sensory Details   As you read "Grendel" from *Beowulf,* you were able to recognize examples of figurative language. List three images that you found especially vivid or compelling. Explain your choices.

DEVELOP YOUR VOCABULARY

Figurative language is language used in a colorful, original way to communicate an idea or feeling. Words used in this way convey a meaning that is different from what you might expect. For example, in the sentence "Henry's face was a *picture of unhappiness,*" Henry's face isn't really a picture. The use of figurative language creates a more vivid impression of Henry's face than would the simple sentence "Henry looked sad."

Look at the following sentences and explain the actual meaning of the italicized figurative language.

1. The hero's *eyes flashed fire* when he heard news of the attack.

2. *Dead tired,* the wounded dragon limped back to his cave.

3. The lone warrior *felt his courage evaporate* at the sight of the approaching army.

4. He had *pinned his hopes* of marrying the princess on his triumph over her enemy's army.

5. The arrows *whistled through the air* toward the enemy.

Learn About

Pilgrims, illustration for Chaucer's *Canterbury Tales.*
Art Resource

READING FOCUS

Identify Figures of Speech   Figurative language uses words in unexpected ways to increase their effect. **Personification** explains a nonhuman object or idea in human terms. **Hyperbole** is an exaggeration used for effect. As you read the story, use your note taking skills to list the figures of speech you identify.   Think about the ways that ~~ese~~ figures of speech increase your ~~'ing~~ enjoyment.

THEME

The **theme** of a work of literature is the central meaning or message that the author of the work tries to communicate to the reader. Theme is the meaning of the work as a whole, not simply an insight about a particular character or event.

Sometimes an author will choose to state a theme directly. Generally, though, the reader must determine the theme on his or her own. To figure out the theme of a literary work, ask yourself: What are the goals of the main character? How does he or she try to achieve them? How does he or she react to important events and other characters in the work? What is the eventual outcome of the character's efforts?

Sometimes, more than one character is responsible for getting across the author's theme. Sometimes, too, the author has more than one theme to get across.

While reading "The Pardoner's Tale," ask yourself:
1. What significant actions do the characters perform?
2. What theme, or meaning, can you determine from these actions?

WRITING CONNECTION

Write a brief paragraph explaining the theme of a magazine article that you have read.

on ▌11

The Pardoner's Tale
from The Canterbury Tales

ADAPTED

by Geoffrey Chaucer

In Flanders[1] once there was a company
Of young folk that were bent on chasing folly;
They danced and played at dice both day and night,
And also ate and drank beyond their might.

5   These rioters three, of whom I will now tell,
Long before the sound of morning bell,
Were sitting in a tavern, talking, drinking,
Till too much drink began to cloud their thinking:
"Let each of us now pledge to both the others

10   That we three are—hic, hic—the best of brothers!"
Then up they jumped and hastened from the village,
Intent on riot, merriment, or pillage.

When they had gone not fully half a mile,
Just as they were about to climb a stile,

15   Among some trees, there lying on the ground,
A mighty heap of golden coins they found.
The pile was huge—bushels, as they thought;
They'd have to haul it off, and not get caught.
Oh, each of them was so glad at the sight

20   Because the florins were so large and bright!
They sat down then beside this precious hoard;
The worst of them, he uttered the first word.

---

rioters (RY ut urz) people who lead a noisy, uncontrolled life
pillage (PIL ij) robbery by force
stile (STYL) one or more steps used to climb over a fence
florin (FLAWR in) any of certain gold or silver coins used in a number of European countries
[1]**Flanders:** a medieval country in northwestern Europe that included a part of France and Belgium

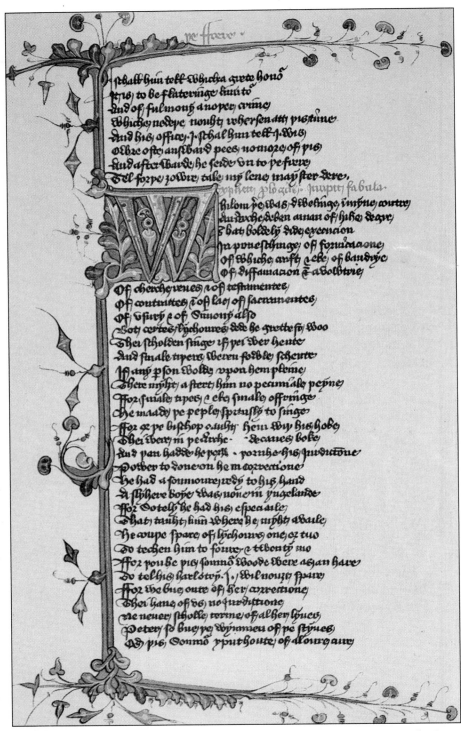

A page from the Lansdowne ms. of Geoffrey Chaucer's *Canterbury Tales*. The Granger Collection

"Brothers," he said, "now hear well what I say;
My mind is clear, although I joke and play.
25 Fortune's given us this precious treasure
So that we may live out our lives in pleasure.
We've got to carry all this gold away,
But surely, it cannot be done by day.

This treasure must be carried off by night,
30 As wisely and as slyly as we might.
Therefore, I think that right now we should all
Draw lots, to see to whom the lot will fall
To run to town, and bring us bread and wine,
So that, before our labor, we may dine.
35 And two of us will keep close watch right here
In case some other rascals might appear."
Then they drew straws, to see whose lot would fall,
And it fell upon the youngest of them all
To make the quick trip back and forth to town.
40 The other two shook hands and sat back down.

Then one of them spoke thus unto the other:
"You know my friend, that you're my best-loved brother.
Let's talk about this gold, just me and you:
Why can't these coins be split between us two?"
45 The other answered, "Fine! Two now, not three!
But I know not just how that's going to be.
He knows the gold is right here with us two.
What shall we say to him? What shall we do?"
"It won't be hard at all," the other said.
50 "We'll stab him through both sides and leave him dead.
And then shall all the gold divided be,
My dearest friend, between yourself and me."

The youngest then, the one who went to town,
Let evil fancies pull him down and down.
55 The beauty of those florins, new and bright!
There had to be a way—some plan that might
Win *all* the gold for him that very night!
And soon it was his very clear intention

---

fancies (FAN seez) ideas; notions; thoughts

To carry out a plan I hate to mention.
60 He hurried on—no longer would he tarry—
And once in town found an apothecary
And asked the man for poison. "To kill rats,"
He said, "and, in my poultry yard, polecats
That raid my chicken coop most every night.
65 I want to kill the vermin, if I might."

"What I have here," said the apothecary,
"Is something that is strong and very scary.
To tell the truth, there is no living creature
It will not kill. And, another feature,
70 A piece no bigger than a grain of wheat
Is all that poor, doomed creature has to eat."
Taking the poison, away the rascal ran
Into the next street, where he met a man
Who sold him three small jugs of rosy wine.
75 Alone again, he marked one jug: "That's mine!
I'll put the poison in the other two;
Then I'll return, and see what it will do!"

Why need this sermon go on any more?
For as the two had planned so well before,
80 Just so they killed him, just like that.
And then, upon the bloody ground they sat.
One said, "Let's have a drink, and make us merry,
And afterward we will his body bury."
And with those words, it happened that he took
85 A bottle with the poison. Then with a look
Of joy he drank, and passed to his good friend
The jug. Mercy! Horrors! What an end!

Thus both were poisoned for their homicide,
And thus the fiendish poisoner also died.

---

apothecary (uh POTH uh ker ee) a person who prepares and sells drugs and medicines
polecat (POHL kat) a European animal somewhat like a weasel
vermin (VUR mun) various small animals that cause harm or destruction
fiendish (FEEN dish) inhumanly wicked or cruel

Geoffrey Chaucer (1340?–1400)

Geoffrey Chaucer, often called "the father of British poetry," was born in London, the son of a successful wine merchant. At about the age of 17, he became a page in a royal household. His talents were recognized at once, and he went on to spend his entire working life in government service. He served as a soldier, as a squire, and as a diplomat to France and Italy. He held such posts as royal forester and clerk to King Richard II.

In Chaucer's time, long before the invention of the printing press, there was no career called *author* or *writer*. For Chaucer, writing was a hobby. He worked hard at it, and several of his works survive. The best known is the great classic *The Canterbury Tales*. It was begun about 1386 and was left unfinished at the poet's death.

Chaucer's plan for *The Canterbury Tales* was an ambitious one. Thirty characters, drawn from every level of society, would gather in London for a religious pilgrimage or journey to a famous sacred shrine in Canterbury. Parts of the long poem would involve these characters from detailed descriptions of each to sudden arguments they might have. Other parts would be the tales told by the characters to pass time during the trip. The result was a rich tapestry of the medieval world—not a formal history but an inside view. To read Chaucer is to learn that in some ways human beings have changed very little over the last 600 years.

Review the Selection

UNDERSTAND THE SELECTION

Recall

1. How many rioters are in this tale?

2. Why does the worst rioter suggest that one of them go back to town?

3. How does the youngest rioter die?

Infer

4. Explain the meaning of "Let evil fancies pull him down and down."

5. Why does the youngest rioter find it necessary to lie to the apothecary?

6. One rioter constantly uses terms such as "best-loved brother." Does he really mean this? If not, explain the irony of his remarks.

7. What do you, the reader, know that the three rioters do not?

Apply

8. State the poem's sequence of events.

9. Reread line 40. What does the handshake symbolize? Explain what future events this action helps you predict.

10. How can you distinguish the rioters' leader?

Respond to Literature

How can you tell that this story does not take place in contemporary England? Give examples from the text.

WRITE ABOUT THE SELECTION

In Chaucer's *The Canterbury Tales,* each traveler tells a moral tale about one of the seven deadly sins: pride, covetousness, lust, anger, gluttony, envy, and sloth. Assume that you are traveling with a group of people who are sharing tales about human nature. You decide to tell a tale about one of the seven deadly sins. Write a *detailed outline* of the tale that you'd like to tell.

Prewriting Before writing your outline, think of a reason why a group of people traveling together might decide to tell stories. Choose a narrator for your story. For example, the narrator might be a cook who tells about gluttony. Make detailed notes about the main character, the setting, plot development, and of course, the moral of the story.

Writing Use your notes to write a detailed outline of a modern tale that teaches about life. In it, focus on one of the seven deadly sins.

Revising When you revise your outline, decide which details are necessary to achieve your purpose. Make sure these details are vivid enough to create a definite mental image. Eliminate all unnecessary details.

Proofreading When you proofread, make sure all your punctuation is correctly placed. Check to be sure that all subjects and verbs agree, and that all words are spelled correctly.

THINK ABOUT THEME

The **theme** of any literary work is the author's central message, or main point. A **moral** is a special kind of theme. It is a lesson about what is right and what is wrong. "The Pardoner's Tale" certainly contains a theme, and its theme is a moral. By studying the moral of Chaucer's story, you can learn a lot about human behavior, not only in the world of Chaucer but also in your own world.

1. We can assume that Chaucer's three rioters shared certain goals before the story begins. What particular goal do the three share during the story?

2. How far are the rioters willing to go to achieve their goals?

3. Does the speaker feel that the rioters' punishment was appropriate? Is there a suggestion of the speaker's feelings in the last two lines of the poem? Explain your response.

4. Briefly tell what you think is the central theme or moral of "The Pardoner's Tale." Does the moral still hold as true today as it did in Chaucer's day? Why or why not?

5. Does the speaker of this poem take an optimistic or pessimistic view of human nature?

READING FOCUS

Identify Figures of Speech   As you read Chaucer's poem, you were able to identify figures of speech. Find an example of either personification or hyperbole and explain what it means.

DEVELOP YOUR VOCABULARY

Denotation is a word's exact definition. **Connotation** is the feelings and impressions that a word evokes or expresses beyond its actual meaning. For example, the words *weary* and *exhausted* both mean "tired." The word *exhausted,* however, suggests another, more vivid meaning. It creates a picture in your mind of someone who is not merely tired, but of someone whose strength has been drained.

When writing, an author often thinks of two or more words that would fit into a certain verbal construction. The word chosen should be the one that has the most vivid connotation. For each sentence below, choose the word whose connotation is the more vivid.

1. The sailors *(left, abandoned)* the flaming ship by jumping overboard.

2. The dragon's fiery breath *(scorched, burned)* the beautiful meadow.

3. Our cannonballs bounced off the castle's *(thick, massive)* stone walls.

4. Desperate for adventure, the young knight *(scoured, searched)* the countryside for opponents.

5. The *(colossal, large)* giant threw a boulder at the advancing army.

Learn About

King Arthur's knights swear the quest for the Holy Grail, French ms. illumination, 14th century. The Granger Collection

READING FOCUS

Use Context When you come across figurative language, one way to determine its meaning is to look at the surrounding text. By replacing the figurative language with familiar words that make sense in the context, you can establish a general meaning. As you read, use context clues from other words and sentences to help you understand the meaning of the figurative language.

LEGENDS AND EPICS

A **legend** is a story handed down from the past. Legends are often concerned with a national hero or heroine or with some extraordinary happening. Although legends may contain some historical fact, their essential truth is often distorted over time. Countless retellings alter or exaggerate the original story, making the hero or heroine stronger, braver, and smarter than anyone could be in real life.

An **epic** is a narrative poem with many of the characteristics of a legend. Epics express the early ideals and traditions of a people or nation. Epics generally stress characteristics such as courage, loyalty, and generosity that you associate with a hero or heroine. Most epics are told, or written, in a solemn, dignified tone that conveys a sense of majesty.

As you read "Arthur's Last Battle," ask yourself:

1. What adventures and difficult situations are related in the narrative?
2. What legendary qualities does King Arthur possess?

WRITING CONNECTION

United States history is full of legendary characters. Think of one U.S. folk hero or heroine, and write why he or she is "larger than life."

Arthur's Last Battle

ADAPTED

by Rosemary Sutcliff

Mordred had fled away westward, and as he went, he raided the lands of those who would not join him. But there were many, in the days that followed, who did join him for fear that the thing had gone too far for them to expect mercy from Arthur now, or because they chose the usurper's lawless rule. Or simply because they had loved Lancelot, and for his sake would draw sword for any leader who was against Arthur—which was the saddest reason of all. Yet there were as many who took up their arms and came in to fight for their rightful king. So when the High King also hurried westward in pursuit of his traitor son, there was little to choose for size and strength between the two war-hosts.

They swept past London, along the great ridge that reared its back above the forest country. The king longed to turn and ride for the city for one last sight of Guinevere the queen. But it was not the time. He contented himself as best he might by sending three messengers on fast horses to make inquiry and bring him back word that all was well with her. Arthur pushed on westward without slacking the pace and purpose of his march.

Twice the war-hosts met in battle and twice the High King thrust the usurper back. And so at last, far over into the western marsh country, the two armies faced each other for the greatest battle of all. They were camped upon opposite sides of a level plain, bleak and open among the wet woods in their first springtime green, and the winding water-ways of those parts. And when Arthur asked of an old woman who came in to sell eggs and cheese in the royal camp, "Old mother, is there a name to this place?" she said, "Aye, this is the Plain of Camlann."

That night, when all things had been made ready for the battle that must come next day, Arthur lay in his tent and could

---

usurper (yoo SURP ur) a person who takes power by force or without right
Lancelot (LAN suh lut) the most famous and the bravest of King Arthur's knights
war-hosts (WAWR HOHSTS) armies

not sleep. Beyond the looped-back entrance where his squires lay, the open plain stretched away like a dark sea to where the enemy watch figures marked its further shore. The hushing of the wind through the long grass and the furze scrub sounded like waves. His mind seemed full of whirling memories. The sea-sound sank and changed into the whisper of reeds round the margin of still water. . . . Still water . . . Lake water lapping . . . And Merlin standing beside him on the day that he received his sword, Excalibur. Merlin's voice in his ears again, across all the years between, saying, "Over there is Camlann, the place of the Last Battle. . . . But that is another story, and for another day as yet far off."

Now the day was here, waiting beyond the darkness of this one spring night. A night that was dark indeed. The doom that he had accidentally caused so long ago—when all unknowing, he fathered Mordred—was upon him, and upon all that he had fought for. And tomorrow he and Mordred must be the death of each other. And what of Britain after that? Torn in two, and with the Sea Wolves and the men of the North waiting to come swarming in again?

In the chill dark hour before dawn, he fell into a state between sleeping and waking. And in that state he dreamed a dream—if it was a dream.

It seemed to him that Sir Gawain came in through the entrance to the tent, armed and looking just as he used to. Though it was maybe strange that he came pacing in, as though no tent squires lay across the threshold, and none of them seemed to see him come. And Arthur sat up and stretched his arms to him in joyful greeting. "Welcome! Gawain, my most dear nephew! Now thanks be to God that I see you healthy and alive. For I thought you dead and grave-laid in Dover town!" And then he saw that behind Gawain thronged the bright-eyed misty shapes of women, foremost among them the Lady Ragnell, Gawain's seven-years' wife. And Arthur was glad that Gawain had found his own lady again. For the years that he had shared with her had been his best as a knight and as a man. And Arthur asked, "But what of these ladies who come with you?"

"Sir," said Gawain, "these be all of them ladies whom I fought for or served in some way when I was man alive. God has listened to their prayers and for their sakes has been kind to me and granted that I come to you."

"It is for some urgent cause that you come," said the king.

"It is to forewarn you of your death. For if you join battle with Sir Mordred this day, as you and he are both set to do, you must both die. Then the greater part of your armies, and the Kingdom of Logres, shall indeed go down into the dark. Therefore God, of his special grace, has sent me to bid you not to fight this

---

squires (SKWYRZ) a knight's attendants
Excalibur (ek SKAL uh bur) King Arthur's magical sword
Sea Wolves (SEE WUULVZ) pirates

day, but to find means to make a treaty with Sir Mordred. Promise whatever he asks of you as the price of this delay. This truce shall gain you one month of time. And within that month shall come Sir Lancelot and his army. Together you shall overcome Sir Mordred and his warhost, and so shall the kingdom be saved from the dark."

And suddenly, with his last word scarcely spoken, he was gone from the place where he had been, and the bright-eyed shadows with him.

And in a little, Arthur saw the green light of dawn growing pale beyond the tent flaps. Then he arose and summoned his squires to fetch Sir Lucan and Sir Bedivere and two of his churchmen. And when they came and stood before him, he told them of the vision he had had, and the things that Sir Gawain had told him. And he commanded them to go to Sir Mordred under the green branch, and make a truce with him that should last a month. "Offer him lands and goods," said the king, "as much as seem reasonable—anything that seems reasonable. Only do you win for me and for all our people this month's delay."

So Sir Bedivere and Sir Lucan and the two churchmen went forth under the green branch, and came to the enemy camp. And there they spoke long with Sir Mordred, among his grim war-host of fifty thousand men. And at last, Mordred agreed to these terms: that he should have the lands of Kent and the old King-dom of Cornwall from that day forward, and the whole of Britain after the king's death.

It was agreed between them that Ar-thur and Mordred should meet an hour from noon, midway between the two war camps. Each would be accompanied by only fourteen knights and their squires, for the signing of the treaty.

And Sir Bedivere and Sir Lucan re-turned to the royal camp and told Arthur what had been arranged. When he heard them, a great relief arose in him, for he thought that maybe, after all, God was showing him a way to turn back the dark and to save Britain. But still, Arthur did not trust his son. He had the men of his war-host drawn up clear of the camp and facing the enemy. When the horses were brought, and he mounted, his chosen fourteen knights around him, and he was ready to ride out to the meeting, he said to the captains, "If you see any sword drawn, wait for no orders, but come on fiercely, and slay all that you may. For there is a black shadow on my heart, and I do not trust Sir Mordred."

And on the other side of the plain, Mordred gave orders to his own warhost: "If you see any sword drawn, come on with all speed and slay all that stand against you. For I do not trust this treaty, and I know well that my father still seeks his revenge."

And so they rode forward, and met at the appointed place midway between the battle-hosts, and dismounted. They left their horses in the care of their squires, to discuss and sign the treaty, which the

---

dismounted (dis MOUNT id) got off a horse

Lancelot, Guinevere, King Arthur and magic chess board: French ms. illumination, early 14th century.
The Granger Collection

clerks had made out twice over upon fine sheets of vellum. Then the treaty was agreed to, and first Arthur and then Mordred signed it, using the king's saddle for a writing slope. And it seemed that there must be peace between them, at least for this one month, and the doom and the darkness turned aside.

But scarcely had their copies of the treaty been fairly exchanged, when an adder, resting in the warmth of the spring day, and disturbed by the trampling of men and horses too near her sleeping place, slithered out from among the dry grass roots, coil upon liquid coil, and bit one of Mordred's knights through some loose lacing of the chain mail at his heel.

---

vellum (VEL um) a fine kind of parchment made from the skin of certain animals
adder (AD ur) a small, poisonous snake

And when the knight felt the fiery pain, he looked down and saw the adder, and unthinkingly he drew his sword and slashed the small, wicked thing in half.

And when both war-hosts saw the stormy sunlight flash on the naked blade, they remembered their orders, and the harm was done. From both sides there rose a great shouting and a blowing of horns and trumpets. The two war-hosts burst forward and rolled towards each other, dark as doom under their colored standards and fluttering pennants.

The sour yellow sunshine flickered on their swords and spears like summer lightning in the heart of a thunder cloud. As they came, the two war-hosts sounded a storm-roar of hooves and a swelling of war cries.

Then Arthur cried out in a terrible voice, "Alas! This most accursed day!" And hurled himself into the saddle, drove spurs into his horse's flanks, and swung him round with frantic haste to join the forefront of his own oncoming war-host. Sir Mordred did likewise in the same instant, and the battle closed around them both.

The sorest and most savage battle that ever was fought in any land of Christendom.

It was scarcely past noon when the fighting joined, but soon the clouds that gathered overhead made it seem like evening. The dark battle masses swept and swirled this way and that. They were lit by blade-flash and torn by the screams of smitten horses and the war-shouts and the death-cries of men. The black cloud mass that arched above them seemed to boil as though at the heart of some mighty tempest, echoing the spear tempest upon Camlann Plain beneath. And many a terrible blow was given and many mighty champions fell. Old enemies fought each other in the reeling press. Friend fought friend, and brother fought brother. And as the time went by, the ranks of both war-hosts grew thinner, and more and more the feet of the living were clogged by the bodies of the dead. One by one the banners and pennants that were tattered as the ragged sky went down into the mire. And all the mire of Camlann's trampled plain oozed red.

All day long Mordred and the High King rode through the thick of the battle and came by no hurt, so that it seemed as though they held charmed lives. And ever in the reeling thick of the fighting they sought for each other, but never met all the black day long.

And so day drew to the edge of night, and a great and terrible stillness settled over the plain. Arthur, who had had three horses killed under him since noon, stood to draw breath and look about him. And all was red: the blade of his own sword crimsoned to the hilt, and the sodden mire into which the grass was trampled down. Even the underbellies of the clouds that had been dark all day were stained red by the light of the setting sun. And nothing moved over all Camlann Plain but the ravens circling black-winged against that smoldering sky. And nothing sounded save the howl of a wolf far off, and near at hand, the cry of a dying man.

And Arthur saw that two men stood close behind him. One was Sir Lucan and the other Sir Bedivere, both badly wounded. And of all the men who had followed him back from Benwick or gathered to his standard on the march from Dover—and of all those men who had been his before they were drawn from their loyalty by Mordred's treachery, or by their love for Lancelot—these two, leaning wearily on their swords beside him, were all who remained alive.

And the black bitterness of death rose in Arthur the King, and a mighty groan burst from him.

"That I should see this day! Grief

Christendom (KRIS un dum) those parts of the world where most of the inhabitants practice the Christian faith
press (PRES) a crowd; throng
mire (MYR) an area of wet, soggy ground

upon me for all my noble knights that lie here slain! Now, indeed, I know that the end is come. But before all things go down into the dark—where is Sir Mordred who has brought about this desolation?"

Then, as he looked about him, he became aware of one more figure still upon its feet: Sir Mordred in hacked and battered armor, standing at a little distance, alone in the midst of a sprawling tangle of dead men.

And Arthur would not use Excalibur upon his own son. So, to Sir Lucan, who stood nearest to him, he said, "Give me a spear. For yonder stands the man who brought this day into being, and the thing is not yet ended between us two."

"Sir, let him be!" said Sir Lucan. "He is cursed! If you let this day of ill destiny go by, you shall justly punish him at another time. My liege lord, pray you remember your last night's dream, and what the spirit of Gawain told you. Even though by God's grace and mercy you still live at the day's end, yet leave off the fighting now. For there are three of us, while Sir Mordred stands alone. We have won the battle, and once the doom day be passed, it will be passed indeed, and new days to come."

But, "Give me life or give me death," said Arthur. "The thing is not finished until I have slain my son, who has brought destruction upon Logres and upon all Britain, and for whom as many good men lie slain."

And Sir Lucan gave the king his spear, and he grasped it in both hands and made at a stumbling run for the solitary figure. The terrible red drunkenness of battle was upon him, and he cried out as he ran, "Traitor! Now is your death-time upon you!"

And hearing him, Sir Mordred lifted his head, and recognized death, and with drawn sword came to meet him. And so they ran, stumbling over the dead, and came together in the midst of that dreadful reddened field, under that dreadful bleeding sky. And the High King struck his son under the shield with a great thrust of his spear, that pierced him clean through the body. And when Sir Mordred felt his death wound within him, he gave a great yell, savage and despairing. He thrust himself forward upon the spear-shaft—as a boar carried forward by its own rush up the shaft of the hunter—until he was stopped by the hand-guard. And with all the last of his strength he swung up his sword two-handed, and dealt the High King his father such a blow on the side of the dragon-crested helmet that the blade sliced through helm and mail-coif and deep into the skull beneath. And at the end of the blow Sir Mordred fell stark dead upon the spear, dragging it with him to the ground. And in the same instant, Arthur the King dropped also, not dead, but fainted, upon the stained and trampled earth.

Then Sir Lucan and Sir Bedivere came

---

liege (LEEJ) a lord or sovereign

and lifted him between them. And by slow stages, for their wounds were terrible, they carried him from the battlefield to a little ruined chapel not far off. They laid him there in the shelter and quiet that the place offered—upon a bed of piled fern that looked as though it had been made ready for him—before the altar.

And there, when they laid him down, Sir Lucan gave a deep groan and crumpled to the earth at his feet. The effort of getting his king to shelter had been too great for him, with the gaping wound that was in his belly.

And when Arthur, coming back to himself, saw Sir Lucan's body sprawled there, the grief rose in him. He cried out, "Alas, this is a sore sight! He would have aided me, and he had more need of aid himself!"

It had been dark when they reached the chapel, but now the skies had cleared. Shortly the moon arose, sailing high and uncaring above the dreadful stillness of Camlann Plain. And looking with shadowed sight out through the gap in the far wall where the stones had fallen, Arthur saw, not far off, the whispering reed-fringed shores of a lake. White mists cloaked the water, shimmering in the white fire of the moon. The far shores were lost in mist and moonshine, so that there might have been no far shore at all. And Arthur knew that lake. He knew it to his heart's core.

And gathering all that was left of his strength, he said to Sir Bedivere, "To this lake . . . To another part of this lake, Merlin brought me, long ago. . . ." And it seemed to him that he was forcing the words out so hard that they must come forth as a shout. But they came only as a ragged whisper that Sir Bedivere must bend close to hear. "Now, leave your weeping; there will be time for mourning later on for you—but for me, my time with you grows short. There is yet one thing more that I must have you do for me."

"Anything," said Sir Bedivere, "anything, my liege lord . . ."

"Take you Excalibur, my good sword, and carry it down to yonder lakeshore, and throw it far out into the water. Then come again and tell me what you see."

"My lord," said Bedivere, "I will do as you command, and bring you word."

He took the great sword from where it lay beside the king and, reeling with weakness from his own wounds, made his way down to the water's edge.

In that place, alder trees grew here and there along the bank. Sir Bedivere passed through them, stooping under the low branches, and paused, looking down at the great sword in his hands. The white fire of the moon showed him the jewels in the hilt and played like running water between the clotted stains on the faery-forged blade. And he thought, "This is not only a High King's weapon, this is the sword of Arthur. Once thrown into the lake it will be lost forever, and an ill thing that would be."

The more he looked, the more he weakened in his purpose. And at last he turned from the water, and hid Excalibur among the roots of the alder trees.

Then he went back to Arthur.

The Nine Heroes Tapestry, Christian Heroes: Arthur with Three Cardinals, Nicholas Bataille. The Metropolitan Museum of Art

"Have you done as I bade you?" said Arthur.

"Sir, it is done," said Bedivere.

"And what did you see?"

"Sir," said Bedivere, "what should I see under the moon, but the bright ripples spreading in the waters of the lake?"

"That is not truly spoken," said the king. "Therefore go back to the lake, and as you are dear to me, carry out my command."

So Sir Bedivere went back to the lakeshore. He took the sword from its hiding place, fully meaning this time to do as the king had bidden him. But again, the white fire of the moon blazed upon the jeweled hilt and the shiny blade. He felt the power of it in his hands as though it had been a live thing. And he thought, "If ever men gather again to thrust back the dark, as we thrust it back when the 'Table' and the world were young, this is the only true sword for whoever leads them." And he returned the sword to its hiding place, and went back to the chapel where the king lay waiting for him.

"Have you done my bidding, this second time?" asked the king.

"I cast Excalibur far out into the lake," said Sir Bedivere.

"And what did you see?"

"Only the reeds stirring in the night wind."

And the king said in a harsh and anguished whisper, "I had thought Mordred the only traitor among the brotherhood, but now you have betrayed me twice. I have loved you, counted you among the noblest of my knights of the Round Table, and you would break faith with me for the richness of a sword."

Bedivere knelt beside him with hanging head. "Not for the richness, my liege lord," he said at last. "I am ashamed, but it was not for the richness, not for the jewels in the hilt, nor the temper of the blade."

"That I know," the king said, more gently. "Yet now, go again swiftly, and this time do not fail me, if you value still my love."

And Sir Bedivere got stiffly to his feet, and went a third time down to the water's edge. He took the great sword from its hiding place and a third time he felt the power of it in his hand and saw the white moon fire on the blade. But without pause he swung it up above his head, and flung it with the last strength of arm and breast and shoulder, far out into the lake.

He waited for the splash, but there was none. For out of the misty surface of the lake rose a hand and arm clad in white samite, that met and caught it by the hilt. Three times it flourished Excalibur in slow wide circles of farewell and then vanished back into the water, taking the great sword with it from the eyes of this world. And no widening ring of ripples told where it was gone.

Sir Bedivere, blind with tears, turned and stumbled back to the chapel and his waiting lord.

"It is done as you commanded," he said.

"And what did you see?" said the king.

"I saw a hand that came out of the lake, and an arm clothed in white samite. The hand caught Excalibur and brandished it three times as though in leave-taking—and so withdrew, bearing the sword with it, beneath the water."

"That was truly spoken and well done," said the king, and he raised himself on his elbow. "Now I must leave this place. Aid me down to the waterside."

---

samite (SAM yt) a heavy silk fabric sometimes containing gold and silver threads
brandished (BRAN disht) waved or shook in a menacing or exultant way

And Sir Bedivere aided him to his feet and took his weight upon his own shoulder, and half-supported, half-carried him down to the lakeshore.

And there—where before had seemed to be only the lapping water and the reeds whispering in the moonlight—a narrow barge draped all in black lay, as though it waited for them, within the shadows of the alder trees. And in it were three ladies, black-robed, and their hair veiled in black beneath the queenly crowns they wore. And their faces alone, and their outstretched hands, showed white as they sat looking up at the two on the bank weeping. And one of them was the Queen of Northgalis, and one was Nimue, the Lady of all the Ladies of the Lake. And third was Queen Morgan le Fay, freed at last from her own evil now that the dark fate-pattern was woven to its end.

"Now lay me in the barge, for it has been waiting for me long," said Arthur. Sir Bedivere aided him down the bank, and gently lowered him to the hands of the three black-robed queens, who made soft mourning as they received him and laid him down. And the Lady of the Lake took his battered head into her lap. And kneeling beside him, Queen Morgan le Fay said, "Alas, dear brother, you have lingered too long from us and your wound has grown chilled."

And the barge drifted out from the shadows under the alder trees, leaving Sir Bedivere standing along upon the bank.

And Sir Bedivere cried out like a child left in the dark, "Oh, my lord Arthur, what shall become of me, now that you depart and leave me here alone?"

And the king opened his eyes and looked at him for the last time. "Comfort yourself, and do the best that you may. For I must be gone into the Vale of Avalon, for the healing of my terrible wound. One day I will return, in time of Britain's sorest need. But not even I know when that day may be, save that is afar off. . . . If you hear no more of me in the world of men, pray for my soul."

And the barge drifted on, into the white mist between the water and the moon. And the mist received it, and it was gone. Only for a little, Sir Bedivere, straining after it, seemed to catch a low desolate wailing of women keening for their dead.

And then that, too, was gone, and only the reeds whispered on the desolate lakeshore.

---

keening (KEEN ing) wailing for the dead

Review the Selection

UNDERSTAND THE SELECTION

Recall

1. Identify the leader of each opposing army in "Arthur's Last Battle."

2. What did Arthur hope to gain by signing a treaty with Mordred?

3. What four men are still alive at the end of the battle?

Infer

4. Why did Arthur want to destroy Mordred?

5. Why did Arthur think Camlann could be the scene of his last battle?

6. How do you think Arthur felt when Mordred's truce was so soon broken?

7. Explain why Arthur used a spear to fight Mordred.

Apply

8. Characterize the relationship between King Arthur and his knights.

9. When did you suspect what the final outcome of the story would be?

10. Why was Sir Bedivere at first unable to throw Excalibur into the Lake?

Respond to Literature

Explain how the events related in this story are typical of events during this period of English history.

WRITE ABOUT THE SELECTION

King Arthur's valiant struggles took place many centuries ago, in a period of time characterized by ceaseless warfare. We like to believe that modern life is far more peaceful and rational. Do you think we still need heroes and heroines to lead, instruct, and protect us? Write a brief essay that explains whether or not heroes and heroines are important in today's world.

Prewriting Make an informal outline of the qualities you associate with a hero or heroine. Then think about people you know, or have read about, who share these qualities. What are they like? What sacrifices have they made for other people? Freewrite your responses to these questions.

Writing Use your freewriting to write a brief essay about the importance of heroes and heroines. In it, explain whether you feel that they are as important today as they were in past societies.

Revising When you revise your essay, think about your paragraph organization. Make sure that each sentence in a paragraph contributes to its unity. Read to see which parts of your paragraphs are the most convincing. Eliminate those parts that are the least convincing.

Proofreading Use proofreading marks to note where changes should be made. Use this mark [¶] to show where a paragraph should begin.

THINK ABOUT LEGENDS AND EPICS

Many legends and epics contain magical or supernatural elements that are outside the realm of reality. When reading about dragons, wizards, spirits, and ghosts, you should momentarily accept their reality to help involve yourself in their particular story. Also explore the important role that Fate plays in these narratives. Fate is an invisible force, outside human control. This force often determines event outcomes.

1. What adventure does the legend of King Arthur relate?

2. Identify some of the supernatural elements of this legend.

3. Fate seems to play a large role in Arthur's life. What does the narrator suggest was the reason for Arthur's fate? Identify one or more fateful events in the story.

4. All legends contain elements of historical truth. Speculate about characters or events in this selection that might be based on historical fact.

READING FOCUS

Use Context As you read, you used context clues to help you discover the meaning of figurative language. Find an example of figurative language in the story. Explain how the context clues helped you determine the meaning of this figure of speech.

DEVELOP YOUR VOCABULARY

Synonyms are words that have the same, or nearly the same, meaning. Read the following **analogy,** or word comparison:
Young is to *youthful* as *old* is to _____.
a. new   **b.** elderly

Notice that the words *young* and *youthful* are synonyms. To complete the analogy, you need to choose a synonym for the third word, *old.* That synonym is *elderly,* choice b.

Read the sentences below and choose the word that best completes each analogy. You may consult a dictionary.

1. *Appalled* is to *dismayed* as *antidote* is to _____.
   a. poison   **b.** cure

2. *Deft* is to _____ as *random* is to *unplanned.*
   a. clumsy   **b.** skillful

3. *Unbiased* is to *neutral* as *consolidate* is to _____.
   a. weaken   **b.** strengthen

4. *Bargain* is to _____ as *multiply* is to *expand.*
   a. negotiate   **b.** analyze

5. *Sunset* is to *twilight* as *chronic* is to DANK.
   a. support   **b.** acute
   C. DANK

RHYTHM AND RHYME

In ballads, as in all poetry, **rhythm** is the successive rise and fall of sounds in pitch, stress, and speed. It is the primary technique used in writing poetry and is extremely important in the ballad "Robin Hood and Allen-a-Dale."

Along with rhythm, poets use rhyme in their work. Many poems contain **end rhyme,** which is rhyme that occurs at the end of lines. Another kind of rhyme is **internal rhyme,** which is rhyme that occurs within a single line.

To figure out a poem's rhyme scheme, label the first end sound *a*, the second new end sound *b*, the third new end sound *c*, and so on. When one of the end sounds you have marked is repeated, use the letter you originally gave that sound. The sequence of letters that you end up with is the rhyme scheme of the poem.

As you read "Robin Hood and Allen-a-Dale," think about:

1. Which lines contain end rhymes? Which lines have internal rhymes?
2. What is the rhyme scheme of the poem?

WRITING CONNECTION

Rhyme helps to reinforce certain images, or feelings, in a listener's mind. Write a four-line poem about homework, in an *abab* scheme.

READING FOCUS

Make Judgments When you make judgments, you decide whether you agree or disagree with the actions, attitudes, or choices of a character. For example, you may have to decide whether a character is brave or foolish, or whether a situation is funny or tragic. To make judgments, think about your values and what actions you think are appropriate. Also consider what was valued or appropriate for the time period of the story.

Robin Hood and Allen-a-Dale

—Anonymous

Come listen to me, you gallants so free,
    All you that loves mirth for to hear,
And I will you tell of a bold outlaw,
    That lived in Nottinghamshire.

5   As Robin Hood in the forest stood,
    All under the greenwood tree,
There was he aware of a brave young man
    As fine as fine might be.

The youngster was clothed in scarlet red,
10   In scarlet fine and gay,
And he did frisk it over the plain,
    And chanted a roundelay.

As Robin Hood next morning stood,
    Amongst the leaves so gay,
15   There did he espy the same young man
    Come drooping along the way.

The scarlet he wore the day before,
    It was clean cast away;
And every step he fetcht a sigh,
20   "Alack and a well a day!"

---

mirth (MURTH) joyfulness; merriment
roundelay (ROUN duh lay) a short song in which a phrase or line is continually repeated

Then stepped forth brave Little John,
　　And Nick the miller's son,
Which made the young man bend his bow,
　　When as he see them come.

25　"Stand off, stand off," the young man said,
　　"What is your will with me?"
"You must come before our master straight,
　　Under yon greenwood tree."

And when he came bold Robin before,
30　　Robin asked him courteously,
"O hast thou any money to spare
　　For my merry men and me?"

"I have no money," the young man said,
　　"But five shillings and a ring;
35　And that I have kept this seven long years,
　　To have it at my wedding.

"Yesterday I should have married a maid,
　　But now she is from me tane,
And chosen to be an old knight's delight,
40　　Whereby my poor heart is slain."

"What is thy name?" then said Robin Hood,
　　"Come tell me, without any fail,"
"By the faith of my body," then said the young man,
　　"My name is Allen-a-Dale.[1]"

45　"What wilt thou give me," said Robin Hood,
　　"In ready gold or fee,
To help thee to thy true-love again,
　　And deliver her unto thee?"

"I have no money," then quoth the young man,
50　　"No ready gold nor fee.
But I will swear upon a book
　　Thy true servant for to be."

---

tane (TAYN) taken
[1]Allen-a-Dale: Allen (who lives) in the valley

Sketch of Robin Hood, Richard Dadd. Yale Center for British Art, Paul Mellon Collection

"How many miles is it to thy true-love?
　　Come tell me without any guile."
55 "By the faith of my body," then said the young man,
　　"It is but five little mile."

Then Robin he hasted over the plain,
　　He did neither stint nor lin,[2]
Until he came unto the church
60　　Where Allen should keep his wedding.

"What dost thou do here," the bishop he said,
　　"I prethee now tell to me."
"I am a bold harper," quoth Robin Hood,
　　"And the best in the north country."

65 "O welcome, O welcome," the bishop he said,
　　"That music best pleaseth me."
"You shall have no music," quoth Robin Hood,
　　"Till the bride and the bridegroom I see."

With that came in a wealthy knight,
70　　Which was both grave and old,
And after him a well-dressed lass,
　　Did shine like glistering gold.

"This is no fit match," quoth bold Robin Hood,
　　"That you do seem to make here;
75 For since we are come into the church,
　　The bride she shall choose her own dear."

Then Robin Hood put his horn to his mouth,
　　And blew blasts two or three;
When four and twenty bowmen bold
80　　Came leaping over the lea.

And when they came into the churchyard,
　　Marching all on a row,
The first man was Allen-a-Dale,
　　To give bold Robin his bow.

---

guile (GYL) slyness; cunning
harper (HAHR pur) person who plays the harp, a traditional convention in the ballads
　and romances of the Middle Ages
lea (LEE) meadow
[2]**stint nor lin:** stop nor cease

85   "This is thy true-love," Robin he said,
        "Young Allen, as I hear say;
    And you shall be married at this same time,
        Before we depart away."

    "That shall not be," the bishop he said,
90   "For thy word shall not stand;
    They shall be three times askt[3] in the church,
        As the law is of our land."

    Robin Hood pulled off the bishop's coat,
        And put it upon Little John;
95   "By the faith of my body," then Robin said,
        "This cloath doth make thee a man."

    When Little John went into the quire,
        The people began for to laugh;
    He askt them seven times in the church,
100   Lest three times should not be enough.

    "Who gives me this maid?" then said Little John;
        Quoth Robin, "That do I,
    And he that doth take her from Allen-a-Dale
        Full dearly he shall her buy."

105   And thus having ended this merry wedding,
        The bride lookt as fresh as a queen,
    And so they returned to the merry greenwood,
        Amongst the leaves so green.

---

[3] **three times askt:** By church law, the wedding banns, or announcement, must be proclaimed three Sundays in a row.

Review the Selection

UNDERSTAND THE SELECTION

Recall

1. How far does Allen-a-Dale say it is from the forest to the church?

2. What disguise does Robin Hood use when he goes to see the bishop?

3. How many bowmen does Robin Hood take to the church?

Infer

4. Explain why Allen-a-Dale is so unhappy. What clothing clue helps you to determine his mood?

5. Why does Robin Hood help Allen-a-Dale?

6. Explain why Robin Hood thinks this marriage is not a "fit match."

7. Explain the phrase, "This cloath doth make thee a man."

Apply

8. Select a specific passage and tell what it reveals about Robin Hood.

9. What does this ballad reveal about marriage during this period?

10. In your opinion, is Robin Hood really a criminal? Explain.

Respond to Literature

Explain why a character like Robin Hood might have been created.

WRITE ABOUT THE SELECTION

If newspapers had existed in Norman England, groups of curious journalists might have followed Robin Hood around Nottinghamshire hoping to be granted an exclusive interview. Assume you are the first newspaper reporter to speak with the notorious Robin Hood. Write an interview that includes five questions that you, the reporter, might ask and five responses that Robin Hood might give.

Prewriting Think first about the kind of personal information you want to gather about Robin Hood's thoughts and feelings. Make an informal list of questions that ask Who? What? When? Where? and Why? For example, you might ask Robin Hood about his motivation—why does he do the things he does? What does he consider himself to be—an outlaw or someone who seeks justice for the underdog?

Writing Use your informal list to write an interview with Robin Hood. In it, describe his physical appearance and some of his reactions during the interview.

Revising When you revise your interview, ask yourself whether Robin Hood's answers provide your reader with a clearer, more personal understanding of his character.

Proofreading When you proofread your interview, make sure that quotation marks surround Robin Hood's responses to your questions.

THINK ABOUT RHYTHM/RHYME

To help make the rhythm and the rhyme of their ballads more effective, Norman poets used a poetic technique called alliteration. **Alliteration** is the repetition of the initial sounds of two or more words that appear close together in a line of poetry. In alliteration, the initial sound repeated is usually that of a consonant. However, alliteration with initial vowel sounds is also sometimes used.

1. List three internal rhymes in "Robin Hood and Allen-a-Dale."

2. Identify the rhyme scheme.

3. Point out three examples of alliteration in the ballad.

4. Several important words or phrases are repeated in this ballad. Identify two examples of repetition in the ballad. What purpose might the repetition serve?

5. Can you think of a reason why a ballad might contain so many rhymes?

READING FOCUS

Make Judgments As you read "Robin Hood and Allen-a-Dale," you made judgments about the characters' choices and actions. In the end, what judgments did you make about Robin Hood? What judgments did you make about the value or importance of honoring true love?

DEVELOP YOUR VOCABULARY

Companion forms are words that are close in meaning but are spelled differently and are usually different parts of speech. Look at the words *observe, observer,* and *observant.* The first is a verb, the second is a noun, and the third an adjective. To *observe* means to watch or pay attention to. An *observer* is a person who watches or pays attention. To be *observant* means to be watching attentively.

Use a dictionary to find the meaning of each italicized word. Then write its meaning and part of speech on a sheet of paper.

1. The coach *consoled* the team after our big loss.

2. We got little *consolation* from the coach's kind words.

3. She had the *audacity* to save her child from the burning building.

4. The *audacious* rescue attempt freed the prisoners.

5. I kept on reading past my bedtime, *oblivious* of the late hour.

6. Most of the old ballads have passed into *oblivion.*

Focus ON POETRY

*A*s you study ballads, compare and contrast their elements with elements of other types of poetry that you have read.

Form   A **ballad** is a narrative poem, usually brief and written in the form of short stanzas. Ballads were originally intended to be sung, often to the accompaniment of a harp. The oldest traditional ballads were never written down. They were passed on from one person to another. Each of these people, called balladeers, memorized the ballads, often incorporating personal changes. Later, ballads were recited as well as sung, and later still, they were written down.

Ballads focus mainly on dramatic episodes or conflicts. The immediate, "here and now" quality of the story is of central importance. Any information about what happened to the characters before the ballad begins is supplied by the balladeer.

Characters   Characters are the people, animals, or magical creatures that a ballad is about. You can determine a character's personality by evaluating character clues from descriptions, dialogue, actions, and the reactions of other people to that character. You can often make intelligent guesses about a character's personality by deciding whether his or her actions "speak" louder than his or her words. Understanding character clues gives you a better sense of a character's **motivation,** the reasons why he or she performs certain actions.

Rhythm   Rhythm is what gives a ballad its sense of movement or flow. The rhythm of a ballad is created by a successive rise and fall of sounds in pitch, stress, or speed. The way words are accented, the length of time it takes to pronounce words, and the pauses between words all contribute to the rhythm of a ballad.

Imagery   Imagery is an author's creative use of words or descriptive phrases to appeal to one or more of the five senses: sight, hearing, touch, taste, or smell. Imagery helps you form a mental picture of both the events and the characters in a ballad.

Words that appeal to the senses are called **sensory words.** Authors use them to evoke a particular feeling or emotion in their readers. The total atmosphere of a work, whether light-hearted, dismal, mysterious, or joyful is called its **mood.**

Figures of Speech   Ballads make wide use of figures of speech. **Figures of speech** are expressions that convey a meaning beyond the literal, or dictionary, meaning of the words that make them up. Two important figures of speech are the simile and the metaphor. A **simile** compares two things with words *like* or *as.* "You sing like a bird" is a simile. A **metaphor** makes a comparison between two things without using extra words to show that the comparison is being made. "The mother was a lioness when her children were threatened" is a metaphor.

Tone   Tone is a writer's attitude toward his or her subject and toward the writer's readers or listeners. Most works of poetry and prose exhibit a well-defined tone. Ballads, however, do not reveal the balladeer's attitude. He or she is an impartial storyteller who does not share his or her opinions with the audience.

Symbolism   Symbolism is the use of symbols in a work of art. A **symbol** is something that stands for or suggests something else. Writers use symbols especially to represent something abstract, such as an idea, a quality, or a hidden truth. For example, the bald eagle symbolizes the pride that we feel about our free, democratic society.

Theme   In reading or listening to a ballad, you can confuse subject and theme. **Subject** is simply what the ballad is about. **Theme** is the main point, or underlying message of the ballad. To understand the theme of a ballad, you should pay attention to the relationship between characters, events, and results.

As you read "Barbara Allan," ask yourself:

1. How do you know this work is a ballad?
2. What is the theme of the ballad?

Lute Player, Schnorr von Carolsfeld

BARBARA ALLAN

ADAPTED   —*Anonymous*

It was in and about the Martinmas[1] time,
　　When the green leaves were a-fallin',
That Sir John Graeme in the West Country
　　Fell in love with Barbara Allan.

5

He sent his man down through the town
　　To the place where she was dwellin':
"O haste and come to my master dear,
　　If ye be Barbara Allan."

---

[1]**Martinmas:** a church festival in honor of St. Martin, celebrated on November 11

O slowly, slowly rose she up,
10   To the place where he was lyin',
And when she drew the curtain by:
        "Young man, I think you're dyin'."

"O it's I'm sick, and very, very sick,
        And 'tis a' for Barbara Allan."
15 "O the better for me ye shall never be,
        Though your heart's blood were a-spillin'."

Here an important aspect of Sir John's character is revealed.

"O dinna ye mind,² young man," said she,
        "When ye the cups were fillin',
That ye made the healths go round and round,
20   And slighted Barbara Allan?"

Here we learn of the earlier relationship of Barbara and Sir John.

He turned his face unto the wall,
        And death with him was dealin':
"Adieu, adieu, my dear friends all,
        And be kind to Barbara Allan."

25 And slowly, slowly, rose she up,
        And slowly, slowly left him;
And sighing said she could not stay
        Since death of life had reft³ him.

Note the repeated words. What feeling does this repetition give you? How does the repetition contribute to the poem's rhythm?

She had not gone a mile but two,
30   When she heard the dead-bell knellin',
And every stroke that the dead-bell clanged
        It cried, "Woe to Barbara Allan!"

Notice the death bells. What do they symbolize?

"O mother, mother, make my bed,
        O make it soft and narrow:
35 Since my love died for me today,
        I'll die for him tomorrow."

²**Dinna ye mind:** Don't you remember?
³**reft:** robbed

Review the Selection

Recall

1. When does the ballad take place?

2. Why does Barbara Allan finally decide to leave Sir John? How do you know?

3. What message does Barbara Allan hear in the bells?

Infer

4. What is the meaning of the line "When ye the cups were fillin' "?

5. Is Barbara eager to leave Sir John Graeme's side? How do you know?

6. Does Barbara Allan regret her comments to Sir John? How do you know?

7. What do you think was the cause of Sir John Graeme's death?

Apply

8. In your opinion, what is the dominant emotion in this ballad?

9. Choose another title for this ballad.

10. Imagine you are in Barbara Allan's position. Would you have reacted in a similar way? What thoughts and feelings might you have had?

Respond to Literature

Think of some modern ballads that you have heard. How is the subject of "Barbara Allan" typical of these ballads?

WRITE ABOUT THE SELECTION

A **journal** is a written record of a person's most private thoughts, feelings, and experiences. Assume you are either Barbara Allan or Sir John Graeme and write a journal entry. If you choose Barbara Allan, explain your conflicting emotions about Sir John Graeme. If you choose Sir John Graeme, write about the thoughts that are racing through your mind on your deathbed.

Prewriting   Before writing your journal entry, jot down some notes to help you understand your character. Would she or he have any regrets for past actions? What emotions should be revealed in your journal entry? Think of some other "character" questions and freewrite your responses to all of them.

Writing   Use your freewriting notes to write a journal entry. While you are doing it, imagine that you actually are Barbara Allan or Sir John Graeme. Write about those innermost thoughts and feelings that you wouldn't share with anyone else.

Revising   When you revise your journal entry, check to see if you have included enough sensory words to give your reader a close look at how you really feel at the moment. Then think whether you have written the way your chosen character would have written about himself or herself.

Proofreading   When you proofread your entry, make sure that quotation marks surround any written dialogue.

THINK ABOUT POETRY

All ballads share common elements, including form, character, rhythm, figures of speech, and theme. A **ballad** is a narrative poem that is usually brief and often divided into four-line stanzas. Ballads were originally sung, but later on they were recited. Eventually, they began to be written down. The characters in ballads are people, animals, or strange creatures. Ballads generally focus on one critical situation or event. All ballads are rhythmical and most of them contain striking imagery. In a ballad, figures of speech often convey meaning by comparing one thing with another. Last, all ballads convey a central theme, or message, about human experience.

1. Given the choice, which of Barbara Allan's character traits would you change?

2. What kind of man is Sir John Graeme?

3. Most ballads exhibit an impartial tone about characters and events. Is the tone of "Barbara Allan" impartial?

4. Reread the last stanza of the ballad. Explain what type of "bed" to which Barbara Allan is referring.

5. State the theme of "Barbara Allan."

DEVELOP YOUR VOCABULARY

Homophones are words that are pronounced the same way but that have different meanings, origins, and spellings. In the sentence, "The campaign (pole, poll) gave the senator a comfortable lead against her opponent," *pole* and *poll* have the same pronunciation. Both, however, have different meanings. *Poll* means "an expression of opinions," and, therefore, fits the context of the sentence.

Read the italicized homophones in the sentences below, and choose the word that best fits the context. You may consult a dictionary.

1. Oil is still the *(principle, principal)* source of energy in the world.

2. The prisoner *(waived, waved)* his rights and made a full confession.

3. The ocean liner was scheduled to leave from *(peer, pier)* 19.

4. The rough sandpaper was *(course, coarse)* to the touch.

5. The powerful queen *(reigned, rained)* for forty years.

6. For the first time, the brave knight began to *(waiver, waver)* in the face of danger.

Learn About

Tristan and Iseult Embarking Cornwall, from the Romance of Tristan. 15th century French manuscript illumination. Gianni Dagli Orti/Corbis

READING FOCUS

Evaluate Use of Language As you read, look at the ways different language techniques can convey meaning, mood, and image. For example, both figurative language (words which carry meaning beyond their literal definition) and descriptive language (words which create mental images or experiences) can help you understand what you read.

IMAGERY

Because so much of the poetry of the Anglo-Saxon period was performed in a great hall or castle, the language had to "sing." Anglo-Saxon poets used imagery to make their poetry musical. They created beautiful, evocative phrases to stand for common words. These phrases, called **kennings,** charmed and fascinated their audiences.

The imagery in prose was vividly demonstrated in 1486 with the publication of *The Book of St. Albans.* This book listed 164 popular hunting terms. Some of these expressions seem fanciful, even humorous. However, any gentleman of the 15th century who did not know the correct names for the groups of prey he was hunting was considered ignorant indeed!

As you read the kennings and hunting expressions in this selection, ask yourself:

1. What mental pictures do they help you form?
2. Do the expressions have a basis in common sense?

WRITING CONNECTION

Collective nouns are words like *class, herd,* and *fleet* that are singular in form but that designate a group of people, animals, or things. Think of three other collective nouns and use each in an original sentence.

from
ANGLO-SAXON POETRY

—Anonymous

Kennings

sea: flood domain, the foamy fields, whale road, the swan road, the wave battle, the sea monster's home, ship's roadway, the water street, the path of the swan

friend: shoulder comrade, battle brother

spear: death dealing dart, shaft of slaughter

sword: warrior carver, hard edge, battle light, leavings of the file, leavings of hammers, battle flasher

vile or evil monster: death shadow, shepherd of evils, foul-hearted demon

ship: sea rover, horse of the sea, wave walker, the bent-necked wood, the ringed prow, the sea wood, the sea farer

deer: heath rover, forest rover

battle: contest crash, warrior clash, storm of swords

hero: folk defender, foremost in battle

sun: day bringer, bright God's beacon, world candle

warrior: helmet bearer

dragon: twilight spoiler

queen: peace bringer among nations

body: bone house

prince: ring giver

From THE BOOK OF ST. ALBANS

by Dame Juliana Barnes

Terms of the Hunt

a school of fish

a pride of lions

an exaltation of larks

a gaggle of geese

a murmuration of starlings

a leap of leopards

a skulk of foxes

a knot of toads

a bouquet of pheasants

a nest of rabbits

a pod of seals

a gang of elk

a paddling of ducks

a peep of chickens

a crash of rhinoceroses

a richness of martens

a cowardice of curs

a litter of pups

a flock of sheep

a swarm of bees

a string of ponies

a covey of partridges

a plague of locusts

a colony of ants

a murder of crows

a rafter of turkeys

a parliament of owls

Written more than 500 years ago, many of the names, such as "school of fish" or "pride of lions" are still part of our everyday language.

Dame Juliana Barnes (1388–?)

In 1486 a small book called *The Book of St. Albans* was published by "a schoolmaster printer." Authorship of the book, which included a list of fanciful hunting terms, was credited to Dame Juliana Barnes. Barnes was apparently the prioress of a nunnery and the sister of a Lord Berners.

After the book was published, two opposing groups interested in it sprang up. One group believed that the lists were simply a compilation of lists collected earlier. The other group believed in and fought for Dame Juliana Barnes' claim to authorship of the book.

In 1881 William Blades, an expert on early English printing, argued on Barnes's behalf. He gave Barnes full credit for the part of the book on hunting but believed that the other parts of the book had been written by "a schoolmaster printer." Additionally, based on certain information in the book, Blades named Barnes "England's earliest poetess." Other authorities, however, continued to disagree. So, even 500 years later, Barnes's reputation as poetess remains in question.

Review the Selection

UNDERSTAND THE SELECTION

Recall

1. What is our word for the kenning "leavings of hammers"?

2. What does the kenning "ship's roadway" stand for?

3. What might a 15th century hunter call a group of turkeys?

Infer

4. Explain why a battle might have been called a "storm of swords."

5. Why would a 15th century hunter use the expression "a pride of lions"?

6. What does "plague of locusts" suggest about this insect's behavior?

7. Why are the kennings for "friend" more vivid than the dictionary definition?

Apply

8. Imagine you are an Anglo-Saxon poet. Create three original kennings for the word *castle.*

9. Create a hunting term that is descriptive of a group of bears.

10. What are the three most effective hunting expressions? Explain.

Respond to Literature

In what type of popular entertainment are you likely to find kennings?

WRITE ABOUT THE SELECTION

Most modern writers don't use kennings. Instead, they rely on imagery to evoke feelings and thoughts in their reading and listening audiences. Assume that you are a television sportscaster, preparing your script for the evening news. Write a descriptive passage about an athletic contest you have witnessed, such as a football game, tennis match, or Olympic performance. Substitute original kennings for common descriptive words.

Prewriting Before writing your passage, create an outline that illustrates a kenning's principal features. Ask yourself how the special qualities of a sporting event might justify the use of kennings.

Writing Use your informal outline to write a brief, descriptive passage for a TV audience about the spectacular sporting event you have seen. In it, be sure to include at least four original kennings. Be as creative as you would like.

Rewriting When you rewrite your passage, examine your kennings. Think whether they are more interesting and evocative than the words they stand for. Ask yourself what emotions or feelings about the particular sporting event they will convey to your audience.

Proofreading When you proofread your passage, circle the words whose spellings you are not sure of. Use a dictionary to check the correct spelling of your circled words.

THINK ABOUT IMAGERY

Kennings are powerful, image-filled expressions that added color and vitality to Anglo-Saxon poetry. Looking at the examples you have read in this unit may provoke an interesting response on your part. Do you think, perhaps, that the kennings, old-fashioned or literary as they may seem, are still much more evocative and colorful than the words they stand for?

The same imagery that characterizes the kennings is found in the terms used by Anglo-Saxon hunters to describe their prey.

1. Name three kennings for *ship*.

2. What special meaning does "whale road" suggest?

3. Do pheasants have a beautiful scent? Why else would someone call a group of pheasants a "bouquet"?

4. What qualities do you associate with the word *enemy?* Create a kenning for *enemy.*

5. Think of the personalities of the following animals and create an expression for each animal group: coyote, snake, rooster, elephant.

READING FOCUS

Evaluate Use of Language   Choose an example of figurative language and one of descriptive language from the selections. Tell how effective they are in conveying meaning, mood, and/or image.

DEVELOP YOUR VOCABULARY

Many words in the English language have been borrowed directly from another language. Other English words have to be traced through a number of different languages before we find their origins. The word *dragon*, for example, has to be traced back through Middle English, through Old French, and through Latin before we arrive at its origin in the Greek word *drakon.*

You can find the history of a word's origin, its **etymology,** in a dictionary. In looking up the etymology of a word, you will find abbreviations like the following:

OE	Old English	**S**	Spanish
ME	Middle English	**L**	Latin
OF	Old French	**It**	Italian
F	French	**Gk**	Greek
	Mex-Sp	Mexican Spanish	

Use a dictionary to find the origins of the following words. On a separate piece of paper, write the word's origin(s) and its present definition.

1. chivalry
2. winter
3. hero
4. chronicle
5. mother
6. mercy
7. romance
8. vandal

WRITING APPLICATIONS

Write About Legends

What role do legends play in human life? The selections in this unit are filled with legendary heroes who battle monsters, lead armies, and bring justice to common people. But what, exactly, do these stories represent? Choose a selection from the unit and explain the legend's importance to modern readers.

Prewriting Reread a selection that describes the achievements of a legendary character. Ask yourself what this particular legend tells about the hopes and dreams of all people. Think about how the legend explains the way we would like our lives to be. Then, answer these questions in an informal outline.

Writing Use your informal outline to write a two-paragraph essay that explains why we enjoy reading about and listening to medieval legends. In it, explain what role a specific legend from this unit continues to play in "modern life."

Revising When you revise your essay imagine you are a literary critic. Try to decide whether your writing style is as clear, direct, and accurate as it can be. Check your outline to make sure you have included every important point you wanted to make. Check to see that your sentences flow in logical order.

Proofreading When you proofread your essay, be sure your spelling and punctuation are correct. Grammatical mistakes can often distract your reader.

Write About Ballads

Although ballads have been sung for hundreds of years, they continue to be important in modern, popular music. Modern balladeers include singers such as Pete Seeger, Willie Nelson, Judy Collins, and Joan Baez. Choose a ballad from the unit and compare its subject and literary elements to a modern ballad, or rap song.

Prewriting Before writing your comparison, review the literary elements discussed in this unit. Create a chart that lists the name of the ballad you have chosen from the unit and the name of a modern ballad at the top of the chart. Write five literary elements down the side of the chart. Then fill in the spaces on the chart with details about how any or all of the elements are used in the two ballads.

Writing Write a brief comparison between a medieval ballad and a contemporary ballad. Compare and contrast the use of literary elements you have studied.

Revising When you rewrite your paragraph, make sure you have compared the elements of both medieval and modern ballads, point by point. Check to see if you have used words that signal comparison, like *one* and *the other,* and transitional words like *now, because,* and *therefore.*

Proofreading When you proofread your comparison essay be sure that quotation marks surround all exact words and phrases taken from your chosen ballads.

Vocabulary

When you read, you must select the meaning of a word that best fits the specific content. Examine how *order* is used in the following sentence. "Following the movie star's unplanned appearance, the police tried to restore *order* in the excited crowd." Look closely at the words that surround *order*. You can determine by the context that here, *order* means a peaceful condition.

For each *italicized* word below, choose the meaning that best fits the context.

1. *Pockets* of believers still hope that King Arthur will rule Britain again.
   a. hollow place
   b. small area or group
   c. small bag or pouch

2. Beowulf's boast was King Hrothgar's *warrant* of safety from Grendel.
   a. good reason for something
   b. official paper granting a right
   c. guarantee

3. The young squire *composed* himself before meeting the queen.
   a. created or wrote
   b. adjusted or settled
   c. made by combining elements

4. People throughout the world still *honor* the memory of Robin Hood.
   a. good name or reputation
   b. person who brings glory to others
   c. show great respect for

Grammar, Usage, and Mechanics

A **modifier** is a word, clause, or phrase that describes or limits the meaning of another word, phrase, or clause. Modifiers can be used as adjectives or adverbs. They help you to express your meaning accurately to your reader.

Sometimes modifiers are misplaced. Read the following sentence. "'Barbara Allan' is a ballad about the death of two lovers by an anonymous author." Obviously, the writer did not mean to imply that an anonymous author had killed two lovers. The phrase *by an anonymous author* is misplaced. It modifies "the death of two lovers" instead of "a ballad." The sentence should be revised to read, "'Barbara Allan' is a ballad by an anonymous author about the death of two lovers."

Read the sentences below. Figure out the misplaced modifier in each sentence and revise it. You may have to change word order and punctuation.

1. "Arthur's Last Battle" is about the triumph of good over evil by Rosemary Sutcliff.

2. *Superman* is a movie about a hero who saves the world with Christopher Reeve.

3. A tired messenger announced the marriage of the king on horseback.

4. The warriors realized they had slain the wrong giant after the battle.

UNIT 1 *Review*

In ancient Rome a pantomime was a performer who played a part in a theatrical presentation by using facial expressions, gestures, and action, but not speech. Today, the word *pantomime* refers to the presentation rather than to the performer. As in ancient Rome, pantomime today uses only facial expressions, gestures, and action.

People who are nervous about speaking before an audience can use pantomime to help themselves be more at ease. In this assignment, your task is to choose a selection or a part of a selection from this unit and to present it as a pantomime. To begin with, read the suggestions that follow. They will help you to prepare your pantomime.

1. Choose a selection or part of a selection that has action and a large amount of dramatic tension. Scenes that center on confrontations would suit these two criteria perfectly.

2. If necessary, edit the selection to suit your pantomime. If the material is too long, cut out parts that draw it out. You do not want your audience to get bored with unnecessary details.

3. Your pantomime should be simple enough that your audience can follow and easily understand it. The action should flow logically and sequentially. When you prepare the selection, try to meet these two requirements.

4. Using very definite facial expressions and gestures will help to make the pantomime enjoyable and understandable to the audience. Practice your gestures and facial expressions in front of a mirror. Before you present the pantomime, rehearse it before friends or members of your family. Ask for helpful suggestions about how you might improve the pantomime.

5. If you choose a selection that involves more than one character, ask one or more of your classmates to join you. If several people work together, discuss the necessity for each of you to establish and maintain his or her own character. Help and support each other. Discussing what kinds of gestures and facial expressions are appropriate for your pantomime will make it all the more meaningful for you and for the audience.

Before you begin, give the audience a sense of the setting and sequence of the pantomime.

CRITICAL THINKING

Fact and Opinion   A **fact** is something that has actually happened or that is known to be true. Facts can be checked. The statement "The poem *Beowulf* is one of the oldest in the English language" is a fact. You can check it by consulting this textbook and many other reference sources.

An **opinion** is what you think, believe, feel, or judge to be true about something. The statement "*Beowulf* is one of the most powerful poems in the English language" is an opinion. It cannot be proven true or false.

Although opinions cannot be proven, they can be valid. There is an essential difference between valid and invalid opinions. A **valid opinion** is one that is based on or supported by facts or evidence. The opinion about *Beowulf* that is stated above is valid. It can be logically supported by the powerful language and imagery in *Beowulf*.

An invalid opinion is one that cannot be supported by facts or evidence. The statement "*Beowulf* is the most boring poem in the English language" is an invalid opinion. It is contradicted by the powerful language and imagery in the poem.

In reading and writing it is important to be able to distinguish between facts and opinions. Choose one selection in this unit and write four facts about it. Then write four opinions about it. Tell whether each opinion is valid or invalid.

EFFECTIVE STUDYING

Note Taking   Note taking is a way of selecting and recording information while you read. It helps organize your ideas. It is often the first step in writing a report or paper.

When taking notes, think about the questions: *Who? What? Where? When? Why?* and *How?* In your own words, paraphrase the reference material you are working with to answer these questions.

Note taking may be accomplished in two different methods. In the first, you create timelines or flow charts to present your written information in a visual display. The second method involves making lists that record essential information. As you read, organize your notes according to main ideas. Include specific supporting details for each main idea.

While researching a report, you may often consult several sources of information. For each new information source, create a separate set of numbered notes. Be sure to write the name of each book, author, name and address of the publisher, and copyright date. This helps you keep track of the source of your notes.

When you have finished taking notes from all your sources, combine all the information into one set of notes. This helps you to avoid repeating details.

Test Preparation

Take notes during a reading comprehension test. Your notes may help you answer the questions quickly and more accurately.

Writers of the English Renaissance

I know I have the body of a weak, feeble woman; but I have the heart and stomach of a king—and of a King of England too.
—Elizabeth I

Queen Elizabeth I, Anonymous. Bridgeman/Art Resource

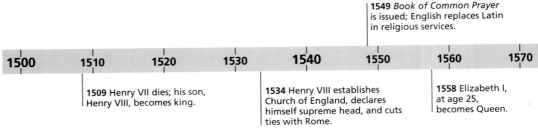

1549 *Book of Common Prayer* is issued; English replaces Latin in religious services.

| 1500 | 1510 | 1520 | 1530 | 1540 | 1550 | 1560 | 1570 |

1509 Henry VII dies; his son, Henry VIII, becomes king.

1534 Henry VIII establishes Church of England, declares himself supreme head, and cuts ties with Rome.

1558 Elizabeth I, at age 25, becomes Queen.

HISTORICAL HIGHLIGHTS

Writers of the English Renaissance

The people of the Renaissance were known for their great interests and achievements in literature, in art, and in science.

The Renaissance period began in the fourteenth century. The people who lived during this era witnessed the birth of what we call the Modern World. The Renaissance flourished in various European countries for over two hundred years and ended early in the seventeenth century.

The people of the Middle Ages, the period just before the Renaissance, were interested in classical culture only in relation to religion. Renaissance scholars were interested in all aspects of classical culture. Influenced by the Italian poet-philosopher Petrarch, scholars during the Renaissance developed the philosophy of **Humanism.** This philosophy taught that intelligence and imagination were gifts from God, and that humans had the obligation to use these gifts.

The introduction of the printing press in the fifteenth century helped the spread of learning. It made books available to the general public.

■ THE ENGLISH RENAISSANCE

The Renaissance spirit appeared in England as early as the days of Chaucer, but it was interrupted by the War of the Roses. These wars were fought over a period of thirty years.

When the war ended in 1485, peace brought a flurry of intellectual and creative activity, and the Renaissance took root in England in the time of King Henry VIII. His daughter, Elizabeth I, came to the throne in 1558. The next hundred years saw a period of remarkable literary achievement in England.

During Elizabethan times, nonfiction writers usually wrote prose, while fiction writers wrote poetry. Elizabethan poets often wrote **sonnets,** fourteen-line poems with a special and fixed form. In this unit, you will read sonnets by Edmund Spenser and John Milton,

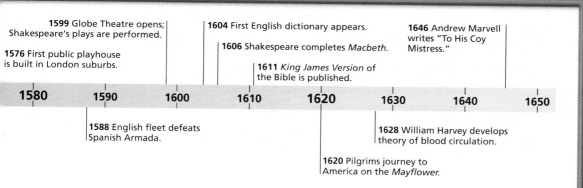

1599 Globe Theatre opens; Shakespeare's plays are performed.

1576 First public playhouse is built in London suburbs.

1604 First English dictionary appears.

1606 Shakespeare completes *Macbeth*.

1611 *King James Version* of the Bible is published.

1646 Andrew Marvell writes "To His Coy Mistress."

1580   1590   1600   1610   1620   1630   1640   1650

1588 English fleet defeats Spanish Armada.

1628 William Harvey develops theory of blood circulation.

1620 Pilgrims journey to America on the *Mayflower*.

two of the great British poets. You will also read four sonnets by William Shakespeare.

Shakespeare is even more famous as a dramatist. He wrote comedies, tragedies, and historical plays. People all the world over recognize Shakespeare's characters by name. You will read an adaptation of one of his most exciting tragedies, *Macbeth.* If you are ever backstage at a theater, do not quote this play or even mention its title. It is considered bad luck.

In this unit, you will also read an excerpt from the King James version of the Bible. The work is a fine example of the Renaissance spirit. It was sponsored by King James, who asked scholars to produce an English translation of the Bible in language that ordinary people could easily understand.

You will also read several lyric poems that express Renaissance ideals.

■ THE END OF THE ENGLISH RENAISSANCE

James I died in 1625, and his son, Charles I, became king. Groups opposed to Charles I began calling for his removal. Poets of the time became involved in the controversy. Milton was against the king, while Herrick and Lovelace, lyric poets, supported him.

In 1646 Charles I was defeated in battle and removed from the throne. In 1649 his opponents beheaded him. For a decade, England was without a king. The ruling party governed by religious authority. The leaders suppressed expression of individual thoughts and ideas that clashed with their own beliefs. The English Renaissance came to an end. However, its influence can still be felt today.

As you read the selections in this unit, ask yourself how each writer expresses the Renaissance trust in intelligence and imagination.

Portrait of a young man, Georg Pencz. Uffizi, Florence, Italy/Art Resource

READING FOCUS

Compare and Contrast Themes The theme of a poem is its main idea or central message. When you read two poems, especially by the same author, you can learn more about the poems and the author by comparing and contrasting their themes. To do this, identify the theme of each poem. Then look at how they are similar and how they differ.

SONNETS

The **sonnet** is one of the major forms of British poetry. Almost every important British poet has tried writing sonnets. They are difficult to write because sonnets require order and discipline.

Sonnets have exactly fourteen lines. They have a fixed rhythm and rhyme scheme that must be followed precisely.

Some sonnets are divided into two parts. The first eight lines present a problem or a question. The final six lines offer a solution or reaction to the first part.

Other sonnets have four parts. Three parts express ideas about a subject. The last two lines offer a conclusion.

All sonnets present personal feelings and thoughts about various aspects of life. Common subjects of sonnets are love, grief, and relationships.

As you read the following sonnets, ask yourself:
1. What problem is presented?
2. What reaction or solution is offered?

WRITING CONNECTION

Write a word such as *love, grief,* or *relationships* on a sheet of paper. Write ten sentences that explore your feelings about the subject. Choose one sentence that might be expanded into a poem.

On His Having Arrived at the Age of Twenty-Three

by John Milton

How soon hath Time, the subtle thief of youth,
   Stolen on his wing my three and twentieth year!
   My hasting days fly on with full career,
   But my late spring no bud or blossom showeth.
5   Perhaps my semblance might deceive the truth
   That I to manhood am arrived so near;
   And inward ripeness doth much less appear,
   That some more timely-happy spirits[1] endueth.
Yet be it less or more, or soon or slow,
10   It shall be still in strictest measure even
   To that same lot, however mean or high,
Toward which Time leads me, and the will of Heaven;
   All is, if I have grace to use it so,
   As ever in my great Task-Master's eye.

---

hath (HATH) *(archaic)* have
hasting (HAYST ing) *(archaic)* moving swiftly
career (kuh RIR) speed
semblance (SEM bluns) outward appearance
deceive (dih SEEV) prove false
endueth (in DOO ith) endoweth
still (STIL) always
lot (LOT) fate
[1]timely-happy spirits: other people who seem to be more accomplished
   poets at the age of twenty-three

ON HIS BLINDNESS

by John Milton

When I consider how my light is spent
Ere half my days in this dark world and wide,
And that one talent which is death to hide
Lodged with me useless, though my soul more bent
5   To serve therewith my Maker, and present
My true account, lest He returning chide;
"Doth God exact day-labor, light denied?"
I fondly ask. But Patience, to prevent
That murmur, soon replies, "God doth not need
10   Either man's work or his own gifts. Who best
Bear his mild yoke, they serve him best. His state
Is kingly: thousands at his bidding speed
And post o'er land and ocean without rest;
They also serve who only stand and wait."

---

ere (AIR) *(archaic)* before; sooner than
doth (DUTH) *(archaic)* does
exact (ig ZAKT) demand
post (POHST) *(archaic)* travel quickly; hasten

John Milton (1608–1674)

At a very early age Milton was encouraged by his father to have an appreciation for music and literature; this would prove to have a lasting influence on him. His early education was at St. Paul's School in London. At sixteen he entered Christ College, Cambridge, where he began to write poetry. He graduated in 1632, but was not convinced that he had learned as much as he could, so he moved to his father's estate where he read on a wide variety of subjects for the next six years.

In 1644, after having supported the cause of the Puritans in the English Civil War by writing pamphlets on their behalf, he wrote a persuasive pamphlet in which he pleaded for freedom of the press. It was called *Areopagitica*. He wrote it to support the cause of the Puritans who wanted religious freedom and a parliamentary form of government without a king. It was a masterful plea for freedom and one of the earliest of its kind.

Oliver Cromwell, who came to power in 1653 after the execution of Charles I, read Milton's work and was so impressed that he appointed Milton as secretary for foreign languages in the new protectorate. Even though Milton had gone blind by 1652, he continued to write and work at his government post with the help of secretaries. When the monarchy was restored in 1660, he retired with his family. It was at this time that he completed the poem for which he is most famous. It is called *Paradise Lost* and is considered the greatest epic poem in the English language. It earned Milton a lasting place in the history of literature as one of England's greatest writers.

Review the Selection

UNDERSTAND THE SELECTION

Recall

1. In Milton's first poem, what does he think has been stolen?

2. Who or what did the stealing?

3. According to "On His Blindness," when did Milton become blind?

Infer

4. What did Milton believe he had accomplished at the age of twenty-three?

5. Why is Milton not totally discouraged by his lack of accomplishments?

6. Is Milton pessimistic or optimistic about his future? Explain.

7. What is Milton's talent and why is it important for him to use it?

Apply

8. What does Milton feel about the worth of blind people?

9. Milton says that "hiding" his talent is like death. How does this apply to your own experience?

10. How do you think Milton managed to create poetry without sight?

Respond to Literature

Write a paragraph discussing how Milton's sonnets reflect the ideas of the Renaissance period.

WRITE ABOUT THE SELECTION

In his poem, "On His Having Arrived at the Age of Twenty-Three," Milton indicates that he had hoped to be a more accomplished poet by that age. He states, however, that he will continue trying to do his best. He did continue, and eventually he accomplished his goal of becoming a recognized poet.

People often set goals they would like to achieve by a certain age. What are some things you wanted to achieve by the age you are now? What do you expect from the future? By the age of twenty-three where would you like to be? Write an essay indicating your goal.

Prewriting Write an outline listing your past and future goals. Number them in the order of importance. Show by what age you accomplished or would like to accomplish each. Include details as to how you achieved or plan to achieve each goal.

Writing Use your informal outline to write an essay explaining your goals in life. Describe which goals are most important and what you hope to accomplish by the age of twenty-three.

Revising As you revise, be sure to add details explaining how you accomplished or will accomplish your goals.

Proofreading Read over your essay. Check for verb-subject agreement problems. Check also for other errors in spelling, usage, and mechanics.

THINK ABOUT SONNETS

Sonnets are fourteen-line poems. They present a poet's feelings and thoughts about personal subjects such as love, grief, success and failure. Sonnets may be written in several different forms; however, the poet must follow the chosen form exactly. In one form, the poet asks a question or presents a problem in the first part of the sonnet. Then the poet answers the question or comments about the problem in the last part of the sonnet.

1. What personal subject does Milton discuss in his sonnet "On His Having Arrived at the Age of Twenty-Three"?

2. What problem does he present in the poem?

3. What conclusion does he give?

4. In the poem "On His Blindness" what question does Milton ask?

5. In the second part of the poem, how was the question answered?

READING FOCUS

Compare and Contrast Themes In reading these sonnets, you looked for similarities and differences in their themes. How are the themes of these two poems similiar? How are they different?

DEVELOP YOUR VOCABULARY

You cannot understand the meaning of a literary work unless you understand the words the author uses. Words frequently have more than one meaning. Sometimes, especially in the works of writers from previous centuries, the meanings of words as written then have changed in modern usage. These out-of-date meanings are called *archaic* today. It is usually wise to check the meaning of an unfamiliar word or unfamiliar use of a known word in a dictionary.

The following words are found in Milton's poems. Their meanings in Milton's time are different from the meanings common today. Using this text and a dictionary, for each word write the meaning Milton intended and the meaning common today. Include an original sentence illustrating each meaning of the word.

1. career
2. still
3. lot

4. spent
5. exact
6. post

Lilium Auratum, John Frederick Lewis. Birmingham City Museums and Art Gallery

READING FOCUS

Compare and Contrast Images Poetry is often filled with rich sensory images. One way to appreciate these images is to compare and contrast them with each other. Such comparisons will also help you to understand the author's tone and the poem's theme. As you read Robert Herrick's poem, think about how his images suggest contrasting ideas.

Learn About

SYMBOLISM

Have you ever experienced the power of suggestion? If you have been fearful while watching a movie or television program, your fear was probably the result of suggestion.

Suppose a scary mood is created with music. The camera moves closer and closer to the image of a partially opened door. What comes to mind?

The partially opened door might suggest something evil in the unknown beyond the door. The door symbolizes this unknown. The door can also, at the same time, symbolize fear and evil.

Symbolism is used in all forms of art, including literature. In **symbolism** an object, place, or person represents itself and at the same time suggests or stands for a thing or idea other than itself.

As you read the following poem, ask yourself:

1. What objects are important in the poem?
2. What does each important object suggest or symbolize beyond itself?

WRITING CONNECTION

Think about an object such as a flower, a football, a jungle cat. Describe it as it actually exists. Write about other ideas or feelings that the object brings to mind.

Counsel to Girls

by Robert Herrick

Gather ye rosebuds while ye may,
　　Old time is still a-flying:
And this same flower that smiles today,
　　Tomorrow will be dying.

5　The glorious lamp of heaven, the sun,
　　The higher he's a-getting,
The sooner will his race be run,
　　And nearer he's to setting.

That age is best which is the first,
10　　When youth and blood are warmer;
But being spent, the worse, and worst
　　Times still succeed the former.

Then be not coy, but use your time,
　　And while ye may, go marry:
15　For having lost but once your prime,
　　You may forever tarry.

---

tarry (TAR ee) *(archaic)* wait

Review the Selection

UNDERSTAND THE SELECTION

Recall

1. In the first verse, what advice does the poet give? Why?

2. What does the poet say happens to the sun?

3. What age does the poet consider best? Why?

Infer

4. In the first verse, what might the rosebuds and flowers symbolize?

5. How does the poet use symbolism in his references to the sun?

6. Why is the sun a good image to represent the passage of time?

7. What does the poet believe about the opportunities women have to marry?

Apply

8. How might women today respond to Herrick's poem?

9. Was Herrick a young man when he wrote this poem? Explain.

10. What advice might Herrick give in a poem entitled "Counsel to Boys"?

Respond to Literature

It has been said that Herrick's poems "please the ear more than the mind." Do you agree or disagree? Why?

WRITE ABOUT THE SELECTION

In "Counsel to Girls," Robert Herrick advises girls to marry while they are young. He believes that "time flies," and they may not have similar opportunities as they grow older. This selection was written in the seventeenth century when women tended to marry at an earlier age.

Suppose that Herrick wrote this poem today. How do you think young women today would respond to it? Do you agree or disagree with his ideas? Suppose you could have a telephone conversation with the poet. Write a dialogue between him and you. Explain why you think a modern woman should or should not follow his advice.

Prewriting   Decide whether you agree or disagree with Robert Herrick's poem. Write a list of reasons for this opinion. Think of examples to support your reasons. Think about how the poet might respond to your ideas.

Writing   Use your list of reasons and examples to write a dialogue between yourself and the poet. State your opinion of his poem and the reasons for your opinion. Include appropriate examples. Tell what the poet says about your ideas.

Revising   Read your dialogue aloud and ask yourself these questions: Have I explained my opinion clearly? Did I give good reasons? Did I include the poet's reactions? How can I improve my dialogue?

Proofreading   Read over your dialogue. Find and correct any errors in spelling.

THINK ABOUT SYMBOLISM

Symbolism is used in literature to suggest ideas and feelings beyond the actual meanings of objects included in the literary work. In the poem "Counsel to Girls," the poet uses objects in two ways. Each object stands for itself, and it also represents a more general idea beyond itself.

1. What relationship do you see between a rose and youth?

2. In what ways is a rose a symbol of youth?

3. What relationships do you see between the following sets of words: youth and morning; old age and evening?

4. For what idea in the poem is the Sun a symbol?

5. Explain the central idea of this poem.

> ### READING FOCUS
>
> **Compare and Contrast Images**   As you read "Counsel to Girls," you compared and contrasted the poet's images. Which image did you find most effective? Why? Compare and contrast this image to a weaker image in the poem.

DEVELOP YOUR VOCABULARY

In the poem "Counsel to Girls," the word *time* is used on several occasions. Each use of the word has a different meaning. For example, in ". . . *the worse, and worst Times*," the word *Times* refers to a particular period in a person's life. Then, in the phrase ". . . *use your time*," the word *time* means an opportunity, a chance.

More than half of all English words are like *time* in that they are multiple-meaning words. Write more than one meaning for each word listed below. Consult the dictionary for meanings you cannot remember. Compare your meanings with dictionary meanings as necessary. Then, locate each word in the poem and tell which meaning applies.

1. still
2. setting
3. age
4. youth
5. succeed
6. coy
7. marry
8. lost

CONFLICT

In a classical tragedy such as the following selection from *The Tragedy of Macbeth,* important struggles, or **conflicts,** are usually internal and psychological. The main character often has a weakness of character or tragic flaw. It is this tragic flaw that brings about the main character's downfall. Usually there is a moment when the main character sees clearly for the first time how his or her own weakness has led to self-destruction. This moment of self-realization is the **climax** or turning point. In classical tragedy, the climax is often followed by the death of the main character. The main character's downfall is not accidental. It results from a tragic choice made as a result of the character's flaw or weakness.

As you read this selection from *The Tragedy of Macbeth,* ask yourself:
1. What is Macbeth's tragic flaw?
2. In what ways did the flaw bring about his downfall?

WRITING CONNECTION

Identify a possible flaw or weakness in this character: "He loved his wife so much that he worried constantly at parties when she spoke to other men." Write two sentences. In one describe a conflict that might arise for the character. In the other describe a possible tragic climax.

READING FOCUS

Compare and Contrast Events When you compare and contrast events in a play or story, it can aid your comprehension. Authors often write about very similar or different events within a play or story. They do this to remind you of characters, settings, or moods that occurred earlier and to sharpen your interest in the work. Keep track of the comparisons and contrasts in events you notice in this play.

from

The Tragedy of Macbeth

ADAPTED

by William Shakespeare

It is the year 1606. You are in London, England. You are very excited about your plans for the evening. You and some friends are going to see William Shakespeare's new play, *The Tragedy of Macbeth,* at the Globe Theater. Everyone in the city knows the name Shakespeare. He is the most famous playwright in the land. For the past fifteen years he has been writing very popular plays.

You remember that when you were younger, you listened as your parents discussed his historical plays. These plays were tales of British kings and the glories of British history. Your parents would laugh as they also described outrageous scenes from his comedies.

Recently, Shakespeare has been writing mostly tragedies. His most recent works have been some of his finest. *The Tragedy of Macbeth* has been the talk of London for weeks. You already know that it is a tale of ambition, murder, and witchcraft.

The character Macbeth is based on a real person who was a Scottish king from the year 1040 until his death in 1057. Macbeth evidently was a brave soldier but he was also a cruel man. As did many people of his time, Macbeth believed in witchcraft.

Macbeth was a thane, or nobleman, in the service of King Duncan. Duncan was a meek, merciful young man. He was reluctant to punish disloyal subjects. Some nobles viewed this kindness as weakness. In the sixth year of Duncan's reign, a rebellion broke out. Macbeth and another thane named Banquo defeated the rebels in battle. In gratitude, Duncan showered Macbeth with honors. He became the second most powerful man in the land. If Macbeth had been content to remain so, he would have been remembered as a hero.

Macbeth, however, killed Duncan; then he claimed the throne for himself. Macbeth ruled for seventeen years, but he found no happiness. He constantly worried that he, too, would be murdered. His reign was one of terror. Little is known about Macbeth's family life.

Now over five hundred years later, Shakespeare has written a new play about this old Scottish king, Macbeth. You and your friends set off for the theater. On the way you discuss what you already know about the history behind the play's characters and setting. You remember that Banquo, the other thane serving King Duncan, was an ancestor of James I. James is now, in 1606, the king of England. You wonder how Shakespeare will treat that character based on the king's ancestor.

The famous Globe Theatre is across London Bridge. It is a tall wooden, eight-sided structure. A flag on top signals that this is a play day. Once inside the theatre, you look around in wonder. The center of the theatre is open to the sky.

Suddenly, from offstage, comes roll after roll of thunder. Drums, you realize. Then, a jet of steam or smoke clouds one side of the stage. In it appear three creatures that look like women, except they have beards. They have withered faces and are dressed like witches. They *are* witches!

FIRST WITCH: When shall we three meet again
    In thunder, lightning, or in rain?
SECOND WITCH: When the hurlyburly's done
    When the battle's lost and won.
THIRD WITCH: That will be ere set of sun.
FIRST WITCH: Where the place?
SECOND WITCH: Upon the heath.
THIRD WITCH: There to meet with Macbeth.
ALL: Fair is foul, and foul is fair;
    Hover through the fog and filthy air.

The witches leave, and as the smoke drifts up and away, the next scene starts almost at once. King Duncan, his son Malcolm,

---

hurlyburly (HUR lee BUR lee) uproar; confusion; (as used here) the battle
ere (AIR) before
heath (HEETH) area of open wasteland

and a group of soldiers enter. Now you learn about the battle mentioned by the witches. A rebellion has been put down. The rebellious Thane of Cawdor has just been defeated in battle by two of King Duncan's loyal lords, Macbeth (Thane of Glamis) and a general named Banquo. Macbeth, it seems, has fought most valiantly. In gratitude, King Duncan orders that the title Thane of Cawdor now be given to Macbeth.

More thunder, more smoke, and the scene shifts back to the witches on the heath:

FIRST WITCH: Where hast thou been, sister?
SECOND WITCH: Killing swine.
THIRD WITCH: Sister, where thou?
FIRST WITCH: Here I have a pilot's thumb,
    Wrecked as homeward he did come.
THIRD WITCH: A drum, a drum!
    Macbeth doth come.

    (Enter MACBETH *and* BANQUO*)*

MACBETH *(entering into smoke):* So foul and fair a day I have not
    seen.
BANQUO *(seeing witches):* What are these,
    So withered, and so wild in their attire,
    That look not like th' inhabitants o' th' earth,
    And yet are on't? You should be women,
    And yet your beards forbid me to interpret
    That you are so.
MACBETH: Speak if you can. What are you?
FIRST WITCH: All hail Macbeth, hail to thee, Thane of Glamis!
SECOND WITCH: All hail Macbeth, hail to thee, Thane of Cawdor!
THIRD WITCH: All hail Macbeth, that shalt be King hereafter.

Both Macbeth and Banquo are amazed at these prophecies. Macbeth, long the Thane of Glamis, has yet had no way to learn that he has just been named Thane of Cawdor, too. And, as for being "King hereafter," Macbeth can only marvel at the news.

---

thane (THAYN) rank of high noble in Scotland
pilot (PY lut) (as used here) any guide or leader
attire (uh TYR) clothing

Banquo then asks the witches what is in store for him. He learns that although he himself will not be the king, he shall be the father of a king. The witches vanish. Macbeth and Banquo start to discuss the prophecies when a messenger from King Duncan arrives. Now Macbeth learns that he has, in fact, been named Thane of Cawdor.

Thane of Cawdor! So the witches told the truth! At first, Macbeth finds himself speechless. Might the prediction of the third witch also come true? Might Macbeth soon find himself king? He becomes obsessed with the thought. He hardly listens to Banquo's warning:

BANQUO: But 'tis strange:
    And oftentimes, to win us to our harm,
    The instruments of darkness tell us truths,
    Win us with honest trifles, to betray us.

Macbeth resolves to stop at nothing on his path to the crown. Sending the news ahead to his wife by speedy messenger, he proceeds to his castle at Dunsinane. Lady Macbeth is overjoyed at the news. Her husband a king! And she a queen. Yet, she has one worry:

LADY MACBETH: Glamis thou art, and Cawdor, and shalt be
    What thou art promised; yet I do fear thy nature,
    It is too full o' th' milk of human kindness
    To catch the nearest way.

To Lady Macbeth, "the nearest way" means only one thing: the murder of King Duncan. Even before Macbeth arrives, she works herself into a state of frenzy on the subject:

LADY MACBETH: Come thick night,
    That my keen knife see not the wound it makes,
    Nor heaven peep through the blanket of the dark,
    To cry, hold, hold!

---

obsessed (ub SEST) dominated; completely ruled in thought and feeling
frenzy (FREN zee) wild excitement

Macbeth then arrives—with more startling news. The king himself is following on his heels, to honor him with an overnight visit. Lady Macbeth's eyes gleam with evil. She declares that King Duncan "never shall tomorrow see." Further, she advises her husband:

LADY MACBETH: Your face, my Thane, is as a book where men
    May read strange matters. To beguile the time,
    Look like the time; bear welcome in your eye,
    Your hand, your tongue: look like th' innocent flower,
    But be the serpent under't.

---

beguile (bih GYL) to mislead; deceive

Seeing that Macbeth is undecided, she tells him that all he has to do is act like an untroubled host: "Leave all the rest to me."

When the good and gentle Duncan arrives, however, Macbeth realizes that he cannot go through with his wife's plan:

MACBETH: If it were done when 'tis done, then 'twere well
It were done quickly. If the assassination . . .
Might be the be-all and the end-all—here,
But here, upon this bank and shoal of time,
We'd jump the life to come. But in these cases
We still have judgment here; that we but teach
Bloody instructions, which being taught, return
To plague the inventor: this even-handed justice
Commends the ingredients of our poisoned chalice
To our own lips. He's here in double trust:
First, as I am his kinsman and his subject,
Strong both against the deed; then, as his host,
Who should against the murderer shut the door,
Not bear the knife myself.

But Lady Macbeth has no patience for such talk. She calls her husband a coward. She pours into his ears reason after reason for proceeding with the murder. Why, the action of just one short night will give all their nights and days the sway and power of royalty! And the deed can be done so easily! For protection, two of Duncan's grooms always sleep in his room. All she has to do is to give these two servants enough drugged wine to ensure a "swinish sleep."

Macbeth knows, better than his wife, that there are risks involved. He knows that King Duncan is so fine a man that his subjects will spare no effort to revenge his murder. He knows, too, he himself has attained his present place only through Duncan's trust. Yet he cannot resist the pull of his own powerful ambition and the pleas of his wife. Suddenly, he finds himself part of the plot. Won't people think, he asks, "when we have marked

---

shoal (SHOHL) piece of rising ground forming a shallow place in a river, sea, etc.
commends (kuh MENDZ) puts in one's hands; entrusts
chalice (CHAL is) a cup; goblet

with blood those sleepy two of his own chamber, and used their very daggers, that they have done it?"

Suspense heightens as the hours drive on toward the murder. Much care is needed: Macbeth knows that the king's son, Malcolm, is also sleeping within his walls. The plan must wait till all is quiet. Then Banquo and his son Fleance arrive unexpectedly. They must be greeted and shown to bed. Macbeth and his wife agree that when everyone seems asleep, she will ring a little bell. That will be the signal.

When silence finally falls upon the castle, Macbeth slowly steals through the dark toward Duncan's room. But suddenly he stops, alarmed. Seemingly suspended in the air ahead of him is a shining, ghostly object.

MACBETH: Is this a dagger which I see before me,
    The handle toward my hand? Come let me clutch thee.
    I have thee not, and yet I see thee still.
    Art thou not, fatal vision, sensible
    To feeling as to sight? Or art thou but
    A dagger of the mind, a false creation,
    Proceeding from a heat-oppressed brain?

(A bell rings in the distance.)

    I go, and it is done. The bell invites me.
    Hear it not Duncan, for it is a knell
    That summons thee to heaven, or to hell.

As Macbeth leaves the stage, you, along with the rest of the audience, await the next scene: the murder. But this is not to be. Instead, the setting shifts to Lady Macbeth's room. She is nervously awaiting Macbeth's return.

MACBETH *(off stage):* Who's there? What ho!
LADY MACBETH: Alack, I am afraid they have awakened,
    And 'tis not done. Th' attempt, and not the deed,

---

sensible (SEN suh bul) (as used here) able to be sensed; perceptible
knell (NEL) warning bell
alack (uh LAK) alas; oh my

Confounds us. Hark! I laid their daggers ready,
He could not miss 'em.—Had he not resembled
My father as he slept, I had done't.

(MACBETH enters, carrying bloody daggers.)

My husband!

MACBETH: I have done the deed. *(Looks at his hands.)*
This is a sorry sight.

LADY MACBETH: These deeds must not be thought
After these ways; so, it will make us mad.

MACBETH: Methought I heard a voice cry, sleep no more.
Macbeth does murder sleep, the innocent sleep,
Sleep that knits up the ravelled sleave of care,
The death of each day's life, sore labor's bath,
Balm of hurt minds, great nature's second course,
Chief nourisher of life's feast.

LADY MACBETH: What do you mean?

MACBETH: Still it cried, sleep no more, to all the house.
Glamis hath murdered sleep, and therefore Cawdor
Shall sleep no more. Macbeth shall sleep no more.

LADY MACBETH: Go get some water,
And wash this filthy witness from your hands.
Why did you bring these daggers from the place?
They must lie there. Go carry them, and smear
The sleepy grooms with blood.

MACBETH: I'll go no more.
I am afraid, to think what I have done.
Look on't again I dare not.

LADY MACBETH: Infirm of purpose!
Give me the daggers. If he do bleed,
I'll gild the faces of the grooms withal,
For it must seem their guilt.

(As she leaves, a loud knocking begins far off.)

---

confound (kun FOUND) confuse; bewilder
ravelled (RAV uld) frayed
sleave (SLEEV) tangle of threads
balm (BAHM) soothing ointment
witness (WIT nis) (as used here) evidence; proof of guilt
gild (GILD) (as used here) cover with blood
withal (with AWL) with it all

MACBETH: To know my deed, 'twere best not know myself.
Wake Duncan with thy knocking. I would thou coulds't.

The next scene is an odd one. In another part of the castle, a drunken porter, lantern in hand, staggers to answer the knocking. He talks to himself.

At last the knocking is answered, the door opened. The early morning visitor turns out to be Macduff, a respected thane. Soon, the murder is discovered. At once the castle bustles with activity. Macbeth and his wife make a great show of grief. Macduff, the dead king's son Malcolm, Banquo and his son Fleance, enter and exit in tumultuous order. Although the evidence seems to be against the two grooms, suspicion begins to fall on Macbeth. Malcolm, fearing for his own life, flees to the south, to England.

Since Malcolm, King Duncan's natural heir, has fled the country, Macbeth, next in line for the throne, is crowned king—but entirely without honor. His troubles continue. He and Lady Macbeth realize they have bloodied their hands for what may be an empty victory. Moreover, they remember the witch's prophecy that Banquo's son—Fleance–will someday be king.

MACBETH: They hailed him father to a line of kings.
Upon my head they placed a fruitless crown
And put a barren scepter in my grip,
Thence to be wrenched with an unlineal hand,
No son of mine succeeding. If it be so,
For Banquo's issue have I filed my mind;
For them the gracious Duncan have I murdered; . . .
To make them kings, the seed of Banquo kings!

What to do? Get rid of Banquo and Fleance of course! A great feast is planned, to which Banquo and Fleance are invited. Macbeth hires murderers to kill his two enemies on their way to the castle. In a thrilling night scene, Banquo is killed, but young Fleance escapes.

---

tumultuous (tuu MUL choo us) disorderly; noisy
scepter (SEP tur) a decorated rod or staff held by rulers as a sign
  of authority
wrenched (RENCHT) pulled or jerked violently
unlineal (un LIN ee ul) (as used here) not in direct line of descent
  from the king

Right afterward Macbeth greets his guests with warm praise. As they are about to sit down at the banquet, Macbeth expresses his regrets that his good friend Banquo is not yet present. But almost as he says these words, the ghost of Banquo, pale and bloody, enters and sits at the table. (You, as a member of the audience, see this ghost. So does Macbeth—but others on the stage do not.) The guests sit down. Macbeth remains standing, staring at the ghost, his face blanching.

MACBETH (*to* BANQUO'S *ghost*): Thou canst not say I did it; Never shake thy gory locks at me.

ROSS: (*a guest*) Gentlemen rise, his Highness is not well.

---

blanching (BLANCH ing) turning white

LADY MACBETH: Sit worthy friends; my lord is often thus,
  And hath been from his youth. Pray you keep seat,
  The fit is momentary, upon a thought
  He will be well again. *(She pulls* MACBETH *aside.)*
  This is the very painting of your fear.
  This is the air-drawn dagger which you said
  Led you to Duncan.

Macbeth speaks to the ghost again before it silently rises and leaves. Then, trying to pull himself together, he excuses his behavior as a "strange infirmity, which is to those that know me." But Lady Macbeth wants to take no more chances. She cancels the banquet at once, and the guests leave in a rush.

Now Macbeth and his lady are troubled by bloody dreams and fears of the future. Macbeth's odd behavior has increased the suspicions of the great lords of Scotland. Moreover, Malcolm and Fleance are still alive and dangerous. Still worse, Macduff has gone to England to raise an army that will put Malcolm on the throne. In desperation, Macbeth decides to return to the witches and learn from them the worst.

With thunder and a cloud of smoke, the three witches appear once again. They are in a cave, preparing a witches' brew in a large caldron.

FIRST WITCH: Round about the caldron go;
  In the poisoned entrails throw.
ALL: Double, double toil and trouble;
  Fire burn, and caldron bubble.
SECOND WITCH: Eye of newt, and toe of frog,
  Wool of bat, and tongue of dog,
THIRD WITCH: Silvered in the moon's eclipse,
  Nose of Turk, and Tartar's lips.
ALL: Double, double toil and trouble;
  Fire burn, and caldron bubble.

---

infirmity (in FUR muh tee) weakness; disease
caldron (KAWL drun) large open kettle or boiler
entrails (EN truhlz) internal parts of body; intestines
newt (NOOT) salamander; small lizard-like creature
Tartar (TAHR tur) member of old eastern European tribe

SECOND WITCH: Cool it with a baboon's blood,
Then the charm is firm and good. . . .
By the pricking of my thumbs,
Something wicked this way comes.
Open locks,
Whoever knocks.

(MACBETH *enters.*)

MACBETH: How now, you secret, black, and midnight hags?
What is't you do?
ALL: A deed without a name.

Macbeth loses no time in asking the witches about his future.
In reply, they produce three apparitions. The first is the likeness of
an armed head. It calls Macbeth by name and tells him to beware
the Thane of Fife (Macduff). The second, which resembles a bloody
child, also addresses Macbeth by name. It tells him to be bloody
and fearless, "for none of woman born shall harm Macbeth." The
third, a crowned child holding a tree, tells him to "take no care"
and that he will be safe "until great Birnam Wood to high Dunsinane Hill shall come." He presses them for more information,
"Shall Banquo's issue ever reign in this kingdom?" An apparition
of eight Kings and Banquo appears. The eighth King has a mirror
in his hand.

MACBETH: Thou art too like the spirit of Banquo. Down!
Thy crown does sear mine eyeballs. And thy hair,
Thou other gold-bound brow, is like the first.
A third is like the former. Filthy hags!
Why do you show me this? A fourth? Start, eyes!
What, will the line stretch out to the crack of doom?
Another yet? A seventh? I'll see no more.
And yet the eighth appears. . .
Now I see 'tis true;
For the blood-boltered Banquo smiles upon me
And points at them for his.

---

apparition (ap uh RISH un) phantom; spirit
sear (SIR) to burn the surface of
blood-boltered (BLUD BOHL turd) (as used here) with blood
   matting his hair

Macbeth leaves the cavern with mixed feelings. If he can be harmed "by none of woman born," why then he can be harmed by no one, for all people have been born of a woman. He knows, too, that Birnam Wood, a forest, can never "unfix his earthbound root" and move to his castle at nearby Dunsinane. It is the first message that worries him: to beware of the Thane of Fife. He decides to act at once.

Thereupon, Macbeth, seething with rage, marches his men to Macduff's castle at Fife. Macduff is not there, but Lady Macduff, her children, and all their relations lose their lives.

Back at Dunsinane, Lady Macbeth, left alone with her guilt, seems more and more oppressed by all the blood she has helped to spill. She sleeps poorly. A woman of her retinue has observed her talking and even writing while sleepwalking. She has asked Lady Macbeth's doctor to witness this behavior.

DOCTOR: I have two nights watched with you, but can perceive no truth in your report. When was it she last walked?

WOMAN: Since his Majesty went into the field. I have seen her rise from her bed, throw her nightgown upon her, unlock her closet, take forth paper, write upon it, read it, afterward seal it, and again return to bed; yet all this while in a most fast sleep.

DOCTOR: What at any time have you heard her say?

WOMAN: That, sir, I will not report after her.

(LADY MACBETH *enters with a candle.*)

Lo you, here she comes. Observe her, stand close.

DOCTOR: You see her eyes are open.

WOMAN: Ay, but their sense are shut.

DOCTOR: What is it she does now? Look how she rubs her hands.

WOMAN: It is an accustomed action with her. I have known her to continue in this a quarter of an hour.

LADY MACBETH: Yet here's a spot.

DOCTOR: Hark, she speaks.

LADY MACBETH: Out damned spot, out I say! What need we fear who knows it, when none can call our power into account?

---

seething (SEE*TH* ing) very angry
retinue (RET un oo) group of servants of an important person

Yet who would have thought the old man to have so much blood in him?

DOCTOR: Do you mark that?

LADY MACBETH: The Thane of Fife had a wife; where is she now? What, will these hands ne'er be clean?

DOCTOR *(thoughtfully, to himself):* You have known what you should not.

WOMAN: She has spoke what she should not, I am sure of that. Heaven knows what she has known.

LADY MACBETH: Here's the smell of the blood still: all the perfumes of Arabia will not sweeten this little hand. Oh, oh, oh!

DOCTOR: This disease is beyond my practice.

LADY MACBETH: Wash your hands, put on your nightgown, look not so pale. I tell you again Banquo's buried; he cannot come out on's grave.

DOCTOR: Even so?

LADY MACBETH: To bed, to bed; there's knocking at the gate. Come, come, come, come, give me your hand. What's done cannot be undone. To bed, to bed, to bed.

DOCTOR: Will she go now to bed?

WOMAN: Directly.

DOCTOR: Foul whisperings are abroad. Unnatural deeds
Do breed unnatural troubles; infected minds
To their deaf pillows will discharge their secrets.
More needs she the divine than the physician.
God, God forgive us all. Look after her.
I think, but dare not speak.

WOMAN: Good night good doctor.

Little time is left. Macbeth, back at Dunsinane, learns that an army led by Malcolm and Macduff is approaching. Even worse, that army is getting ever larger as lords from all over Scotland join it to oppose Macbeth. Now the army has reached Birnam Wood. Now it is marching on the castle. Macbeth tries to take comfort in the memory of the words about "none of woman born" and "Birnam Wood." He assures his forces that the attackers will be defeated.

---

on's (AHNZ) of his
abroad (uh BRAWD) (as used here) about; spread around
divine (duh VYN) priest or other clergyman

Just at this tense moment, word reaches Macbeth that Lady Macbeth has killed herself. He is stunned:

MACBETH: She should have died hereafter;
   There would have been a time for such a word.
   To-morrow, and to-morrow, and to-morrow,
   Creeps in this petty pace from day to day,
   To the last syllable of recorded time;
   And all our yesterdays have lighted fools
   The way to dusty death. Out, out, brief candle!
   Life's but a walking shadow, a poor player,
   That struts and frets his hour upon the stage,
   And then is heard no more. It is a tale
   Told by an idiot, full of sound and fury
   Signifying nothing.

Life has now lost all meaning for Macbeth, and the audience senses that the play is nearly over. Macbeth learns Malcolm's troops have cut limbs off trees in Birnam Wood to camouflage themselves as they march on the castle. Thus, Birnam Wood has come to Dunsinane. In despair, Macbeth prepares to meet his enemies in battle:

MACBETH: I begin to be aweary of the sun,
   and wish the estate of the world were now undone.
   Ring the alarum bell! Blow wind, come wrack!
   At least we'll die with harness on our back.

The scene shifts to the battlefield. Characters enter and exit quickly as the battle rages. Macduff seeks out Macbeth to avenge the killing of his wife and children. At last, they meet:

MACDUFF: Turn, hell-hound, turn!
MACBETH: Of all men else I have avoided thee.
   But get thee back! My soul is too much charged
   With blood of thine already.
MACDUFF: I have no words:
   My voice is in my sword.

---

petty (PET ee) small or slow
wrack (RAK) wreck; destroy
harness (HAHR nis) (as used here) armor

Macbeth warns Macduff that no man "of woman born" can kill him. Macduff shouts back that he was "from his mother's womb untimely ripped" by Caesarean section, not born in the natural way. Macbeth is shaken, but he will not surrender:

MACBETH: I will not yield,
  To kiss the ground before young Malcolm's feet
  And to be baited with the rabble's curse.
  Though Birnam Wood be come to Dunsinane,
  And thou opposed, being of no woman born,
  Yet I will try the last. Before my body
  I throw my warlike shield. Lay on, Macduff,
  And damned be him that first cries "Hold, enough!"

The two exit the stage fighting. Malcolm and the other lords enter. Macduff reappears, having slain Macbeth. He hails Malcolm as the new king. The play ends with Malcolm pledging to restore peace and order.

As you leave the theater, you find yourself saddened—and yet strangely thrilled at the same time.

---

rabble (RAB ul) common people; the masses

William Shakespeare (1564–1616)

William Shakespeare was probably the greatest writer ever to use the English language. He left 37 plays and a book of poems. Unfortunately, he wrote almost nothing about his own life, and what little we know comes from sketchy 400-year-old official records and the writings of a few friends.

Shakespeare was born in Stratford, England, in April, 1564. His father, a glove maker, was an active town leader. The boy probably went to the free local school, but nothing is known for sure about his education. Records show that at 18 he married Anne Hathaway, a woman of 26. The births of three children are recorded. The next facts about Shakespeare's life come from London. He is referred to as an actor in 1592, and soon after as a playwright. He was also part owner of the theater company with which he worked. His plays were popular, and in about 1612 he retired to Stratford a wealthy man. In the words of his friends, he was "handsome," "open and free," "very good company," and "gentle"—but "a poor speller."

Shakespeare usually wrote in blank verse, or unrhymed poetry with five strong vocal stresses per line. Although he wrote for the common playgoer, his language is sometimes hard for the reader of today to understand. This is because English is in a constant process of change.

In *Macbeth,* you read words like *ere, withal,* and *on's,* all common in Shakespeare's time. (On the other hand, many of our most-used words, including *its,* were not used by Shakespeare.) In spite of the change in language, however, many words and expressions invented by Shakespeare live on in our everyday speech: "flaming youth," "method in his madness," "an itching palm," "a fool's paradise," "cold comfort," "out of the question," "a spotless reputation," and even "it was Greek to me."

Review the Selection

UNDERSTAND THE SELECTION

Recall

1. What prophecies did the witches make at the beginning of the play?

2. What act clears the way for Macbeth to become King of Scotland?

3. Who eventually killed Macbeth?

Infer

4. How was Macbeth's character honorable and how was it flawed?

5. What do you think is the meaning of the voice Macbeth imagines he hears?

6. What do you think Banquo's ghost represents?

7. What does the "spot" on Lady Macbeth's hand represent?

Apply

8. Predict what might have happened if Macbeth had not killed Duncan.

9. How might Banquo have acted if he had been told he would be king?

10. How might King James I have reacted to a performance of *Macbeth*?

Respond to Literature

What have you learned from Shakespeare's characters that applies to human beings in general?

WRITE ABOUT THE SELECTION

After hearing the prophecies of the three witches, Macbeth becomes obsessed with the idea of becoming king. However, the witches had also made another prediction that same day. They prophesied that Banquo would one day be father of a king. Banquo's son Fleance was a threat to Macbeth. He sent murderers to kill both father and son, but they succeeded in killing only Banquo. Fleance escaped.

At the conclusion of the play *Macbeth,* it is not clear what has happened to Fleance. Write another scene to the play explaining what happened to Fleance and telling if the witches' predictions were correct.

Prewriting   Write a list of events that might have happened to Fleance. Include details of how he escaped, who might have helped him, where he went, and what he did. Decide whether or not he became king. Include those events.

Writing   Use your list to write your scene. Explain what happened to Fleance and tell about the events that led to his becoming king or not becoming king.

Revising   Before revising, read your scene aloud. Add specific details that will make the characters come to life.

Proofreading   Read your scene again. Look for contractions. Make sure you have used an apostrophe in every contraction.

THINK ABOUT CONFLICT

In classical tragedy, the conflict is often represented by an internal struggle in the mind of the main character. A flaw or weakness in the character's personality causes him or her to commit a treacherous act. The story comes to a climax when the main character realizes his or her error. A story with these elements is considered a **tragedy**. It is a tragedy because the main character who is a hero at the beginning of the story loses those qualities that made him a hero.

1. What actions justify calling Macbeth a hero at the beginning of the play?

2. How would you describe Macbeth's internal conflicts?

3. What is Macbeth's flaw or weakness of character?

4. How does Macbeth's flaw bring about his downfall?

5. When does Macbeth realize his errors? Why is it too late?

READING FOCUS

Compare and Contrast Events   As you read *The Tragedy of Macbeth,* you compared and contrasted events to understand the drama. Think back now. How were the prophecies presented by the witches the same as or different from the realities that came to pass?

DEVELOP YOUR VOCABULARY

A **synonym** is a word that has almost the same meaning as another word. *Warrior* is a synonym for *soldier.* As in the case of *warrior* and *soldier,* all synonyms are a shade different in meaning. Sometimes one synonym will express the writer's meaning better than all the other synonyms. For example, find the word *petty* in the following quote from *Macbeth:*

> "To-morrow, and to-morrow, and tomorrow,
> Creeps in this petty pace from day to day. . . "

Shakespeare chose the word *petty* instead of a synonym for several reasons. The meaning of *petty* more exactly expressed what he wanted to say. It fit the rhythm of his line, and *petty* and *pace* created alliteration.

Find a synonym for each of the following words in a thesaurus or a dictionary. Write an original sentence for each word. Then rewrite the sentence substituting the synonym for the word. Check which of the two sentences better expresses your meaning.

1. strut
2. foul
3. attire
4. fret
5. deed
6. worthy
7. gory
8. entrails
9. apparition
10. taunt

Learn About

Our English Coasts (Strayed Sheep), William Holman Hunt. The Granger Collection

READING FOCUS

Compare and Contrast Authors' Viewpoints Poems, as well as prose selections, usually reflect the author's viewpoint or attitude toward the subject. This viewpoint may be communicated by the speaker or narrator, a character, or an outside observer. As you read the poems in this selection, decide who is speaking and his or her attitude toward the subject.

LYRIC POETRY

The lyric is one of the oldest forms of poetry. The name comes from an ancient musical instrument, the lyre. In its original meaning, the lyric was a poem that could be set to music or sung. In its modern meaning, the **lyric** is a poem expressing direct, intense personal feeling. Many lyric poems celebrate nature or love.

A lyric poem often does not tell a story. It presents an experience, a single effect, or a feeling. There are many different types of lyric poems. An **elegy** is a lyric poem that expresses the feeling of sorrow, especially for a person who has died. Another kind of lyric is an ode. An **ode** is a poem of praise. **Pastorals** are lyric poems that celebrate the beauty and pleasure of country life. **Ballads** tell stories of romance and adventure.

As you read these selections, ask yourself:

1. Could the words be set to music?
2. Is the poet presenting an intense, personal feeling, creating an effect, or telling a story?

WRITING CONNECTION

Lyric poetry often celebrates country life. Think of the most beautiful country place you know. List five features you remember. Describe the pleasures each feature provides.

The Passionate Shepherd to His Love

by Christopher Marlowe

Come live with me, and be my love,
And we will all the pleasures prove
That hills and valleys, dales and fields,
And all the craggy mountains yields.

5   And we will sit upon the rocks,
Seeing the shepherds feed their flocks
By shallow rivers, to whose falls
Melodious birds sings madrigals.

And I will make thee beds of roses,
10   And a thousand fragrant posies,
A cap of flowers and a kirtle
Embroidered all with leaves of myrtle.

A gown made of the finest wool
Which from our pretty lambs we pull,
15   Fair lined slippers for the cold,
With buckles of the purest gold;

A belt of straw and ivy-buds,
With coral clasps and amber studs,
And if these pleasures may thee move,
20   Come live with me, and be my love.

---

prove (PROOV) *(archaic)* experience
madrigals (MAD rih gulz) songs with parts for several voices
posies (POH zeez) flowers
kirtle (KUR tul) *(archaic)* skirt

The Hireling Shepherd, William Holman Hunt. Manchester City Art Galleries

Thy silver dishes for thy meat,
As precious as the gods do eat,
Shall on an ivory table be
Prepared each day for thee and me.

25   The shepherd swains shall dance and sing
For thy delight each May-morning;
If these delights thy mind may move,
Then live with me, and be my love.

---

swain (SWAYN) *(archaic)* boy; youth

The Nymph's Reply to the Shepherd

by Sir Walter Raleigh

If all the world and love were young,
And truth in every shepherd's tongue,
These pretty pleasures might me move
To live with thee and be thy love.

5   But time drives the flocks from field to fold,
When rivers rage and rocks grow cold;
And Philomel becometh dumb;
The rest complains of cares to come.

The flowers do fade, and wanton fields
10   To wayward winter reckoning yields:
A honey tongue, a heart of gall,
Is fancy's spring, but sorrow's fall.

Thy gowns, thy shoes, thy beds of roses,
Thy cap, thy kirtle, and thy posies,
15   Soon break, soon wither, soon forgotten,—
In folly ripe, in reason rotten.

Thy belt of straw and ivy buds,
Thy coral clasps and amber studs,—
All those in me no means can move
20   To come to thee and be thy love.

But could youth last, and love still breed;
Had joys no date, nor age no need;
Then those delights my mind might move
To live with thee and be thy love.

Philomel (FIL uh mel) the nightingale
wanton (WAHN tun) luxurious; lavish
gall (GAWL) bitterness
fancy (FAN see) love
posies (POH zeez) flowers
date (DAYT) ending

The Bait *by John Donne*

Come live with me, and be my love,
And we will some new pleasures prove
Of golden sands, and crystal brooks,
With silken lines, and silver hooks.

5   There will the river whispering run
Warmed by thine eyes, more than the sun.
And there th' enamored fish will stay,
Begging themselves they may betray.

When thou wilt swim in that live bath,
10 Each fish, which every channel hath,
Will amorously to thee swim,
Gladder to catch thee, than thou him.

If thou, to be so seen, beest loath,
By sun, or moon, thou darkenest both,
15 And if myself have leave to see,
I need not their light, having thee.

Let others freeze with angling reeds,
And cut their legs, with shells and weeds,
Or treacherously poor fish beset
20 With strangling snare, or windowy net:

Let coarse bold hands, from slimy nest
The bedded fish in banks out-wrest,
Or curious traitors, sleave-silk flies[1]
Bewitch poor fishes' wandering eyes.

25 For thee, thou needest no such deceit,
For thou thyself art thine own bait;
That fish, that is not catched thereby,
Alas, is wiser far than I.

---

prove (PROOV) *(archaic)* experience
amorously (AM ur us lee) as if in love
loath (LOHTH) reluctant
beset (bih SET) surround
[1]**sleave-silk flies:** fishing flies of unraveled, floss-silk

Sir Walter Raleigh (c.1552–1618)

Legend has it that Sir Walter Raleigh gained favor with the Queen of England, Elizabeth I, by chivalrously spreading his cape over a muddy spot in the road so she would not get wet. In return the Queen granted him large parcels of land in both England and Ireland and knighted him in 1584. Whatever the reasons for her favor, Raleigh fell out of favor in 1592 when he married one of her maids of honor. For several years he was forbidden at court.

Besides being a writer and poet, he was also a mariner and colonizer. He traveled extensively to South America and set up three colonies on the islands off North Carolina. A lot of this exploration was motivated in part by his trying to stop the Spanish rule in the New World. Toward that end, he also participated in two attacks against the Spanish: in 1596 at Cadiz and in 1597 on the Azores.

Unfortunately, when James I succeeded Elizabeth, Raleigh was accused of trying to overthrow the King and was convicted of treason. He stayed in the Tower of London for thirteen years where he spent a great deal of time writing. He wrote about many subjects, but perhaps his most impressive writing was the *History of the World* which he wrote while he was there. It was never finished; however, it was such a fascinating book that eleven editions were printed.

Finally, Raleigh persuaded James I to release him by telling him that he knew the location of valuable gold mines in South America. When Raleigh arrived in Guiana, he was sick, and so sent his crew ahead to search for the mines. His crew fought against the Spanish, which James I had ordered Raleigh not to do. Upon hearing this, James I arrested Raleigh upon his return and had him beheaded on October 29, 1618.

Review the Selection

Recall

1. What does the passionate shepherd in Marlowe's poem offer?

2. In "The Nymph's Reply to the Shepherd," who is the speaker?

3. In Raleigh's poem, how does the woman feel about the offer?

Infer

4. What are the similarities and differences in Marlowe's and Raleigh's poems?

5. Under what conditions would the young woman agree to the shepherd's request?

6. What is the subject of "The Bait"?

7. In what ways does the poet compare love to fishing?

Apply

8. What gifts of nature might the shepherd promise a woman today?

9. How would someone reply to the shepherd today?

10. If you were one of the characters in "The Bait," how would you feel about being compared to a fish?

Respond to Literature
In what ways do modern song lyrics and poems celebrate the same things that Renaissance poems do?

WRITE ABOUT THE SELECTION

The three poems in this selection are all lyrical. Each has a musical quality and all three consider feelings of love.

Suppose you are a songwriter creating lyrics for a love song. In your song a young man speaks of his feelings of love for a young woman. The woman replies.

Prewriting Use the technique of clustering to jot down ideas, words, and phrases that come to mind for your lyrics. You may want to start with two circles, one labeled *man* and one labeled *woman.* Think about how you might feel if you were a young man in love. What words might he use to describe his feelings? What might he offer to his love? Think about how a young woman might feel about his offers. Jot down words and phrases she might use to respond.

Writing Use the notes in your cluster to write two verses of a song lyric. Have a young man speak in the first verse and a young woman speak in the second. Have each person tell about his or her feelings.

Revising Read your lyric aloud. Think about changes you could make to improve it. Have you used the same words or phrases too often?

Proofreading Read your lyric again and identify all pronouns. Make sure you have included an antecedent for each pronoun.

THINK ABOUT THE LYRIC

The **lyric** is a poem expressing direct, intense personal feeling. Because it expresses passionate feeling, the lyric is often characterized by extreme or exaggerated claims.

1. What seems extreme or exaggerated about the shepherd's offer? Explain.

2. What pleasures of country life does Marlowe present in his poem? Give examples of sights, sounds, and smells.

3. What seems extreme or exaggerated about Raleigh's poem? Explain.

4. What seems extreme or exaggerated about Donne's poem? Explain your answer with examples.

5. In "The Bait," what sights, sounds, and physical sensations of the country are present?

READING FOCUS

Compare and Contrast Authors' Viewpoints Identify the speaker of each poem. Explain how the speakers' attitudes toward the subject of love in these three poems are the same or different.

DEVELOP YOUR VOCABULARY

Collective nouns are words like *class, herd,* and *fleet* that are singular in form, but that designate a group of people, animals, or things. In "The Passionate Shepherd to His Love," Christopher Marlowe refers to "flocks." In this case, he is talking about groups of sheep. A *flock* could also be a group of other mammals or birds that live or are herded together. Other specialized collective nouns listed below refer to specific groups of animals. Use a dictionary to identify the group of animals with which each word is associated. Write an original sentence for each word using the meaning you found in the dictionary.

1. school
2. gaggle
3. pack
4. swarm
5. litter
6. herd
7. colony
8. covey
9. brood
10. pride
11. bevy
12. plague

Learn About

THEME

As a reader you can enjoy a literary work on several different levels. On one level you read to understand what happens in the work. On a second level you can try to understand the idea an author had in mind as he or she wrote a work. Each author usually tries to communicate something he or she thinks is true or important about human beings. This truth or important idea is central to the work, and it is called **theme.**

Sometimes the theme is stated so you know exactly what an author thinks about the subject. In fiction, though, the theme is more likely expressed indirectly, or **implied.** You must use literary clues to draw your own conclusions as to the meaning of the work.

As you read the selection, ask yourself:

1. What clues to the author's thoughts and feelings appear in the work?
2. What truth about human beings do you think the author had in mind when he or she created the work?

WRITING CONNECTION

Sometimes writers choose a theme. Then they write a story that illustrates that theme. Make a list of human truths that might make good themes for stories.

READING FOCUS

Compare and Contrast Characters
When you compare and contrast two or more characters, you learn how these characters are similar to and different from one another. Notice how two characters behave in a similar situation and you will discover the underlying traits of each. As you read this parable, remember that the characters are meant to teach readers something. Comparing and contrasting these characters helps you understand the lessons the author or work intends to teach.

The Parable of the Prodigal Son

ADAPTED *from the King James Bible*

A certain man had two sons. The younger of them said, "Father, may I have those goods that are to be mine now rather than waiting until after your death?" The father said, "Yes." He then divided his goods, giving half to his younger son.

Several days later, the younger son took what was his and journeyed to a far country. There, he wasted what was his in riotous living. When his goods were gone, a mighty famine arose in that land. The son was in want. He went to work as a servant in that country. His master had him feed the swine in the fields. He was so poorly fed that he would have been happy to fill his belly with the corn husks that the swine ate.

He soon came to his senses and asked himself, "How many hired servants of my father's have bread enough and to spare, while I perish with hunger! I will arise and go to my father. I will say unto him, "Father, I have sinned against heaven, and before thee. I am no longer worthy to be called thy son. Make me as one of thy hired servants."

---

parable (PAR uh bul) short story with a moral lesson
prodigal (PROD ih gul) recklessly wasteful
swine (SWYN) pigs

So he arose and went back to his father's home. When he was still a great way off, his father saw him coming. His father was filled with compassion. He ran to his son and hugged him. The son said, "Father, I have sinned against heaven, and in thy sight. I am no longer worthy to be called thy son."

However, the father said to his servants, "Bring forth the best robe, and put it on him. Put a ring on his hand and shoes on his feet. Bring the fatted calf here and kill it. Let us eat and be merry for this, my son, who was dead, is alive again. . ." And they began to make merry.

Now the elder son had been in the fields. As he came home and drew near the house, he heard music and dancing. He called

---

compassion (kum PASH un) sympathy

to one of the servants, and asked what all this meant. The servant replied, "Thy brother has come home. Thy father has killed the fatted calf in thanks for his safe return."

The elder son became angry. He refused to enter the house. Therefore, his father came out and entreated the elder son to join the party. The elder son replied, "Lo these many years, I have served thee. At no time did I transgress thy commandments. Yet thou never gave me even a small goat that I might make merry with my friends. When the prodigal son returns, after squandering his inheritance, you butcher for him the fatted calf."

The father said unto him, "Son, thou art always with me, and all that I have is thine. It was meet that we should make merry and be glad because thy brother, who was dead, is alive again. He, who was lost is now found."

entreat (en TREET) plead with to persuade; beg
transgress (trans GRES) break
squander (SKWAHN dur) to spend foolishly or wastefully

Review the Selection

UNDERSTAND THE SELECTION

Recall

1. What did the younger son do with the inheritance from his father?

2. What did the older son do?

3. How did the father react when the younger son returned home?

Infer

4. Why was the father happy to see his younger son?

5. How did the older brother treat the younger brother?

6. Why was the older brother angry?

7. In what two ways was the younger son "lost and then found"?

Apply

8. What lesson does this parable teach?

9. If the older son had been the prodigal son, how might the father's reaction have been different?

10. How might the prodigal son and the elder son react toward one another?

Respond to Literature

What important ideas in this parable still hold true today?

WRITE ABOUT THE SELECTION

In this selection, the prodigal son decides to return home without contacting his family prior to his arrival. What if he had written to his brother asking for help? Assume that he has written a letter to you, his brother, explaining what has happened. In it he asks you to approach your father and inquire whether or not he may come home. Are you angry at his request? What does your father say when you talk to him? What advice do you want to give to your brother? Write a letter answering your prodigal brother's request.

Prewriting   Brainstorm ideas for the letter to your brother. Jot down as many ideas, words, and phrases as you can think of about your brother's situation. Include how you feel and any advice you want to give him.

Writing   Use your notes to write a first draft of a letter to your brother. Include your own and your father's reactions to your brother's request.

Revising   Reread your letter. Think about how it will make your brother feel. Revise parts that do not communicate the feelings or ideas you intended.

Proofreading   Read over your letter. If you have quoted your father exactly, make sure you have placed the quotation marks correctly.

THINK ABOUT THEME

Theme is rarely stated in fiction. However, fictional works often contain thematic passages. **Thematic passages** are episodes or dialogue that bring the central idea into sharp focus. Thematic passages help the readers identify the underlying theme of the work.

1. What clues to the theme can you infer from the prodigal son's experiences in the far country?

2. What does the prodigal son's decision to return home tell you about the theme?

3. What information about the theme can you learn from the father's words and actions after his son's return?

4. Can you identify a thematic passage in this work? Explain your answer.

5. In your own words, explain the theme of "The Parable of the Prodigal Son."

READING FOCUS

Compare and Contrast Characters In reading this parable, you studied similarities and differences between the main characters. Briefly summarize the key similarities and differences between two of these characters.

DEVELOP YOUR VOCABULARY

In the year 1066, William the Conqueror defeated the descendants of the Angles. After his victory, William became king of the region known as England. Since he and his followers were from France, they spoke French. It became the language of business, the courts, and the upper classes. The language of the Angles, Old English, was still used by the peasants. Eventually modern English developed combining the two languages.

In the list below, the first word in each pair appears in the selection. The second is a synonym. Guess which of the two words originally was used by the upper classes. Which of the two was used by peasants? Use a dictionary to check your guesses and to note which words are of French and of Germanic origin.

1. far   distant
2. belly   stomach
3. sin   transgress
4. son   heir
5. hire   employ
6. kill   butcher

Young Girl Arranging Flowers, Gustave Courbet. The Granger Collection

READING FOCUS

Compare and Contrast Themes The theme is the main idea or message in a piece of literature. When you read several works by the same author, you can compare and contrast the author's messages. While reading Shakespeare's sonnets, ask yourself how his theme varies from one sonnet to the next.

RHYME

Rhyme refers to the repeated use of words containing the same sounds. A vowel usually creates the rhyming sound *(day* and *May).* Sometimes, letters in combination produce the rhyme *(brings* and *kings).* The last syllable is usually the rhymed unit *(despising* and *arising).* In poetry, rhyme is most commonly employed at the end of a poetic line.

Rhyme scheme refers to the arrangement of rhyme in a stanza or verse within a poem. The simplest form of rhyme scheme is the couplet. A **couplet** is a two-line rhyming unit.

Following are four Shakespearean sonnets. Think of each sonnet as three four-line stanzas or **quatrains,** and a concluding couplet. In each quatrain, the last syllables in the first and third lines rhyme. The last syllables in the second and fourth lines also rhyme.

As you read the selections, ask yourself:

1. Which rhyming words use identical sounds to create the rhyme?
2. Which words use similar, but not identical, sounds to create the rhyme?

WRITING CONNECTION

Choose a subject and write four pairs of rhyming words that describe the subject.

SONNET 18

by William Shakespeare

Shall I compare thee to a summer's day?
Thou art more lovely and more temperate:
Rough winds do shake the darling buds of May,
And summer's lease hath all too short a date:
5   Sometime too hot the eye of heaven shines,
And often is his gold complexion dimmed;
And every fair from fair sometime declines,
By chance or nature's changing course untrimmed;[1]
But thy eternal summer shall not fade,
10   Nor lose possession of that fair thou ow'st;
Nor shall death brag thou wander'st in his shade,
When in eternal lines to time thou grow'st:
     So long as men can breathe, or eyes can see,
     So long lives this, and this gives life to thee.[2]

---

ow'st (OHST) ownest
[1]**changing course untrimmed:** stripped of gay apparel
[2]**gives life to thee:** boast of immortality

SONNET 29

by William Shakespeare

When in disgrace with fortune and men's eyes
I all alone beweep my outcast state,
And trouble deaf heaven with my bootless cries,
And look upon myself, and curse my fate,
5   Wishing me like to one more rich in hope,
Featured like him, like him with friends possessed,
Desiring this man's art, and that man's scope,
With what I most enjoy contented least;
Yet in these thoughts myself almost despising,
10   Haply I think on thee,—and then my state,
Like to the lark at break of day arising
From sullen earth, sings hymns at heaven's gate;
    For thy sweet love remembered such wealth brings
    That then I scorn to change my state with kings.

---

bootless (BOOT lis) futile

Only a Lock of Hair, Sir John Everett Millais. Manchester City Art Galleries

SONNET 116

by William Shakespeare

Let me not to the marriage of true minds
Admit impediments. Love is not love
Which alters when it alteration finds,
Or bends with the remover to remove:
5 O, no! it is an ever-fixed mark,
That looks on tempests and is never shaken;
It is the star to every wandering bark,[1]
Whose worth's unknown, although his height be taken.
Love's not Time's fool, though rosy lips and cheeks
10 Within his bending sickle's compass come;
Love alters not with his brief hours and weeks,
But bears it out even to the edge of doom.
     If this be error, and upon me proved,
     I never writ, nor no man ever loved.

---

impediments (im PED uh munts) hindrances; obstacles; (as used here) reasons why a marriage
   should not be allowed to take place
sickle (SIK ul) crescent-shaped tool for cutting grain
doom (DOOM) Judgment Day
[1]**star. . .bark:** the star that guides every wandering ship; the North star

SONNET 130

by William Shakespeare

My mistress' eyes are nothing like the sun;
Coral is far more red than her lips' red:
If snow be white, why then her breasts are dun;
If hairs be wires, black wires grow on her head.
5   I have seen roses damasked, red and white,
But no such roses see I in her cheeks;
And in some perfumes is there more delight
Than in the breath that from my mistress reeks.
I love to hear her speak, yet well I know
10   That music hath a far more pleasing sound:
I grant I never saw a goddess go,—
My mistress, when she walks, treads on the ground:
    And yet, by heaven, I think my love as rare
    As any she belied with false compare.

---

dun (DUN) dull, grayish brown
damasked (DAM uskt) varied in appearance
reeks (REEKS) emanates; comes out
go (GOH) walk

Review the Selection

UNDERSTAND THE SELECTION

Recall

1. In Sonnet 18, how does the poet feel about the subject?

2. How does the poet guarantee eternal life to his love?

3. At the beginning of Sonnet 29, in what kind of mood is the poet? Why?

Infer

4. How and why does the poet's mood change by the end of Sonnet 29?

5. In Sonnet 116, how is true love compared to the North Star?

6. In Sonnet 116, what connection does the poet see between true love and youth and good looks?

7. In Sonnet 130, what does Shakespeare suggest about the importance of physical perfection?

Apply

8. Describe the personality of the individual portrayed in Sonnet 18.

9. What would you retitle Sonnet 29?

10. Compare the themes of Sonnets 116 and 130. What is similar about them?

Respond to Literature

Explain how Shakespeare's sonnets demonstrate the Renaissance trust in intelligence and imagination.

WRITE ABOUT THE SELECTION

The poems in this section explain Shakespeare's feelings for people he knew. Identities remain a mystery as the poet never revealed names.

Each sonnet immortalized his feelings toward the individual described. He often indicates how permanent his feelings are. How would you feel if someone immortalized you in poetry or prose? By whom would you choose to be remembered?

Select one person for whom you have strong feelings. You cannot reveal the individual's name. Assume you have an opportunity to immortalize the person. Decide what qualities you want others to remember about the individual and why. You may choose to write four lines of original poetry or a prose paragraph.

Prewriting Write a list of the qualities you admire and examples of how this person exhibits those qualities. Include your feelings about these qualities and why.

Writing Use your list of qualities, examples, and feelings to write your poem or paragraph. Describe the person you have chosen. Include your impressions and feelings and add details that give a strong sense of what the person is like.

Revising In revising, make sure that you have included specific details that create a vivid picture of the person.

Proofreading Read over your poem or paragraph. Be sure to add any words that you might have missed in your final draft.

THINK ABOUT RHYME

Rhyme scheme refers to the pattern of the rhyme. A **couplet** is two lines of a poem that go together. The two lines often rhyme. A **quatrain** is four lines of a poem that go together. The rhyme scheme of a quatrain varies with the poet.

1. In each quatrain of Shakespeare's sonnets, which other line rhymes with the first?

2. Which other line rhymes with the second in each quatrain?

3. Give examples from the sonnets of rhymes created using identical sounds.

4. Give examples of rhymes created using similar, but not identical, sounds.

5. Choose any one of Shakespeare's four sonnets. Explain how the final rhyming couplet summarizes the thoughts or answers the questions asked in the preceding three quatrains.

READING FOCUS

Compare and Contrast Themes Think about the theme of each sonnet. Summarize each theme in one sentence. Then explain how the themes in the sonnets are similar and different.

DEVELOP YOUR VOCABULARY

Between the 8th and 11th centuries people from Scandinavia began raiding the English coastline. The Scandinavians left an influence on the English language. For example, when Shakespeare uses *give* and *scorn,* he is using words of Scandinavian origin.

Nouns with the following characteristics are usually, though not always, borrowed from Scandinavian languages. They begin with a hard *sc* or *sk* sound that is followed by a vowel; for example, *scorn.* (This sound can be distinguished from the soft sound of the "sc" in a word like *scene* which is not Scandinavian in origin.)

Following are English words of Scandinavian origin. Notice that they consist of one syllable and end in a consonant. Find the meanings of these words in a dictionary and then write an original sentence for each.

1. scalp
2. scant
3. scar
4. scold

5. skill
6. skin
7. skirt
8. skull

Focus ON POETRY

How can you improve your understanding of poetry? One good method is to think about the elements of a poem as you read it. The elements of a poem include: rhyme, rhythm, imagery, figurative language, symbolism, form and theme. A poet may use some or all of these elements to create a feeling, or emotional response, in the reader or listener.

Rhyme   Rhyme is the repeated use of words containing the same ending sounds. In poetry, rhyme is most commonly used at the end of a poetic line. To aid understanding of a poem, poets will often change the rhyme at the end of each completed thought.

Rhythm   Rhythm in poetry is similar to rhythm in music. Instead of using notes to create a regular beat, a poet uses syllables in a pattern. Within the pattern certain syllables are stressed or accented and others are not stressed or unaccented. The arrangement of these syllables is called **meter.**

Stressed syllables cause a rising sound. Unstressed syllables cause a falling sound. By alternating the rise and fall of sounds, the poet creates rhythm.

Imagery   Imagery is vivid descriptions which produce mental pictures, or images, in the reader's mind. Poets often use imagery to express an unfamiliar idea in a way that enables the reader to picture the idea in his or her mind. Imagery is also used to create pleasant or unpleasant associations for the reader.

Figurative Language   Figurative language refers to a group of literary devices a poet uses to create images.

Personification is one type of figurative language. Sometimes a poet will explain a nonhuman object or idea in human terms. The poet is personifying the object or idea.

Similes and metaphors are two other types of figurative language. Both similes and metaphors make comparisons. **Similes** make direct comparisons using the words *like* or *as*. A **metaphor** is an indirect comparison that does not use the words *like* or *as*.

Alliteration is another type of figurative language. **Alliteration** is the repetition of initial consonant sounds. "I love to laugh" is an example of alliteration.

Symbolism   A symbol is an object that represents itself and at the same time represents an idea other than itself. Poets often use symbols to assist a reader in understanding the theme or central idea in a poem. Often images and symbols create emotional responses in addition to visualizing ideas.

Form   Form refers to the structure of a literary work. The lyric and the sonnet are two of many poetic forms. A **lyric** expresses intense personal feeling.

A **sonnet** is always fourteen lines. Many sonnets have three **quatrains,** or four line stanzas, and one **couplet,** or two line stanza. In a sonnet, the poet begins by posing a problem and concludes by offering a solution.

Theme   Theme is the central idea in a literary work. The theme usually involves an important idea or truth the poet knows about life. In poetry, theme is usually implied.

As you read Spenser's "Sonnet 75," pay attention to the various elements of poetry. Think about these questions:

1. What images form in your mind as you read the poem?
2. Do the images create pleasant or unpleasant associations?

SONNET 75

by Edmund Spenser

One day I wrote her name upon the strand,
but came the waves and washed it away:
again I wrote it with a second hand,
but came the tide, and made my pains his prey.

"Wrote . . . waves . . . washed" are examples of alliteration.

5   "Vain man," said she, "that dost in vain assay,
a mortal thing so to immortalize,
for I myself shall like to this decay,
and eek my name be wiped out likewise."
"Not so," quod I, "let baser things devise

The tide is personified as a hunter who pursues his prey, or victim, and destroys it. The tide pursues what is written on the beach, its prey, and victimizes it.

10   to die in dust, but you shall live by fame:
my verse your virtues rare shall eternize,
and in the heavens write your glorious name.
Where whenas death shall all the world subdue,
our love shall live, and later life renew."

The poet states his conclusion and suggests the theme in the couplet, or last two lines of the sonnet.

---

strand (STRAND) beach
assay (uh SAY) *(archaic)* attempt
eek (EEK) *(archaic)* also
quod (KWOHD) *(archaic)* said
baser (BAYS ur) of relatively little value

Review the Selection

UNDERSTAND THE SELECTION

Recall

1. Whose name did the speaker write?

2. Where did he write the name?

3. What happened to the name?

Infer

4. Who is the poem's second speaker?

5. How did she react to having her name written on the beach?

6. Why did the first speaker write his love's name on the beach?

7. How was he finally successful in immortalizing her?

Apply

8. What disadvantages and advantages do you see to writing something in sand?

9. Besides writing a poem about a person, how else do you think you could give someone immortality?

10. If the poet gave his love a copy of this sonnet, what do you think she did with it?

Respond to Literature

Writers during the English Renaissance explored themes about human feelings, and they experimented with new ways to use language. How does Spenser's "Sonnet 75" illustrate these two developments?

WRITE ABOUT THE SELECTION

You have been studying the elements of poetry in this unit. It is now time for you to switch from being a student to being a literary critic. Evaluate the author, Edmund Spenser. Decide which of the literary elements you learned about in this unit Spenser uses most effectively. Which elements contributed most to your response to and enjoyment of the poem? Write a literary review which answers this question.

Prewriting   Make a chart for recording information about the poetic elements. List the literary elements (rhyme, rhythm, imagery, symbolism, form, theme, and figurative language) down one side of the chart. Think about how these elements were used in this poem. Record examples of as many of the elements as you can find in the poem.

Writing   Use the information in your chart to write a one-paragraph literary review about the poetic elements in Edmund Spenser's "Sonnet 75." Be sure you explain how the poetic elements contributed to your own response to the poem.

Revising   Think about adding examples from the poem that illustrate each poetic element.

Proofreading   Check each example you have included from the poem. If you are quoting the poem, make sure you copy the quotation exactly as it appears in the poem, including punctuation.

THINK ABOUT POETRY

Elements of poetry are rhyme, rhythm, imagery, symbolism, form, theme, and figurative language (such as personification, alliteration, simile, and metaphor). As you grow to recognize these elements in poems, poetry will become more enjoyable to read and easier to understand.

1. Find at least three examples of alliteration in Spenser's "Sonnet 75."

2. Think about the theme of Spenser's "Sonnet 75." What idea do you think the poet wants to communicate about feelings of love?

3. Find the line "But came the tide, and made my pains his prey." Explain how the line is an example of personification. Tell what two things are being compared and what feature in each is linked to the other.

4. Find words that rhyme in the sonnet. Explain how the rhyming words form a pattern. How does the pattern change in the last two lines?

DEVELOP YOUR VOCABULARY

A word can sometimes be used as a noun or a verb. A **noun** is a word that names a person, place, idea, or object. For example, in this selection, Spenser says ". . .heavens write your glorious name." *Name,* in this case, is a noun referring to the distinctive word or words a person is called. *Name* is also a verb. A **verb** is a word that expresses action or a state of being. In the sentence, "The president will *name* his Cabinet members," the word *name* is a verb meaning "appoint" or "designate."

The following words are found in this selection. Each can be used as a noun or verb. Check the dictionary for definitions of what each word means as a noun and what each means as a verb. Write an original sentence using each word as a noun. Then, write another sentence using each word as a verb.

1. hand
2. pains
3. waves
4. decay
5. dust
6. strand

William of Orange Landing at Torbay, Anonymous.
The Royal Collection, Stable Yard House, St. James's
Palace, London

READING FOCUS

Compare and Contrast Moods Every
piece of writing has a mood or moods
associated with it. Mood is the atmosphere of the work—angry, frightening,
light-hearted, and so on. In poetry,
mood is often created by the rhythm
and rhyme as well as the language and
images the poet uses. As you read the
four poems in this selection, notice the
mood or feeling in each poem.

Learn About

FIGURATIVE LANGUAGE

Figurative language uses words and
phrases to create interesting literary
effects. Poets often use figurative
language to create vivid, memorable
images in a reader's mind.

Similes and metaphors are two of the
most frequently used figures of speech.
Both similes and metaphors make comparisons between two objects or ideas
that are basically different.

A **simile** compares objects directly
connecting them with the words *like* or
as. The connectors *like* or *as* appear
between the two objects or ideas being
compared. A **metaphor** on the other
hand compares objects and ideas indirectly. A metaphor does not include connectors such as *like* or *as.*

As you read these selections, ask
yourself:
1. What comparisons are made
   between things that are different?
2. Do these comparisons use the
   connectors *like* or *as?*

WRITING CONNECTION

Select two objects or ideas that are basically different. In a sentence, compare
the two things using *like* or *as.* Select
two more things. In a sentence, compare
them. Do not use a connector such as
like or *as* in the second sentence.

To His Coy Mistress

by Andrew Marvell

Had we but world enough, and time,
This coyness, lady, were no crime.
We would sit down, and think which way
To walk, and pass our long love's day.
5 Thou by the Indian Ganges' side
Should'st rubies find: I by the tide
of Humber[1] would complain. I would
Love you ten years before the Flood,
And you should, if you please, refuse
10 Till the conversion of the Jews:[2]
My vegetable love should grow
Vaster than empires and more slow;
An hundred years should go to praise
Thine eyes, and on thy forehead gaze;
15 Two hundred to adore each breast,
But thirty thousand to the rest;
An age at least to every part,
And the last age should show your heart.
For, lady, you deserve this state;
20 Nor would I love at lower rate.
    But at my back I always hear
Time's winged chariot hurrying near;
And yonder all before us lie
Deserts of vast eternity.
25 Thy beauty shall no more be found,
Nor in thy marble vault shall sound

---

state (STAYT) dignity
[1]**Humber:** river flowing through Hull, Marvell's hometown
[2]**conversion of the Jews:** according to Christian tradition, the Jews were to be converted
  immediately before the Last Judgment

Lady Lilith, Dante Gabriel Rossetti. Samuel and Mary R. Bancroft Collection, Delaware Art Museum

My echoing song; then worms shall try
That long preserved virginity;
And your quaint honor turn to dust,
30 And into ashes all my lust:
The grave's a fine and private place,
But none, I think, do there embrace.
    Now therefore, while the youthful hue
Sits on thy skin like morning dew,
35 And while thy willing soul transpires
At every pore with instant fires,

---

transpires (tran SPYRZ) breathes out

Now let us sport us while we may,
And now, like amorous birds of prey,
Rather at once our time devour
40 Than languish in his slow-chapped[1] power,
Let us roll all our strength and all
Our sweetness up into one ball,
And tear our pleasures with rough strife
Thorough[2] the iron gates of life:
45 Thus, though we cannot make our sun
Stand still, yet we will make him run.

To Lucasta, on Going to the Wars

by Richard Lovelace

Tell me not, sweet, I am unkind,
    That from the nunnery
Of thy chaste breast and quiet mind
    To war and arms I fly.

5 True, a new mistress now I chase,
    The first foe in the field;
And with a stronger faith embrace
    A sword, a horse, a shield.

10 Yet this inconstancy is such
    As you too shall adore;
I could not love thee, dear, so much,
    Loved I not honor more.

---

amorous (AM ur us) in love
languish (LANG gwish) to lose vigor; become weak
chaste (CHAYST) pure in thought and act; virtuous
inconstancy (in KON stun see) unsteadiness in affection or loyalties
[1]**slow-chapped:** *(archaic)* slowly aging
[2]**thorough:** *(archaic)* through

Song: To Celia

by Ben Jonson

Drink to me only with thine eyes,
And I will pledge with mine;
Or leave a kiss but in the cup,
And I'll not look for wine.

5   The thirst that from the soul doth rise
Doth ask a drink divine;
But might I of Jove's[1] nectar sup,
I would not change for thine.

I sent thee last[2] a rosy wreath,
10   Not so much honoring thee
As giving it a hope that there
It could not withered be;
But thou thereon didst only breathe,
And sent'st it back to me;
15   Since when it grows, and smells, I swear,
Not of itself but thee!

---

[1] **Jove:** Jupiter
[2] **last:** late, recently

Still to Be Neat

by Ben Jonson

Still to be neat, still to be dressed,
As you were going to a feast;
Still to be powdered, still perfumed:
Lady, it is to be presumed,
5   Though arts hid causes are not found,
All is not sweet, all is not sound.

Give me a look, give me a face
That makes simplicity a grace;
Robes loosely flowing, hair as free:
10   Such sweet neglect more taketh me
Than all th'adulteries of art;
They strike mine eyes, but not my heart.

---

adulteries (uh DUL tuh reez) impurities; not genuine substances

Review the Selection

UNDERSTAND THE SELECTION

Recall

1. What does Marvell always hear?

2. What does Richard Lovelace love even more than Lucasta?

3. What did Ben Jonson send to Celia?

Infer

4. Under what circumstances does Marvell think his lady could be coy?

5. Did Lovelace discuss his decision with Lucasta before making it? Explain.

6. What clues tell you if Celia loves or does not love the speaker?

7. In "Still to Be Neat," tell what the speaker is saying to his love.

Apply

8. How do the lines "But at my back I always hear/Time's winged chariot hurrying near" apply today?

9. What might Lucasta have written in reply to Lovelace's poem?

10. What might you imagine to be the reply to "Still to Be Neat"?

Respond to Literature

How might a poem written today about going to war differ from Lovelace's poem? In what ways might it be the same?

WRITE ABOUT THE SELECTION

This selection contains four different poems. In each, the poet expresses feelings about his love for a woman.

Today, people express their feelings of love in many ways. One way is to take a special photograph and write a message on the back. Choose one of the four poems to express a feeling you may want to convey to another person. Think of a scene or image that best illustrates your feeling. (You do not have to take a picture.) Briefly describe the picture you would like to send. Then write a paragraph that you would enclose with the photograph.

Prewrite   Reread the poem you selected. Make a list of words and phrases from the poem that appeal to you. Jot down ideas, phrases, and words of your own that you might use in your paragraph. Include details about your feelings.

Writing   Use your notes to write a paragraph expressing your feelings. Include words and phrases from the poem if they apply.

Revising   Make sure the reader of your paragraph will clearly understand the message you are trying to convey.

Proofreading   Read over your selection to check for errors in spelling and punctuation.

THINK ABOUT LANGUAGE

The emotional power of poetry stems in part from its concentrated use of language. The poet says a great deal in few words. For this reason, metaphor and simile are important elements of poetry. Through them, the poet can often create vivid images in very few words.

1. In your words explain the meaning of Marvell's comparison between a "vegetable" and "love."

2. What link did Marvell find to compare "birds of prey" and "people living life to the fullest"?

3. How does Lovelace's mention of "the nunnery" make his destination even more striking?

4. In what ways does Lovelace say war is similar to a mistress?

5. In what way is the line "Robes loosely flowing, hair as free" a metaphor?

READING FOCUS

Compare and Contrast Moods   As you read the four poems, you identified the mood of each. Choose two of the poems and compare and contrast their moods.

DEVELOP YOUR VOCABULARY

A **suffix** is a letter or combination of letters added at the end of a word or to a word root. A suffix added to a root word may change that word's part of speech. A suffix also alters or changes the meaning of the word.

The suffix *ery* or *ory* added to a word or word root indicates a place. For example, Lovelace uses the word *nunnery* in his poem, "To Lucasta, on Going to the Wars." *Nunnery* is a place where a nun lives. The following words end with the suffix *ery* or *ory*. Find the root word in each of these words and then add "place of or for" to the meaning of the root. Check your definition in the dictionary. Finish by writing an original sentence for each word.

1. bakery
2. winery
3. fishery
4. observatory
5. crematory
6. eatery
7. beanery

UNIT 2 Review

Write About Poets

Suppose that you are living in Renaissance England. You are hosting a discussion in a theater. You have invited three poets from this unit to discuss how the Renaissance influenced their writing. What might each poet say? Write their comments and responses as a discussion about the Renaissance. State a point of view for each poet. Have the other poets comment positively or negatively on each point-of-view statement.

Prewriting   Before you begin to write, review the work of each author in the unit. Choose three poets you think would give the most interesting responses to the question. Freewrite your question and each response. After you have written the responses, decide how the other poets will comment. Freewrite those comments.

Writing   Use your freewriting as a basis for writing a short discussion. You may want to set the scene by briefly discussing the characteristics of the Renaissance. Then, arrange the poets' statements and responses in the order that you think will be most lively.

Revising   Since the speakers in your discussion are poets, they probably would be very aware of their own language. To make them sound more realistic, eliminate unnecessary words. Also try to use figurative language in their responses.

Proofreading   Names are important to people. Make sure you have spelled all the names correctly.

Write About Poetry

Suppose that you are living in Renaissance England. You have traveled to the exciting city of London. In London you have seen a new play and have read copies of poems printed on a newly invented printing press. Write to a friend describing the new literature you have discovered in London.

Prewriting   Make a chart. At the top, write the names of at least four poems or selections in the unit. Down the side, list the elements of poetry studied in this unit. Fill in the spaces on the chart with details you remember about each element from each selection.

Writing   Select at least three literary elements you think most vividly illustrate the characteristics of the new Renaissance literature. Write a letter to your friend telling him or her about the new literature, the four specific works you have chosen to write about, and your thoughts about the poetic elements demonstrated in each work. Write at least one paragraph about each work.

Revising   Read your letter to make sure you have made your points clearly. Add examples that will illustrate your ideas for your friend.

Proofreading   Make sure your letter includes a salutation and a complimentary close. The salutation is the word *Dear* before the person's name. The complimentary close above your signature may be *Yours truly,* or something similar.

BUILD LANGUAGE SKILLS

Vocabulary

When you read literature from earlier periods, sometimes you will notice words that are no longer in common usage. You may also notice words that are still in use but whose meanings have changed over the years. Words or word meanings that are no longer in use are called *archaic.*

In this unit you have been introduced to some archaic words and meanings. To understand certain selections, you have had to learn the meanings for the words at the time the author was writing. Words with archaic meanings are identified following each selection. The archaic meanings are also listed in a dictionary.

Each of the following words can be found in this unit. Read the archaic meaning of each word. Use it in an original sentence. Then see what other archaic words or meanings you can add to this list.

1. hasting
2. tarry
3. prove
4. kirtle
5. swain
6. assay

Grammar, Usage, and Mechanics

When you are writing about literary works it is important to identify the title of the book by underlining it. A particular selection within a book is identified with quotation marks (""). Quotation marks are also used to identify titles of shorter works such as lyric poems, sonnets, and stories. Plays, epics, collections of poems, and titles of longer works as well as books are underlined. Example: "The Bait" appears as a selection in *The Collected Works of John Donne.*

Correctly identify all the literary works mentioned in the following sentences.

1. Macbeth is one of Shakespeare's most exciting tragedies.

2. Milton's On His Blindness is a sonnet about using one's own talents.

3. Ben Jonson wrote both the lyric poem Song: To Celia and the play Volpone.

4. The Parable of the Prodigal Son is an excerpt from The King James Bible.

SPEAKING AND LISTENING

A **monologue** is a speech, a play, a scene from a play, or a recitation given by one person. *Monologue* literally means speaking alone. It is a popular type of oral presentation because it has such variety. Monologues can be as humorous as the ones delivered by Bill Cosby or they can be as serious as those written by Shakespeare.

Practice your dramatic ability by presenting a monologue to your classmates. The ideas and suggestions below will help to make your performance easy and enjoyable.

1. Choose a selection from this unit that is suitable for a monologue. Select something that appeals to you and that you think might entertain or interest your classmates. Familiarize yourself with the selection and with its feeling by reading it several times both silently and aloud. Picture yourself as the person who is speaking in the selection. How does that person look? What emotions is the person feeling as he or she speaks?

2. Memorize three or four sentences. When you know them, learn three or four more. Recite the two sets of lines together smoothly before proceeding to a third set of three or four lines. Continue the process until you have memorized the entire monologue. Pay attention to pauses and words or phrases that should be emphasized.

3. Practice the monologue with gestures, facial expressions, and voice changes. This process could help you remember the lines because you will associate the gesture or expression with the words of the monologue.

4. Rehearse in front of an imaginary audience, a mirror, and your family. Ask those who watch you for comments or suggestions as to how you can improve your delivery. Make adjustments based only on those suggestions that you think will improve your presentation. Be aware that you have your own style, and take that style into consideration as you polish your monologue.

5. When you present your monologue, imagine that you are actually the character or person you are portraying. Make believe you are talking to another character who is in the back row of the class. Speak across the top of your classmates' heads, conveying the feeling of the monologue.

Limit the monologue to about two minutes. After you have finished, analyze your performance. Identify which parts of the performance were most successful and why. Decide how you might improve your next presentation. If reading the monologue is a more comfortable way for you to present it, remember to glance at your audience from time to time to emphasize an idea or convey a feeling.

CRITICAL THINKING

Figurative Language One element of poetry is figurative language. This element frequently involves a comparison of two basically different things. For example, in the poem "To Lucasta, on Going to the Wars" the poet compares war with having a mistress. The reader must think about the comparison and try to understand the link between the two objects or ideas that the poet is writing about.

In "To His Coy Mistress" Marvell states that he and his love should sport like amorous birds of prey. He is not suggesting they should grow feathers and talons of birds or that they hunt small game. Marvell is suggesting that he and his love should aggressively seize every opportunity life offers because time passes quickly.

Choose one poem from this unit that uses a figurative comparison. Answer the following questions about the comparison you choose.

1. What is one idea being compared?

2. What is the other object or idea being compared?

3. What is the link or feature of comparison? Look for other images or context clues within the poem that can help you answer the question.

4. What idea is the poet suggesting by using this comparison?

5. How does the poet's idea relate to your own life and experience?

EFFECTIVE STUDYING

Summarizing One good way to avoid extra work and to prepare efficiently for a test is to keep a record in a notebook of the poems you have read. After you read each poem, write the title and the author's name in a notebook. Also list the elements of poetry identified in the "Focus on Poetry" section of this unit. Beside each element that applies to the poem briefly summarize how the poet made use of the element in this particular poem.

Example:
Sonnet 75 by Edmund Spenser
Form: Sonnet
Figures of Speech: Personification—the tide is spoken of as a hunter.
Alliteration—wrote . . . waves . . . washed; die in dust; verse your virtues; love . . . live . . . later life
Theme: True love is immortal.

The summaries will help you remember the poem and understand the elements of poetry. They can also be a time-saving study guide for a final exam.

Test Preparation

When taking a reading comprehension test, summarize the events of each story after you read. This will help you remember the story details when answering the questions.

The Rise of the Romantics

Amidst the storm they sang,
  And the stars heard and the sea!
And the sounding aisles of the dim woods rang
  To the anthem of the free!
                —Felicia Dorothea Hemans

Calais Pier: An English Packet Arriving, J.M.W. Turner. The Granger Collection

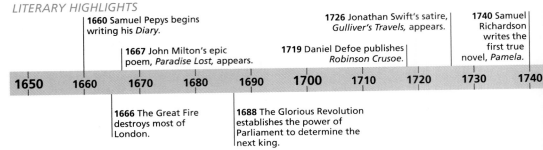

1660 Samuel Pepys begins writing his *Diary.*

1667 John Milton's epic poem, *Paradise Lost,* appears.

1726 Jonathan Swift's satire, *Gulliver's Travels,* appears.

1719 Daniel Defoe publishes *Robinson Crusoe.*

1740 Samuel Richardson writes the first true novel, *Pamela.*

| 1650 | 1660 | 1670 | 1680 | 1690 | 1700 | 1710 | 1720 | 1730 | 1740 |

1666 The Great Fire destroys most of London.

1688 The Glorious Revolution establishes the power of Parliament to determine the next king.

HISTORICAL HIGHLIGHTS

The Rise of the Romantics

Do you prefer to think logically or to follow your imagination? Probably at different times you use different types of thinking. So did the writers of 17th- and 18th-century England.

■ THE RESTORATION

If you had lived in 17th century England during the years 1650–1660, your imagination might have led you into trouble. The ruling Puritan party, headed by Oliver Cromwell, did not tolerate any disagreement with its own ideas. The Protectorate, as the government was called, even closed the theaters because the plays might take people's minds off more serious matters.

Cromwell died in 1658. In 1660 Charles II became king of England. His reign and that of his brother, James II, who followed him, are called the Restoration. When James II seemed to be ignoring the limits the people had set for their monarchs, Parliament, the governing body, sent him into exile. His daughter Mary and her husband, William of Orange, were put in his place. This is known as the Glorious Revolution of 1688 and led to a new era called the Enlightenment.

■ THE ENLIGHTENMENT

The people's new beliefs belonged to a period called the Enlightenment, which lasted through much of the 18th century, and to a philosophy called **rationalism.** Rationalists thought that humans should depend on reason. They did not trust the imagination.

Science was popular during the Enlightenment. People scanned the sky through telescopes. They explored the world of the microbe through microscopes. They invented new machines. These machines began the Industrial Age. With machine-made goods came mass production and more trade with other lands. England changed from a farming society to a commercial and industrial power.

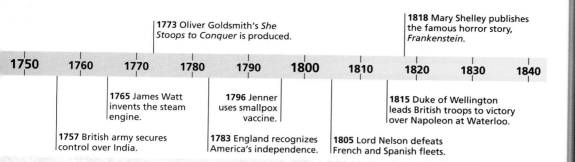

1773 Oliver Goldsmith's *She Stoops to Conquer* is produced.

1818 Mary Shelley publishes the famous horror story, *Frankenstein*.

1750   1760   1770   1780   1790   1800   1810   1820   1830   1840

1765 James Watt invents the steam engine.

1796 Jenner uses smallpox vaccine.

1815 Duke of Wellington leads British troops to victory over Napoleon at Waterloo.

1757 British army secures control over India.

1783 England recognizes America's independence.

1805 Lord Nelson defeats French and Spanish fleets.

◼ LITERATURE AND THE ENLIGHTENMENT

When Charles II became king, the theaters reopened. You will read the comedy *She Stoops to Conquer,* a good example of a Restoration-style play written during the time of the Enlightenment.

Outside the theater, literature was more serious. Two sad events of the time were the Plague and the Great Fire of London. Excerpts from Samuel Pepys's *Diary* will provide an eyewitness account of these calamities.

Alexander Pope wrote about contemporary habits and beliefs. You will read some of his witty remarks here.

◼ LITERATURE AND THE ROMANTICS

Toward the end of the 18th century, writers known as the Romantics rebelled against the Enlightenment. The Romantics stressed the power of the imagination.

The Romantics often wrote about people living a simple life in the country. Their characters might be ordinary folk who had rejected the values of society. Sometimes the Romantics wrote about supernatural events.

In this unit, you will sample the poetry of two early Romantics, Robert Burns and William Blake. You will read "I wandered lonely as a cloud" by William Wordsworth and an excerpt from his sister Dorothy's journal.

Wordsworth inspired younger poets, including Percy Bysshe Shelley and John Keats. You will read "Ozymandias" and "On First Looking into Chapman's Homer," two of the finest examples of Romantic poetry.

Frankenstein is a gothic thriller. Jane Austen's *Pride and Prejudice* is nothing like it. It is a quiet, humorous look at small town society. When you read the excerpt, see if you can tell why *Pride and Prejudice* is considered part of the Enlightenment rather than the Romantic tradition.

As you read this unit, think about whether you prefer the writers of the Enlightenment or the Romantics. What are the reasons for your choice?

PLOT

Plot is the series of events in a literary work. **Conflict** provides the dramatic action in the story. The **climax** is the moment at which the conflict is resolved.

A comedy is a light and amusing drama. Farce is a form of comedy. In a **farce,** the plot is often an improbable or ridiculous series of events.

Mistaken identity sometimes forms the basis for humor in a farce. Sometimes certain characters are mistaken about their surroundings. They say or do things that would be appropriate in a different social situation but are inappropriate in their current surroundings. The resulting confusion leads to a silly series of events.

The confusion of the characters causes ridiculous conflicts. The climax arrives when the characters learn the truth.

As you read the selection, ask yourself the following questions:

1. Which characters are confused about their surroundings?
2. What conflicts are caused by the confusion?

WRITING CONNECTION

Imagine that you are at home but think you are in school. Write a paragraph describing your behavior.

READING FOCUS

Make Inferences About Characters
Sometimes authors tell you about their characters directly through description or narration. Other times you have to make a logical guess, or an inference, about characters. As you read, think about what each character does and says. Consider what these actions and words reveal about the characters' personalities.

SHE STOOPS TO CONQUER

ADAPTED   *by Oliver Goldsmith*

CHARACTERS

MR. HARDCASTLE: *Squire of an English manor house*

MISS KATE HARDCASTLE: *Mr. Hardcastle's daughter by a previous marriage*

MRS. HARDCASTLE: *Wife of the squire*

TONY LUMPKIN: *Mrs. Hardcastle's son by a previous marriage*

MISS CONSTANCE NEVILLE: *Mrs. Hardcastle's niece*

CHARLES MARLOW: *Suitor of Miss Hardcastle*

SIR CHARLES MARLOW: *Young Marlow's father and a friend of Mr. Hardcastle*

GEORGE HASTINGS: *Suitor of Miss Neville and a friend of Charles Marlow*

SERVANTS, MAID, LANDLORD, AND OTHERS

---

squire (SKWYR) country gentleman
suitor (SOOT ur) man who courts a woman

ACT ONE

Scene 1: a room in HARDCASTLE's manor

(Enter MRS. HARDCASTLE *and* MR. HARDCASTLE*)*

MRS. HARDCASTLE: I say again, Mr. Hardcastle, you're very particular. Is there a creature in the whole county but ourselves that doesn't take a trip to London now and then, to rub off the rust a little? There's our neighbor, Mrs. Grigsby—she goes for a month's polishing every winter.

HARDCASTLE: Aye, and brings back enough fine clothes and foolishness to last the whole year. I wonder why London cannot keep its own fools at home. In my time, the follies of the town crept slowly among us, but now they travel faster than a stagecoach.

MRS. HARDCASTLE: Aye, *your* times were very fine times, indeed. You have been telling us of *them* for many a long year. Here we live in an old rambling mansion, that looks for all the world like an inn, but we never see company. All our entertainment is your old stories of Prince Eugene and the Duke of Marlborough. I hate such old-fashioned nonsense.

HARDCASTLE: And I love it! I love everything that's old: old friends, old times, old manners, old books, old wine. And, I believe, Dorothy *(taking her hand),* you'll agree I've been pretty fond of an old wife.

MRS. HARDCASTLE: Lord, Mr. Hardcastle! I'm not so old as you'd make me by more than one good year. Add twenty to twenty, and make money of that.

HARDCASTLE: Let me see: twenty added to twenty—makes just fifty and seven!

MRS. HARDCASTLE: It's false, Mr. Hardcastle! I was but twenty when I gave birth to Tony, that I had by Mr. Lumpkin, my first husband. And he's not come to years of discretion yet.

HARDCASTLE: Nor ever will, I say.

MRS. HARDCASTLE: No matter. Tony Lumpkin has a good fortune. I don't think a boy needs too much discretion to spend fifteen hundred a year. Come, Mr. Hardcastle, you must allow the boy a little fun.

HARDCASTLE: If burning the footman's shoes, frightening the maids, and worrying the kittens is fun, he has it! It was only

yesterday he fastened my wig to the back of my chair, and when I went to make a bow, I popped my bald head in Mrs. Frizzle's face!

MRS. HARDCASTLE: Am I to blame? The poor boy was always too sickly to do any good, even to go to school.

HARDCASTLE: School for him! A cat and a fiddle! No, no, the alehouse and the stable are the only schools he'll ever go to.

MRS. HARDCASTLE: Well, we must not snub the poor boy now, for I believe we shan't have him long among us. Anybody that looks in his face can see he's consumptive.

HARDCASTLE: Aye, if growing too fat is one of the symptoms.

MRS. HARDCASTLE: He coughs sometimes.

HARDCASTLE: Yes, when his liquor goes the wrong way. Sometimes he whoops like a trumpet, too. (TONY *whoops behind the scene.*) Oh, here he comes.

(*Enter* TONY, *crossing the stage*)

MRS. HARDCASTLE: Tony, where are you going, my charmer? Won't you give Papa and me a little of your company?

TONY: I'm in haste, Mother. I cannot stay.

---

consumptive (kun SUMP tiv) afflicted with tuberculosis, a serious lung disease

MRS. HARDCASTLE: You shan't venture out on this raw evening, my dear.

TONY: I can't stay, I tell you. *The Three Pigeons* expects me down any moment. There's some fun going on.

HARDCASTLE: Aye, the alehouse. I thought so.

MRS. HARDCASTLE: Please, my dear, disappoint your friends for one night, at least.

TONY: As for disappointing *them*, I shouldn't much mind. But I can't stand to disappoint *myself*.

MRS. HARDCASTLE *(grabbing his arm):* You shan't go!

TONY: I will, I tell you!

MRS. HARDCASTLE: I say you shan't!

TONY: We'll see who is stronger, you or I! *(Exit, hauling her out)*

HARDCASTLE *(to himself):* Aye, there goes a pair that only spoil each other. But isn't the whole age we live in enough to drive sense and discretion out of anyone? Ah, *(looking off)* there's my pretty darling, Kate. The fashions of the times have infected her, too. By living a year or two in London, she's as fond of silk and French foolishness as the best of them.

(Enter MISS HARDCASTLE, very dressed up)

HARDCASTLE: Dressed up as usual, my Kate! Goodness!

MISS HARDCASTLE: You know our agreement, sir. You allow me in the morning to receive and pay visits, and to dress in my own manner. And in the evening, I put on my plain old housedress, to please you.

HARDCASTLE: Well, remember I insist on the terms of our agreement. And by the way, I believe I'll have a chance to test your obedience this very evening.

MISS HARDCASTLE: What, sir? I don't understand your meaning.

HARDCASTLE: Then, to be plain with you, Kate, I expect the young gentleman I have chosen to be your husband to arrive this very day. I have his father's letter, in which he informs me that his son has set out from London, and that he intends to follow shortly after.

MISS HARDCASTLE: Indeed! I wish I had known something of this before. How shall I behave? It's a thousand to one I shan't like him. Our meeting will be so formal, so like a thing of business. I fear I shall find no room for friendship, not to speak of love.

HARDCASTLE: Depend upon it, child, I'll never control your choice. But Mr. Marlow, whom I have picked for you, is the son of my old friend, Sir Charles Marlow. The young man has been a good student and is headed for excellent employment. I'm told he's a man of generous character.

MISS HARDCASTLE: Is he?

HARDCASTLE: Very generous.

MISS HARDCASTLE: I believe I shall like him.

HARDCASTLE: Young and brave.

MISS HARDCASTLE: I'm sure I shall like him!

HARDCASTLE: And very handsome.

MISS HARDCASTLE: My dear Papa, say no more (*kissing his hand*). He's mine! I'll have him!

HARDCASTLE: And to top it all, Kate, he's one of the most bashful and reserved young fellows in all the world.

MISS HARDCASTLE: You have frozen me to death again. That word *reserved* has undone all the rest. A reserved lover, it is said, always makes a suspicious husband.

HARDCASTLE: No, just the opposite. Modesty seldom occurs in a dishonest or suspecting person. It was this very feature of his character that first struck me.

MISS HARDCASTLE: He must have more striking features to catch me, I promise you. However, if he's so young, so handsome, and so everything, I think I'll have him. At least, I'll have a look.

HARDCASTLE: That's the spirit! I'll go prepare the servants for his arrival. As we seldom have company, they'll need some training. (*Exit*)

MISS HARDCASTLE (*to herself*): Young, handsome—these he put last. But I put them first. *Sensible, good natured*—I like all that. But then *reserved* and *sheepish*—that's much against him.

(*Enter* MISS NEVILLE)

MISS HARDCASTLE: I'm glad you've come, Neville, my dear. Tell me, Constance, how do I look today? Is this one of my better days? Am I in face?

MISS NEVILLE: You look fine, my dear. Yet, now I look again—

---

reserved (rih ZURVD) quiet and formal in manner

bless me!—you *do* look excited. Has the cat or your brother been meddling? Or has the last novel been too moving?

MISS HARDCASTLE: No, nothing like that. I have been threatened— I can scarcely get it out—I have been threatened with a lover!

MISS NEVILLE: And his name—

MISS HARDCASTLE: Is Marlow.

MISS NEVILLE: Indeed!

MISS HARDCASTLE: The son of Sir Charles Marlow.

MISS NEVILLE: As I live, he's the best friend of Mr. Hastings, *my* admirer! I believe you must have seen him when we lived in London.

MISS HARDCASTLE: Never.

MISS NEVILLE: He's a very strange character, I assure you. Among women of reputation and virtue, he's the most modest man alive. But I hear he has a very different character among women of another kind. You understand me?

MISS HARDCASTLE: An odd character, indeed! What shall I do? Oh, I'll think no more of him, but trust to luck for success. But how goes your own affair, my dear? Has my mother been courting you for my brother Tony, as usual?

MISS NEVILLE: Yes, I've just come from her. She's been saying a hundred tender things, and setting off her monster of a son as the very pink of perfection.

MISS HARDCASTLE: And she actually thinks him so! A fortune like yours is no small temptation. Besides, as she still has control over it, she'll do all she can to keep it in the family. That's one reason she wants you to marry your cousin.

MISS NEVILLE: A fortune like mine, which is mostly jewels, is no such huge temptation. And at any rate, my dear Hastings is the one I hope to marry. But to keep the peace, I let Mrs. Hardcastle think that I'm in love with her son Tony, and she never once dreams that I dream of another.

MISS HARDCASTLE: My good brother holds out against her plans, though. I could almost love him for hating you so.

MISS NEVILLE: There—my aunt's bell rings for our afternoon walk. Good-bye. Courage is necessary, as our lives are nearing an important point. *(Exit)*

MISS HARDCASTLE: I wish it all were over, and all were well.

Scene 2: an alehouse room, with TONY *and his friends*

TONY *is at the head of a table.*

ALL: Hurrah, hurrah, bravo!

FIRST FELLOW: Now, gentlemen, silence for a song. Our friend Tony Lumpkin is going to knock himself out with a song.

SECOND FELLOW: Aye, a song, a song.

TONY: Then I'll sing you a song I just made up about this alehouse, *The Three Pigeons (sings):* Let schoolmasters puzzle their brains, with grammar, and nonsense, and learning *(looks off and stops)*. Well, Stingo, what's the matter?

(Enter LANDLORD*)*

LANDLORD: There are two gentlemen in a large carriage at the door. They have lost their way, and are saying something about Mr. Hardcastle.

TONY: As sure as can be, one of them must be the gentleman that's coming down to court my sister. Do they seem like Londoners?

LANDLORD: I believe so.

TONY: Then ask them to step this way, and I'll set them right in a flash. *(Exit* LANDLORD*)* Gentlemen, they might not be good enough company for you. If you step out a moment, I'll be with you in the squeezing of a lemon. *(Exeunt all but* TONY*)*

TONY *(to himself)*: My stepfather has been calling me a lazy dog this half year. Now, if I pleased, I could get my revenge. But then I'm afraid—afraid of what? I shall soon be worth fifteen hundred a year, and let him frighten me out of *that* if he can!

(Enter LANDLORD, *with* MARLOW *and* HASTINGS*)*

MARLOW: What a day we've had of it! We were told it was forty miles across the county, and we've come more than sixty.

HASTINGS: And all, Marlow, because of that shyness of yours. It wouldn't let us inquire more often along the way.

TONY: No offense, gentlemen. But I'm told you've been inquiring for one Mr. Hardcastle in these parts. Do you know what part of the county you are in?

HASTINGS: Not in the least, sir. But we would thank you for information.

TONY: Nor the way you came?

HASTINGS: No, sir. But if you can inform us—

TONY: Why, gentlemen, if you know neither the road you are on, nor where you are, the first thing I have to inform you is that— you have lost your way.

MARLOW: We needed no genius to tell us that.

TONY: Gentlemen, may I be so bold as to ask the place you came from?

MARLOW: That is not necessary for directing as where we want to go.

TONY: No offense. But question for question is fair, you know. Now, gentlemen, is not this same Hardcastle an old-fashioned, stubborn fellow with an ugly face, a daughter, and a handsome son?

HASTINGS: We have not seen the gentleman, but he has the family you mention.

TONY: The daughter, a tall, talkative beanpole. The son, a well-bred, agreeable youth that everybody is fond of.

MARLOW: Our information differs. The daughter is said to be

---

exeunt (EK see unt) go offstage (a plural of exit)

well-bred and beautiful; the son, an awkward fool, reared up and spoiled at his mother's apron string.

TONY: He-he-hem—then, gentlemen, all I have to tell you is this: You won't reach Mr. Hardcastle's house this night, I believe.

HASTINGS: Unfortunate!

TONY: It's a long, dark, dirty, and dangerous way.

HASTINGS: What's to be done, Marlow?

MARLOW: Perhaps this landlord can put us up.

LANDLORD: No, master. We have but one spare bed in the whole house.

TONY: And to my knowledge, that's taken up by three guests already. *(After a pause)* I have it! Don't you think, Stingo, that you could let these gentlemen have the fireside, with three chairs and a pillow?

HASTINGS: I hate sleeping by the fireside.

MARLOW: And I detest your three chairs and a pillow.

TONY: You do, do you? Then let me see—if you go on a mile farther, to the Buck's Head. . . . Yes, the old Buck's Head Inn, one of the best in the whole county!

LANDLORD *(apart to Tony)*: Surely, you aren't sending them to your stepfather's house as an inn, are you?

TONY: Mum's the word, you. Let *them* find that out. *(To them)* You have only to keep on straight forward till you come to a large old house by the roadside. You'll see a pair of large horns over the door. That's the sign. Drive up in the yard, and call loudly.

HASTINGS: Sir, we're obliged to you. Our servants can't miss the way?

TONY: No, no. But let me warn you about the landlord at the Buck's Head. He's grown rich, and he's going to get out of the business soon. So he wants to be thought of as a gentleman, he! he! he! He'll be for giving you his company, as well as his rooms.

LANDLORD: A troublesome old fool, to be sure. But he keeps as good meat and beds as any in the county.

MARLOW: Well, if he supplies us with those, we shall want no more. We are to turn to the right, did you say?

TONY: No, no, straight forward. I'll just step outside myself and show you a piece of the way. *(To Landlord)* Mum, now.

LANDLORD: Ah, bless your heart. *(Exeunt)*

ACT TWO

Back at HARDCASTLE'S *manor house*

(Enter HARDCASTLE, *followed by three or four awkward* SERVANTS*)*

HARDCASTLE: Well, I hope you're perfect in the table exercises I have been teaching you. You all know your places, and can act as if you've been used to good company.

ALL: Aye, aye.

HARDCASTLE: When company comes, you're not to pop out and stare, and then run in again, like frighted rabbits.

ALL: No, no.

HARDCASTLE: You, Diggory, whom I have taken from the barn, are to make a show at the side table. And you, Roger, whom I have advanced from the plow, are to place yourself behind *my* chair. But you're not to stand so, with your hands in your pockets. Take your hands from your pockets, Roger. And from your head, you blockhead, you. But don't I hear a coach drive into the yard? To your posts, you blockheads! I'll go in the meantime and give my old friend's son a warm reception at the gate. *(Exit)*

FIRST SERVANT: What now? My place is gone quite out of my head!

SECOND SERVANT: I know that my place is to be everywhere!

THIRD SERVANT: Where the devil is mine?

FOURTH SERVANT: My place is to be nowhere at all, and so I'll go about my business! *(Exeunt* SERVANTS, *running about as if frighted, different ways)*

(Enter SERVANT *with candles, showing in* MARLOW *and* HASTINGS*)*

SERVANT: Welcome, gentlemen, very welcome. This way.

HASTINGS: After the disappointments of the day, welcome once more, Charles, to the comforts of a clean room and a good fire. Upon my word, a very good-looking house. Antique but comfortable.

MARLOW: The usual fate of a large mansion. Having first ruined the master with expenses, it at last comes to collect contributions as an inn.

HASTINGS: You have lived at inns a good deal. In truth, I have been surprised that a person like you, who has seen so much of the world, never became more self-confident.

MARLOW: The Englishman's malady. But tell me, George, where could I have learned that self-confidence you talk of? Most of my life has been spent at schools, or staying at an inn. I've always lived far from that lovely part of the creation that chiefly teaches men confidence. I don't know that I was ever really acquainted with a single modest woman—except my mother. But among females of another class, you know—

HASTINGS: Aye, among them you are confident enough!

MARLOW: They are like *us,* you know.

HASTINGS: But in the company of women of reputation I never saw such an idiot. You look for all the world as if you wanted a chance to sneak out of the room.

MARLOW: Why, man, that's because I *do* want to sneak out of the room. I have often made a resolution to break the ice, and rattle away at a great rate. But I don't know how. A single glance from a pair of fine eyes has totally ruined my resolutions. A confident fellow can fake modesty, but I'll be hanged if a modest man can ever fake confidence.

HASTINGS: If you could only say half the things to them that I have heard you say to the barmaid of an inn, or even to a college cleaning—

MARLOW: But, George, I *can't* say *anything* to them! I freeze. They petrify me. To me, a modest woman, dressed out in all her finery, is the most frightening object of the whole creation.

HASTINGS: Ha! ha! ha! At this rate, man, how can you ever expect to marry!

MARLOW: Never, unless, as among kings and princes, my bride were just to be given to me. If one were to be introduced to a wife he never saw before, it might be endured. But to go through all the terrors of a formal courtship, together with the aunts, grandmothers and cousins, and at last to blurt out the question *Madam, will you marry me?* No, no, that's a strain much above me, I assure you!

HASTINGS: I pity you. But how do you intend behaving to the lady you have come down to visit at the request of your father?

MARLOW: As I behave to all other ladies. Bow very low. Answer yes, or no, to all her demands. But for the rest, I don't think I'll dare to look at her face till I see my father's again.

HASTINGS: I'm surprised that one who is so warm a friend can be so cool a lover.

MARLOW: To be clear, my dear Hastings, my chief reason for coming was your happiness, not my own. Miss Neville loves you, the family doesn't know you, as my friend you are sure of a welcome. Aw, this fellow again to interrupt us!

(Enter HARDCASTLE*)*

HARDCASTLE: Gentlemen, once more you are welcome. Which is Mr. Marlow? Sir, you're most welcome. It's not my way, you see, to receive my friends with my back to the fire. I like to give them a good reception, in the old style, at my gate. I like to see their horses and trunks taken care of.

MARLOW: *(aside)* He has got our names from the servants already. *(To him)* We approve your hospitality, sir. *(To* HASTINGS*)* I have been thinking, George, of changing our traveling clothes in the morning. I'm growing ashamed of mine.

HARDCASTLE: Mr. Marlow, you'll not have to dress up in this house.

HASTINGS: George, you're right. With the women, your first appearance is important. The first shot is half the battle. I intend opening the campaign with the white and gold.

HARDCASTLE: Mr. Marlow—Mr. Hastings—gentlemen—please be informal in this house. This is Liberty Hall, gentlemen. You may do just as you please here.

MARLOW: Yet, George, if we start the campaign with too much strength, we may need ammunition before it is over. I think I'll reserve the gold for after a retreat.

HARDCASTLE: Your talking of a retreat, Mr. Marlow, puts me in mind of the Duke of Marlborough, when we went to conquer Denain. He first summoned the garrison—

MARLOW: Don't you think my yellow jacket will do with the brown pants?

HARDCASTLE: He first summoned the garrison, which consisted of about five thousand men—

---

aside (uh SYD) an actor's words heard by the audience but supposedly not heard by certain other actors

HASTINGS: I think not. Brown and yellow mix very poorly.

HARDCASTLE: I say, gentlemen, as I was telling you, he summoned the garrison, about five thousand men—

MARLOW: The girls like yellow.

HARDCASTLE: About five thousand men, well provided with ammunition. "Now," says the Duke of Marlborough to George Brooks, who stood next to him—you must have heard of George Brooks. "I'll pawn my dukedom," says he, "but I'll take that garrison without spilling a drop of blood!" So—

MARLOW (*to* HARDCASTLE): What, my good friend. If you gave us a glass of punch in the meantime, it would help us to carry on the battle with vigor.

HARDCASTLE (*aside*): Punch, sir!—This is the strangest kind of modesty I ever met with!

MARLOW: Yes, sir, punch! A glass of punch, after our journey, will be comfortable. This is Liberty Hall, you know.

HARDCASTLE (*filling three glasses*): I hope you'll find this to your liking. I have prepared it with my own hands, and I believe you'll agree the ingredients are good. Here, Mr. Marlow, here is to our better acquaintance! (*Drinks*)

HASTINGS (*aside*): I see this fellow wants to give us his company, and forgets that he's only an innkeeper, not a gentleman. Here's your health, my philosopher. (*Drinks*)

HARDCASTLE: Good, very good, thank you; ha! ha! Your talk puts me in mind of Prince Eugene, when he fought the Turks at the battle of Belgrade. You shall hear—

MARLOW: Instead of the battle of Belgrade, I believe it's almost time to talk about supper. What has your philosophy got in the house for supper?

HARDCASTLE (*aside*): For supper, sir!—Was there ever such a request to a man in his own house!

MARLOW: Yes, sir, supper, sir; I begin to feel an appetite.

HARDCASTLE (*aside*): Such a demanding dog, surely, never my eyes beheld. (*To him*) Why, really, sir, as for supper I can't well tell. My wife Dorothy and the cook settle these things between them. I leave these kinds of things entirely to them.

MARLOW: You do, do you?

HARDCASTLE: Entirely. By the way, I believe they are talking about what's for supper this moment in the kitchen.

MARLOW: Then I beg they'll admit *me* to their meeting. It's a way

I have. When I travel, I always choose to regulate my own supper.

HARDCASTLE: I beg you'll leave all that to me. You shall not stir a step.

MARLOW: Leave that to you! I protest, sir. You must excuse me, I always look to these things myself.

HARDCASTLE (*aside*): Well, sir, I'm determined at least to go with you. This may be modern modesty, but I never saw anything look so like old-fashioned rudeness. (*Exeunt* MARLOW *and* HARDCASTLE)

HASTINGS (*to himself*): I find this fellow's friendship begins to grow troublesome. Ha! What do I see? Miss Neville, by all that's happy!

(*Enter* MISS NEVILLE)

MISS NEVILLE: My dear Hastings! What unexpected good fortune! What accident have I to thank for this happy meeting?

HASTINGS: Rather let *me* ask the same question. I could never have hoped to meet my dearest Constance at this inn.

MISS NEVILLE: An inn! Surely you make a mistake! My aunt and guardian, Mrs. Hardcastle, lives here. What could make you think this house an inn?

HASTINGS: My friend, Mr. Marlow, and I have been sent here as to an inn, I assure you. A young fellow we accidentally met at an alehouse directed us here.

MISS NEVILLE: Oh, no! This must be one of my nasty cousin's tricks, ha! ha! ha! ha!

HASTINGS: The cousin your aunt intends for you to marry? The one I'm worried about?

MISS NEVILLE: You have nothing to fear from him, I assure you. You'd adore him if you knew how much he despises me.

HASTINGS: You must know, Constance, of my plans. I have used the excuse of my friend's visit to get admittance into the family. The horses that brought us down will soon be refreshed. And then my dearest girl must trust in her faithful Hastings. We shall soon be landed in France, where the laws of marriage are respected as well as here.

MISS NEVILLE: Mr. Hastings, I have often told you that I'm ready to obey you. But I don't want to leave my little fortune behind. The greatest part of it was left me by my uncle, and chiefly consists of jewels. I have been for some time persuading my aunt to let me wear them. I think I'm very near succeeding. The instant they are put into my hands, you shall find me ready to make them and myself yours.

HASTINGS: Forget the jewels! Your person is all I desire. In the meantime, my friend Marlow must not know about this mistake. I know the strange shyness of his nature. If suddenly informed of it, he would instantly leave the house before our plan was ripe.

MISS NEVILLE: But Miss Hardcastle has just returned from walking. This, this way—(They confer)

(Enter MARLOW)

MARLOW: The fine friendship of these people is more than I can take. My host seems to think it ill manners to leave me alone. He and his old-fashioned wife talk of coming to eat with us, too. What have we got here!

HASTINGS: My dear Charles! Let me congratulate you!—The most fortunate accident! Who do you think has just arrived?

MARLOW: Cannot guess.

HASTINGS: Our mistresses, boy, Miss Hardcastle and Miss Neville. Give me leave to introduce Miss Constance Neville to your acquaintance. They happened to dine in the neighborhood. Then they stopped, on their return, to take fresh horses here. Miss Hardcastle has just stepped into the next room, and will be back in an instant. Wasn't it lucky?

MARLOW (*aside*): Here comes something to complete my embarrassment.

HASTINGS: Well! But wasn't it the most fortunate thing in the world?

MARLOW: Oh, yes! Very fortunate—most joyful. But our clothes, George, you know, are in disorder. What if we should postpone the happiness till tomorrow? Tomorrow at her own house— It will be every bit as convenient—Tomorrow let it be. (*Starts to go*)

MISS NEVILLE: By no means, sir. Your leaving will displease her. The disorder of your clothes will show the force of your impatience. Besides, she knows you are in the house, and will permit you to see her.

MARLOW: Oh, the devil! Hem! hem! Hastings, you must not leave me. You are to assist me, you know. I shall look ridiculous. Yet, hang it, I'll take courage! Hem!

HASTINGS: Man, it's but the first plunge, and all's over! She's but a woman, you know.

MARLOW: And of all women she that I dread most to meet!

(*Enter* MISS HARDCASTLE, *as returned from walking, wearing a large bonnet that nearly hides her face*)

HASTINGS (*introducing them*): Miss Hardcastle, Mr. Marlow. I'm proud of bringing two persons of such merit together.

MISS HARDCASTLE (*aside*): Now for meeting my modest gentleman. And I must meet him in quite his own manner. (*After a pause, in which he appears very uneasy*) I'm glad of your safe arrival, sir. I'm told you had some accidents on the way.

MARLOW (*hardly looking at her directly, as throughout the meeting*): Only a few, madam. Yes, we had some. Yes, madam, a good many accidents, but should be sorry—madam—or rather glad of any accidents—that are so wonderfully ended. Hem!

HASTINGS (*to him*): You never spoke better in your whole life! Keep it up, and I'll guarantee you the victory.

MISS HARDCASTLE: I'm afraid you flatter, sir. You who have seen so much of the finest company can find little entertainment in this forgotten corner of the country.

MARLOW *(gathering courage):* I have lived, indeed, in the world, madam. But I have kept very little company. I have been but an observer upon life, madam, while others were enjoying it.

MISS NEVILLE: But that, I am told, is the way to enjoy it at last.

HASTINGS *(to him):* No one ever spoke better. Once more, and you are a confident man for life.

MARLOW *(to him):* Hem! Stand by me, then, and when I'm down, throw in a word or two to set me up again.

HASTINGS: Well, Miss Hardcastle, I see that you and Mr. Marlow are going to be very good company. I believe our being here will only embarrass the two of you.

MARLOW: Not in the least, Mr. Hastings. We like your company! *(To him)* Zounds, George! How can you leave us?

HASTINGS: Our presence will only spoil conversation, so we'll retire to the next room. *(To him)* Don't you realize, man, that we want a little meeting of our own? *(Exeunt* HASTINGS *with* MISS NEVILLE*)*

MISS HARDCASTLE *(after a pause):* But you have not always been just an observer upon life, sir. The ladies, I should hope, have received some part of your attention.

MARLOW *(again very timid):* Pardon me, madam, I—I—I—as yet have tried—only—to—deserve them.

MISS HARDCASTLE: And that, some say, is the very worst way to please them.

MARLOW: Perhaps so, madam. But I love to converse only with the more serious and sensible members of the sex. Ah, I'm afraid I grow tiresome.

MISS HARDCASTLE: Not at all, sir. There is nothing I like so much as serious conversation myself. I could hear it forever. Indeed, I have often been surprised how a man of *quality* could ever admire those light, airy pleasures, where nothing reaches the heart.

MARLOW: It's—a disease—of the mind, madam. In the variety of tastes there must be some who, wanting—um-a-um.

MISS HARDCASTLE: I understand you, sir. There must be some, who, wanting certain pleasures, pretend to despise what they are not capable of getting.

MARLOW: My meaning, madam, but much better expressed. And I can't help observing—a—

MISS HARDCASTLE *(aside):* Who could ever suppose this fellow rude upon some occasions? *(To him)* You were going to observe, sir—

MARLOW: I was observing, madam—I protest, madam. I forget what I was going to observe.

MISS HARDCASTLE: You were observing, sir, that in this age of hypocrisy—something about hypocrisy, sir.

MARLOW: Yes, madam. In this age of hypocrisy, there are few who do not—a—a—

MISS HARDCASTLE: I understand you perfectly, sir.

MARLOW *(aside):* Egad, and that's more than I do myself!

MISS HARDCASTLE: You mean that in this age of hypocrisy, there are few who do not condemn in public what they practice in private.

MARLOW: True, madam. Those who have most—a—a—virtue in their—um, a—But I'm sure I tire you, madam.

MISS HARDCASTLE: Not in the least, sir. There's something so agreeable and lively in your manner, such life and force! Please, sir, go on.

MARLOW: Yes, madam, I was saying—that there are some occasions—when a total lack of courage, madam, destroys all the—and puts us—upon a—a—a—

MISS HARDCASTLE: I agree with you entirely. A lack of courage sometimes looks like ignorance, and makes us fail when we most want to succeed. I beg you to proceed.

MARLOW: Yes, madam. But I see Miss Neville wants us in the next room. I would not wish to keep her waiting.

MISS HARDCASTLE: I protest, sir. I never was more agreeably entertained in all my life. Please go on.

MARLOW: Yes, madam. I was—but she waves for us to join her.

MISS HARDCASTLE: Well, then, I'll follow.

MARLOW *(aside):* This conversation has ruined my chances. *(Exit)*

MISS HARDCASTLE *(to herself):* Ha! ha! ha! Was there ever such a sober, serious interview? I'm certain he scarcely looked at my face the whole time. Yet the fellow, but for his bashfulness,

---

hypocrisy (hih POK ruh see) pretending to be what one is not, or to feel what one does not feel

has good sense. If I could teach him a little confidence, it would be doing somebody that I know of a favor. But who is that somebody? Well, that's a question I can scarcely answer. *(Exit)*

(Enter TONY *and* MISS NEVILLE, *followed by* MRS. HARDCASTLE *and* HASTINGS)*

TONY: What do you follow me for, Cousin Con?

MISS NEVILLE: I hope, cousin, that I can speak to one of my own relations, and not be to blame.

TONY: Aye, I know what sort of a relation you want to make me! But I won't do. I tell you, Cousin Con, it won't do; so I beg you to keep your distance. I want no nearer relationship. *(She follows him to the back scene.)*

MRS. HARDCASTLE: Well Mr. Hastings, you are very entertaining. There's nothing in the world I love to talk of so much as London, and the fashions, though I was never there myself.

HASTINGS: Never there! You amaze me! From your air and manner, I concluded you went to London often.

MRS. HARDCASTLE: Please, Mr. Hastings, what do you take to be the most fashionable age in London now?

HASTINGS: Some time ago forty was all the style. But I'm told the ladies intended to bring up fifty for the coming winter.

MRS. HARDCASTLE: Seriously? Then I shall be too young for the fashion!

HASTINGS: No real lady now wears jewels till she's past forty. For instance, that young woman there, in London society, would be considered a child.

MRS. HARDCASTLE: And yet my niece thinks herself as a woman. Why, she's as fond of jewels as the oldest of us all.

HASTINGS: Your niece, is she? And that young gentleman—a brother of yours, I should think?

MRS. HARDCASTLE: My son, sir. They are engaged to each other. Observe their little games. They fall in and out ten times a day, as if they were man and wife already. *(To them)* Well, Tony my child, what soft things are you saying to your Cousin Constance this evening?

TONY: I have been saying no soft things!

MRS. HARDCASTLE: Never mind him, Con, my dear. He's another person behind your back.

TONY: That's a—crack.

MRS. HARDCASTLE: Ah, he's a sly one! Don't you think they resemble each other about the mouth, Mr. Hastings? They're of a size too. Back to back, my pretties, so Mr. Hastings may see you. Come, Tony.

TONY: You had better not make me, I tell you.

MRS. HARDCASTLE: Was ever the like? But I see he wants to break my heart, I see he does.

HASTINGS: Dear madam, permit me to lecture the young gentleman a little. I'm certain I can persuade him to do his duty.

MRS. HARDCASTLE: Well! I must go. Come Constance, my love, You see, Mr. Hastings, the misery of my situation. Was ever a poor woman so bothered by a dear, sweet, undutiful boy? *(Exeunt* MRS. HARDCASTLE *and* MISS NEVILLE*)*

TONY: Don't mind her. Let her cry. It's the comfort of her heart. I have seen her and sister cry over a book for an hour together, and they said they liked the book the better the more it made them cry.

HASTINGS: Then you're no friend to the ladies, my young gentleman?

TONY: Well, I'm a friend to *some.*

HASTINGS: Not to her of your mother's choosing, then. And yet she appears to me a pretty, well-tempered girl.

TONY: That's because you don't know her as well as I do.

HASTINGS: Well, but you must allow her a little beauty.—Yes, you must allow her some beauty.

TONY: Make-up! She's all a made-up thing, man. Ah! If you could see Bet Bouncer of these parts, you might then talk of beauty. She has two eyes as black as sloes, and cheeks as broad and red as a pulpit cushion. She'd make two of Cousin Con.

HASTINGS: Well, what would you think of a friend who would take this bitter bargain off your hands?

TONY: Speak on.

HASTINGS: Would you thank someone who would take Miss Neville, and leave you to happiness and your dear Betsy?

TONY: Aye, but where is there such a friend? Who would take *her?*

HASTINGS: I am he. If you'll only help me, I'll try to whip her off to France, and you'll never hear more of her.

TONY: Assist you! I will, to the last drop of my blood. I'll get you a pair of horses that shall carry you off in a twinkling. And maybe, I'll get you a part of her fortune besides, in jewels that you little dream of.

HASTINGS: My dear friend, you look like a lad of spirit.

TONY: Come along then, and you shall see more of my spirit before you have done with me.

ACT THREE

The house

(Enter HARDCASTLE, *alone*)

HARDCASTLE: What could my old friend Sir Charles mean by recommending his son as the most modest young man in town? That fellow, modest? He has taken over my easy chair by the fireside already. He took off his boots, and told me to take care of them. I'm curious to know how his rudeness affects my daughter. She will certainly be shocked at it.

---

sloe (SLOH) kind of small black fruit

(Enter MISS HARDCASTLE; *quite simply dressed)*

HARDCASTLE: Well, my Kate, I see you have changed your dress as I told you. And yet, I believe there was no great reason—particularly when I recommended my *modest* gentleman to you as a lover today.

MISS HARDCASTLE: You taught me to expect something unusual, and I found that the original was even more than the description!

HARDCASTLE: I was never so surprised in my life!

MISS HARDCASTLE: I never saw anything like it! And a man of the world, too!

HARDCASTLE: Aye, he learned it all abroad. What a fool was I, to think a young man could learn modesty by traveling. I fear he's been a good deal assisted by bad company and a French dancing master!

MISS HARDCASTLE: You're mistaken, Papa! A French dancing master could never have taught him that timid look—that awkward speech—that bashful manner—

HARDCASTLE: Whose look? Whose manner, child?

MISS HARDCASTLE: Mr. Marlow's. His timidity struck me at the first sight.

HARDCASTLE: Then your first sight deceived you.

MISS HARDCASTLE: He met me with a respectful bow, a stammering voice, and a look fixed on the ground.

HARDCASTLE: He met me with a loud voice, a lordy air, and a friendliness that made my blood freeze.

MISS HARDCASTLE: One of us must certainly be mistaken.

HARDCASTLE: If he really is what he has shown himself to be, he shall never have my consent.

MISS HARDCASTLE: And if he really is the sheepish thing I saw, he shall never have mine.

HARDCASTLE: In one thing then we are agreed—to reject him.

MISS HARDCASTLE: Yes. But upon conditions. For you might find him less rude, and I more confident—I don't know—the fellow is good looking.

HARDCASTLE: If we should find him so—but that's impossible!

MISS HARDCASTLE: And as one of us must be mistaken, what if we go on to make further discoveries?

HARDCASTLE: Agreed. But depend on it—I'm in the right.

MISS HARDCASTLE: And depend on it—I'm not much in the wrong. *(Exeunt)*

(Enter TONY, *running in with a box)*

TONY: I have got them! Here they are. My Cousin Con's jewels, necklaces and all. My mother shan't cheat the poor souls out of their fortune now. Oh! Is that you?

(Enter HASTINGS*)*

HASTINGS: My dear friend, how have you managed with your mother? I hope you have amused her with pretending love for your cousin Constance. Our horses will be ready in a short time, and we shall soon set off.

TONY: And here's something to take with you *(giving the box)*, your sweetheart's jewels.

HASTINGS: But how have you got them from your mother?

TONY: Ask me no questions, and I'll tell you no fibs. If I didn't have a key to every drawer in Mother's bureau, how could I go to the alehouse so often as I do? Zounds! Here they are! Go! Hurry! *(Exit* Hastings*)*

(Enter MRS. HARDCASTLE *and* MISS NEVILLE*)*

MRS. HARDCASTLE: Indeed, Constance, you amaze me. Such a girl as you want jewels? There will be time enough for jewels, my dear, twenty years from now, when your beauty begins to want repairs.

MISS NEVILLE: But what will repair beauty at forty will certainly improve it at twenty, madam.

MRS. HARDCASTLE: Besides, I believe I can't easily get at them. They may be missing, for all I know.

TONY (*apart to* MRS. HARDCASTLE): Then why don't you tell her so at once? Say they're lost, and call me to bear witness.

MRS. HARDCASTLE (*apart to* TONY): You know, my dear, I'm only keeping them for you, when you two marry. So if I say they're gone, you'll bear me witness, will you? He! he! he!

TONY (*apart to* MRS. HARDCASTLE): Never fear! I'll say I saw them taken with my own eyes.

MISS NEVILLE: I desire them but for a day, madam. Just to look at.

MRS. HARDCASTLE: My dear Constance, if I could find them, you should have them. They're missing, I assure you. Lost, for all I know. But we must have patience, wherever they are.

TONY: That I can bear witness to. They are missing, and not to be found.

MRS. HARDCASTLE: You must learn patience, my dear. For though we lose our fortune, we should not lose our patience. See me, how calm I am.

MISS NEVILLE: Aye, people are generally calm at the misfortune of others.

MRS. HARDCASTLE: We shall soon find them. In the meantime, you shall make use of my garnets till your jewels are found.

MISS NEVILLE: I detest garnets!

MRS. HARDCASTLE: I will get them. (*Exit*)

MISS NEVILLE: I dislike them of all things.

TONY: Don't be a fool. If she gives you the garnets, take what you can get. The jewels are your own already. I have stolen them out of her bureau, and she doesn't know it. Fly to your Hastings. He'll tell you more of the matter. Leave me to manage here.

MISS NEVILLE: My dear cousin!

TONY: Vanish! She's here, and has missed them already. (*Exit* MISS NEVILLE)

---

garnet (GAHR nit) kind of red gem

(Enter MRS. HARDCASTLE*)*

MRS. HARDCASTLE: Confusion! Thieves! Robbers! We are cheated, broke open, undone!

TONY: What's the matter, Mamma?

MRS. HARDCASTLE: My bureau has been broke open, the jewels taken out, and I'm undone!

TONY: Stick to that! Ha, ha, ha! Stick to that! I'll bear witness, you know. Call me to bear witness.

MRS. HARDCASTLE: I tell you, Tony, by all that's precious, the jewels are gone!

TONY: Sure, I know they're gone, and I am here to say so.

MRS. HARDCASTLE: My dearest Tony, hear me! They're *gone,* I say.

TONY: That's right!—that's right! Keep being that disturbed about it, and nobody will suspect either of us. I'll bear witness that they are gone.

MRS. HARDCASTLE: Oh! Was ever poor woman so beset with fools on one hand, and thieves on the other?

TONY: I can bear witness to that. *(He runs off; she follows him)*

(Enter MISS HARDCASTLE *and* MAID*)*

MISS HARDCASTLE: What a character that brother of mine is, to send them to this house as an inn! Ha! ha! I don't wonder at Mr. Marlow's behavior.

MAID: But what's more, as you passed by in that dress you have on now, Mr. Marlow asked me if you were the barmaid. He mistook you for the barmaid, madam!

MISS HARDCASTLE: Did he? Then as I live, I'm going to keep the fun alive. Are you sure he doesn't remember my face or size?

MAID: Certain of it!

MISS HARDCASTLE: I think so too. For though we spoke for some time together, his fears were such that he never once looked at me. Indeed, if he had, my bonnet would have kept him from seeing my face.

MAID: But are you sure you can act your part? Can you disguise your voice? He has to mistake that now too, you know.

MISS HARDCASTLE: Never fear. I think I know how to speak bar

---

beset (bih SET) bothered; troubled

language. (*Acting the part*)—Did your honor call?—Attend the gentleman there.—Pipe and tobacco for the squire.

MAID: It will do, madam. But he's here.

(*Exit* MAID)

(*Enter* MARLOW)

MARLOW: What an inn this is! I have scarcely a moment's peace. If I go to the best room, there I find my host and his stories. If I fly to the gallery, there we have my hostess with all her courtesy. Finally I have a moment to myself, and now for some thought. (*Walks and muses*)

MISS HARDCASTLE: Did you call, sir? Did your honor call?

MARLOW (*musing*): As for Miss Hardcastle, she's much too serious for me.

MISS HARDCASTLE: Did your honor call? (*She places herself before him, he turning away*)

MARLOW: No, child! (*Musing*) Besides, from the glimpse I had of her, I think she squints.

MISS HARDCASTLE: I'm sure, sir, that I heard the bell ring.

---

muse (MYOOZ) think; ponder

MARLOW: No, no! (*Musing*) I have pleased my father, however, by coming down here. And tomorrow I'll please myself by returning.

MISS HARDCASTLE: Perhaps the other gentleman called, sir?

MARLOW: I tell you no.

MISS HARDCASTLE: I should be glad to know, sir.

MARLOW: No, no, I tell you. (*Looks full in her face*) Yes, child, I think I did call. I wanted—I wanted—I see, child, you are a real beauty.

MISS HARDCASTLE: Oh la, sir, you'll make me ashamed.

MARLOW: I never saw a more lively, devilish eye. Yes, yes, my dear. I did call. Suppose I should call for a taste, just by way of trial, of the nectar of your lips. Might I be disappointed in that?

MISS HARDCASTLE: Nectar? Nectar? That's a drink there's no call for in these parts. French, I suppose. We keep no French wines here, sir.

MARLOW: Of true English growth, I assure you.

MISS HARDCASTLE: Then it's odd I should not know it. We brew all sorts of wines in this house, and I have lived here these eighteen years.

MARLOW: Eighteen years! Why one would think, child, you kept the bar before you were born. How old are you?

MISS HARDCASTLE: Oh, sir! I must not tell my age. They say women and music should never be dated.

MARLOW: To guess at this distance, you can't be much above forty. (*Approaching*) Yet nearer, I think not so old. (*Approaching*) By coming close to some women, they look younger still. But when we come very close indeed—(*Attempting to kiss her*)

MISS HARDCASTLE: Pray, sir, keep your distance. One would think you wanted to know a person's age as they do horses, by checking their teeth.

MARLOW: I protest, child. If you keep me at this distance, how is it possible you and I can be ever acquainted?

MISS HARDCASTLE: And who wants to be acquainted with you? I want no such acquaintance, not I. I'm sure you didn't treat Miss Hardcastle a while ago in this flirtatious manner. Before her you looked embarrassed, and kept bowing to the ground.

MARLOW: Before Miss Hardcastle, child? Ha! ha! ha! She's only

---

nectar (NEK tur) in mythology, the life-giving drink of the gods

an awkward, squinting thing! No, no! I find you don't know me. I laughed and cheered her up a little. But I was unwilling to be as serious as she was.

MISS HARDCASTLE: Then, sir, you're a real favorite among the ladies?

MARLOW: Yes, my dear, a great favorite. And yet, I don't really see what they find in me. At the Ladies Club in town I'm called their agreeable Rattle. Rattle, child, is not my real name, but one I'm known by. My name is Solomons. Mr. Solomons, my dear, at your service. *(Making a sweep with his arm before reaching for her shoulders)*

MISS HARDCASTLE *(stepping back)*: Wait, sir! You were introducing me to your club, not to yourself. And you're a great favorite there, you say?

MARLOW: Yes, my dear. There's Mrs. Mantrap, Lady Betty Blackleg, the Countess of Sligo, Mrs. Longhorns, Miss Biddy Buckskin, and your humble servant, to keep up the spirit of the place.

MISS HARDCASTLE: Then it's a very merry place, I suppose?

MARLOW: Yes, as merry as cards, suppers, and women can make me.

MISS HARDCASTLE: And their agreeable Rattle. Ha! ha! ha!

MARLOW *(aside)*: Egad! I don't quite like this talk. She looks knowing, I think. *(To her)* You laugh, child!

MISS HARDCASTLE: I can't help laughing when I think what little time all those ladies have for their work or their family.

MARLOW *(aside)*: All's well. She doesn't laugh at me. *(To her)* Do you ever work, child?

MISS HARDCASTLE: Aye, sure. There's not a pillow or a quilt in the whole house but what can bear witness to that.

MARLOW: Oh, so! Then you must show me your embroidery. I embroider and draw patterns myself a little. If you want a judge of your work you must apply to me. *(Seizing her hand)*

(Enter HARDCASTLE, *who stands in surprise)*

MISS HARDCASTLE: Aye, but the colors don't look well by candlelight. You shall see all in the morning. *(Struggling)*

MARLOW: And why not now, my angel? Such beauty fires up beyond my power to resist. Oh, no! The innkeeper here! My old luck. *(Exit)*

HARDCASTLE: So, madam! So I find *this* is your *modest* lover! This is your humble admirer who kept his eyes on the ground and only adored at distance. Kate, Kate, aren't you ashamed to deceive your father so?

MISS HARDCASTLE: Trust me, dear Papa, that he's still the modest man I first took him for. You'll be convinced of it soon, I promise.

HARDCASTLE: But didn't I see him seize your hand? Didn't I see him haul you about like a milkmaid? And now you talk of his respect and his modesty!

MISS HARDCASTLE: But soon I'll convince you of his modesty. If you see that his faults will pass off with time, and that his virtues will improve with age, I hope you'll forgive him.

HARDCASTLE: This girl would actually make me run mad! I tell you, I'll not be convinced. Or rather, I *am* convinced. My son-in-law, madam, must have very different qualifications.

MISS HARDCASTLE: Sir, I ask only this evening to convince you.

HARDCASTLE: You shall not have half the time. I have thoughts of turning him out of my house this very hour.

MISS HARDCASTLE: Give me that hour then, and I hope to satisfy you.

HARDCASTLE: Well, an hour let it be then. But I'll have no trifling with your father. All fair and open, do you hear me?

MISS HARDCASTLE: Of course, sir. I have always considered your commands to be your kindness.

ACT FOUR

The house

(*Enter* HASTINGS *and* MISS NEVILLE)

HASTINGS: You surprise me! Sir Charles Marlow expected here this night? Where have you got your information?

MISS NEVILLE: You may depend upon it. I just saw his letter to Mr. Hardcastle. Sir Charles writes that he intends setting out a few hours after his son.

HASTINGS: Then, my Constance, all must be completed before he arrives. He knows me. If he should find me here, he might tell my plans to the rest of the family.

MISS NEVILLE: The jewels, I hope, are safe.

HASTINGS: Yes, yes. I have sent them to Marlow, who keeps the keys of our baggage. In the meantime, I'll go to prepare for our elopement. I have had the promise of a fresh pair of horses. *(Exit)*

MISS NEVILLE: Well, success be with you! In the meantime, I'll go amuse my aunt with the old story of a violent passion for my cousin. *(Exit)*

(Enter MARLOW *followed by a* SERVANT*)*

MARLOW: I wonder what Hastings could mean by sending a valuable box of jewels to keep for him. Have you deposited the box with the landlady, as I ordered you? Have you put it into her own hands?

SERVANT: Yes, your honor.

MARLOW: She said she'd keep it safe, did she?

SERVANT: Yes. Those were her very words: *"I'll keep it safe enough."* *(Exit)*

MARLOW: Ha! Ha! Ha! They're safe, however. What a set of people at this inn. That little barmaid, though, runs in my head most strangely. She's mine, she must be mine, or I'm greatly mistaken.

(Enter HASTINGS*)*

HASTINGS: Bless me! Marlow here, and looking happy too.

MARLOW: Give me joy, George! Crown me! After all, we modest fellows don't always lack success among the women.

HASTINGS: But what success?

MARLOW: Didn't you see the tempting, brisk, lovely little thing that runs about the house with a bunch of keys?

HASTINGS: Well! And what then?

MARLOW: She's mine, you rascal, you. Such fire, such motion, such eyes, such lips! But egad! She would not let me kiss them though.

HASTINGS: But are you sure, so very sure of her?

MARLOW: Why, man, she talked of showing me her embroidery upstairs.

HASTINGS: Well—we'll see what happens. You have taken care, I hope, of the box I sent you to lock up? It's in safety?

MARLOW: Yes, yes. It's safe enough. I have taken care of it. But how could you think our baggage a place of safety? Ah! I have taken even better care of it—I have—

HASTINGS: What?

MARLOW: I have sent it to the landlady to keep for you.

HASTINGS: To the landlady!

MARLOW: The landlady.

HASTINGS: You did!

MARLOW: Wasn't I right?

HASTINGS *(aside):* He must not see my uneasiness.

MARLOW: You seem a little disturbed, I think. Surely nothing has happened?

HASTINGS: No, nothing. I was never in better spirits in all my life. After all, the jewels are safe.

MARLOW: As in a miser's purse.

HASTINGS *(aside):* So now all hopes of fortune are at an end, and we must elope without it. *(To him)* Well, Charles, I'll leave you to your pretty barmaid. He! he! he! May you be as successful for yourself as you have been for me. *(Exit)*

MARLOW: Thanks, George! I ask no more. Ha! ha! ha! *(Enter* HARDCASTLE*)*

HARDCASTLE *(to himself):* I no longer know my own house. It's turned all topsy-turvy. His servants have got drunk already.

I'll stand it no longer—and yet, from my respect for his father, I'll be calm. *(To him)* Mr. Marlow, I have submitted to your rudeness for more than four hours. I see no likelihood of its coming to an end. I'm the master here, sir. And I desire that you and your drunken pack leave my house directly.

MARLOW: Leave your house! Surely, you cannot be serious! At this time of night, and such a night!

HARDCASTLE: I tell you, sir, I'm serious. I say this house is mine, sir. This house is mine, and I command you to leave it directly.

MARLOW: Ha! ha! ha!

HARDCASTLE: Young man, young man, listen. From your father's letter to me, I was led to expect a well-bred, modest man as a visitor here. But now I find him no better than a bully. I tell you, Sir Charles will be here soon, and he shall hear all of it! *(Exit)*

MARLOW: How's this! Surely, I have not mistaken the house. Everything looks like an inn. The servants cry, "Coming." The barmaid, too, to attend us. But she's here, and will tell me more.

(Enter MISS HARDCASTLE*)*

MARLOW: Why so fast, child? A word with you.

MISS HARDCASTLE: Let it be short then. I'm in a hurry. *(Aside)* I believe he begins to find out his mistake.

MARLOW: Child, answer me one question. Who are you, and what may your business in this house be?

MISS HARDCASTLE: A relation of the family, sir.

MARLOW: What! A poor relation?

MISS HARDCASTLE: Yes, sir. A poor relation appointed to keep the keys, and to see that the guests lack nothing in my power to give them.

MARLOW: That is, you act as the barmaid of this inn.

MISS HARDCASTLE: Inn! What brought that in your head? Does one of the best families in the county keep an inn! Ha, ha, ha. Old Mr. Hardcastle's house an inn!

MARLOW: Mr. Hardcastle's house! Is this house Mr. Hardcastle's house, child?

MISS HARDCASTLE: Aye, sure. Whose else would it be?

MARLOW: So then all's out in the open. I have been fooled for some reason. I shall be laughed at forever. To mistake this house, of all others, for an inn! And my father's old friend for an innkeeper! What a rude bully must he take me for! What a silly puppy do I find myself! There again, may I be hanged, my dear, but I mistook you for a common barmaid! And you're really a relation of Mr. Hardcastle's!

MISS HARDCASTLE: Dear me! I'm sure there was nothing in my *behavior* to make you think—

MARLOW: Nothing, my dear, nothing. I was in for a list of mistakes. My stupidity saw everything the wrong way. But it's over— this house I'll no more show *my* face in!

MISS HARDCASTLE: I hope, sir, I have done nothing to displease you. I'm sure I should be sorry to anger any gentleman who has said so many nice things to me. I'm sure I should be sorry *(pretending to cry)* if he left the family upon my account.

MARLOW *(aside):* By heaven, she weeps! This is the first sign of tenderness I ever had from a modest woman, and it touches me. *(To her)* Excuse me, my lovely girl. You are the only part of the family I leave with pain. But the difference of our birth, fortune, and education makes an honorable connection impossible. And I could never think of bringing ruin upon one whose only fault was being too lovely.

MISS HARDCASTLE *(aside):* Generous man! I now begin to admire him. *(To him)* But I'm sure my family is as good as Miss Hardcastle's. And though I'm poor, that's no great misfortune. Why, until this moment, I never thought that it was bad to lack a fortune.

MARLOW: And why now, my pretty one?

MISS HARDCASTLE: Because it puts me at a distance from a person whom, if I had a thousand pounds, I would give it all to.

MARLOW *(aside):* This girl bewitches me! If I stay, I'm undone! I must make one bold effort and leave her. *(To her)* Your words, my dear, touch me most tenderly. If I could live for myself alone, I could easily fix my choice. But I owe too much to the opinion of the world, too much to the authority of a father.— I can scarcely speak of how—all this—affects me! Farewell! *(Exit)*

MISS HARDCASTLE: I never knew half his merit till now. He shan't go. Not if I can help it. I'll still keep the character in which I stooped to conquer. But I'll tell all to my father, who perhaps can laugh him out of his plans. *(Exit)*

(Enter TONY, MISS NEVILLE*)*

TONY: Aye, you may steal for yourselves the next time. I have done my duty. My mother has got the jewels again, that's a sure thing. But she believes it was all a mistake of the servants.

MISS NEVILLE: My dear cousin, surely you won't forsake us in this distress. If she suspects that I am going off, I shall certainly be locked up—or sent to my Aunt Pedigree's, which is ten times worse.

TONY: But what can I do? I have got you a pair of horses that will fly. Here she comes. We must act our parts a bit more, or she'll suspect us. *(They retire, and seem to fondle.)*

(Enter MRS. HARDCASTLE*)*

MRS. HARDCASTLE: Well, I was greatly annoyed, to be sure. But my son tells me it was all a mistake of the servants. Ah, what do I see! Fondling together, as I'm alive! Ah, have I caught you, my pretty doves?

MISS NEVILLE: Cousin Tony promises to give us more of his company at home. Indeed, he shan't leave us any more.

TONY: I'm sure I always loved Cousin Con's hazel eyes, and her pretty long fingers. Oh, pretty creature.

MRS. HARDCASTLE: Ah, he would charm the bird from the tree. I was never so happy before. The jewels, my dear Con, shall be yours. You shall have them. Isn't he a sweet boy, my dear? You shall be married tomorrow.

(Enter SERVANT*)*

SERVANT *(to* TONY*):* I have a letter for your worship.

TONY: Give it to my mamma. She reads all my letters first.

SERVANT: I had orders to deliver it into your own hands. *(Exit)*

MISS NEVILLE *(aside):* Undone, undone! A letter to him from Hastings. I know the hand. If my aunt sees it, we are ruined forever!

TONY: Here, mother. *(Giving* MRS. HARDCASTLE *the letter)*

MRS. HARDCASTLE: How's this! *(Reads)* "Dear Tony, I'm now waiting for Miss Neville at the bottom of the garden. But I find my horses yet unable to perform the journey. I expect you'll assist us with a pair of fresh horses, as you promised.

Speed is necessary, as the *hag, (aye, the hag)* your mother, will otherwise suspect me. Yours, Hastings." Give me patience! My rage chokes me!

MISS NEVILLE: I hope, madam—

MRS. HARDCASTLE (*to* TONY): And you, you great oaf! Were you, too, joined against me? But I'll defeat all your plots in a moment. As for you, madam, since you have a pair of fresh horses ready, it would be cruel to disappoint them. So, if you please, forget your plan of running away with your Hastings. Instead, prepare, this very moment, to run off with *me.* Your old Aunt Pedigree will keep you secure, I'm sure. You too, my son, may mount your horse, and guard us upon the way. (*Exit*)

MISS NEVILLE: So now I'm completely ruined.

TONY: Aye, that's a sure thing.

MISS NEVILLE: What better could be expected from such a stupid fool as you!

TONY: No miss, it was your own cleverness, not my stupidity. You were so nice and smiling with me—I thought you could never be making believe. And her words: "Married tomorrow!"

(*Enter* HASTINGS)

HASTINGS: So, sir, I find from my servant that you have shown my letter and betrayed us!

TONY: Ask miss there who betrayed you. It was her doing, not mine.

(*Enter* MARLOW)

MARLOW: So I have been laughed at here among you! Made to look the fool! Insulted!

MISS NEVILLE: And there, sir, is the gentleman who caused every part of this madness.

TONY: Baw!

MARLOW: What can I say to him, a mere boy, an idiot!

HASTINGS: A poor fool, not worth my breath.

MISS NEVILLE: Yet with enough evil tricks to make himself merry with all our embarrassments.

(*Enter* SERVANT)

SERVANT: My mistress desires you'll get ready immediately,

madam. The horses are ready. Your hat and things are in the next room. We are to go thirty miles before morning.

MISS NEVILLE: Well, I'll come presently.

MARLOW (to HASTINGS): Was it all done, sir, to make me look ridiculous? Depend upon it, sir, I shall expect an explanation.

MISS NEVILLE: Mr. Hastings. Mr. Marlow. Why will you increase my distress by this silly dispute? I beg you—

SERVANT: Your cloak, madam. My mistress is impatient.

MISS NEVILLE: Oh, Mr. Marlow! If you knew all my poor Mr. Hastings has been through, I'm sure it would change your anger into pity.

MARLOW: I don't know what I know. Forgive me, madam. George, forgive me. You know my hasty temper.

HASTINGS: The torture of my situation is my only excuse.

MRS. HARDCASTLE (within): Miss Neville! Constance, why, Constance, I say.

MISS NEVILLE: I'm coming. (Exit, followed by SERVANT)

HASTINGS: My heart! How can I stand this! To be so near happiness, and such happiness!

MARLOW (to TONY): You see now, young gentleman, the results of your tricks. What might be amusement to you is here disappointment, and even distress.

TONY (from a trance): Egad, I have hit it! It's here! Your hands. Yours, and yours (shaking hands with both). Meet me two hours from now at the bottom of the garden. And if you don't find Tony Lumpkin a better fellow than you thought, I'll give you my best horse, and Bet Bouncer in the bargain! Come along. (Exeunt)

ACT FIVE

Scene 1: the house

(*Enter* HASTINGS *and* SERVANT)

HASTINGS: You saw the old lady and Miss Neville drive off, you say?

SERVANT: Yes, your honor. They went off in a coach, and master

Tony Lumpkin went on horseback. They're thirty miles off by this time.

HASTINGS: Then all my hopes are over.

SERVANT: Yes, sir. Old Sir Charles Marlow has arrived. He and the old gentleman of the house have been laughing at young Marlow's mistakes. Oh, they're coming this way.

HASTINGS: Then I must not be seen. So now to my fruitless appointment at the bottom of the garden. This is about the time. *(Exit)*

(Enter SIR CHARLES *and* HARDCASTLE*)*

HARDCASTLE: Ha! ha! ha! The tone in which he gave me his commands! And yet he might have seen something in me above the common innkeeper, too.

SIR CHARLES: Yes, Dick, but he mistook you for an uncommon innkeeper, ha! ha! ha!

HARDCASTLE: Well, I'm too happy now to think of anything but joy. Yes, my dear friend, this union of our families will make our personal friendship hereditary. And though my daughter's fortune is but small—

SIR CHARLES: Why, Dick, will you talk of fortune to *me?* My son has more than a little money already. He can want nothing but a good and virtuous girl to share his happiness and increase it. If they like each other, as you say they do—

HARDCASTLE: *If,* man. I tell you they *do* like each other. My daughter as good as told me so.

SIR CHARLES: But girls are apt to flatter themselves, you know.

HARDCASTLE: I saw him grasp her hand in the warmest manner myself. And here he comes to put you out of your *ifs. (Enter* MARLOW*)*

MARLOW: I come, sir, once more, to ask pardon for my very strange conduct.

HARDCASTLE: It was nothing, boy. You take it too seriously. An hour or two of laughing with my daughter will set all to rights again. She'll never like you the worse for it.

MARLOW: Sir, I shall always be proud of her approval.

HARDCASTLE: *Approval* is too cold a word, Mr. Marlow. If I'm not deceived, you have something more than just approval from her right now. You understand me?

MARLOW: Really, sir, I have not that happiness.

HARDCASTLE: Come, boy. I'm an old fellow, but I know what's what as well as a younger man. I know what has passed between you two.

MARLOW: Sir, nothing has passed between us but the most profound respect and serious discussion. You can't think, sir, that my impudence to you has been passed on to the rest of the family.

HARDCASTLE: Impudence? No, I don't say that—it's not quite impudence. Girls like to be flirted with, and rumpled a little, too, sometimes. But she has told no tales, I assure you.

MARLOW: I never gave her the slightest cause.

HARDCASTLE: Well, well, I like modesty in its place. But this is overacting, my young gentleman. You may be honest with us. Your father and I will like you the better for it.

MARLOW: Dear sir—I protest, sir—

HARDCASTLE: I see no reason why you two should not be joined as fast as the parson can tie you.

MARLOW: But hear me, sir—

HARDCASTLE: Your father approves the match, and I admire it.

MARLOW: But why won't you hear me? By all that's just and true, I never gave Miss Hardcastle the most distant hint of affection. We had but one interview, and that was formal and uninteresting.

HARDCASTLE *(aside):* This fellow's formal, modest impudence is beyond bearing.

SIR CHARLES: And you never grasped her hand or made any talk of love?

MARLOW: As Heaven is my witness, *no! (Exit)*

SIR CHARLES: I'm astonished at the air of sincerity with which he parted.

HARDCASTLE: And I'm astonished that his odd behavior goes on and on.

SIR CHARLES: I dare pledge my life and honor upon his truth.

HARDCASTLE: Here comes my daughter, and I would stake my happiness upon *her* truth.

(Enter MISS HARDCASTLE*)*

---

impudence (IM pyuh duns) rudeness; disregard of others

HARDCASTLE: Kate, come here, child. Answer us sincerely. Has Mr. Marlow made to you any show of love and affection?

MISS HARDCASTLE: The question is very abrupt, sir! But since you require sincerity, I think he has.

HARDCASTLE (*to* SIR CHARLES)*:* You see!

SIR CHARLES: And tell us, madam, have you and my son had more than one interview?

MISS HARDCASTLE: Yes, sir, several.

HARDCASTLE (*to* SIR CHARLES)*:* You see!

SIR CHARLES: But did he talk of love?

MISS HARDCASTLE: Much sir.

SIR CHARLES: Amazing. And all this in earnest?

MISS HARDCASTLE: In earnest.

HARDCASTLE: Now, my friend, I hope you are satisfied.

SIR CHARLES: And how did he behave, madam?

MISS HARDCASTLE: As most admirers do. Said some nice things about my face; talked much of his lack of merit, and the greatness of mine; mentioned his heart; gave a short speech of pretended—

SIR CHARLES: *Indeed, no!* I know his conversation with women to be most modest. This bold, talkative manner by no means describes him. I am confident he never sat for the picture.

MISS HARDCASTLE: Then what, sir, if I should convince you of my sincerity? If you and my papa, in about half an hour, will place yourselves behind that screen, you shall hear him declare his passion to me in person.

SIR CHARLES: Agreed. And if I find him what you describe, all my happiness in him must have an end. (*Exit*)

MISS HARDCASTLE: And if you don't find him what I described—I fear my happiness will never have a beginning. (*Exeunt*)

Scene 2: the back of the garden

(*Enter* HASTINGS)

HASTINGS: What an idiot I am, to wait here for a fellow who probably takes great delight in tricking me.

(*Enter* TONY, *booted and spattered*)

HASTINGS: My honest friend! I now find you a man of your word!

TONY: Aye, I'm your friend.

HASTINGS: But where did you leave your fellow travelers? Are they in safety?

TONY: Leave them? Why, where should I leave them but where I found them?

HASTINGS: This is a riddle.

TONY: Riddle me this, then. What goes round and round the house, and never touches the house?

HASTINGS: I'm still astray.

TONY: You shall hear. First I took them round and round the house on this dark night. They've been within five miles these two hours. At the end, I nearly dumped them in the horse pond over there.

HASTINGS: By no accident, I hope.

TONY: No, no. Only Mother is frightened. She thinks herself forty miles off. So, if your own horses are ready, you can whip off with Cousin Con toward France, I'll be sure that no one here will follow you.

HASTINGS: My dear friend, how can I show my gratitude? *(Exit)*

(Enter MRS. HARDCASTLE*)*

MRS. HARDCASTLE: Oh Tony, I'm killed! Shook! Bettered to death! I shall never survive it.

TONY: Alas, Mama, it was all your own fault. You would be for running away by night, without knowing one inch of the way.

MRS. HARDCASTLE: I wish we were at home again. I never met so many accidents on such a short journey. Overturned in a ditch, stuck fast in the mud, jolted to a jelly, and at last to lose our way? Where do you think we are, Tony?

TONY: By my guess we should be upon Crackskull Common, about forty miles from home.

(Enter HARDCASTLE, *holding lamp, to one side)*

HARDCASTLE: I thought I heard a voice down here. I'd be glad to know where it came from.

MRS. HARDCASTLE: Mr. Hardcastle, as I'm alive! My fears blinded me. But who, my dear, could have expected to meet you here, in this frightful place, so far from home? What has brought you to follow us?

HARDCASTLE: Surely, Dorothy, you have not lost your wits? So far from home, when you are within forty yards of your own door! *(To* TONY*)* This is one of your old tricks, you rascal, you. *(To her)* Don't you know the gate, and the mulberry tree? And don't you remember the horse pond, my dear?

MRS. HARDCASTLE: That's—that's *our* horse pond? Then I shall remember the horse pond as long as I live! I have caught my death in it! *(To* TONY*)* And it is to you, you graceless son of mine, that I owe all this? I'll teach you to abuse your mother, I will!

TONY: Now, Mother, all the county says you spoiled me, and so you must take the results of it.

MRS. HARDCASTLE: I'll spoil you, I will! *(Chases him off the stage)*

HARDCASTLE: There's some sense, however, in his reply. *(Exit)*

(Enter HASTINGS *and* MISS NEVILLE*)*

HASTINGS: My dear Constance, if we delay a moment, all is lost forever. Pluck up a little courage, and we shall soon be out of her reach.

MISS NEVILLE: No, I find it impossible. My spirits are so sunk with all I have suffered. I am unable to face any new danger.

HASTINGS: Let us fly, my charmer. Let us date our happiness from this very moment. Forget your fortune. Love and joy will increase what we possess beyond the fortune of a king.

MISS NEVILLE: No, Mr. Hastings, no. Good sense once more comes to my relief, and I will obey it. In a moment of passion, fortune may be despised, but it can never be regained. I'm determined to apply to Mr. Hardcastle's justice and sense of fair play.

HASTINGS: I have no hopes. But since you insist, I must obey you. *(Exeunt)*

Scene 3: a room at MR. HARDCASTLE'S

(Enter HARDCASTLE, SIR CHARLES *and* MISS HARDCASTLE*)*

SIR CHARLES *(to* MISS HARDCASTLE*)*: What a situation I am in! If what you say is true, I shall then find a guilty son. But if what he says is true, I shall then lose the girl I most wanted for a daughter.

MISS HARDCASTLE: I am proud of your approval. And to show I merit it, if you place yourself as I directed, you shall hear his very declaration of love to me. But he comes!

HARDCASTLE: Quick, my friend, behind the screen. *(They go there.)*
(Enter MARLOW*)*

MARLOW: Though prepared for setting out, I come once more to say goodbye. Till this moment, I never knew the pain I'd feel in separation.

MISS HARDCASTLE *(in her own natural manner)*: I believe your suffering cannot be very great, sir. Why, you can so easily remove the pain. Staying a day or two longer, perhaps, might bring some relief.

MARLOW *(aside)*: This girl every moment improves upon me. *(To her)* That must not be, madam. I have already played too long with my heart. My very pride begins to submit to my passion. The difference between us in education and fortune, and the anger of a parent, begin to lose their weight. Nothing can ease the situation now—but that I leave.

MISS HARDCASTLE: Then go, sir. I'll not detain you. Remember, though, that my family is as good as hers you came down to visit. And my education, I hope, is not inferior. But what are these things worth without an equal fortune? I must be content with only the sight of your back as you leave, while all your serious aims are fixed on fortune.

SIR CHARLES *(from behind)*: Ah, what is this?

HARDCASTLE: Shhh, make no noise. I'll bet my Kate covers him with confusion at last.

MARLOW: By the heavens, madam! Fortune was ever my smallest thought. Your beauty first caught my eye. Who could see that without emotion? Even now, every moment that I converse with you brings some new attraction.

SIR CHARLES: What can it mean? He amazes me!

HARDCASTLE: I told you how it would be. Hush.

MARLOW *(with great self-confidence)*: I am now determined to stay, madam. The fortune means nothing. And I think I know my father's taste in women. When he sees you, his approval is certain.

MISS HARDCASTLE: No, Mr. Marlow. I will not, I cannot detain you. How could I agree to a connection with the slightest room for doubt? How could I take advantage of a passing passion to load you with confusion? Do you think I could ever enjoy my own happiness by lessening yours?

MARLOW: By all that's good, I can have no happiness but what's in your power to give me! I will stay, even against your wishes. And even if you shun me, my behavior will make up for the levity of my past conduct.

MISS HARDCASTLE: Sir, I must beg you to change your mind. As our acquaintance began, so let it end—with no strong attachment. Once, I might have given an hour or two to levity. But seriously, Mr. Marlow, do you think I could ever agree to a connection? What would people think? I might appear greedy for money, and you lacking in judgment.

MARLOW *(kneeling)*: Does this look like poor judgment? No, madam, your merit only increases my confidence that my judgment is—

SIR CHARLES *(coming from behind screen)*: I can hold it no longer. Charles! How you have deceived me! Is this what you call uninteresting conversation?

---

levity (LEV ih tee) lightness of mind, conduct or speech; lack of seriousness

HARDCASTLE: Your cold behavior! Your formal interview! What have you to say now?

MARLOW: That I'm all amazement. What can this mean?

HARDCASTLE: It means that you can say and unsay things as you wish. That you can court a lady in private, and deny it in public. That you have one story for us, and another for my daughter!

MARLOW: Daughter!—this lady, your daughter!

HARDCASTLE: Yes, sir, my only daughter, my Kate. Whose else should she be?

MARLOW: Oh, the devil!

MISS HARDCASTLE: Yes, sir, the very same tall, squinting lady you were pleased to take me for. (*Curtsying*) She that you approached as the mild, shy, and serious man, and also as the bold, confident, Rattle of the Ladies Club, ha! ha! ha!

MARLOW: I can't stand this. It's worse than death!

MISS HARDCASTLE: In which of your characters, sir, shall we now address you? As the gentleman who looks on the ground, speaks just to be heard, and hates hypocrisy? Or as the loud, confident creature that rattles away with Mrs. Mantrap and Miss Biddy Buckskin till three in the morning, ha! ha! ha!

MARLOW: Oh, curse my noisy head. I must be gone.

HARDCASTLE: By the hand of my body, you shall not go! I see it was all a mistake, and I am happy to find it so. You shall not go, sir, I tell you. I know she'll forgive you. Won't you forgive him, Kate? We all forgive you. Take courage, man. (MARLOW *and* MISS HARDCASTLE *retire, talking together, to the back of the scene.*)

(*Enter* MRS. HARDCASTLE *and* TONY)

MRS. HARDCASTLE: So, so, they've gone off. Let them go. I care not.

HARDCASTLE: Who's gone?

MRS. HARDCASTLE: My niece Constance and her gentleman, Mr. Hastings.

SIR CHARLES: Who? My honest George Hastings? As worthy a fellow as lives, and the girl could not have made a better choice.

HARDCASTLE: Then, by the hand of my body, I'm proud of the connection.

MRS. HARDCASTLE: Well, if he has taken away the lady, he has not taken her fortune. That remains in this family to make up for her loss.

HARDCASTLE: Surely, Dorothy, you would not be so money-minded.

MRS. HARDCASTLE: Aye, and that's my affair, not yours.

HARDCASTLE: But you know, if your son, when he comes of age, refuses to marry his cousin, her whole fortune is then her own.

MRS. HARDCASTLE: Aye, but he's not of age, and Constance has not thought proper to wait for his refusal.

(Enter HASTINGS *and* MISS NEVILLE*)*

MRS. HARDCASTLE: What! Returned so soon? I begin not to like it.

HASTINGS *(to* HARDCASTLE*):* Sir, I regret my recent attempt to fly off with your niece. Let my present confusion be my punishment. We have now come back, to appeal to your justice and your humanity.

MISS NEVILLE: In an hour of folly, I was even ready to give up my fortune to marry Mr. Hastings. But I'm now recovered, and appeal to your tenderness.

MRS. HARDCASTLE: Oh, all this sounds like the whining end of a modern novel.

HARDCASTLE: Be it what it will, I'm glad they've come back to make things right. Come here, Tony, boy. Do you refuse to marry this lady I now offer you?

TONY: What means my refusing? You know I can't refuse her till I'm of legal age, Father.

HARDCASTLE: Boy, when I thought that hiding your age was likely to lead to your improvement, I agreed with your mother's desire to keep it a secret. But since I find she turns it to a wrong use, I must now declare that you have been of age for three months.

TONY: Of age? Am I of legal age, Father?

HARDCASTLE: More than three months.

TONY: Then you'll see the first use I make of my liberty. *(Taking* MISS NEVILLE'S *hand)* Witness all men, that I, Anthony Lumpkin, of BLANK place, now refuse you Constance Neville, of no place at all, for my true and lawful wife. So Constance Neville may marry whom she pleases, and Tony Lumpkin is his own man again!

SIR CHARLES: O brave young man!

HASTINGS: My worthy friend!

MRS. HARDCASTLE: My undutiful child!

MARLOW: Joy, my dear George, I give you joy sincerely. And if I could persuade my little tyrant here to now accept *me*, I would be the happiest man alive.

HASTINGS *(to* MISS HARDCASTLE*)*: Come, madam, you are now driven to the very last scene of all your play acting. I know you love him. I'm sure he loves you. Now, you must and shall have him.

HARDCASTLE *(joining their hands as* MISS HARDCASTLE *smiles)*: And I say so too. Mr. Marlow, if she makes as good a wife as she has a daughter, I don't believe you'll ever regret your bargain. So now to supper. Tomorrow we shall gather all the neighborhood together, and the Mistakes of the Night shall be crowned with a merry morning. So, boy, take her. And as you have been mistaken in the mistress, my wish is that you'll never be mistaken in the wife.

Oliver Goldsmith (1730?–1774)

Seldom has success and failure fought for control of a person's life as in the case of the Irish-born author Oliver Goldsmith. Early in life, Goldsmith studied religion, but he was never permitted to become a clergyman, partly because of his fun-loving and careless habits. He moved to Scotland and studied medicine, only to fail as a doctor. He turned to teaching, with no success. When he was nearly 30, he began writing. He peddled an assortment of his writings to magazines.

Then, quite suddenly, a literary genius emerged. A long poem, "The Deserted Village," was a success. *The Vicar of Wakefield* became a popular novel of the 18th century. Plays he wrote, such as *She Stoops to Conquer*, were greatly enjoyed by audiences. Goldsmith even wrote a two-volume *History of England*.

Success with money did not come as easily, however. It seemed to flow through Goldsmith's fingers as quickly as it came. Some of the money he gambled away. Some he spent on pleasures. Much he simply gave away to people in need. His habits kept him a poor man, and he died at an early age.

Today, Goldsmith lives on through his words. Like William Shakespeare, he is sometimes quoted unknowingly. In *She Stoops to Conquer*, for instance, you'll read "the very pink of perfection" and "Ask me no questions, and I'll tell you no fibs."

Two lines of Goldsmith's poetry seem to fit his own life well:

His best companions, innocence and
    health;
And his best riches, ignorance of wealth.

Oliver Goldsmith, James Boswell, and Samuel Johnson at the Mitre Tavern in London, Anonymous. The Granger Collection

Review the Selection

UNDERSTAND THE SELECTION

Recall

1. Why did Marlow act so rudely in the Hardcastle home?

2. Who really loves Constance Neville?

3. Why did Mrs. Hardcastle resist giving Constance her jewels?

Infer

4. Which character's actions started the "Mistakes of the Night"?

5. Did distinct social classes exist during this time? How can you tell?

6. What does the play's title mean?

7. Which character acts foolishly throughout the play? What examples let you know?

Apply

8. What two events could have changed the outcome of this story?

9. What might have happened if Marlow had quickly recognized Kate?

10. If this story were set in modern times, would Mr. Hardcastle arrange for his friend's son to meet his daughter?

Respond to Literature

In what way is *She Stoops to Conquer* representative of Restoration-style plays? Look back at pages 134 and 135 for a summary of the Restoration.

WRITE ABOUT THE SELECTION

At the end of this play, Tony Lumpkin learns that he had come of age three months earlier. His mother, Mrs. Hardcastle, had kept this information from him for her own selfish reasons. She had hoped that Tony would agree to marry Constance and that the jewels would remain in the family. Tony, of course, had different plans for his life. Until this discovery of his true age, Tony had been rebellious and prankish. Now that he has come of age, he is entitled to his inheritance. Do you think he will change his outlook on life? Will he become more responsible or remain rebellious? Add a brief episode to the play of one or two paragraphs indicating how you think Tony will react.

Prewriting Think about how Tony will react. Write an informal outline of what steps he takes toward maturing or what he does instead. Include details of what he will do with his new-found freedom and money. Freewrite some conversation among the characters.

Writing Use your informal outline to write your conclusions in play form. Be sure to include dialogue involving other characters.

Revising When you revise, be sure to add stage directions to help readers follow the action.

Proofreading Read over your selection. Be sure you have identified each speaking part with the character's name.

THINK ABOUT PLOT

In a farce, the plot is often an improbable or ridiculous series of events. Because it is a play, the audience accepts that these events could really happen. The audience agrees to this in order to enjoy the humor that results from the ridiculous events on stage. This agreement is called the **willing suspension of disbelief.**

1. In what way does the mistaken belief that the Hardcastle residence is the inn illustrate farce?

2. The plot depends on the unlikely mistake in question 1. Why does the audience believe this mistake could happen?

3. If this were a serious play, what might Mr. Hardcastle have said when meeting Hastings and Marlow?

4. In what ways does this selection illustrate the use of complex plot and rapid action in farce?

5. In real life, do you think that Marlow would have acted as he did? Would Kate have agreed to marry him after seeing him act as he did?

READING FOCUS

Make Inferences About Character As you read this play, you used clues to piece together each character's personality. Now use those clues to briefly describe each character.

DEVELOP YOUR VOCABULARY

The humor in the play *She Stoops to Conquer* is evident even to this day. Many of the words or terms used reflect the times in which it was written. This language helps you sense what it was like to live in the 18th century. For example, Mr. Hardcastle's statement ". . . but now they travel faster than a stagecoach" tells you about travel in this period. If this play were written today, he might say ". . .faster than a plane." Below are questions about some of the 18th-century terms used in the play. Answer each question with a complete sentence stating what term could be used in a modern-day version.

1. Would Hastings and Marlow arrive by *carriage?*

2. Would Tony go to an *alehouse?*

3. Would a guest be brought into a home through the use of *candlelight?*

4. Would Constance refer to George Hastings as her *suitor?*

5. Would Constance and Hastings plan to elope on *horseback?*

DENOTATION AND CONNOTATION

Denotation refers to the literal meaning of a word. **Connotation** refers to the images suggested by a word.

Denotation includes the qualities that belong to the object being defined. A dog is a four-legged mammal closely related to the common wolf. The word *dog* denotes those characteristics. Connotation includes the ideas and images people associate with the object being defined. A dog is friendly, loyal and playful. The word *dog* connotes those traits.

Denotation describes an object as it is, independent of human emotion. Connotation expresses our feelings about an object. Denotation is objective; connotation is subjective.

As you read the selection, ask yourself:

1. Does the poet rely on denotation or connotation to express his theme?
2. How does his use of adjectives help you determine whether he is using denotation or connotation?

WRITING CONNECTION

Choose any three nouns. For each, write two original sentences. One sentence should illustrate denotation, and the second should illustrate connotation.

READING FOCUS

Make Inferences from Actions You can find out much about a character from his or her actions. You can often make inferences more by action than by words. Notice how distinctly the writer describes the actions of the mouse and the speaker of the poem. What do their actions reveal about their characters?

TO A MOUSE

On Turning Her Up in Her Nest with the Plow, November, 1785

ADAPTED   *by Robert Burns*

Wee sleek and cowering fearful beastie,
O, what a panic's in thy breastie!
Thou need not start away so hasty,
    With scurrying scamper!
5   I would be loath to run and chase thee,
      Your life to tamper!

---

cowering (KOU ur ing) crouching fearfully,
  shrinking from
loath (LOHTH) unwilling; reluctant
tamper (TAM pur) to interfere with

I'm sure that sometimes thou may thieve;
So what? poor beastie, thou must live!
A grain or two occasionally
10   'S a small request;
The rest's a blessing come to me,
  So I'll never miss it!

Thy tiny housie, too, in ruin!
Its silly walls the winds are strewin'!
15 And nothing, now, to build a new one,
  No foliage green!
And bleak December's winds ensuin'
  Biting and keen!

---

foliage (FOH lee ij) leaves of one or more plants
ensuing (en SOO ing) taking place afterward or as a result

Thou saw the fields laid bare and waste,
20 And weary winter coming fast,
And cozy here, beneath the blast,
  Thou thought to dwell—
Till crash! the cruel plowshare passed
  Right through thy cell.

25 That wee bit heap of leaves and stubble
Has cost thee many a weary nibble!
Now thou's turned out for all thy trouble,
  Without a home
To bear the winter's sleety dribble
30   And frozen loam!

But Mousie, thou art not alone,
In proving foresight may be vain;
The best-laid schemes of mice and men
  Gang aft agley,
35 And leave us nought but grief and pain,
  For promised joy!

Still thou art blest, compared with me!
The present only toucheth thee:
But oh! I backward cast my eye,
40   On prospects drear!
And forward, though I cannot see,
  I guess and fear!

---

plowshare (PLOU shair) blade of a plow
loam (LOHM) rich soil
gang aft agley (GANG AFT uh GLEE) go often astray

Review the Selection

Recall

1. What destroyed the mouse's nest?

2 What was the mouse's nest made of?

3. According to the author, what often happens to the best-laid schemes of mice and men?

Infer

4. Why did the mouse run away?

5. When did this event occur?

6. What was the poet's reaction when he saw the mouse?

7. Why did Robert Burns think the mouse was luckier than he?

Apply

8. Predict what happened to the mouse after its nest was destroyed.

9. How do you think Burns would have reacted if he had found the mouse living in his home rather than the field?

10. Suppose you uncovered a mouse in its nest. How would you react?

Respond to Literature

How does Burns's choice of his subject illustrate characteristics of the Romantic period?

WRITE ABOUT THE SELECTION

In this selection, you saw Robert Burns's concern for the tiny mouse whose home he accidentally destroyed. You also learned about this event from the poet's point of view. Assume that the mouse could talk. How would it respond to Burns? What would it do? Where would it go once its home had been destroyed? Write an explanation of this incident from the mouse's point of view.

Prewriting In your "mind's eye," place yourself in the body of the tiny mouse. How do you see your surroundings now? How do you feel about this giant man who has just unearthed your home? Make an idea cluster of what you see and how you feel about what has occurred. Add specific details of the mouse's reactions to the destruction of its home.

Writing Use your informal outline to write a paragraph of this event from the mouse's point of view. Include details about how you view the man who has just destroyed your home.

Revising When you revise your paragraph, be sure to include specific details about the mouse's immediate plans for the future.

Proofreading Read over your selection. Be sure all your words are spelled correctly.

THINK ABOUT CONNOTATION

Poets try to create a specific emotional response in the reader. The use of connotation is one way in which poets achieve that goal. Poets may suggest images that are traditionally associated with objects. They may also express feelings not usually linked with an object.

1. What feelings do you usually associate with mice?

2. What feelings do you associate with the mouse in Burns's poem?

3. Do you think this poem would have been as effective if Burns had written it to another animal, such as a dog? Explain your answer.

4. How is the life of the mouse similar to, yet different from, human existence?

5. What connotations of mice does the poet use to make the poem effective? Compare these with your feelings about mice.

READING FOCUS
Make Inferences from Actions Think about the actions described in the poem. What inferences did you make about how the speaker feels about his life? What actions helped you decide?

DEVELOP YOUR VOCABULARY

Sometimes a specialized vocabulary develops from a place or occupation. New words or new meanings for existing words become part of this specialized vocabulary. For example, if you hear the words *doctor, nurse, ambulance, emergency room,* you may think of a hospital.

Robert Burns was a farmer as well as a poet. A farm was the setting for this poem. As a result, words commonly associated with a farm are found in this selection. The following words are related to a farm setting. Write an original paragraph using each word at least once. If you are not certain of the meaning or pronunciation of some of these words, check them in a dictionary.

1. plowshare
2. till
3. furrows
4. loam
5. seedlings
6. fertilizer
7. irrigation
8. sickle
9. harvester
10. crops

Learn About

The Lamb from Songs of Innocence and Experience, William Blake. The Granger Collection

SYMBOLISM

A symbol is something that represents or stands for something else. The word or image used as a symbol has two levels of meaning. It has a **concrete or literal meaning.** This meaning includes those traits denoted by the word or image. It also has an **abstract or symbolic meaning.** This meaning includes the traits connoted by the word or image.

The bald eagle is a large bird of prey noted for its strength, size, grace, and power of flight. This is the concrete or literal meaning of eagle. When used symbolically, we add connotations such as independence, bravery, dignity, and wisdom. These connotations are suggested by the symbol of the bald eagle.

As you read the selection, ask yourself the following questions:

1. What does the lamb symbolize?
2. What does the tiger symbolize?

WRITING CONNECTION

On a sheet of paper, write your school's mascot or nickname. Write the denotative definition found in the dictionary. List the symbolic or connotative characteristics that come to mind when you hear that name.

READING FOCUS

Make Inferences About Author's Viewpoint You can use text clues to make inferences not just about characters but also about the author. Think about Blake's choice of subject and about the message in each of his poems. Notice the imagery he uses to describe the animals in his poems. Then ask yourself how he feels about the world in which he lives.

THE LAMB

by William Blake

> Little Lamb who made thee?
> Dost thou know who made thee?
> Gave thee life, and bid thee feed,
> By the stream and o'er the mead;
> 5   Gave thee clothing of delight,
> Softest clothing, woolly, bright;
> Gave thee such a tender voice,
> Making all the vales rejoice?
> Little Lamb who made thee?
> 10   Dost thou know who made thee?
>
> Little Lamb, I'll tell thee.
> Little Lamb, I'll tell thee:
> He is called by thy name,
> For He calls Himself a Lamb.
> 15   He is meek, and He is mild;
> He became a little child.
> I a child, and thou a lamb,
> We are called by His name.
> Little Lamb, God bless thee!
> 20   Little Lamb, God bless thee!

---

mead (MEED) meadow
vales (VAYLZ) small valleys

The Tyger: color relief etching, William Blake. The Granger Collection

THE TYGER

by William Blake

Tyger! Tyger! burning bright
In the forests of the night,
What immortal hand or eye
Could frame thy fearful symmetry?

5   In what distant deeps or skies
Burnt the fire of thine eyes?
On what wings dare he aspire?
What the hand dare seize the fire?

And what shoulder, and what art,
10   Could twist the sinews of thy heart?
And when thy heart began to beat,
What dread hand? and what dread feet?

What the hammer? what the chain?
In what furnace was thy brain?
15   What the anvil? what dread grasp
Dare its deadly terrors clasp?

When the stars threw down their spears,
And watered heaven with their tears,
Did he smile his work to see?
20   Did he who made the Lamb make thee?

Tyger! Tyger! burning bright
In the forests of the night,
What immortal hand or eye,
Dare frame thy fearful symmetry?

---

tyger (TI gər) Blake's spelling of *tiger.*
aspire (uh SPYR) ascend; soar

Review the Selection

Recall

1. According to Blake, what kind of covering does a lamb have?

2. What kind of voice does the lamb have?

3. What response does the tiger provoke?

Infer

4. What characteristics do the lamb and the lamb's creator share?

5. Who is the lamb's maker?

6. What qualities does Blake suggest the tiger shares with its creator?

7. Why does Blake have difficulty understanding that the same creator could have made both animals?

Apply

8. What animal would you select to represent "good"? Why?

9. What if you were selecting an animal to represent "evil"? What animal would you select? Why?

10. What might Blake have said was the reason for the tiger's existence?

Respond to Literature

What Romantic elements are present in "The Lamb" and "The Tyger"?

WRITE ABOUT THE SELECTION

In this selection you read two poems by William Blake. You saw how Blake not only described the characteristics of a lamb and a tiger but used these characteristics to represent the abstract concepts of good and evil. He accomplished this through his careful selection of adjectives.

Each person has a slightly differing idea of what abstract concepts suggest. For example, what do you think of when you hear the terms *loyalty, liberty, wisdom,* and *independence?* Select one of the abstract concepts mentioned here and then choose an animal you feel would best describe the characteristics you associate with that concept.

Prewriting After you have selected one abstract concept, develop an idea cluster of the qualities you think it represents. Then select an animal whose characteristics are good examples of these qualities. List these characteristics in your outline.

Writing Use the ideas from your cluster to write a paragraph which describes the animal you have selected. Carefully choose adjectives that portray your feelings about this animal.

Revising When you revise your paragraph, add specific details to the animal's description to convey your impressions of the abstract concept.

Proofreading Read over your selection. Be sure all punctuation is correct.

THINK ABOUT SYMBOLISM

Concentrated use of language is a characteristic of poetry. The poet says a great deal in a few words. Symbolism is one way to accomplish this. One word or image used in a symbolic way has the effect of several words or phrases.

1. What is the literal meaning of *lamb?*

2. What abstract ideas are suggested by the word *lamb?*

3. What is the literal meaning of *tiger?*

4. What abstract ideas are suggested by the word *tiger?*

5. How do your answers to questions 1 through 4 illustrate the use of symbolism and concentrated language in poetry?

READING FOCUS

Make Inferences About Author's Viewpoint What inferences did you make about how Blake views his world? Support your response with specific examples from the poem.

DEVELOP YOUR VOCABULARY

Words that sound alike, but have different spellings and meanings, are called **homophones.** For example, the words *eye* and *I* are homophones. Blake uses the word *eye*, meaning the organ of sight. If you use *I*, referring to yourself, you are using a homophone of *eye.*

The following groups of words are homophones. The first word in each group appears in the poems by Blake. Use each homophone group to write original sentences. If you are not certain of the meaning of a word, check a dictionary.

1. vales–veils
2. made–maid
3. know–no
4. seize–sees–seas
5. to–two–too
6. beat–beet
7. feet–feat
8. there–their

EPIGRAMS

Epigram is a literary form. The term *epigram* comes from a Greek word meaning "to write on or inscribe." A literary **epigram** is a brief expression dealing with a single thought or event.

An epigram is short and to the point. It may contain wise counsel or express a beautiful thought. The epigram may be a satirical comment, ridiculing human vice and folly. An epigram may contain a paradox. A **paradox** is a statement which at first seems contradictory or nonsensical, but on closer examination reveals a truth.

The epigram may be written in verse or prose. Its length can vary. In poetry it is most frequently expressed as a **couplet,** or two-line rhyming verse. The epigram may be a complete work in itself. It may also be a part of a longer work.

As you read each epigram, ask yourself:

1. Does the epigram contain a beautiful or wise thought?
2. Does the epigram include a satirical comment or a paradox?

WRITING CONNECTION

Refer to any other selection you have read in this text. Write the theme of that work as a two-line prose epigram.

READING FOCUS

Make Inferences About Motives When you understand why an author wrote something—what he or she felt about the issue—you can more fully respond to the ideas. As you read, ask yourself what Alexander Pope's motives might have been for writing these epigrams. Ask yourself why he wrote about these particular issues and how he felt about each of them. Draw from your own experiences and opinions about the subject of each epigram to make your inferences.

EPIGRAMS

by Alexander Pope

1

'Tis education forms the common mind,
Just as the twig is bent, the tree's inclined.
—*Moral Essays*
Epistle I, lines 149–150

2

For fools rush in where angels fear to tread.
—*An Essay on Criticism*
Part III, line 66

3

Be not the first by whom the new are tried,
Nor yet the last to lay the old aside.
—*An Essay on Criticism*
Part II, lines 135–136

4

Hope springs eternal in the human breast:
Man never Is, but always To be, blest.
—*An Essay on Man*
Epistle I, lines 95–96

---

inclined (in KLYND) to have a particular disposition; have a tendency

Alexander Pope, attributed to Charles Jervas. The Granger Collection

5

All nature is but art, unknown to thee
All chance, direction, which thou canst not see;
All discord, harmony not understood;
All partial evil, universal good:
And, spite of pride, in erring reason's spite,
One truth is clear, Whatever is, is right.

　　　　　　　—*An Essay on Man*
　　　　　　　Epistle I, lines 289–294

6

A wit's a feather, and a chief's a rod;
An honest man's the noblest work of God.
—*An Essay on Man*
Epistle IV, lines 247–248

7

A little learning is a dangerous thing;
Drink deep, or taste not the Pierian spring:
There shallow drafts intoxicate the brain,
And drinking largely sobers us again.
—*An Essay on Criticism*
Part II, lines 15–18

8

Know then thyself, presume not God to scan,
The proper study of mankind is man.
—*An Essay on Man*
Epistle II, lines 1–2

9

To err is human, to forgive, divine.
—*An Essay on Criticism*
Part II, line 325

Pierian spring (py IR ee un SPRING) a spring in Macedonia; According to legend, drinking from it inspired learning.
drafts (DRAFTS) drinks

Review the Selection

Recall

1. According to Pope, what happens to a child who is not educated?

2. According to Pope, what should be the focus of contemplation?

3. What is God's noblest creation?

Infer

4. Why does the author say that all chance is direction you cannot see?

5. Why should a person not be the first to try something new?

6. What does the author mean by "to err is human, to forgive, divine"?

7. Why is a little learning dangerous?

Apply

8. Explain how the second and third epigrams could support two different sides of an argument.

9. Would Pope agree with the statement, "This is the best of all possible worlds!"? Explain your answer.

10. Examine the seventh epigram. What might happen if you learned all there was to know about a subject?

Respond to Literature

How does Pope's emphasis on education illustrate Enlightenment beliefs?

WRITE ABOUT THE SELECTION

In this selection, you read nine of Alexander Pope's epigrams. You may have found it easier to relate to some more than others. Choose your favorite epigram from this selection and explain how it relates to a personal experience you have had.

Prewriting Write an informal outline of an experience you have had and show how it relates to the message of the epigram. Did the experience involve only you, or were others involved? Where did the experience take place? What did it mean to you? What did you learn from it? Keep these questions in mind as you form your outline.

Writing Indicate which epigram you selected. Use your informal outline to write a paragraph about your related experience. Be sure to state the reason or reasons why you chose the epigram. Add details about other people who may have been involved and any other details that add to the clarity of the scene you are trying to create.

Revising When you revise your paragraph, be sure to add specific details of your experience that relate to the message of the epigram.

Proofreading Read over your selection. Be sure you add any words that you might have missed in your revised draft.

THINK ABOUT EPIGRAMS

Didactic literature is writing intended to instruct or to teach a lesson. Epigrams are often didactic. The lesson may be advice offered in a straightforward manner. In a satirical epigram, the reader may have to infer the lesson from the ridicule directed at a vice or folly.

1. In what way are Pope's epigrams didactic?

2. Are these epigrams straightforward or satirical?

3. In your own words, compare the lesson in the first epigram with the lesson in the seventh epigram.

4. In what way does the fifth epigram illustrate the use of paradox?

5. In your own words, state the lesson in the last epigram.

READING FOCUS

Make Inferences About Motives In reading these epigrams, you looked for clues to the author's feelings, thoughts, and motives. Review these clues. Then choose one epigram and explain why you think Pope wrote it. What was his motive? Support your inference with clues from the text and from your life experiences.

DEVELOP YOUR VOCABULARY

A **root** is a word or word part that is used to form other words. The root usually carries the central meaning of the word. For example, the meaning of the root, *-graph,* and one of the meanings of the root, *-gram,* is to write or to draw for description. Many times you can use these roots to help you determine the meaning of a larger word.

Following are words containing the root *-gram* or *-graph.* Use these roots to help you figure out the meaning of each word. Check your answers in a dictionary, and then use each word to write an original sentence.

1. epigram
2. telegram
3. grammar
4. audiogram
5. chronogram
6. telegraph
7. polygraph
8. autograph
9. graphite
10. epigraph

POINT OF VIEW

Point of view is the position the writer takes in relation to the subject matter. The writer may speak to the reader from the viewpoint of a participant in the events described in the work. This is called first-person point of view. Diaries are written in the first person.

A **diary** is a record of events, transactions, or observations often kept daily. The narrator describes those events which have been witnessed that day. A diary is not written with publication in mind. Therefore, it is not revised for dramatic effect. The drama results from the realization that the author is experiencing firsthand the events described.

As you read the selection, ask yourself:

1. How does the author's uncertainty about his own chances of surviving the Plague heighten the dramatic effect of his diary?
2. When does Pepys understand the destruction of the London Fire?

The Great Fire of London, detail, 1666. Contemporary painting, Dutch School, The Granger Collection

READING FOCUS

Predict Outcomes Predicting outcomes is a useful way to check your reading comprehension. It also helps you stay involved in your reading. When you ask yourself what will happen next, you predict what seems likely or possible given what has already happened. Use your own life experiences along with text clues to make your predictions.

WRITING CONNECTION

Before you leave school today, write three diary entries. Wait one week. Reread the entries and think about what other information you have learned in the meantime.

from
The Diary

ADAPTED

by Samuel Pepys

The Plague

Sept. 3, 1665. (Sunday). After services, several of us met in the
church hall to discuss preventing the spread of the Plague.
Funeral processions were forbidden. Still, crowds of the morbidly
curious would follow as victims were carried to the grave. We
agreed on some steps that could be taken to prevent this madness.

Alderman Hooker told us of a saddle maker and his wife who
had begged a friend to save their youngest child. Their other children had all died of the Plague. The man and wife had lost all
hope of surviving themselves. The friend had taken the youngest
child, dressed in uncontaminated clothing, to the town of Green-
wich. A complaint had been lodged against the friend for having
removed the child from an infected house. We all agreed the
complaint should be dismissed, and the child permitted to stay in
the town.

Sept. 14, 1665. I arrived home with mixed feelings of joy and
sadness. On one hand, my stolen property had been found and
returned. Furthermore, my income had increased unexpectedly.
Most importantly, the death toll decreased by over 500 last week.
This is the first such decrease since the outbreak of the Plague.
There are great hopes for an even greater decline next week.

On the other hand, the burial count may be down, but the size
of the infected area continues to grow. It is getting close to our
house. Funeral processions passed close by this afternoon. A
person infected with sores drove by me on the street. The Angell
Tavern at the foot of the hill is boarded up. The other night I

stopped at a nearby alehouse to write a letter. The innkeeper's wife was saying that someone she knew was very ill, but she did not think it was the Plague.

More and more acquaintances are dying. Payne, the waiter, has buried a child and is dying himself. A laborer I sent on an errand just the other day is dead. A ferryman, who often carried me across the river, fell sick on reaching land last Friday and died of the Plague.

I myself had been on the river the night before the ferryman's death. Captains Lambert and Cuttle died after taking these ferries. Montague is running a high fever. Both my servants have recently lost their fathers to the Plague. These thoughts, with good reason, frighten and sadden me.

I try not to think about it. Instead, I try to keep up my wife's spirits. After eating a fine fish dinner, we are going to bed.

The Fire of London

Sept. 2, 1666. (Sunday). About three o'clock in the morning, Jane, one of the servants, awoke us. She had seen a great fire from her window. I looked. The fire was not that far away, but I saw no threat to us and returned to bed.

I rose at seven. The fire appeared smaller and farther away. Jane said she had heard that over 400 houses had been destroyed during the night, and the fire was still raging near London Bridge. Curious, I went to have a look.

From a high point near the Tower of London, I could see a huge fire raging on both sides of the bridge. We had friends who lived in that area. Worried, I approached the bridge.

An intense fire was raging out of control. People were desperately trying to save their belongings, loading them in boats or flinging them into the river. Some stayed in their homes until the fire nearly touched them before making their escape. Pigeons, paralyzed with fear, hovered about balconies, until, their wings burned, they fell to the ground.

A high wind was driving the fire deeper into the city. Seeing no attempt to put it out, I sped to the King's castle. After telling what I had seen, I was ushered before his Majesty. At my suggestion, the King commanded that houses in the immediate path

The Great Fire of London, 1666. Contemporary painting, Dutch School.
The Granger Collection

of the fire be torn down. In this way, we hoped to control its spread. I left to take the King's message to the Mayor.

I found him in Canning Street. As we spoke, crowds laden with possessions streamed by. To the King's message, the mayor replied, "What can I do? People will not obey me. I have been pulling houses down, but the fire moves faster than we do."

He left me, and I walked home. No one could think of a way to stop the fire. It seemed to feed on all it found: pitch and tar in the homes; oil, wines and brandy in the warehouses, and other things. The people I passed seemed distracted. Many file into churches, not to worship, but to store their goods. Others loaded carts with their belongings. Ready to run down anyone in their path, they fled from street to street.

Sparks fell from the sky like rain. Smoke filled the sky. A horrid, malicious, bloody flame leaped as far as the eye could see. Its noise was a horrid, cracking sound. At home, my wife and I packed those valuables we could and prepared to evacuate.

3rd. At four o'clock this morning, we were told to wait no longer. Even at that hour, the streets and highways were packed with refugees. At length, we found a haven in the home of a friend, but there was no rest for my wife or me that night.

Review the Selection

UNDERSTAND THE SELECTION

Recall

1. What two major events are recounted in this diary excerpt?

2. What suggestion did Pepys make about controlling the fire?

3. Why were Pepys and his family awakened at four o'clock in the morning?

Infer

4. Did many people die during the Plague? Explain your answer.

5. Do you think any of the author's family died during the Plague?

6. At first, why was Pepys not concerned about the fire?

7. Why did the fire spread so rapidly?

Apply

8. If Samuel Pepys were living today, what major events might he record?

9. How would you have reacted if you witnessed the London Fire?

10. Do you agree with the decision to remove the child from an infected house? Explain.

Respond to Literature

Pepys wrote his diary in shorthand which was later transcribed by others. How is this different from most diaries?

WRITE ABOUT THE SELECTION

A diary relates how a person feels about his or her experiences and what significance he or she places on the events of the day. In this selection, you were able to see how one person reacted to what later were seen as important historical events—the Plague and the Great Fire of London. The events that touch your life may one day be history. One person's point of view on events happening today can be of significance years, even centuries, from now.

For the next three days, keep a diary of personal events in your life. Also include current national or international events.

Prewriting Each day, jot down some notes about those events you feel are most significant to you. Do this as soon as possible after they occur. Include details about how you feel and how you think others involved reacted.

Writing Each evening before you go to bed, use your notes to write one or two paragraphs about your experiences of the day. Add details you may not have included in your notes.

Revising At the end of the third day, review what you have written. Add specific details that clarify your response to what you have experienced.

Proofreading Read over your selections. Be sure each sentence ends with a period, question mark, or exclamation point.

THINK ABOUT POINT OF VIEW

A **diary** is a record of events or observations kept by a person on a daily basis. The diary keeper is living the experiences described. History is a written chronological record of significant events, often including an explanation of their causes and effects. An historian records events after they happen with the benefit of knowing their outcome.

1. In what ways are a diary and history similar?

2. What is the difference between a diary and history in point of view?

3. What advantages does the diary keeper have that the historian does not?

4. What advantages does the historian have that the diary keeper does not?

5. Would you expect the diary or the history to be more dramatic? Explain your answer.

READING FOCUS

Predict Outcomes As you read these diary excerpts, you used text clues to make predictions. How, if at all, did you revise your predictions as new clues arose?

DEVELOP YOUR VOCABULARY

An **adverb** is a word that modifies a verb, adjective, or another adverb. Adverbs usually answer one of the following questions: *How? When? Where? How often? How much?* One common indicator of an adverb is the suffix *-ly* added to an adjective. For example, in the sentence, "The *impatient* young man waited on the doorstep," *impatient* is an adjective. In the sentence, "The young man waited *impatiently* outside," *impatiently* is an adverb.

The following adverbs were used in this selection. Find the adjective within each adverb. If you are not certain of the meaning of an adverb ending in *-ly,* you can discover its meaning by finding the meaning of the related adjective in a dictionary. When you are certain that you understand both forms of the word, use each to write an original sentence.

1. morbidly
2. recently
3. rarely
4. desperately
5. unexpectedly
6. importantly

THE GOTHIC ROMANCE

The 18th century is sometimes called the Age of Reason. The writers of that period believed in common sense and social order. They distrusted the undisciplined imagination. As the century drew to a close, some writers began rebelling against those beliefs. They were the Romantics. The Gothic Romance is one example of this literary rebellion.

A **Gothic Romance** is a tale of mystery and terror. The setting is distant in time or place. The plot incidents are often grisly and violent. The characters often include individuals who are considered social outcasts.

The authors of Gothic Romances set out to shock 18th-century readers. They created a fictional world in which common sense provided no safety against terror lurking in the dark.

As you read this selection, ask yourself:
1. What is the setting?
2. What grisly elements are present in the plot?

WRITING CONNECTION

The time is midnight. You are alone in a dark castle. Using elements of the Gothic Romance, write a paragraph describing what happens next.

READING FOCUS

Make Inferences About Characters
You can make inferences or educated guesses about characters by studying their actions and words. You can also make inferences by looking at how characters respond to one another in a story or play. Think about the personality traits that would lead to the character's actions or would be likely to inspire another character's reactions. Check your own experiences to verify your inferences.

from FRANKENSTEIN

ADAPTED

by Mary Shelley

I packed only absolute necessities: food, blankets and a gun. I had only a few desperate hours. If I failed, Justine had only two more days to live.

I knew where to begin my search. A few days ago, I had seen the monster swinging above the rock face of Plainpalais. It could not be far away. Having neither the strength nor the agility of my creation, I was forced to take a slower but easier path to that place.

From time to time I questioned cottagers along the way. There was no need to ask if they had encountered a madman's nightmare. If they had, the mountainside would have been buzzing with a new nightmare to frighten children. Instead, I asked if they had noticed anything unusual.

"Have there been any unexplained sounds at night, unexpected shadows, thefts of food, missing livestock?"

I met nothing but blank looks. Every question was answered "no" or by that suspiciously soothing nonsense reserved for an idiot.

The creature had learned to keep away from people. I continued my search far from human dwellings. I followed the light of the moon. An error in judgement or twisted foot and my climb would have ended at the bottom of a valley. However, I pressed on. Eventually, I had to sleep.

I awoke with the first rays of the sun. Had I dreamt or heard that whisper, "Frankenstein"? Something white and delicate fell at my feet. It was a sprig of edelweiss.

I looked around but found no sign of life. I shouted but only echoes replied. Then, on the rock space above my head, I saw the imprint of a giant hand. The creature had been here.

I felt fear then triumph. I had tracked it down. Justine would be saved.

A slight fall of stones rattled down from above. I followed these traces higher and higher. The day wore on. It was late afternoon when I passed a river of ice. Mist covered the surrounding mountain. Ahead, I heard a low laugh more chilling than the cold of any glacier. I realized I was the prey, not the hunter.

---

edelweiss (AYD ul vys) a small perennial herb with tiny white flowers that grows high in the Alps

I had no choice but to go on. I had my pistol. Failing all else, I might avenge William's death. A light breeze dispersed the clouds as I climbed down the surface of the glacier. With my back to the cliff, I gazed at the river of ice, winding between mountains whose glittering peaks were bloodied by the setting sun. Then, I saw the figure of a man bearing down on me with superhuman speed.

As he approached, I realized how much bigger he was than a man. I had made him that way. As he drew closer, I recognized only too well those misshapen features.

I felt faint. Only at the last minute was I able to raise my hand and shoot. Too late. With a leap even I had not thought possible, he knocked the pistol away.

"I know guns," he croaked hoarsely.

"You want to kill me." His voice had a flat impersonal quality, like a machine.

"Devil," I shouted. "What else do you deserve?"

"I expected this greeting." His withered lips were twisted in an evil grin. "I have learned to live with every hand against me."

Rage overcoming fear, I leaped at him. He merely stepped aside and said, "You know I am stronger, faster than you. My life may be misery, but I will defend it."

"Murderer," I shrieked, "I curse the day I created you. I hate you."

In reply, he placed an immense hand over my eyes. I struggled to no avail. "Listen," he said in a slow creaking voice. "You will learn what you have done. Then you will decide what is to be done."

He took away his hand. I turned my head to avoid that hideous face. The scars were no longer livid, but this made the crude matching of dead flesh even more repulsive.

The creature built a fire. "I learn quickly," he said as the flames leaped up. "Sit."

"The first thing I remember is light. It hurt my eyes. When light and darkness came together, they made shapes. The shapes became a face. Then the face was gone. Confusion followed. I saw, felt, heard and smelled at the same time.

"I was lying down. I sat up. Around me were shapes that meant nothing. Close by me was a little wavering thing on a white stick. I put out my finger and touched it. There was pain."

"I found that I could stand up. I knocked over things as I learned balance. I walked into the darkness. Then I saw the face again. I cannot say what I felt. It was not something I could see, or hear, or smell or touch or taste. Love is a word I learned much later. I would never forget your face, Frankenstein."

"You looked at me. You made a noise like the one I made when I burned my finger. The light was gone, and I could see nothing.

"The light was gone. In the dark I

---

dispersed (dih SPURST) to cause to spread widely; to evaporate
croaked (KROHKT) made a deep, harsh sound

began to bump into things again. Some of them hurt me. Anger is another word I learned later, but that is what led me to break the things that hurt me.

"After a long time the room became light again. I do not know how, but I found my way out into the forest. I became more confused. The sounds and smells were strange. I felt hunger and thirst. I crammed things in my mouth. I drank from a brook.

"I realized the light came from two objects. The sun I could not bear to look at, but the moon lit my path at night. From time to time I slept. When I did not, I walked on.

"Soon I came to a hut. An old man sat there. When he saw me, he made a loud noise and ran away. I was delighted with the hut. The fire was warm, and I had learned not to put my fingers into the flame. I ate what the man had left then lay down and went to sleep.

"I was awakened by the sound of voices. There was a group of men at the door. They carried objects like the leafless branches of trees. I tried to signal that I meant no harm, but they could not understand the noises that I made. They struck at me with the objects. I ran away and did not stop until they could no longer see me. Then I walked on avoiding the places where men lived.

"As light was fading, I came to a small shelter. It was so low that I could not stand upright inside, but at least it gave me protection from the cold, wet weather.

"I slept there until light came, then crept out to see if I could find a way of staying hidden in this shelter. The shelter had been built against the back wall of another place. On one side was a place for animals and on the other was a pool of water. Using wood and stones, I covered every gap through which I might be seen.

"The back wall was warm. There must have been a fire on the other side. Later, looking round my shelter, I discovered a crack in the wood through which I could see into the other place.

"As time went by I learned about the people who lived in that room. There was an old man, a young man, and a girl. The young man left each morning to work outdoors. The girl worked in the cottage and the surrounding yard. She would dig up plants. Some she threw away. Others she put into a pot over the fire. When the sky was nearly dark, the young man would return with wood he had cut.

"When the three were together, they would eat the food the girl had put in the pot. Afterwards, the old man would put a stick to this mouth and make sounds sweeter than any bird I had ever heard.

"At first, I took some of their food while they slept. Then I noticed that sometimes the younger ones would put food in front of the old man when they had nothing for themselves. When I realized I was hurting them, I stopped taking their food. Instead, I picked berries and nuts.

"Sometimes, I would cut wood and add it to their pile. This made them happy. The young man would not go away on those days. He stayed and helped the girl.

"Slowly, I realized these people used special sounds to mean certain things. By listening and watching, I learned these words. I also learned the names of the people. The old man was called father. The young man was sometimes called son and sometimes called brother. The girl was daughter or sister. I practiced saying the words myself.

"In this way the winter passed. Often I longed to join them, but I was afraid. They did not seem like the other men, but I thought it best to remain hidden.

"The sun grew warmer. Leaves came out on trees. Sometimes I would listen as the old man made music. He had to feel his way as he walked. I realized he could not see.

"Feelings I did not understand came over me. I knew I was different. I was stronger and faster than them. I also was ugly. I had seen my face in the water.

"Where was my family? All my past

life was a nothing. I had no father or mother. All I could remember was a face. Could there by any other creature like me? Or was I a thing alone?

"The more I saw these people, the more I wanted to know them. I knew how they would react if I startled them. One day when the leaves were turning red and falling, the young ones went out. Even though I knew the old man could not see me, I took a long time finding the courage to knock at the door.

" 'Come in,' said the old man.

"I asked if I might sit for a moment by his fire. He made me welcome.

" 'My children are out, and I am blind. It will not be easy, but I will try to find food for you.'

"I told him that was not necessary. I said I hoped to meet some people who had never seen me before and knew little about me. I hoped they would see me as I really am. I wanted them to understand I meant no harm. I only wanted to be friends. I began to sob.

"At this moment, I heard footsteps. I knelt by the old man and cried, 'Help me. You are my friends. Do not turn me away.'

"The old man exclaimed, 'Good God. Who are you?'

"The door opened. The girl screamed. The young man ran at with me a stick. I could have torn him limb from limb. What good would it have done? My plan had come to nothing. Howling with dis-appointment, I ran into the woods.

"I wanted to destroy everything around me. Then I remembered your face. At that moment I began to hate you, my creator.

"I lay in thinking all day. Maybe if they had had time to be prepared for my appearance. I made up my mind to go back. There was a thing on wheels outside the cottage. It was piled with their belongings.

"The young man was talking to another. 'Don't ask us to stay. You did not see that monster.'

"They left, and I was alone. I entered the empty cottage. Rage overcame me. I could not harm anything human, so I turned my anger on things. I burned the cottage to the ground. I shouted and danced as it burned. Then I left."

By now I realized that I, Victor Frankenstein, was at least partly to blame for the creature's sufferings. I had brought this misshapen thing to life, and all he had to thank me for was that enormous body and unnatural strength. The wavering light of the fire distorted even further a face more grotesque than any carved stone devil's.

"If my creator is afraid to look at me, why should anyone else?" he rasped. He moved behind me where he could not be seen.

"After some days, I came to the edge of the forest. There I was stopped by a wide stretch of running water. As I won-dered what to do, I heard a girl's voice. I

---

misshapen (mis SHAY pun) not correctly shaped

hid behind a tree. She was running and looking behind her laughing all the while. She tripped and fell into the water. In the space of one frightened scream, she was swept away.

"I threw myself into the water after her. I had to struggle, but I caught her and dragged her to shore. I climbed with her in my arms onto the river bank. There I came face to face with a man.

"He was probably the one she had been running from in play. In his hand he carried what I thought was a large stick. I recognized the look on his face. I had seen it before.

"I put the girl down at his feet and held out my arms to him. I wanted to explain that there was nothing to fear. He did not even wait for me to speak. He raised the stick.

"There was a flash and a loud noise. Then something hit me like a blow. Its force hit me like a blow and threw me back into the water. I was carried away.

"I saved myself, but in the next weeks I felt pain as I had never felt before. Not only in my broken bones, but in my head. Every feeling of gentleness gave way to burning rage. I thought only of revenge. Revenge for all the agony I had felt. And my chief suffering came from knowing that my entire life would be spent like this: with every man's hand against me.

"Do you wonder why I hate you, Frankenstein?"

I did not answer. In spite of the fire, I felt cold. The sky beyond the cave seemed pitch black.

"Go on," I whispered. "Why did you come here?"

"Fate, maybe. Perhaps I followed the sun. Growing time came again, but that only made my dark thoughts darker. I took care not to be seen, but I watched your race—two by two. And I was alone." The creature's voice was hoarse in the gloom.

"Perhaps it was fate that brought me to the woods by the lake. There I saw a young boy. Suddenly I had an idea. He had lived too short a time to have been taught to fear my ugliness. If I took him away, I could bring him up as my friend. I would no longer be alone.

"Impulsively, I seized him. He put his hands over his eyes and screamed.

"I forced his hands down and said, 'I don't want to hurt you. Just listen to me.'

"He struggled, shouting, 'My father is Mr. Frankenstein. He will have you arrested, Monster. You want to tear me to pieces. You're ugly, ugly. . . .'

"I only meant to silence him, but in a moment, he lay dead at my feet."

The creature shuffled to the mouth of the cave and stood looking out. I groaned. I had a confession from the murderer's own mouth and could do nothing. The creature continued.

"As I looked down at the body, I saw a shining chain. Hanging on the chain was your picture. At last, the face I hated had a name. Frankenstein. I saw how like you the boy looked, and I was glad of what I had done. Here was my revenge. I could make you suffer.

The creature turned with a look of

unholy glee. "Kill me," I said, "and be done with it."

The thing laughed a laugh as dreadful as its appearance.

"No, I am not done with you. I took the picture and went in search of a hiding place. I found a barn that appeared to be empty, but a young woman lay asleep on some straw. As I gazed at her, I thought, 'If only she would smile for me.' I whispered, 'Here is one who would give his life for one loving look.'

"She stirred, and I was terrified. I could imagine her screams if she opened her eyes. The thought aroused the demon in me. I thought, 'Let her suffer, too.' So I hid your picture in her dress and fled. I don't know what happened to her, but from what I have seen of men it will be devilish."

"She will die at daybreak tomorrow unless I can prove that she is innocent."

"Then she will die."

I hurled myself at him, but he held me off with one contemptuous hand.

"I have more work for you, Frankenstein. My misery comes from being alone. I want a companion, and you will create her."

I tore myself from his grasp, howling, "Never."

"There are others you love. Do you

---

contemptuous (kun TEMP choo us) feeling or expressing hate

want them to die also? They will, if you refuse. I shall not rest until you are as alone in the world as I am."

"I'll kill myself first."

"That will not save them. Kill yourself and you condemn them."

My mind was in a whirl. William was dead already. Dare I risk the lives of others? The creature could hide from any pursuit. He could strike when he chose and disappear. Would anyone believe my story?

"I'll do it on one condition. That you will go to an uninhabited area and not return. Swear to that, and I will create a companion to share your exile."

"I swear. Do that and no man will ever see me again. But start soon. I shall be watching your progress."

The first blush of dawn had appeared in the night sky.

"If mankind had not put an end to all pity in me, I might feel sorry for the one your fellow men will kill today."

His evil laughter faded as he ran down the mountainside. My own journey would take much longer, but there was no need to hurry. I had failed to save Justine—the monster's second victim.

And I had agreed to create a mate for the thing. In the warm rays of the morning sun, I fell to my knees and wept.

Mary Shelley (1797–1851)

Mary Shelley was the daughter of two writers. Her mother, Mary Wollstonecraft wrote enthusiastically in the late 1700s about the importance of woman's independence, along with other books about education and politics. Her father, William Godwin, was a philosopher. Though Wollstonecraft died shortly after the child was born, Mary Shelley followed closely in her mother's footsteps. In her lifetime, she wrote seven novels, two dozen ghost stories, travel books, and newspaper articles. At nineteen she had already written *Frankenstein,* the novel for which she is best remembered.

Unfortunately her life was marked by terrible personal tragedy. She married the poet Percy Shelley in 1816. They had four children. Three of the children died young. Then, six years after they married, Shelley died by drowning in a boating accident off the coast of Italy. He was only thirty years old.

After Percy Shelley's death, which devastated her, Mary moved with her surviving child to Genoa, Italy, where she lived until she returned to England about a year later. She continued to write to support herself and her child. In addition to her usual writing, she began to edit Shelley's work and continued to write in her journal, which she kept for most of her life.

Mary and Percy Shelley had been part of an acclaimed literary circle. When Mary Shelley wrote *Frankenstein,* many of her friends were interested in the scientific speculations about nature and the origins of life. She was very much influenced by their ideas. *Frankenstein* is really a story about the power of the scientist to restructure nature. Mary Shelley's incredibly imaginative skills enabled her to write a book which has remained of great interest to many generations of readers.

Review the Selection

UNDERSTAND THE SELECTION

Recall

1. Where did the monster lead the narrator?

2. Whom had the monster killed?

3. Who was the narrator of this story?

Infer

4. Why did the creature hide Frankenstein's picture in the girl's pocket?

5. How had the monster learned to talk?

6. Why was the narrator trying to find the monster?

7. Why did Dr. Frankenstein agree to create a companion for the monster?

Apply

8. Predict what might have happened if people had not judged the monster solely by his appearance.

9. Imagine that you are the monster. Why would you want a companion who was like you?

10. If you were a scientist who had the knowledge to create a human being in a laboratory, would you put this knowledge to work? Why or why not?

Respond to Literature

How do the characters in *Frankenstein* typify Romantic writing?

WRITE ABOUT THE SELECTION

At the end of this selection, Dr. Frankenstein reluctantly agrees to create a companion for the monster. How will he accomplish this task? What will she look like? How will the monster react when he first sees her? How will she react to him? Will they "live happily ever after"? Add an episode of about two paragraphs to "Frankenstein" explaining what you think happens.

Prewriting Write a list of events in time order telling what happens after Dr. Frankenstein's promise. Include details to tell how he creates this companion and what her appearance is like when he has finished. Freewrite some conversation between characters.

Writing Use your informal outline to write your episode. In it, explain where and when the monster and his companion meet and how they react to one another.

Revising When you revise your episode, be sure to add specific details that convey Dr. Frankenstein's reactions and what you think the outcome will be for the couple. Eliminate any details that do not contribute to your explanation of what happens in this episode.

Proofreading Read over your selection. Be sure that the episode shows coherence. Sentences should flow smoothly into each other. Be sure you have enclosed any direct conversation between the characters using correct quotation marks.

THINK ABOUT GOTHIC ROMANCE

Gothic Romances were the inspiration for the modern suspense story. In *Frankenstein,* Mary Shelley introduced a now familiar character, the scientist, whose experiments lead to disaster. Thus, *Frankenstein* can also be considered an early forerunner of the modern science-fiction story.

1. In what way is the setting of *Frankenstein* typical of the Gothic Romance?

2. Why do you think the setting is a place far from civilized society?

3. How is Dr. Frankenstein's creation an example of the supernatural element in Gothic Romance?

4. How do you think Shelley's readers reacted to Dr. Frankenstein's failure to save Justine? Explain your answer.

5. In what way did *Frankenstein* reject social order or acceptable behavior?

READING FOCUS

Make Inferences About Characters
After reading this excerpt and studying its clues, what did you infer about Frankenstein's capabilities as a scientist? On what did you base these inferences?

DEVELOP YOUR VOCABULARY

Sometimes writers create characters whose impact on the minds of the audience is so great that the names become part of the language. People apply the name of the character to individuals who exhibit the same personality traits. Shakespeare's Romeo is an example. The term *Romeo* is used to describe any young man deeply in love.

Use the dictionary to find the origin and current meaning of the words below. Each is a noun or adjective which can be traced to a memorable fictional character. Use each word in an original sentence. Note the curious way in which Frankenstein has come to represent both the scientist and his creation. For number 1, write a separate sentence to illustrate both uses. Write one sentence for each of the remaining words.

1. Frankenstein
2. Scrooge
3. quixotic
4. Cinderella
5. Jekyll and Hyde
6. Shylock
7. Babbitt
8. Pollyanna

Focus on Fiction

*O*ne way to improve your understanding of fiction is to think about the elements of fiction. Since these elements work together, they are best studied in connection with a single work. The elements of fiction that appear in the following selection include setting, character, plot, theme, point of view, and tone.

Setting   Setting is the locale in a literary work. Setting refers to both the time and the place of the action. It tells where and when the story takes place.

Setting in a contemporary novel may be used for effect. The action may take place anywhere from a small town to a desolate glacier. The reader learns about characters through a description of their lifestyles or possessions. However, the contemporary author may include only a brief sketch of the setting and concentrate on revealing the character through dialogue and narrative.

Character   Characters inhabit the fictional world the author has created. Characters have physical features and personalities. The author may use physical features to shed light on character.

The thoughts, words, and deeds may be those of the character or of the people with whom the character interacts. Occasionally, the author may interpret character for the reader. When this is done, the reader must understand that this information is not available to the other characters in the story.

Some characters are well-developed and believable. A **round** character is complex, with strengths and weaknesses like a real person. In a successful work, the major characters are always round. Minor characters may be stereotyped or **flat.** These characters are not well developed. They are introduced more to shed light on the character of a major figure.

Plot   Plot is the series of events or story line in a literary work. **Conflict** provides the dramatic action that advances the plot. Conflict may arise between characters or between a character and an external force. Conflict may also exist within the character.

Theme   Theme is the central idea in a literary work. In nonfiction, theme is often stated as a topic for discussion. Theme is rarely stated in fiction. The author combines the elements of fiction to communicate the central or dominating idea in the work.

Point of View   Point of view is the position the author takes in relation to the reader and the subject matter. Point of view may be first person or third person.

First-person point of view is always **limited.** The narrator is a character or participant in the action. The narrator can only relate what is seen and heard first-hand.

The third-person point of view may also be limited. The action is seen from the point of view of a character or characters. The narrator, however, speaks in the third person as an observer of the action.

Third-person point of view can also be **omniscient** or all-knowing. The omniscient narrator speaks as an observer, not as a participant.

Tone   Tone refers to the writer's style or manner of expression. Often the tone of a work is humorous. In a humorous work, the author often points out human foibles or failings. This is called **satire.** The tone of a satire may be savage or gentle.

If the tone is savage, the author must be careful in the presentation of character. In a **savage satire,** the characters are usually flat. They are not so much human as concrete representations of a characteristic. In a **gentle satire,** the author presents round characters. Their intentions may be good. The author pokes fun not at the people but at their behavior.

As you read the excerpt from *Pride and Prejudice,* keep in mind the elements of literature that are present. Ask yourself these questions:

1. How does the writer employ satire? Is it savage or gentle?
2. Which characters are flat? Which ones are round?
3. Which elements are most important in this selection?

from
PRIDE AND PREJUDICE

ADAPTED

by Jane Austen

Everyone knows a rich bachelor needs a wife. Neighbors may know nothing else about him, but they know that. To parents of eligible daughters, he is the rightful property of one of their girls.

"Mr. Bennet," said his wife, "did you know the house in Netherfield Park has been rented?"

Mr. Bennet did not answer.

"Aren't you curious about the new tenant?" asked his wife impatiently.

"You want to tell me, and I have no objection to hearing it."

"His name is Bingley. He is a rich bachelor from the north of England. He arrived in horse-drawn carriage and will take possession before Michaelmas. What a fine thing for our girls!"

"How so?"

"Mr. Bennet," said his wife, "you must know that I am thinking of marrying one of them to him."

"Is that why he moved here?"

"Nonsense! Still if he meets one he may fall in love. You must visit him right away."

"Me? He won't fall in love with me. You and the girls go."

"Sir, you must go and see Mr. Bingley. Think of your daughters. They cannot visit a bachelor unless they have first been properly introduced."

"Why not? I'm sure he will be glad to see them. I'll send a note along telling him he has my consent to marry whichever one he chooses. I must tell him, though, that Lizzie's the best choice."

Michaelmas (MIK ul mus) the feast of the archangel Michael, celebrated
on September 29

Conversation in a Park, Thomas Gainsborough. Louvre Museum Art Resource

"Lizzie has always been your favorite!"

"I love them all, but Lizzie is the smartest."

"Little good that will do her if you won't visit Mr. Bingley."

"Depend upon it, my dear, I will visit him."

Mrs. Bennet was satisfied. Her goal in life was to get her daughters married. Visiting and news were the means to that goal.

The point of view is omniscient.

Mr. Bennet had always intended to visit his new neighbor. He did so the next morning, but saw no reason to tell his wife until that night. The family was gathered in the living room. The girls were discussing Mr. Bingley.

"Stop it!," cried Mrs. Bennet. "I am sick of Mr. Bingley."

"I am sorry to hear that," said Mr. Bennet. "Why didn't you tell me sooner? I certainly would not have called on him this morning."

The astonishment of the ladies was just what he had wished. His wife was the most surprised. When the first tumult of joy was over, she addressed her daughters.

"What an excellent father you have, girls. I do not know how you will ever repay his kindness. At our time of life, it is not so pleasant, I can tell you, to be making new acquaintances every day. Still, for your sakes, we would do anything."

The rest of the evening was spent wondering when Mr. Bingley would return the visit and deciding when they would invite him to dinner.

Over the next few days, Mrs. Bennet and the girls tried to draw from Mr. Bennet a description of their new neighbor. They attacked him in various ways: direct questions; sly conjecture; distant musings. It was all to no avail. They had to rely on second-hand intelligence.

Their neighbor, Lady Lucas, had not actually seen him, but her husband had. According to Sir William Lucas, Mr. Bingley was quite young, extremely handsome, and very pleasant. To top it all, he meant to attend the next dance with several friends. Mrs. Bennet was delighted. In her mind, a fondness for dancing was a certain step towards falling in love.

Note that the author uses very little description in establishing the setting.

A few days later, Mr. Bingley returned Mr. Bennet's visit and sat for about ten minutes in the library. The young man had hoped to see the young ladies of the house. He had heard they were beautiful. He saw only their father, though. The girls were a little luckier. From an upstairs window, they could at least see that he wore a blue coat and rode a black horse.

The night of the dance soon arrived. Mr. Bingley came, accompanied by his two sisters, a brother-in-law, and another young man. He was all Lady Lucas had reported. Still, it was his friend Mr. Darcy who became the center of attention. He was tall, handsome, and distinguished. Rumor spread that he was very wealthy. He was the topic of much favorable comment until it

Again, note the gently satirical tone.

---

tumult (TOO mult) commotion; noisy activity
conjecture (kun JEK chur) guess; inference; supposition
musings (MYOO zingz) ponderings; meditations

became apparent that he thought himself above the rest of the company. Opinion turned to how disagreeable he was, an unworthy companion for the unaffected Mr. Bingley.

Mr. Bingley spoke with all the men and danced with all of the ladies. Mr. Darcy mingled only with his own party. At one point, Elizabeth Bennet, who was sitting nearby overheard the following exchange.

Character is revealed through word and deed.

"Come, Darcy," said Mr. Bingley. "Dance. I hate to see you standing about in this stupid manner."

"You know I detest dancing with strangers," replied Darcy. "Besides, dancing with any woman in this room except your sisters would be a punishment."

"Ridiculous! I have never met so many pleasant girls in my life, and several of them are uncommonly pretty."

"You have been dancing with the only handsome girl in the room." Darcy was looking directly at Jane as he spoke.

"She is beautiful, but one of her sisters is sitting right over there. She is very pretty and quite pleasant. Let me introduce you."

"Which do you mean?" Darcy stared at Elizabeth until, catching her eye, he withdrew his own and said coldly, "Tolerable, but not pretty enough to tempt me. Besides, I am in no humor to dance with young ladies who are being slighted by other men. Return to your partner. You are wasting your time with me."

The two men separated. Elizabeth remained with not very cordial feelings toward Darcy. She had a quick wit, though, and told her friends the story, emphasizing how ridiculous Darcy's snobbery was.

Character is supplied by the omniscient narrator.

Mr. Bennet was in the library reading when his family returned home. He had rather hoped that his wife would be disappointed in Mr. Bingley. His hopes were dashed when she spoke.

Mrs. Bennet talked glowingly of the new neighbor. Her praise of Mr. Bingley made her distaste for Mr. Darcy stand out in contrast.

After describing (with some exaggeration) his rudeness, she concluded by saying:

"I can assure you Lizzie does not lose much by not suiting his fancy. He is a horrid man not worth pleasing. He fancies himself so great. I wish you had been there, my dear, to put him down. I quite detest the man."

Review the Selection

UNDERSTAND THE SELECTION

Recall

1. Who was the Bennets' new neighbor?

2. Which daughter was Mr. Bennet's favorite? Why?

3. What did Mrs. Bennet hope Mr. Bingley would do?

Infer

4. Why did Mr. Bingley visit Mr. Bennet?

5. Why didn't Mr. Darcy ask Elizabeth (Lizzie) to dance?

6. Why did Mrs. Bennet dislike Mr. Darcy?

7. How do Darcy and Bingley's actions at the dance reveal their different characters?

Apply

8. Suppose that you are one of the Bennet daughters. Why would you want to meet Mr. Bingley?

9. Assume that you are Mr. Bingley. How would you have reacted to Mr. Darcy's attitude toward Elizabeth?

10. Predict what might happen if Mr. Darcy were to meet Elizabeth again.

Respond to Literature

Is *Pride and Prejudice* a Romantic work? Explain your answer.

WRITE ABOUT THE SELECTION

At the end of the excerpt, Mrs. Bennet and her daughters are in agreement in their distaste for Mr. Darcy. Do you think that attitude continues throughout the novel? Describe their next meeting. Keep in mind that Elizabeth has inherited Mr. Bennet's sharp wit. Imagine the effect of Elizabeth's intelligence on Mr. Darcy. Include Mrs. Bennet's feeling in your episode.

Prewriting Decide on the setting. Remember that setting in this novel is sketchy. Write the name of each character who will appear in the scene. Make notes on their conversation.

Writing Briefly establish the setting at the outset. Write the episode as a conversation among the characters. Be sure the meeting has a beginning, a middle and an end.

Revising Be certain each person stays in character throughout the conversation. Allow your conclusion to lead to a sequel. The characters should not part on terms that make another conversation impossible. This meeting should be the second of many.

Proofreading It is not necessary to include the character's name if the reader understands who is speaking. If there is any doubt about the identity of the speaker, add the character's name with verbs such as *said* or *replied.*

THINK ABOUT FICTION

Fiction is literature which comes from the author's imagination. There are many different genres, or types of fiction. These genres share a number of fictional elements. Among these are setting, plot, character, theme, point of view, and tone.

1. The events in *Pride and Prejudice* take place in the late 18th century. Was it written as an historical or a contemporary novel? Explain your answer.

2. Darcy is presented as a flat character in this excerpt. Do you think he remains so throughout the novel? Explain your answer.

3. Is plot the most important element in this selection? Explain your answer.

4. What is the point of view in this selection? Explain your answer.

5. Is this a gentle or a savage satire? Explain your answer, using Mrs. Bennet as an example.

DEVELOP YOUR VOCABULARY

Some words can be used as nouns or as verbs. A **noun** is a word that names a person, object, place, or idea. For example, in the sentence, "Mr. Darcy's *comment* was not taken seriously," *comment* is a noun meaning *remark*. A **verb** is a word that expresses action or a state of being. For example, in the sentence, "Elizabeth will *comment* on his remarks after the dance," *comment* is a verb meaning *explain* or *interpret*.

The following words are found in this selection. Each can be used as a noun or as a verb. If you are not certain of the meanings of each word, find the definitions in a dictionary. Write two original sentences for each word. In the first, use the word as a noun; in the second, use the word as a verb.

1. rent
2. address
3. dance
4. prejudice
5. exchange
6. visit

The Fairy Tale, William Merritt Chase. The Granger Collection

READING FOCUS

Make Reasonable Inferences You have now studied and practiced making inferences about many elements of literature. Remember, however, that the inferences you make must be reasonable. They must make sense within the context of the literary work. To ensure this, think carefully about the inference you are making. Confirm that the events in the selection support your inferences.

DESCRIPTION

Technique is a method of accomplishing a desired aim. Description is one technique of fiction. Through description, the writer provides the reader with a mental image of a person, an object, or a scene.

Selective detail is one way in which this mental image is created. The writer chooses characteristics which will produce a desired image in the reader's mind.

Specific language is another feature of description. The writer describes the selected characteristics in specific terms. The specific terms are concrete. They identify features that can be seen, heard, smelled, or touched.

Through selective detail and specific language, the writer creates a dominant impression in the reader's mind. The **dominant impression** is the effect the description has upon the reader.

As you read the selection, ask yourself:

1. What kinds of details does Wordsworth select for her description?
2. What concrete terms does she use in her description?

WRITING CONNECTION

Write a journal entry describing three things you saw today. Be sure each description has enough detail to create a definite mental image.

from JOURNALS OF DOROTHY WORDSWORTH

by Dorothy Wordsworth

Thursday 15th, April 1802. It was a threatening, misty morning, but mild. We set off after dinner from Eusemere. Mrs. Clarkson went a short way with us, but turned back. The wind was furious, and we thought we must have returned. We first rested in the large boat-house, then under a furze bush opposite Mr. Clarkson's. Saw the plough going in the field. The wind seized our breath. The Lake was rough. There was a boat by itself floating in the middle of the bay below Water Millock. We rested again in the Water Millock Lane. The hawthorns are black and green, the birches here and there greenish, but there is yet more of purple to be seen on the twigs. We got over into a field to avoid some cows—people working. A few primroses by the roadside, wood—sorrel flower, the anemone, scentless violets, strawberries, and that starry yellow flower which Mrs. C. calls pile wort. When we were in the woods beyond Gowbarrow Park we saw a few daffodils close to the water side. We fancied that the lake had floated the seeds ashore, and that the little colony had so sprung up. But as we went along there were more and yet more; and at last, under

---

furze (FURZ) an evergreen shrub with dark-green spines and yellow flowers

hawthorn (HAW thawrn) any of a group of spiny shrubs or small trees of the rose family with glossy leaves, white or pink fragrant flowers, and small red fruits

birch (BURCH) any of a family of small deciduous trees and shrubs characterized by their peeling bark

anemone (uh NEM uh nee) a flower of the buttercup family known for its bright medium-sized blooms; sometimes called "wind flower"

pile wort (PYL wort) a plant of the crowfoot family with a grainlike, underground stem; sometimes referred to as the lesser celandine

the boughs of the trees, we saw that there was a long belt of them along the shore, about the breadth of a country turnpike road. I never saw daffodils so beautiful. They grew among the mossy stones about and about them; some rested their heads upon these stones as on a pillow for weariness; and the rest tossed and reeled and danced, and seemed as if they verily laughed with the wind, that blew upon them over the lake, they looked so gay, ever glancing, ever changing. This wind blew directly over the lake to them. There was here and there a little knot, and a few stragglers a few yards higher up, but they were so few as not to disturb the simplicity, unity, and life of that one busy highway. We rested again and again. The bays were stormy, and we heard the waves at different distances, and in the middle of the water, like the sea. Rain came on—we were wet when we reached Luffs, but we called in. Luckily all was cheerless and gloomy, so we faced the storm— we *must* have been wet if we had waited—put on dry clothes at Dobson's. I was very kindly treated by a young woman, the landlady looked sour but it is her way. She gave us a goodish supper. Excellent ham and potatoes. We paid 7/= when we came away. William was sitting by a bright fire when I came downstairs. He soon made his way to the library, piled up in a corner of the window. He brought out a volume of Enfield's *Speaker*, another miscellany, and an odd volume of Congreve's plays. We had a glass of warm rum and water. We enjoyed ourselves, and wished for Mary. It rained and blew, when we went to bed. N.B. Deer in Gowbarrow Park like skeletons.

---

verily (VER uh lee) truly; certainly
miscellany (MIS uh lay nee) a collection of writings on various subjects; separate writings collected in one volume

Dorothy Wordsworth (1771–1855)

When Dorothy Wordsworth was twelve, her father died, leaving her and three brothers orphaned. Dorothy, along with John and Christopher, was sent to live with Sir James Lowther in a cheerless home. William, her other brother, was sent away to school. Dorothy described these dismal, lonely years in her letters to William, thus beginning her writing career.

William sent for Dorothy in 1795 when he inherited some money. She went to live with him and his wife at Alfoxden in Somerset to be near the poet Samuel Coleridge. William had always been fond of his sister, and now she became his trusted confidante and close companion. She lived with her brother until he died in 1850.

Dorothy began her first journal in 1798, and although most of it has been lost, the remaining entries for January to April reveal her love of nature as well as the important friendship between her brother and Coleridge.

In another journal, known as the *Grasmere Journal,* written in 1800 to 1803, she vividly describes the world around the Wordsworths and their daily activities. This particular journal, containing precise descriptions of the weather, the seasons, and the landscape, was written especially for William, who used Dorothy's writing as a source for his own.

View in Hampshire, Patrick Nasmyth. Guildhall Art Gallery, London. The Bridgeman Art Library

Review the Selection

UNDERSTAND THE SELECTION

Recall

1. When was this selection written?

2. What did Dorothy Wordsworth discover on the bank beside the lake?

3. After the rain, where did Dorothy change her clothes?

Infer

4. When Dorothy refers to "we," who is her companion?

5. How do you know this selection was written in the springtime?

6. How were the Wordsworths traveling? Explain your answer.

7. How do you know that Dorothy was impressed with the daffodils?

Apply

8. In the description of the daffodils, which sensory images are most effective?

9. Suppose the Wordsworths had been traveling by carriage. How might the description vary?

10. What might William have been thinking about while sitting by the fire?

Respond to Literature
How does the setting of this journal illustrate Romantic interests?

WRITE ABOUT THE SELECTION

Writers can paint a picture of their surroundings through their choice of words. As you read this selection, you might feel that you were accompanying Dorothy on her walk that spring afternoon in 1802. The writer creates this impression through her use of vivid details. She was particularly impressed by the daffodils that she and her brother William discovered that day. You will see William's impressions of those same daffodils later in this unit.

Many times in your life, you will view a scene that you would like to share with others. If you live in or near a city, visit a local park or a zoo. If you live in the country, take a walk through a woods or a meadow. Then write a paragraph describing your experience and the things that impressed you.

Prewriting Take a notepad and pencil with you on your walk. Make notes in sequence about what impresses you as you move about. Include details of scenes that most impress you.

Writing Use your notes to write about your walk. Add details that allow your reader to visualize what you saw.

Revising When you revise your paragraph, be sure to add specific details that make your readers feel they are accompanying you on your walk.

Proofreading Read over your selection. Be sure each thought is a complete sentence with a subject and a predicate.

THINK ABOUT DESCRIPTION

Concrete language is one characteristic of description. **Specific terms** are one form of concrete language. The writer may identify the particular shape, sound, smell, or feel of an object. Sometimes, the writer may use a **figure of speech** to describe what an object resembles.

1. Is "misty morning" a specific term or a figure of speech? Explain your answer.

2. Is "the wind was furious" a specific term or a figure of speech? Explain your answer.

3. Does the description of the pile wort use figures of speech? Explain your answer.

4. How does the description of daffodils use figures of speech?

5. How does the dominant impression of the lake contrast with the dominant impression of the library?

READING FOCUS

Make Reasonable Inferences As you read Dorothy Wordsworth's journals, you made inferences about her. Use these inferences to briefly describe what she was like. What facts and details in the selection support your inferences?

DEVELOP YOUR VOCABULARY

An **adjective** is a word that modifies a noun. Adjectives are extremely important when you are writing a description. They help the reader visualize what is being described. A writer can also use an adjective to give an opinion of a noun. For example, in the sentence, "The *beautiful, tiny, golden-yellow* blossoms covered the tree," *beautiful* is an adjective that is an opinion. The adjectives, *tiny* and *golden-yellow,* describe the size and color of the noun *blossoms.*

The following words are nouns. Select two adjectives that describe each noun. Then, use each set of adjectives and nouns in a sentence. Underline the adjectives you use in each sentence.

1. flower
2. road
3. house
4. man
5. woman
6. lake
7. tree
8. bird
9. deer
10. sky

FIGURES OF SPEECH

Figurative language is an element of poetry. Poets often use figurative language to create a vivid image in the reader's mind. This image brings out an emotional response that helps the reader understand the underlying theme of the poem. **Figure of speech** is the term used to describe specific examples of figurative language.

A figure of speech is used to convey meaning or to heighten effect. Giving a thing or an abstract idea human characteristics is one way to convey meaning as in "daffodils . . . dancing in the breeze." This technique is called personification. Figures of speech can also be used to heighten effect. For example, using a facial expression to represent the entire person is one way to **heighten effect** as in "sneer of cold command."

As you read these selections, ask yourself:

1. How do the authors use figures of speech to convey meaning?
2. How do the authors use figures of speech to heighten effect?

READING FOCUS

Paraphrase Poetry When you paraphrase you restate the speaker's experiences and feelings in your own words. Restating the lines or stanzas of a poem will help you to clarify their meaning.

As you read the next three poems, practice paraphrasing the lines of each one.

WRITING CONNECTION

Write the words *lonely, daffodils,* and *sneer* on a sheet of paper. Use each in an original sentence that contains a figure of speech.

I wandered lonely as a cloud

by William Wordsworth

I wandered lonely as a cloud
That floats on high o'er vales and hills,
When all at once I saw a crowd,
A host of golden daffodils;
5   Beside the lake, beneath the trees,
Fluttering and dancing in the breeze.

Continuous as the stars that shine
And twinkle on the milky way,
They stretched in never-ending line
10   Along the margin of a bay:
Ten thousand saw I at a glance,
Tossing their heads in sprightly dance.

The waves beside them danced, but they
Out-did the sparkling waves in glee:—
15   A poet could not but be gay,
In such a jocund company;
I gazed—and gazed—but little thought
What wealth the show to me had brought:

For oft, when on my couch I lie
20   In vacant or in pensive mood,
They flash upon that inward eye
Which is the bliss of solitude;
And then my heart with pleasure fills,
And dances with the Daffodils.

---

vale (VAYL) small valley
host (HOHST) great number
sprightly (SPRYT lee) lively; joyful
jocund (JOK und) joyous; jolly
pensive (PEN siv) deeply thoughtful

OZYMANDIAS

by Percy Bysshe Shelley

I met a traveler from an antique land
Who said: Two vast and trunkless legs of stone
Stand in the desert. Near them on the sand,
Half sunk, a shattered visage lies, whose frown
5 And wrinkled lip and sneer of cold command
Tell that its sculptor well those passions read
Which yet survive, stamped on these lifeless things,
The hand that mocked them, and the heart that fed;
And on the pedestal these words appear:
10 "My name is Ozymandias, king of kings:
Look on my works, ye Mighty, and despair!"
Nothing beside remains. Round the decay
Of that colossal wreck, boundless and bare,
The lone and level sands stretch far away.

Ozymandias (oz uh MAN dee us) a powerful Egyptian king who died about 1258 B.C.
  He was a great builder of palaces, temples, and statues of himself.
trunkless (TRUNK lis) without the torso, or main part of the body.
visage (VIZ ij) face
pedestal (PED uh stul) base of a statue

ON FIRST LOOKING INTO CHAPMAN'S HOMER

by John Keats

Much have I traveled in the realms of gold,
    And many goodly states and kingdoms seen;
    Round many western islands have I been
Which bards in fealty to Apollo[1] hold.
5   Oft of one wide expanse had I been told
    That deep-browed Homer ruled as his demesne;
    Yet did I never breathe its pure serene
Till I heard Chapman speak out loud and bold:
Then felt I like some watcher of the skies
10   When a new planet swims into his ken;
Or like stout Cortez[2] when with eagle eyes
    He stared at the Pacific—and all his men
Looked at each other with a wild surmise—
    Silent, upon a peak in Darien.[3]

---

bard (BAHRD) poet or singer who composes heroic or epic verse
fealty (FEE ul tee) (archaic or poetic) fidelity; loyalty
demesne (dih MAYN) realm
serene (suh REEN) calm; (in this selection) clean air
ken (KEN) range of vision; view
surmise (sur MYZ) a thought or idea based on scanty evidence
[1]**Apollo:** in Greek and Roman mythology, the god of music, poetry, and medicine
[2]**Cortez:** Here, Keats was mistaken. The Pacific Ocean was discovered in 1513 by Balboa, not Cortez.
[3]**Darien:** the Isthmus of Panama

Percy Bysshe Shelley (1792–1822)

As a young boy Shelley liked to make up incredible tales about imaginary creatures for his brothers and sister. He was also very interested in science and spent a lot of time experimenting. His Eton classmates teased him cruelly for his ideas and strange ways.

In 1810 Shelley went to Oxford where he published a pamphlet called *The Necessity of Atheism.* He was expelled when he refused to admit that he had written it. He was briefly married at nineteen to Harriett Westbrook. He met Mary Godwin, whom he married in 1816 when his first wife, Harriet, drowned. He and Mary moved to Italy where they developed a friendship with Lord Byron, among other literary figures.

Shelley had an intense desire to reform the world. His idealism is reflected in his early poems. However, as he matured, his poetry began to balance his doubts with his desire for a perfect world. His most famous poem, and perhaps his greatest accomplishment, was *Prometheus Unbound,* published in 1820. Shelley used a well-known story from Greek mythology about Prometheus who stole fire from Olympus to give to humans. It is considered one of the greatest English Romantic mythological poems. Shelley also wrote many famous odes, such as "Ode to Heaven," "Ode to the West Wind," and "To a Skylark." Shelley died at the age of thirty in a boating accident.

Review the Selection

UNDERSTAND THE SELECTION

Recall

1. To what object does Wordsworth compare himself?

2. According to the words on the pedestal, who is Ozymandias?

3. Who does Keats mistakenly identify as the discoverer of the Pacific Ocean?

Infer

4. How does Wordsworth feel when he remembers the daffodils?

5. What has happened to the statue?

6. In what way are the words on the pedestal of the statue ironic?

7. To what kind of experience is reading "Chapman's Homer" compared?

Apply

8. What impression might you have gotten from viewing the daffodils?

9. If you were viewing the statue of Ozymandias, what might your response be?

10. How would you describe your response to reading a selection that excited you?

Respond to Literature

In what way does Keats's form show the Romantic tradition?

WRITE ABOUT THE SELECTION

In this section, you have seen how three different poets reacted to an experience that changed their perspective on life or a particular subject. Everyone has experiences which shape or change his or her opinion or way of viewing an idea, object, or person. Think about an experience you have had that changed your perspective or your beliefs. Write about the experience and how it changed your perspective.

Prewriting Write an informal outline of your experience. Present the events of your experience in chronological order. In other words, tell what happened first, then what happened next, and so forth. Include details about how you felt before this experience and how you changed afterward.

Writing Use your informal outline to write a paragraph about your experience. In it, give a clear explanation of what occurred and why the experience had an impact on your thinking. Be sure to tell whether others were involved, as well as what you learned from the experience.

Revising When you revise, be sure to add details that make clear how you felt before and after your experience.

Proofreading Read over your paragraph to check for errors. Be sure you have used a capital letter to begin each sentence and each proper noun.

THINK ABOUT FIGURES OF SPEECH

Metaphor, simile, personification, and synecdoche are kinds of figures of speech. **Metaphors** describe one thing in terms usually associated with another. **Similes** compare two different things and are introduced by the word *like* or *as*. **Personification** describes objects or ideas in human terms. **Synecdoche** uses one part of something to represent the whole.

The following examples are taken from the poems you have just read. For each, identify the figure of speech being used. Explain the meaning conveyed in your own words.

1. Then felt I like some watcher of the skies

2. eagle eyes

3. sneer of cold command

4. a crowd, a host of golden daffodils

5. continuous as the stars that shine

READING FOCUS

Paraphrase Poetry   Paraphrase one of the poems you just read. Then tell how restating the poem in your own words helped to make the meaning clearer.

DEVELOP YOUR VOCABULARY

Dialect is a regional or local variety of language. **Dialect** is distinguished from the standard language of a country and from other dialects by several features. These include vocabulary, grammar, and pronunciation.

Dialect is often the spoken language of the common people. Romantic poets, such as the three in these selections, occasionally flavored their poems with the dialect of the common folk in whom they were interested.

Below are several terms that began as dialect but have found their way into the standard usage. Use a dictionary. Beside each word, write its origin in dialect and its meaning. Then use each in an original sentence.

1. ken
2. blarney
3. galore
4. donnybrook
5. bonnie
6. auld lang syne
7. smithereens
8. loch

UNIT 3 Review

Write About Literary Changes

Imagine that you are a contemporary of Samuel Pepys. You are a writer and are also keeping a diary. You have been noticing various changes taking place in the literature of the time. You write about these changes in your diary. Choose one of the many literary changes you have witnessed during your lifetime in the late 17th and the 18th centuries.

Prewriting Before you begin to write, decide which literary change you will write about. Freewrite at least three points you wish to make about this change. Locate examples or direct quotes from selections in this unit that support your points.

Writing Use your freewriting as the basis for your diary entry. Write your ideas as though each one were a diary entry made at the end of a different day. Include the month and the year in which you are recording your literary observations in your diary. Include authors' names and selection titles of literary examples or direct quotes you use.

Revising Be sure you explain the change that is taking place, then state your opinion about that literary change. Finally, include a conclusion.

Proofreading This is an informal diary entry; however, make certain all your sentences are complete and you have no misspelled words. Polish other aspects of your language as necessary.

Write About Literary Elements

When people analyze writing, they often examine the elements of literature that apply. In this unit, you have studied plot, character, point of view, setting, tone, theme, symbolism, and figurative language. Choose two selections. One should be typical of Restoration or Enlightenment literature. The other should exhibit characteristics of the Romantic period. You will compare and contrast the literary elements of the two works.

Prewriting Review the work you did for each "Think About" section in this unit. Then make a chart with the names of the two selections you have chosen at the top. On the side of the chart list the literary elements named above. Fill in as many of the spaces as possible with details about each element as it applies to each selection.

Writing Decide which literary element will be least important in your discussion and which will be most important. Number your most effective point 1 and continue numbering to 4 for your least effective argument. When you make your draft, write your points in that order.

Revising Think about adding direct quotes from each selection to support your arguments. Direct quotes will help to strengthen your arguments.

Proofreading Be certain you have followed the rules of punctuation that apply to direct quotations in your writing.

BUILD LANGUAGE SKILLS

Vocabulary

The writers of the Restoration, the Enlightenment, and the Romantic periods were influenced by Classical literature. The term **Classical** refers to the cultures of ancient Greece and Rome. Many of the terms we use to describe literature originally come from Latin terms or from the Romance languages. The **Romance languages** are languages that developed from Latin. These include Italian, French, and Spanish.

The English word *poem,* for example, comes from a French word *poeme* and a Latin word *poema,* as well as a Greek word *poiema.*

Use the dictionary to check the origins of the literary terms below. Then write a short explanation of each term. In your explanation tell what the term means and the origin of the word. Use each term in an original sentence. In each sentence, try to illustrate either the meaning or the history of the word.

1. farce
2. romance
3. lyric (lyre)
4. comedy
5. sonnet
6. novel
7. essay
8. journal
9. drama
10. scene

Grammar, Usage, and Mechanics

Every language follows an orderly pattern of word arrangement. This is called **syntax.** Syntax may vary from language to language. In English, the normal basic pattern of a sentence is subject—verb—object/adverbial modifiers.

Writers sometimes vary this pattern. Poets, in particular, may use a nontypical arrangement to heighten effect or to sustain rhythm. In the sentences below, note the word arrangement. Then rewrite the sentences using normal English syntax. Add or delete words as necessary to have the sentences make sense.

1. In what distant deeps or skies burnt the fire of thine eyes?

2. And forward, though I cannot see, I guess and fear.

3. Its sculptor well those passions read which yet survive.

4. Just as the twig is bent the tree's inclined.

5. Then felt I like some watcher of the skies when a new planet swims into his ken.

SPEAKING AND LISTENING

You give speeches, short ones at least, every day of your life. You give someone directions to your house, you coax your parents to buy you something new, or you give a friend details about a movie you saw. But, when you are asked to give a speech in front of your class, you may tense up. This is a pretty typical reaction, but you do not need to let fear prevent you from making a speech. Here are some pointers on how to relax and what to be aware of when you speak. Read them; they will help you with this assignment and in all your efforts to communicate.

1. The opening words of your speech are important, so give them special consideration. They should be interesting enough so that they grab the audience's attention. They should also explain the focus of your speech.

2. The major points of your speech will be included in the "body." Since this speech will be a short one (about three minutes), you will probably focus on one main idea and have several minor ideas that support it.

3. Jot down major and minor ideas. Decide in what order you will present them in your speech. Your time limit will regulate the amount of time you give to the minor points.

4. Make your last statement as clear as you can. It should sum up your main point, give your opinion and perhaps make a recommendation. A good ending should also leave the audience with something to think about.

5. As you prepare your speech, be aware of the phrases and vocabulary you use. Certain precise words and phrases will help convey your ideas and will add "punch" to your speech.

6. Delivering your speech requires you to relax. Rehearse before a mirror or a supportive friend to get over "stage fright." When your body is relaxed, your voice will be smooth and natural. Practice so that you know your speech so well that you don't have to read it.

From the selections in this unit, choose a person or a character you admire and give reasons for your choice in a speech. Your purpose is to convince the audience that your choice is a good one. Use note cards to help you recall supporting ideas and to keep you on topic for the two or three minutes you will talk.

CRITICAL THINKING

Theme is the dominating or central idea in a literary work. In fiction, theme is almost always implied or stated indirectly.

Fiction writers often include thematic passages in their works. Thematic passages may appear as dialogue or narrative. **Thematic passages** state an idea that focuses the reader's attention on the central idea in the work.

Thematic passages are usually straightforward in tone. Occasionally, however, a writer may include thematic passages that are not straightforward in tone. The narrator or a character may say things that are the opposite of the message the writer wants to communicate to the reader. This technique is often found in satire.

Choose one selection from Unit 3 in which you think you can identify a thematic passage. Then answer the following questions:

1. In your own words, what is the literal meaning of this passage?

2. Is the thematic passage related by a character in the work? If so, what is the writer's attitude toward that character?

3. If the thematic passage is related by the narrator, what is the tone of the narration? Does the narrator seem to speak humorously or seriously?

4. Do you agree with the literal meaning of the passage? Explain.

EFFECTIVE STUDYING

Drama   In this unit, you read the play *She Stoops to Conquer.* At times, this comedy may have seemed complicated. If you have trouble following a complicated plot, you may not enjoy the literary work. To better understand and enjoy reading a play, take the following steps:

1. Remember that a play was meant to be performed by live actors on a stage. As you read, attempt to envision a scene and how the characters might move and act.

2. After you have read each act, list the main characters and briefly describe what you thought were the most important actions taken by each.

3. At the end of each act, select and reread the most important lines spoken by each character.

4. When you have finished the play, review your notes. If you are not certain of what happened in a particular act, reread it.

Test Preparation

If you are to be tested on a play, study with several friends. Take parts and read the play aloud. Discuss opinions of each part.

Expressions of the Victorian Era

Resolve to be thyself; and know that he,
Who finds himself, loses his misery!
— Matthew Arnold

The Baleful Head, Sir Edward Burne-Jones. Staatsgalerie, Stuttgart.
Bridgeman Art Library, Art Resource

LITERARY HIGHLIGHTS

1838 Charles Dicken's
Oliver Twist and *Nicholas
Nickleby* are bestsellers.

1847 Charlotte
Brontë's *Jane Eyre*
and Emily Brontë's
Wuthering Heights appear.

1850 Elizabeth Bar
Browning publishe
*Sonnets from the
Portuguese.*

| 1820 | 1825 | 1830 | 1835 | **1840** | 1845 | 1850 | **1855** |

1833 Slavery is abolished
in the British Empire.

1837 Victoria becomes
Queen of England.

1854 Britain enters
Crimean War.

1847 Factory Act limits
women and children to
ten-hour workday.

HISTORICAL HIGHLIGHTS

Expressions of the Victorian Era

You may have seen Victorian furniture: heavy cabinets, overstuffed velvet sofas. Who was Victoria?

■ QUEEN VICTORIA

Victoria became queen of England in 1837, at age 18. She ruled over the British Empire until her death in 1901. She was strong-minded, accused by some of being domineering and admired by others for setting high standards. She was as complicated as the times she lived in.

■ LIFE IN THE VICTORIAN AGE

During Victoria's reign, England achieved the greatest position of world power that any nation has ever known. This was mainly because of the Industrial Revolution, which began in England, giving the country a tremendous advantage over the rest of the world.

Factories were built, and great cities grew up. The population of London more than tripled, to 6.5 million. Major advances were made in transportation and communications. The economy changed from one based on farming to one based on manufacturing and trade.

■ A GOOD TIME FOR WRITERS

More printed material became available, and more people were able to read it. Readers came from all classes. They read not just for entertainment but for explanations. They expected writers to answer questions such as: Are the technological advances really so wonderful, or do they create more problems than they solve?

■ THREE TYPES OF LITERATURE

Victorian literature covered a wide range of themes and writing styles. In the early part of the period, most of the literature was **romantic.** Themes were optimistic—individual worth, love, and the beauty of

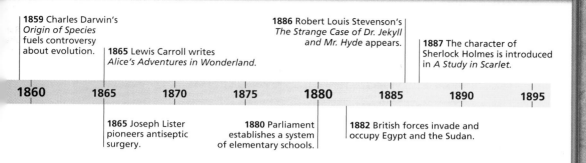

1859 Charles Darwin's *Origin of Species* fuels controversy about evolution.

1865 Lewis Carroll writes *Alice's Adventures in Wonderland.*

1886 Robert Louis Stevenson's *The Strange Case of Dr. Jekyll and Mr. Hyde* appears.

1887 The character of Sherlock Holmes is introduced in *A Study in Scarlet.*

1860 1865 1870 1875 1880 1885 1890 1895

1865 Joseph Lister pioneers antiseptic surgery.

1880 Parliament establishes a system of elementary schools.

1882 British forces invade and occupy Egypt and the Sudan.

nature. Writers wrote more about with the way things should be than the way things were.

Later, especially after 1870, a different kind of literature became dominant. It was called **realism.** It was concerned with life as it really was.

By the end of the century, realism was replaced by a movement called **naturalism.** Its followers were interested in how scientific theories can be applied to human nature.

■ READING VICTORIAN LITERATURE

Charles Dickens was one of the most popular writers of his day. You will read *A Christmas Carol,* which provides a picture of the working class's difficulties.

Matthew Arnold was another critic of society. His "Dover Beach" uses images of nature to present a pessimistic view of the world.

Alfred, Lord Tennyson, was named England's Poet Laureate, or chief poet, in 1850; it was a great honor. Tennyson liked to write about King Arthur's time, but when you read "The Lady of Shalott," you will find that it also raises questions about happiness and the quality of life.

Do you like love stories? Charlotte Brontë's *Jane Eyre* is one. It is also a comment on the moral values of the age. Do you like mysteries? You will enjoy Arthur Conan Doyle's "The Second Stain." Sherlock Holmes was so popular that Victorian readers would not let Doyle kill him off.

There was humor in the period, too. A. E. Housman's poems often have ironic themes, as you will see when you read "When I was one-and-twenty." Lewis Carroll and Edward Lear were the age's foremost humorists. You will read Carroll's "The Walrus and the Carpenter" and Lear's "Three Recipes for Domestic Cookery."

The Victorian period in British history was significant in world history as well. As you read, ask yourself how each selection relates to the life of the era.

Character

The characters, or people, in a story carry the action of the plot. The more important a character is, the more you need to know about him or her. You can learn about characters in the following two ways: the author tells you directly; or the author tells you through character clues.

Characters may be either round or flat. **Round** characters are individuals with many-sided, fully-developed personalities. The main characters are usually round. **Flat** characters are one-sided stereotypes. They basically express a single quality.

The main character in a story is known as the **protagonist**. The protagonist is not necessarily a "good guy," but simply the most important figure.

Sometimes there is a character who stands directly opposed to the protagonist. This character is called the **antagonist**, and is the second most important character.

As you read "Sherlock Holmes and the Second Stain," try to:

1. Form an image of each character.
2. Solve the mystery.

READING FOCUS

Make Predictions Authors do not always tell you how the story will end. Authors of detective stories try to keep you guessing until the last minute. However, they do give you clues along the way. As you read, watch for clues and try to predict what will happen next. As you continue reading, you can change your prediction as needed.

WRITING CONNECTION

Think of a character in your favorite story. Write a paragraph that describes that character, telling whether he or she is the protagonist or the antagonist.

SHERLOCK HOLMES
AND THE
SECOND STAIN

DRAMATIZED · *by Arthur Conan Doyle*

CHARACTERS

SHERLOCK HOLMES, *the famous detective*
DR. WATSON, *his assistant*
THE PRIME MINISTER[1] **OF ENGLAND**
THE HONORABLE TRELAWNEY HOPE, *Secretary for European Affairs*
LADY HILDA TRELAWNEY HOPE, *his wife*
BUTLER
MRS. HUDSON, *Holmes's housekeeper*
SUPERINTENDENT LESTRADE, *member of the police force*
OFFICER MACPHERSON, *member of the police force*

SCENE 1

SETTING: HOLMES'S *rooms.*

AT RISE: SHERLOCK HOLMES *is seen seated in a leather chair, right, in his Baker Street rooms. A small littered sofa stands left of center, where there is a table with books and papers and a lamp on it. Left and right there are several comfortable but rather shabby leather and upholstered chairs, and a coatrack stands far right.* DR. WATSON *enters right.*

---

[1]**prime minister:** head of British government
secretary (SEK ruh ter ee) high government official in charge of a particular department

DR. WATSON: Well, Holmes, it looks as if some important business is coming our way. The Prime Minister and Mr. Trelawney Hope, the Secretary for European Affairs, have arrived, and they seem very troubled.

HOLMES: Show them in, my dear Watson, and we'll see what's bothering them. (DR. WATSON *exits briefly and returns with the* PRIME MINISTER *and* TRELAWNEY HOPE.)

WATSON: Gentlemen, please come in. (HOLMES *stands up, and the* PRIME MINISTER *walks over to him and shakes hands.*)

PRIME MINISTER: Mr. Holmes, you were good to see us at such short notice. This is Mr. Trelawney Hope, our Secretary for European Affairs.

HOLMES (*walking toward* HOPE): I'm glad to see you both. (*They shake hands.*) Won't you please sit down? (HOLMES *sits back down, and others sit right and left of him.*) You know my friend, Dr. Watson, of course? (*They nod, and* WATSON *sits in chair slightly behind* HOLMES.) Now, gentlemen, please tell me how I may be of service.

PRIME MINISTER: Early this morning, Mr. Hope arrived at my home to report the loss of a very important government document. The disappearance of this paper can bring about international trouble. But I would like the European Secretary to tell you the story in detail.

HOLMES: Very well. (*He leans forward and looks at* HOPE.) Please proceed, Mr. Secretary.

HOPE (*fidgeting nervously with his watch chain*): When I discovered the loss of this document, which was at eight o'clock this morning, I at once informed the Prime Minister. He suggested that we come to you for help in recovering it.

HOLMES: Have you informed the police?

PRIME MINISTER (*quickly*): No, sir, for to do so would in the long run mean informing the public. This we must avoid at all costs.

HOLMES: And why, sir?

PRIME MINISTER: Because the document in question is of such great importance. Its publication might lead to serious trouble for all of Europe. Unless this document can be recovered in secrecy, it may as well not be recovered at all!

HOLMES: I understand. (*To* HOPE) Can you tell me exactly how this document disappeared?

HOPE: This can be done in a few words, Mr. Holmes. The letter— for the document in question is a letter—was received six days ago from a foreign ruler. After showing it to the Prime Minister, I placed it in my private dispatch box, not in my safe, and each evening I have taken it to my home in Whitehall Terrace. The box was always locked, and at night I kept it on my dressing table. The only key is in my pocket. The letter was in the dispatch box last night. Of that I am certain, for I opened it when I was dressing for dinner and saw it. This morning it was gone. I am a light sleeper and so is my wife, and we are both prepared to swear that no one could have entered the room during the night without our knowledge. Yet, the paper is missing.

HOLMES: What time did you eat?

HOPE: Half-past seven.

HOLMES: And when did you go to bed?

HOPE: My wife had gone to the theater. I waited up for her, and we went to bed at eleven-thirty.

HOLMES: Then for four hours the box was unguarded?

HOPE: Yes. But no one enters our room at night except my valet and my wife's maid. Both are old and trusted servants. Moreover, as I never discuss politics in the house, no one could possibly know there was anything more valuable than my ordinary papers in the box.

HOLMES: Who *did* know of the existence of that letter?

HOPE: No one in the house.

HOLMES: Surely you have told your wife?

HOPE: I said nothing to my wife till I missed it this morning.

HOLMES: Who in England knew of its existence?

HOPE: The Cabinet Ministers—all under a pledge of secrecy, of course—and two or three Department officers.

HOLMES: Who knew of the document abroad?

HOPE: Only the man who wrote it.

HOLMES: What was in it, exactly?

PRIME MINISTER: The envelope is a long, thin, pale-blue one, with a seal of red wax—

HOLMES: What was *in* the *letter?*

---

dispatch (dih SPACH) official message
valet (VAL it) personal servant who takes care of a man's clothing

PRIME MINISTER *(stiffly)*: These are government secrets, Mr. Holmes.

HOLMES *(with a smile)*: Then I regret I cannot help you.

PRIME MINISTER *(jumping to his feet; angrily rising)*: I am not ac-customed, sir—*(Controlling himself)* I see we must accept your terms, Mr. Holmes. *(Slight pause)* The letter, then, is from a foreign ruler who has been angered by certain actions of this country. The letter is so nasty that its publication would un-doubtedly stir up strong feeling in this country. Within a week we might find ourselves close to war. *(HOLMES writes something on a slip of paper he has taken from table and hands it to the PRIME MINISTER, who reads it, then nods.)* Yes, that is the name of the man who wrote the letter which may well cost this country millions, and the loss of thousands of men.

HOLMES: I assume, then, it is the enemies of this ruler who wish to get the letter and make it public, causing trouble between his country and ours.

PRIME MINISTER *(nodding)*: Exactly.

HOLMES: And to whom would these thieves send the letter if they are successful in stealing it?

PRIME MINISTER: To one of the great nations of Europe. *(Bitterly)* It is probably on its way there now.

HOLMES *(sadly)*: Then, sir, prepare for war.

HOPE: Are you quite sure?

HOLMES: Consider the facts. It could not have been taken after eleven-thirty, since, as I understand it, Mr. Hope and his wife were both in their room from that time until the loss was dis-covered this morning. It therefore had to be taken between seven-thirty, when they left the room to go to dinner, and eleven-thirty, when they returned—probably nearer seven-thirty, since the thief knew it was there and would want to get it as soon as possible after the Hopes left. *(Standing up and pacing back and forth)* But where can it be now? It must already be on its way to those who would want it.

PRIME MINISTER: I feel that it is beyond our reach.

HOLMES *(thoughtfully)*: Let us assume, for argument's sake, that the document was taken by a maid or the valet—

HOPE *(breaking in)*: They are both tried and true servants.

HOLMES *(to HOPE)*: Where in your house is your room located, Mr. Secretary?

HOPE: On the second floor. There is no entrance from outside, and no one could go up from the inside without being seen or heard.

HOLMES: It must, then, be somebody inside the house who has taken it.

WATSON: To whom would the thief take the letter, Holmes?

HOLMES: Elementary, my dear Watson—to one of the three chief international spies who may be said to be the best in the world. My first job is to find out if each of these is here in London as usual. If one is missing—especially if he has disappeared since last night—we shall have some clue as to where the document has gone.

PRIME MINISTER: Why should he be missing? Would he not have taken the letter to an embassy in London?

HOLMES: I think not. These agents work by themselves. They are often not on good terms with the embassies.

PRIME MINISTER: I believe you are right, Mr. Holmes. He would deliver so valuable a prize with his own hands. (*Rising*) Hope and I must return to our other duties. If anything new happens during the day, we shall communicate with you. And you, no doubt, will let us know if you discover something important.

HOLMES: Certainly.

PRIME MINISTER: Then good morning for now, and thank you a thousand times for your help. (WATSON *and* HOPE *rise. The* PRIME MINISTER *and* HOPE *go off, followed by* HOLMES. WATSON *picks up newspaper from table, then sits down again and begins to read.* HOLMES *re-enters, takes pipe from his jacket pocket and puts it into his mouth, then sits down, and is soon deep in thought.*)

HOLMES (*half to himself*): The situation is desperate, but not hopeless. If I could be sure which of them had taken the letter, it is just possible that it has not yet passed out of his hands. After all, it is a question of money with these fellows, and I have the British treasury behind me. If the letter is on the market, I'll buy it, even if it means another penny on the income tax.

WATSON (*looking up from the newspaper*): Which three agents did you have in mind?

HOLMES: There are only three who would play so dangerous a game—Oberstein, La Rothiere, and Eduardo Lucas.

WATSON: Is that the Eduardo Lucas of Godolphin Street?

HOLMES: Yes.

WATSON: You will not see him.

HOLMES: Why not?

WATSON: According to this paper, he was murdered in his house last night.

HOLMES (*jumping up*): Good heavens! (*He seizes paper and reads eagerly.*) "A crime of a mysterious kind was committed last night at 16 Godolphin Street, the home of Mr. Eduardo Lucas, well known in society circles." (*Looks up with a smile*) They

---

embassy (EM buh see) a country's official headquarters in another country

generally are! (*Scans paper quickly*) I note the household consisted only of Lucas, his housekeeper, Mrs. Pringle, and his valet, Mitton. Apparently Mrs. Pringle had gone to bed early, to her room on the top floor of the house. Mitton was visiting a friend in Hammersmith. Well, they should be able to check that alibi. (*Reading from newspaper*) "At a quarter to twelve, Police Officer Barrett, passing along Godolphin Street, saw that the door of Number 16 was open." (*Breaking off*) That points to an unexpected visitor, Watson, but *one who had a key.*

WATSON: Perhaps Mitton went back and did his master in.

HOLMES: Don't jump to the obvious conclusions, Watson. That would be much too neat a solution! Cases seldom run like that. (*Reading paper again*) Barrett went in and found the front room lighted, in wild disorder, with a chair overturned, and the body of Lucas beside it—"stabbed to the heart," it says here, with "a curved Indian dagger, obviously taken from a display of weapons on the wall. There was no sign of robbery." Well, Watson, what do you make of this?

WATSON: It's an amazing coincidence.

HOLMES: Coincidence! Here is one of the three possible actors in our drama, found murdered during the very hours when we know that drama was happening. (*Pacing about*) No, my dear Watson. This is no coincidence. The stealing of the letter and this murder are connected—*must* be connected. It is for us to find that connection.

WATSON: But now the police must know all.

HOLMES: Not at all. They know all they see at Godolphin Street. They know nothing of the events at Whitehall Terrace. Nor shall they. Only we know of both events, and can find the connection between them. (*Sits down*) You know, Watson, I'd have thought of Lucas, in any case. He lives only a few minutes' walk from Whitehall Terrace. The other two agents live in the West End. (MRS. HUDSON *enters, holding a tray with a card on it. She walks center to* HOLMES.)

MRS. HUDSON (*holding tray toward* HOLMES): You have a visitor, Mr. Holmes.

---

conclusion (kun KLOO zhun) judgment; guess based on available facts
coincidence (koh IN suh duns) two unrelated events accidentally occurring at the same time

HOLMES (*taking card from tray and glancing at it quickly*): Hullo! What have we here? (*He raises his eyebrows in surprise, then passes card to* WATSON.) Will you please ask Lady Hilda Trelawney Hope to come up, Mrs. Hudson?

MRS. HUDSON: Right away, Mr. Holmes. (*She exits, and in a moment* LADY HILDA TRELAWNEY HOPE *enters, a dignified young woman, but obviously nervous.* HOLMES *and* WATSON *rise, as she walks center.*)

LADY HILDA (*anxiously*): Has my husband been here, Mr. Holmes?

HOLMES: Yes, madam.

LADY HILDA: Mr. Holmes, I beg you not to tell him I have come to see you.

HOLMES: Your ladyship places me in a very delicate position. (*Motioning to chair*) Please sit down and tell me what you wish, but I fear that I cannot make any promise. (*She walks to chair farthest from* HOLMES *and sits in dim light.*)

LADY HILDA: Mr. Holmes, there is complete faith between my husband and me, except on politics. On that he tells me nothing. Now I know there was a disturbing occurrence in our house last night. A paper has disappeared, and now I must understand the importance of this. I beg you, Mr. Holmes, to tell me exactly what happened and what it will lead to. (*With earnestness*) I assure you it is in my husband's best interests for me to know all. What *was* this paper?

HOLMES: Madam, you ask what is impossible for me to tell you. It is your husband you must ask.

LADY HILDA: I have done so, but all in vain. Can you at least tell me one thing—is my husband's political career likely to suffer as a result of this?

HOLMES: Unless it is set right, there may be very unfortunate results.

LADY HILDA (*drawing in her breath sharply*): And I understand that terrible things may occur for the country from the loss of this document?

HOLMES: You ask me more than I can answer.

LADY HILDA: Then I will take up no more of your time. (*Rises*) Please, I beg you, say nothing of my visit. (*She walks to exit, looks back at them, then goes out.*)

HOLMES: Now, Watson, what was the fair lady's game? What did she really want?

WATSON: Surely her statement was clear.

HOLMES: Hm-m. Think of her appearance—tense, excited. And she comes from a class of people who rarely show emotion. And what did she mean by saying that it was best for her husband that she knew all? And she sat there in the dim light where we could not read her expression.

WATSON: She probably sat in the shadow because she had no powder on her nose.

HOLMES: Exactly. *(Rising)* Well, good morning, Watson.

WATSON: You're off?

HOLMES: Just down to Godolphin Street. With Lucas lies our solution. So stand on guard, my good Watson, and receive any new visitors, I'll join you here for lunch, if I can.

WATSON: Right-o, Holmes. *(Curtain)*

SCENE 2

TIME: *A few days later.*

SETTING: *The home of* EDUARDO LUCAS. *It is furnished in luxurious style, with a large table with drawer, center, and some large chairs and sofas about. At rear of stage, center, there is a fireplace over which hang Oriental weapons on the wall. There is a door, left, a loose carpet on the floor, a bookcase on right wall, and a straight-backed chair in front of table.*

AT RISE: SUPERINTENDENT LESTRADE *is sitting at table, reading a newspaper.* HOLMES *and* WATSON *enter.*

LESTRADE: Ah, here you are, Holmes. Glad you got my note. Seen the Paris news?

HOLMES: Yes. It's an interesting happening.

LESTRADE: Our French friends seem to have touched the spot this time. Evidently this fellow Lucas lived a double life—Eduardo Lucas here, bachelor, and M. Henri Fournaye in Paris, with a wife who seems to have been very excitable. The papers say she was likely to get violent fits of jealousy.

WATSON: She probably had cause!

LESTRADE: No doubt, sir, no doubt. Why did he pose as a bachelor here? Probably to give himself just that bit of rope she'd never allow him over there.

HOLMES: But what, I wonder, sent her dashing over here on that particular night?

LESTRADE: My guess, sir, is that she had just discovered that he was living here as Eduardo Lucas. Now that, to a jealous woman, would only suggest one thing—that he had a little lady friend tucked away in London. So she comes rushing over from Paris, surprises him, they have one flaming fight, and in a wild fit she seizes one of the daggers on the wall— you can see where it was hanging—*(Points to wall)* and goes for him. Evidently, from the state of the room, he'd picked up a chair to defend himself, but too late—she got in with the dagger.

HOLMES: It all fits neatly. And the paper states someone fitting her description had been seen watching this house from the other side of Godolphin Street.

LESTRADE: Yes. And the fingerprints on the dagger are hers. Also, she arrived back in Paris in a state of great excitement after the murder. I should say, however, that this murder doesn't look like a planned one.

HOLMES: But she seems to have chosen a very convenient night, when he was alone.

LESTRADE: Oh, no doubt she would do that to pick a fight with him when the coast was clear. If she was watching, she would have seen the valet go out, and noticed the light go on in the housekeeper's room. Then in she'd pop. *(OFFICER MACPHERSON enters.)*

MACPHERSON: Excuse me, sir, but there's an offficer with a message for you outside.

LESTRADE: All right, I'll speak to him. *(To* HOLMES *and* WATSON*)* I'll be with you in a moment, gentlemen. *(LESTRADE and* MACPHERSON *exit.)*

WATSON: What do you make of this, Holmes?

HOLMES: Make of it? Nothing.

WATSON: But they seem to have cleared up Lucas's death neatly.

HOLMES: My dear Watson, the man's death is only a small part of our real job—to find that letter and save Europe from war. Only one important thing has happened in the past three days—and that is, that *nothing* has happened! I get reports almost hourly, and it's certain that nowhere in Europe is there any sign of trouble. Now, where *can* this letter be? Who has it? Why was it held back? Was it a coincidence that Lucas was murdered the very night the document disappeared? Did it ever reach him? If so, why is it not among his papers? Did his jealous wife carry it off to Paris? How can I search her house there without making the French police suspicious? Stumped at every turn! *(LESTRADE enters.)*

LESTRADE: Yes, Mr. Holmes, we've got it all as clear as if we'd seen it.

HOLMES *(raising eyebrows):* And yet you have sent for me?

LESTRADE: Ah yes, that's another matter—a small one, but strange, you know, and freakish. But it doesn't affect the main point.

HOLMES: What is it, then?

LESTRADE: Well, you know that after a crime we're very careful to keep things in their position. There's an officer in charge here night and day. But this morning, the investigation being over, we thought we'd tidy up a bit. You see this carpet? *(Pointing)* It's not fastened down, just laid there loose. We raised it, and we found—

HOLMES *(tensely):* Yes?

LESTRADE: You see that stain on it? Well, with a man bleeding to death, a great deal of blood must have soaked through, wouldn't you say so?

WATSON: A great deal.

LESTRADE: Then you'll be surprised to hear there's no stain on the wood floor underneath.

HOLMES AND WATSON *(together):* No *stain?* There must be!

LESTRADE: So you'd say. The fact remains there isn't! *(He takes up carpet and points. Eagerly they bend over it.)*

WATSON *(examining carpet with magnifying glass he takes from his pocket):* But the underside of the carpet is as stained as the top. It must have left a mark!

LESTRADE *(chuckling):* Now, I'll show you the explanation. There is a second stain, but it's right here. *(He lifts another portion of carpet, uncovering a stain on floor. They examine this carefully.)*

WATSON: Yes, that would go with the stain over there.

LESTRADE: Now, what do you make of that, Mr. Holmes?

HOLMES: Elementary. The two stains did go together, but the carpet has been turned around.

LESTRADE: The police don't need you, Mr. Holmes, to tell them the carpet has been turned around. What I want to know is, *who* shifted the carpet, and *why?*

HOLMES *(in great excitement):* Look here, Lestrade, has that officer in the hallway been in charge all the time?

LESTRADE: Yes.

HOLMES: Well, take my advice. Examine him carefully, in private. You'll be more likely to get a confession out of him alone. Ask him how he dared to admit people to this room and then leave them here alone. Don't *ask* him if he has done it. Take it for granted that he has. Tell him you *know* someone has been in the room and that a full confession is his only chance.

LESTRADE: By George, I'll have it out of him! *(He rushes off.)*

HOLMES *(anxiously):* Now, Watson, now! Help me with this rug! *(He bends over rug and throws back one end, as* WATSON *turns back the other corner.)* Try these squares of wood and see if any of them seems loose or in any way different from the others. *(He kneels and taps on floor boards, examining them carefully.)*

WATSON *(kneeling down beside* HOLMES*):* What are we looking for, Holmes?

HOLMES *(with sudden happiness):* I think I can show you now, Watson! *(Tapping floor)* This section is hollow. *(As he lifts back lid of hinged "box")* It should be here. *(He reaches in, but quickly draws his hand out, empty.)* Empty! It can't be! *(Voices are heard from offstage.)*

LESTRADE *(from offstage):* You come in here, MacPherson.

HOLMES *(closing down lid of hinged section):* Quick, Watson, we must put this all back as it was! *(They quickly replace carpet, and* HOLMES *jumps up. He takes pipe from pocket and begins puffing on it, as* WATSON *sits in chair.* LESTRADE *and* MACPHERSON *enter.)*

LESTRADE: I'm sorry for the delay, Mr. Holmes. I can see that you are bored with the whole affair. Now, MacPherson, tell these gentlemen what you told me of your conduct.

MACPHERSON *(uneasily):* I meant no harm, sir, I'm sure. You see, sir, this young woman came to the door last evening—

HOLMES *(sharply):* What young woman?

MACPHERSON: A very respectable, well-spoken young woman, sir. She mistook the house. It was lonesome, and well, we got to talking. She wanted to see where the crime was done— she'd read about it in the papers.

HOLMES: And you let her in?

MACPHERSON: I saw no harm in letting her have a peep. But when she saw the stain, the mark on the rug, she fell down in a dead faint. I ran to the kitchen to get her some water, but couldn't bring her to. So I ran around the corner for some smelling salts.[2] But by the time I had come back, she had recovered and was off. I guess she was too embarrassed to face me.

HOLMES: Could you see if this rug *(pointing to small carpet)* had been moved while you were out?

MACPHERSON: Well, sir, it was a bit rumpled. You see, she fell on

---

[2]**smelling salts** powder to cure dizziness, fainting, or nausea

it when she fainted, and the floor under it is polished, with nothing to keep the rug in place. I straightened it out.

LESTRADE *(to* MACPHERSON*):* It's lucky for you, my man, that nothing is missing, or you'd be in jail by now.

MACPHERSON: I *am* sorry, sir.

HOLMES: Has this girl been here only once?

MACPHERSON: Yes, sir.

HOLMES: Have you any idea who she was?

MACPHERSON: None at all, sir. She said she was answering some advertisement for typewriting and came to the wrong number. A very pleasant lady she seemed, sir.

HOLMES: Tall? Good-looking?

MACPHERSON: She was that, sir! Some might say *very* good-looking. She had very pretty, coaxing ways.

WATSON: No doubt.

HOLMES: How was she dressed?

MACPHERSON: Quiet, sir—a long coat down to her feet.

HOLMES: What time was it?

MACPHERSON: It was just dusk. They were lighting the lamps as I came back to the house.

HOLMES: Very good. Come, Watson, we have more important work elsewhere. (HOLMES *and* WATSON *go to door, and* MAC-PHERSON *opens door to let them out.)*

LESTRADE: I'm sorry to have called you out over such unimportant business, Mr. Holmes, but I thought you would find the matter of the second stain interesting.

HOLMES *(turning briefly):* It was indeed, *most* interesting! *(As* LES-TRADE *bends to straighten rug,* HOLMES *takes something from his pocket, holds it so that* MACPHERSON *can see it, then puts it back into his pocket, as* MACPHERSON *stares in amazement.)*

MACPHERSON: Good Lord, sir! (HOLMES *puts his finger to his lips and exits quickly with* WATSON, *as curtain falls.)*

SCENE 3

TIME: *Later that morning.*

SETTING: *Sitting room in the home of* TRELAWNEY HOPE. *A small table stands center, and a writing desk with straight chair at left. Odd chairs are placed right and left. There is a door left, with a bell rope hanging on wall next to it.*

AT RISE: BUTLER *enters, followed by* HOLMES *and* WATSON.

BUTLER: If you will sit down, sirs, I shall tell her ladyship that you are here. (BUTLER *exits, and* HOLMES *and* WATSON *sit down.*)

HOLMES: Well, Watson, the curtain rings up on the last act. You will be relieved that our friend Trelawney Hope will suffer no setback in his brilliant career. And the Prime Minister will have no European war on his hands. In fact, with a little tact on our part, no one will be a penny the worse for what might have been very ugly.

WATSON (*amazed*): You have solved it?

HOLMES: Not quite, Watson. There are still a few points to clear up. (LADY HILDA *enters, obviously nervous.* WATSON *and* HOLMES *rise.*)

LADY HILDA (*angrily*): Mr. Holmes, this is most unfair of you. I begged you to keep my visit to you a secret so that my husband would not think I was snooping into his affairs. Now you come here, and he will surely know.

HOLMES: Unfortunately, madam, I had no other choice. I have been asked to recover this very important paper, and I must therefore ask you to place it in my hands. (LADY HILDA *sways, then grasps back of chair to steady herself, and straightens up.*)

LADY HILDA (*in a controlled, angry voice*): You—you insult me, Mr. Holmes.

HOLMES: Come, come, madam, it is useless. Give me the letter. (*She moves swiftly to the bell rope next to door.*)

LADY HILDA: The butler will show you out.

HOLMES: Do not ring, Lady Hilda. If you do, all my efforts to prevent further trouble will be for nothing. Give up the letter and all will be set right. If you work *with* me, I can arrange everything. If you work *against* me, I must expose you.

LADY HILDA (*proudly, with her hand still on bell rope*): You are trying to frighten me, Mr. Holmes. (*Changing her tone*) You say you know something. Just what is it?

HOLMES: Pray sit down, madam. (*She walks to chair, left, and sits.*) Thank you.

LADY HILDA: Well, Mr. Holmes, I give you five minutes.

HOLMES: One is enough. (*Quickly*) I know of your visit to

---

tact (TAKT) wise kindness

Eduardo Lucas. I also know of your clever return to his house last evening and of the manner in which you took the letter from its hiding place under the carpet.

LADY HILDA (obviously upset): You are mad, Mr. Holmes, mad! (HOLMES draws a small piece of cardboard from his pocket. It has a picture of a woman's face on it.)

HOLMES (showing picture to LADY HILDA): I have carried this picture with me because I thought it might be useful. The policeman on duty last night at the Lucas house recognized it! (LADY HILDA gasps and falls back in chair.) Come, Lady Hilda, you have the letter. My duty ends when I have returned it to your husband. Be honest with me.

LADY HILDA (hurt, but still trying): I tell you again, Mr. Holmes, that you are very, very wrong.

HOLMES (rising and walking toward bell pull): I am sorry for you, Lady Hilda. I have done my best for you. (He pulls bell rope.) I can see that it is all in vain. (BUTLER enters.) Is Mr. Trelawney Hope at home?

BUTLER: He will be at home, sir, at a quarter to one.

HOLMES (glancing at watch): Still a quarter of an hour. Very good. I shall wait. (BUTLER exits.)

LADY HILDA (wringing her hands in great distress): Oh, Mr. Holmes, Mr. Holmes! For heaven's sake don't tell him! I love him so much! This would break his heart!

HOLMES: I am thankful, madam, you have come to your senses at last. (Quickly) There is not a moment to lose. Where is the letter? (She hurries to the writing desk, unlocks it, and draws out a long, blue envelope.)

LADY HILDA (handing envelope to HOLMES): Here it is.

HOLMES (examining it briefly): How can we return it to his dispatch box? We must think of some way! Where is the dispatch box?

LADY HILDA: Still in his bedroom.

HOLMES: Good. Quickly, bring it here. (She hurries out.)

WATSON: How did you arrive at the truth?

HOLMES: Elementary, my dear Watson. (He paces about.) I only hope her husband doesn't arrive back too soon. (LADY HILDA re-enters carrying a flat, red box. HOLMES takes it and puts it onto table.) Now, Lady Hilda, how did you open it? Of course

—you have another key. Quickly—open it. *(She takes a small key from her pocket and opens box.)*

LADY HILDA: It belongs here. *(Puts her finger between papers in box.)*

HOLMES *(pushing some papers back and slipping blue envelope between other documents):* There. *(He shuts the box quickly.)* Now lock it and return it quickly to your bedroom. *(LADY HILDA locks it and puts key back into her pocket. She picks up box and rushes out.)*

WATSON: And to think she had it all the time!

HOLMES: Yes. *(Resumes pacing)* But why did she take it, Watson? That's what she must tell us.

WATSON: Lucas was well known in society circles—rather a lady's man. Do you think he worked up some sort of romance with her, in order to get the document out of her?

HOLMES: Could be, but—no. She's not the type. I think there's something more to the whole thing. Something we haven't got as yet. (LADY HILDA *re-enters.*)

LADY HILDA: Thank heaven it's back there at last!

HOLMES: Now we are ready for him. I am going far to protect you, Lady Hilda, but you must be honest with me.

LADY HILDA: Mr. Holmes, I will tell you everything. I love my husband very much and would not give him a moment of sorrow. Yet, if he knew how I have acted, how I have been forced to act, he would never forgive me. I beg you to help me. His happiness, my happiness, our very lives are at stake!

HOLMES: Quickly, madam, time grows short!

LADY HILDA: It all began with a letter of mine, a love letter I wrote before I was married—the letter of a young and foolish girl to an older man who had paid me much attention. He turned my head and I was flattered, and I wrote him a note. If you were to read it now, you might think I was having an affair with him. I learned much later that he was married and had a dreadful reputation with women. It all happened years ago and I thought the whole matter was forgotten. Somehow or other, this man Lucas got hold of the letter. He came to me and told me that he would show it to my husband, unless I gave him a certain document, which he described, from my husband's dispatch box. He had a spy in the office who knew of the document and where my husband kept it. Put yourself in my position, Mr. Holmes. What would you have done?

HOLMES: So, blackmail? But why did you not let him send it to your husband, and explain to him?

LADY HILDA: Oh, Mr. Holmes! My dear Mr. Holmes! You don't know husbands! Trelawney loves me, really. He thinks I'm perfect. He would have forgiven me, but the seed of suspicion planted in his mind when he received that letter might grow and I couldn't risk that! Well, I got the document from my husband's dispatch box. I took an impression of the key, and this man Lucas had another one made. I opened the box, took the paper, and went with it to Godolphin Street.

HOLMES: What happened when you went there?

---

impression (im PRESH un) copy made by pressure on some sort of mold to show shape

LADY HILDA: Lucas was alone. I remember seeing a woman outside when I went in. I handed him the document. He gave me the letter. Suddenly there was a sound outside in the hallway. Lucas quickly turned back the carpet, put the envelope into some hiding place there, and pulled the rug back over it. What happened next was a nightmare. I remember a dark, angry face peering in, a woman's voice shrieking, "At last! At last! I have found you with her!" Then there was a fearful scene. The woman rushed in, and she and Lucas started talking in French. The woman sounded quite crazy. She seized a dagger from the wall, and Lucas picked up a chair—I rushed from the horrible scene. It was not till next morning in the paper that I learned the dreadful result. I realized then that I had only exchanged one trouble for another. My husband's distress at the loss of the document went to my heart. I could hardly keep from telling him what I had done, but that would have meant a confession of the past. I realized that I had to get that document back. I knew it must still be where Lucas had hidden it, but how was I to get into the room? For two days I watched the house, but the door was never left open. Then I thought of pretending that I had mistaken the house for another, and asked the policeman to let me see the room.

HOLMES: And we know how you managed to get the envelope from the hiding place under the rug.

WATSON: Quite clever, madam.

LADY HILDA: When I brought the paper back here with me, I thought of destroying it, for I could see no way of returning it to the dispatch case without confessing my guilt. (*Sounds of footsteps and voices are heard from offstage.*) I hear my husband coming now. (TRELAWNEY HOPE *rushes into room.*)

HOPE (*excitedly*): Any news, Mr. Holmes? Any news?

HOLMES: I have distinct hopes.

HOPE: Thank heaven! The Prime Minister is lunching with us. May he share your hopes?

HOLMES: Certainly. (HOPE *goes to door and speaks to* BUTLER *off.*)

HOPE (*to* BUTLER, *off*): Will you please ask the Prime Minister to join us. (*Walks back center and takes* LADY HILDA'S *hands.*) How are you, my dear?

LADY HILDA: Glad that you are home and may expect good news from Mr. Holmes.

HOPE: My dear, this is a matter of politics. We shall join you shortly in the dining room. (LADY HILDA *smiles and exits. In a moment, the* PRIME MINISTER *enters.*)

PRIME MINISTER (*walking over to* HOLMES): Have you something to report, Mr. Holmes?

HOLMES: Nothing has been discovered, as yet. But I have inquired at *every point,* and I am sure there is no danger.

PRIME MINISTER: But we cannot live forever on the edge of a volcano!

HOLMES: I am—in hopes of getting the letter. The more I think, the more I am sure that it has never left the house.

PRIME MINISTER AND HOPE (*together*): Mr. Holmes!

HOLMES: If it had been taken from here, it would have been made public by now.

HOPE: But why should anyone take it and then do nothing with it?

HOLMES: There is no proof that anyone did take it.

PRIME MINISTER: Then how could it leave the dispatch box?

HOLMES: There is no proof that it ever did leave the dispatch box.

HOPE: You have my word that it left the box.

HOLMES: Have you examined the box since Tuesday?

HOPE: No, it was not necessary.

HOLMES: You may have overlooked it.

HOPE: Impossible! I took everything out.

HOLMES: Such things have happened. It may have been mixed with the other papers there.

HOPE: It was on the top.

HOLMES: Someone may have shaken the box and changed the position of the letter.

PRIME MINISTER: It is easily decided. Let us have the dispatch box brought in.

HOPE: I will get it myself. But it is a waste of time. (*Exits.*)

WATSON: I have known some strange cases of papers sometimes getting stuck together.

PRIME MINISTER: Yes, but this was such an unusual envelope. Blue—and right on top. I can hardly see how anything like that could have happened—(HOPE *re-enters carrying dispatch box. He puts it onto table, takes key from his pocket and unlocks box.*)

HOPE (*opening box and taking out some papers*): Now, we will make a search. (*Going through more papers*) A letter from Lord Merrow; the report from Sir Charles—

PRIME MINISTER *(impatiently):* But the letter—is it there?

HOPE: Not yet. *(continues going through papers, putting each on table as he identifies it)* Letter from Belgrade; a note on German grain taxes; a letter from Madrid—*(Suddenly stopping, as he picks up blue envelope)* Good heavens—Yes, this is it!

PRIME MINISTER *(snatching envelope and examining it):* Yes, this is the blue envelope—*(Taking letter out of envelope)* And the letter is here! Hope, I congratulate you.

HOPE: What a weight from my heart! But it is impossible! Mr. Holmes, you are a wizard! How did you know it was here?

HOLMES: Because I knew it was nowhere else.

HOPE: I cannot believe my eyes. Oh, I must tell my wife that all is well! *(He rushes excitedly to door, calling.)* Hilda! Hilda! *(He exits.)*

PRIME MINISTER *(looking at* HOLMES *with confusion and amusement):* Come, Holmes. There is more here than meets the eye. How came the letter back in the box? *(*HOLMES *turns away, smiling.)*

HOLMES *(as he picks up his hat and starts toward door):* We also have our diplomatic secrets. *(Turning to* WATSON*)* Come, Watson, we must be off. *(*WATSON *gets up. Curtain.)*

---

diplomatic (dip luh MAT ik) concerning relationships between countries; also skillful in handling people's feelings

Review the Selection

UNDERSTAND THE SELECTION

Recall

1. Why did the Prime Minister and Mr. Hope come to see Sherlock Holmes?

2. Why was the letter so important?

3. Why did Mrs. Hope give the letter to Lucas?

Infer

4. Of the three international spies, explain why Holmes suspected Lucas.

5. How did Holmes know that Lucas was murdered during the time when the envelope was stolen?

6. What was the significance of the second stain?

7. What is one difference and one similarity between the two letters?

Apply

8. If you were Dr. Watson, how would you have answered Holmes when he asked you about the real purpose of Mrs. Hope's visit to his office?

9. What do you think Holmes showed Officer MacPherson on his way out?

10. Were you able to solve the case? What did you think had happened?

Respond to Literature

Discuss the clues that tell you where and when this story is taking place.

WRITE ABOUT THE SELECTION

Imagine that Mrs. Hope had not returned the blue envelope back to the dispatch box in time and had to confess to her husband. How do you think she would have told him? What do you think his reaction would have been? What would he have thought about her love letter? Write a different ending to the story that answers all these questions.

Prewriting Make two lists, side by side, one with the heading *Mr. Hope,* the other with the heading *Mrs. Hope.* Under each heading, write what you know about each character's personality traits and values. When you have listed everything you can think of, compare the two lists. This will tell you what the two characters have in common.

Writing Compare the similarities and differences between the two characters. This will give you a good idea of how to answer the questions listed above. Write a new ending to the story on this basis.

Revising As you revise, be sure any dialogue you have written is reflective of how the characters speak and what they would say. If you did not include dialogue in your ending, add it where it would be most effective.

Proofreading Check your revised ending. Make sure that any character's action or expression you have described is placed in parentheses.

THINK ABOUT CHARACTER

Round characters have full personalities and show several facets as the story progresses. **Flat characters** are one-sided and usually not as important. Characters may also be dynamic or static. A **dynamic character** changes in some way during the course of the story. A **static character** remains basically the same throughout the story.

In short stories and plays, many characters are static. This is simply because the works are not long enough to show changes in all of the characters.

1. There is one dynamic character in the story. Who is it? How can you tell?

2. Which characters do you consider round and which do you consider flat? Explain your answer.

3. Explain the characters involved and the nature of the story's major conflict.

4. Which character is the protagonist? Which is the antagonist? Explain.

5. This selection was adapted for performance as a play. How does this affect the way in which you learn about the characters?

READING FOCUS

Make Predictions Give a specific prediction you made and tell what details you based the prediction on.

DEVELOP YOUR VOCABULARY

To understanding the meaning of a word, it is important to know what part of speech the word is. Below are the eight parts of speech. Read the following lists.

Noun—names a person, place, or thing
   examples: teacher, school, book

Pronoun—replaces a noun
   examples: it, we, they

Verb—names an action, or a state of being
   examples: run, think, is

Adjective—describes a noun
   examples: red, new, nice

Adverb—modifies a verb
   examples: quickly, nicely

Article—a special adjective
   examples: a, an, the

Preposition—introduces a phrase
   examples: of, at, in

Conjunction—connects parts of a sentence
   examples: and, or, but

All but one of the following words or terms have something in common. Which one is different? How do you know?

1. prime minister
2. secretary
3. dispatch
4. valet
5. embassy
6. coincidence
7. smelling salts
8. tact
9. impression
10. diplomatic

FOCUS ON DRAMA

Drama is a literary form that tells a story through action and dialogue and is written to be performed on the stage by actors. Some of the major elements of drama that are the same as those in stories and novels are: plot, conflict, climax, character, setting, symbolism, allegory, and theme. Imagery, irony, metaphor, and simile are also often used in stories, novels, poems, and plays. An element that is unique to drama is **dramatic technique.** This includes dialogue, soliloquy, asides, and stage directions.

Plot   The plot is the action of the play or story. It involves the unfolding of the story's events. As the plot develops, questions are raised and answered. Longer works often contain **subplots,** the minor stories that take place within the framework of the major story. For example, in "The Second Stain," the main plot follows the mystery of the disappearing letter. The subplot focuses on the murder of Lucas, the secret agent.

Conflict   Conflict is a struggle between opposing forces. It can involve a conflict between two characters or a conflict between a character and a force of nature or society. Conflict can also occur inside a character. In *A Christmas Carol*, Scrooge experiences a conflict between facets of his own character.

Climax   The climax is the turning point of the story. At this point the conflict is most intense, but the reader can see that it will be resolved. The rising action of the plot usually involves a heightening of the conflict before the climax. After the climax, the action usually falls off.

Character   The characters in a piece of literature are its people or animals. There are several ways in which the author can tell the reader about the characters. You might learn about the characters through what they say or do, through what other characters say about them, or through narration by the author.

Some characters are **static.** They do not change during the course of the story. Other characters are **dynamic.** They, like Scrooge in *A Christmas Carol,* are different at the end of the piece from the way they were at the beginning.

Characters can also be round or flat. A **round** character has a complete personality with many aspects to it. A **flat** character is not fully developed. This kind of character is often a stereotype and is presented as a contrast to the main character, or **protagonist.** If a character is involved in a major conflict with the protagonist, he or she is the **antagonist.** Major characters are usually round, and minor characters are usually flat.

Setting   The place and time in which the action occurs is the setting. Setting can help make other elements of a story more real and believable. It can help the reader understand the characters and help establish a general feeling in which the action unfolds.

Dramatic Technique   Dialogue and soliloquy are the words spoken by the characters. The action of a play unfolds through dialogue. When a character is making a speech alone on the stage, it is called a **soliloquy.** In a **dialogue,** one character speaks to another. An **aside** is the direct address of the audience by a character. In an aside, the other characters do not hear what is being said. It is spoken directly to the audience and often temporarily breaks the illusion that what is happening on the stage is not a play, but reality.

Stage directions indicate the areas of the stage in which the actors move and stand. They establish the physical setting and suggest how the actors speak some of the lines. Stage directions help the reader of a play visualize how it would be performed. They are also guidelines for the play's production on a stage.

As you read *A Christmas Carol,* think about the following questions:

1. What major conflict takes place?
2. What dramatic techniques are used?

A Christmas Carol

by Charles Dickens
adapted by Israel Horovitz

FOCUS ON
DRAMA
STUDY
HINTS

List of
characters

THE PEOPLE OF THE PLAY

JACOB MARLEY, *a specter*

EBENEZER SCROOGE, *not yet dead, which is to say still alive*

BOB CRATCHIT, SCROOGE'S *clerk*

FRED, SCROOGE'S *nephew*

THIN DO-GOODER

PORTLY DO-GOODER

SPECTERS (VARIOUS), *carrying moneyboxes*

THE GHOST OF CHRISTMAS PAST

FOUR JOCUND TRAVELERS

A BAND OF SINGERS

A BAND OF DANCERS

LITTLE BOY SCROOGE

YOUNG MAN SCROOGE

FAN, SCROOGE'S *little sister*

THE SCHOOLMASTER

SCHOOLMATES

FEZZIWIG, *a fine and fair employer*

DICK, *young* SCROOGE'S *co-worker*

YOUNG SCROOGE

A FIDDLER

MORE DANCERS

SCROOGE'S LOST LOVE

SCROOGE'S LOST LOVE'S DAUGHTER

SCROOGE'S LOST LOVE'S HUSBAND

THE GHOST OF CHRISTMAS PRESENT

SOME BAKERS

MRS. CRATCHIT, BOB CRATCHIT'S *wife*

BELINDA CRATCHIT, *a daughter*

MARTHA CRATCHIT, *another daughter*

PETER CRATCHIT, *a son*

TINY TIM CRATCHIT, *another son*

SCROOGE'S NIECE, FRED'S *wife*

THE GHOST OF CHRISTMAS FUTURE, *a mute Phantom*

THREE MEN OF BUSINESS

DRINKERS, SCOUNDRELS, WOMEN OF THE STREETS

A CHARWOMAN

MRS. DILBER

JOE, *an old second-hand goods dealer*

A CORPSE, *very like* SCROOGE

AN INDEBTED FAMILY

ADAM, *a young boy*

A POULTERER

A GENTLEWOMAN

SOME MORE MEN OF BUSINESS

THE PLACE OF THE PLAY: *Various locations in and around the City of London, including Scrooge's Chambers and Offices; the Cratchit Home; Fred's Home; Scrooge's School; Fezziwig's Offices; Old Joe's Hide-a-Way.*

THE TIME OF THE PLAY: *The entire action of the play takes place on Christmas Eve, Christmas Day, and the morning after Christmas, 1843.*

ACT I, SCENE 1

(Ghostly music in auditorium. A single spotlight on JACOB MAR-LEY, D.C. *He is ancient; awful, dead-eyed. He speaks straight out to auditorium.)*

MARLEY *(cackle-voiced):* My name is Jacob Marley and I am dead. *(He laughs.)* Oh, no, there's no doubt that I am dead. The register of my burial was signed by the clergyman, the clerk, the undertaker . . . and by my chief mourner . . . Ebenezer Scrooge . . . *(pause; remembers)* I am dead as a doornail.

(A spotlight fades up, Stage Right, on SCROOGE *in his counting-house,*[1] *counting. Lettering on the window behind* SCROOGE *reads: "SCROOGE AND MARLEY, LTD." The spotlight is tight on* SCROOGE'S *head and shoulders. We shall not yet see into the offices and setting. Ghostly music continues, under.* MARLEY *looks across at* SCROOGE; *pitifully. After a moment's pause)*

I present him to you: Ebenezer Scrooge . . . England's most tightfisted hand at the grindstone, Scrooge! a squeezing, wrenching, grasping, scraping, clutching, covetous, old sinner! secret, and self-contained, and solitary as an oyster. The cold within him freezes his old features, nips his pointed nose, shrivels his cheek, stiffens his gait; makes his eyes red, his thin lips blue; and speaks out shrewdly in his grating voice. Look at him. Look at him . . .

(SCROOGE counts and mumbles.)

---

[1]**counting-house:** an office for keeping financial records and writing business letters

SCROOGE: They owe me money and I will collect. I will have them jailed, if I have to. They owe me money and I will collect what is due me. (MARLEY *moves towards* SCROOGE; *two steps. The spotlight stays with him.*)

MARLEY (*disgusted*): He and I were partners for I don't know how many years. Scrooge was my sole executor, my sole administrator, my sole assign, my sole residuary legatee, my sole friend and my sole mourner. But Scrooge was not so cut up by the sad event of my death, but that he was an excellent man of business on the very day of my funeral, and solemnized it with an undoubted bargain. (*Pauses again in disgust*) He never painted out my name from the window. There it stands, on the window and above the warehouse door: Scrooge and Marley. Sometimes people new to our business call him Scrooge and sometimes they call him Marley. He answers to both names. It's all the same to him. And it's cheaper than painting in a new sign, isn't it? (*Pauses; moves closer to* SCROOGE) Nobody has ever stopped him in the street to say, with gladsome looks, "My dear Scrooge, how are you? When will you come to see me?" No beggars implored him to bestow a trifle, no children ever ask him what it is o'clock, no man or woman now, or ever in his life, not once, inquire the way to such and such a place. (MARLEY *stands next to* SCROOGE *now. They share, so it seems, a spotlight.*) But what does Scrooge care of any of this? It is the very thing he likes! To edge his way along the crowded paths of life, warning all human sympathy to keep its distance.

More exposition

Irony: saying one thing, implying another (Scrooge gave Marley a cheap funeral.)

(*A ghostly bell rings in the distance.* MARLEY *moves away from* SCROOGE, *now, heading D. again. As he does, he "takes" the light:* SCROOGE *has disappeared into the black void beyond.* MARLEY *walks D.C., talking directly to the audience. Pauses*)

Stage directions (D., D.C., etc.): instructions for actors. U = upstage; D = downstage; R,L,C = right, left, center

The bell tolls and I must take my leave. You must stay a while with Scrooge and watch him play out his scroogey life. It is now the story: the once-upon-a-time. Scrooge is busy in his counting-house. Where else? Christmas Eve and Scrooge is busy in his counting-house. It is cold, bleak, biting weather

---

solemnized (SOL um nyzd) honored or remembered; Marley is being ironic

outside: foggy withal: and, if you listen closely, you can hear the people in the court go wheezing up and down, beating their hands upon their breasts, and stamping their feet upon the pavement stones to warm them . . .

(The clocks outside strike three.)

Only three! and quite dark outside already: it has not been light all day this day.

(This ghostly bell rings in the distance again. MARLEY *looks about him. Music in.* MARLEY *flies away.)* (Author's Note: Marley's comings and goings should, from time to time, induce the explosion of the odd flash-pot.)

SCENE 2

(Christmas music in, sung by a live chorus, full. At conclusion of song, sound fades under and into the distance. Lights up in set: offices of Scrooge and Marley, Ltd. SCROOGE *sits at his desk, at work. Near him is a tiny fire. His door is open and in his line of vision, we see* SCROOGE'S *clerk,* BOB CRATCHIT, *who sits in a dismal tank of a cubicle, copying letters. Near* CRATCHIT *is a fire so tiny as to barely cast a light: perhaps it is one pitifully glowing coal?* CRATCHIT *rubs his hands together, puts on a white comforter and tries to heat his hands around his candle.* SCROOGE'S NEPHEW *enters, unseen.)*

Rising action—
complication begins—
first plot event/conflict

SCROOGE: What are you doing, Cratchit? Acting cold, are you? Next, you'll be asking to replenish your coal from my coal-box, won't you? Well, save your breath, Cratchit! Unless you're prepared to find employ elsewhere!

NEPHEW *(cheerfully; surprising* SCROOGE): A merry Christmas to you, Uncle! God save you!

SCROOGE: Bah! Humbug!

More complication—
second conflict

NEPHEW: Christmas a "humbug," Uncle? I'm sure you don't mean that.

SCROOGE: I do! Merry Christmas? What right do you have to be merry? What reason have you to be merry? You're poor enough!

comforter (KUM fur tur) a long, woolen scarf
Humbug (HUM bug) Nonsense!

NEPHEW: Come, then. What right have you to be dismal? What reason have you to be morose? You're rich enough.

SCROOGE: Bah! Humbug!

NEPHEW: Don't be cross, Uncle.

SCROOGE: What else can I be? Eh? When I live in a world of fools such as this? Merry Christmas? What's Christmas time to you but a time of paying bills without any money; a time for finding yourself a year older, but not an hour richer. If I could work my will, every idiot who goes about with "Merry Christmas" on his lips, should be boiled with his own pudding, and buried with a stake of holly through his heart. He should!

Character clues—more exposition

NEPHEW: Uncle!

SCROOGE: Nephew! You keep Christmas in your own way and let me keep it in mine.

NEPHEW: Keep it! But you don't keep it, Uncle.

SCROOGE: Let me leave it alone, then. Much good it has ever done you!

NEPHEW: There are many things from which I have derived good, by which I have not profited, I dare say. Christmas among the rest. But I am sure that I always thought of Christmas time, when it has come round—as a good time: the only time I know of, when men and women seem to open their shut-up hearts freely, and to think of people below them as if they really were fellow-passengers to the grave, and not another race of creatures bound on other journeys. And therefore, Uncle, though it has never put a scrap of gold or silver in my pocket, I believe that it *has* done me good, and that it *will* do me good; and I say, God bless it!

Imagery

(The CLERK *in the tank applauds, looks at the furious* SCROOGE *and pokes out his tiny fire, as if in exchange for the moment of impropriety.* SCROOGE *yells at him.)*

Further conflict

SCROOGE *(to the* CLERK*):* Let me hear another sound from *you* and you'll keep your Christmas by losing your situation. *(To the* NEPHEW*)* You're quite a powerful speaker, sir. I wonder you don't go into Parliament.[2]

---

[2]**Parliament:** the national legislative body of Great Britain, in some ways like the American Congress

NEPHEW: Don't be angry, Uncle. Come! Dine with us tomorrow.

SCROOGE: I'd rather see myself dead than see myself with your family!

NEPHEW: But, why? Why?

SCROOGE: Why did you get married?

NEPHEW: Because I fell in love.

SCROOGE: That, sir, is the only thing that you have said to me in your entire lifetime which is even more ridiculous than "Merry Christmas"! *(Turns from* NEPHEW*)* Good afternoon.

NEPHEW: Nay, Uncle, you never came to see me before I married either. Why give it as a reason for not coming now?

SCROOGE: Good afternoon, Nephew!

NEPHEW: I want nothing from you; I ask nothing of you; why cannot we be friends?

SCROOGE: Good afternoon!

NEPHEW: I am sorry with all my heart, to find you so resolute. But I have made the trial in homage to Christmas, and I'll keep my Christmas humor to the last. So a Merry Christmas, Uncle!

SCROOGE: Good afternoon!

NEPHEW: And a Happy New Year!

SCROOGE: Good afternoon!

NEPHEW *(he stands facing* SCROOGE*):* Uncle, you are the most . . . *(Pauses)* No, I shan't. My Christmas humor is intact . . . *(Pause)* God bless you, Uncle . . . (NEPHEW *turns and starts for the door; he stops at* CRATCHIT'S *cage.)* Merry Christmas, Bob Cratchit . . .

CRATCHIT: Merry Christmas to you sir, and a very, very happy New Year . . .

Exposition: Do you think Cratchit is well-paid?

SCROOGE *(calling across to them):* Oh, fine, a perfection, just fine . . . to see the perfect pair of you: husbands, with wives and children to support . . . my clerk there earning fifteen shillings a week . . . and the perfect pair of you, talking about a Merry Christmas! *(Pauses)* I'll retire to Bedlam![3]

NEPHEW *(to* CRATCHIT*):* He's impossible!

CRATCHIT: Oh, mind him not, sir. He's getting on in years, and he's alone. He's noticed your visit. I'll wager your visit has warmed him.

---

[3]**Bedlam:** a hospital in London for the mentally ill

NEPHEW: Him? Uncle Ebenezer Scrooge? *Warmed?* You are a better Christian than I am, sir.

CRATCHIT *(Opening the door for* NEPHEW*: two* DO-GOODERS *will enter, as* NEPHEW *exits):* Good day to you, sir, and God bless.

NEPHEW: God bless . . . *(One man who enters is portly, the other is thin. Both are pleasant.)*

CRATCHIT: Can I help you, gentlemen?

THIN MAN *(carrying papers and books; looks around* CRATCHIT *to* SCROOGE*):* Scrooge and Marley's, I believe. Have I the pleasure of addressing Mr. Scrooge, or Mr. Marley?

SCROOGE: Mr. Marley has been dead these seven years. He died seven years ago this very night.

PORTLY MAN: We have no doubt his liberality is well represented by his surviving partner . . . *(offers his calling card)*

SCROOGE *(handing back the card; unlooked at):* . . . Good afternoon.

THIN MAN: This will take but a moment, sir . . .

Plot question: Can you see more conflict coming?

PORTLY MAN: At this festive season of the year, Mr. Scrooge, it is more than usually desirable that we should make some slight provision for the poor and destitute, who suffer greatly at the present time. Many thousands are in want of common necessities; hundreds of thousands are in want of common comforts, sir.

SCROOGE: Are there no prisons?

PORTLY MAN: Plenty of prisons.

SCROOGE: And aren't the Union workhouses still in operation?

THIN MAN: They are. Still, I wish that I could say that they are not.

SCROOGE: The Treadmill[4] and the Poor Law[5] are in full vigor, then?

THIN MAN: Both very busy, sir.

SCROOGE: Ohhh, I see. I was afraid, from what you said at first, that something had occurred to stop them from their useful course. *(Pauses)* I'm glad to hear it.

PORTLY MAN: Under the impression that they scarcely furnish Christian cheer of mind or body to the multitude, a few of us are endeavoring to raise a fund to buy the Poor some meat and drink, and means of warmth. We choose this time, because it is a time, of all others, when Want is keenly felt, and Abundance rejoices. *(Pen in hand; as well as notepad)* What shall I put you down for, sir?

Answer to plot question

SCROOGE: Nothing!

PORTLY MAN: You wish to be left anonymous?

SCROOGE: I wish to be left alone! *(Pauses; turns away; turns back to them)* Since you ask me what I wish, gentlemen, that is my answer. I help to support the establishments that I have mentioned: they cost enough: and those who are badly off must go there.

THIN MAN: Many can't go there; and many would rather die.

SCROOGE: If they would rather die, they had better do it, and

---

[4]**Treadmill:** a kind of mill wheel turned by the weight of persons treading steps arranged around it; this device was used to punish prisoners in jails.

[5]**the Poor Law:** A series of laws were passed in England from the 17th century on to help the poor; changes to the law in 1834 gave responsibility for this relief to the national government but did not provide much aid for the poor.

decrease the surplus population. Besides—excuse me—I don't know that.

THIN MAN: But you might know it!

SCROOGE: It's not my business. It's enough for a man to understand his own business, and not to interfere with other people's. Mine occupies me constantly. Good afternoon, gentlemen! (SCROOGE *turns his back on the gentlemen and returns to his desk.*)

PORTLY MAN: But, sir, Mr. Scrooge . . . think of the poor.

SCROOGE (*turns suddenly to them. Pauses*): Take your leave of my offices, sirs, while I am still smiling.

(*The* THIN MAN *looks at the* PORTLY MAN. *They are undone. They shrug. They move to door.* CRATCHIT *hops up to open it for them.*)

THIN MAN: Good day, sir . . . (*To* CRATCHIT) A Merry Christmas to you, sir . . .

CRATCHIT: Yes. A Merry Christmas to both of you . . .

PORTLY MAN: Merry Christmas . . .

(CRATCHIT *silently squeezes something into the hand of the* THIN MAN.)

THIN MAN: What's this?

CRATCHIT: Shhhh . . .

(CRATCHIT *opens the door; wind and snow whistle into the room.*)

THIN MAN: Thank you, sir, thank you.

Character clue: What do you think it is? Why did Cratchit say "Shhhh . . ."?

(CRATCHIT *closes the door and returns to his workplace.* SCROOGE *is at his own counting table. He talks to* CRATCHIT *without looking up.*)

SCROOGE: It's less of a time of year for being merry, and more a time of year for being loony . . . if you ask me.

CRATCHIT: Well, I don't know, sir . . . (*The clock's bell strikes six o'clock.*) Well, there it is, eh, six?

SCROOGE: Saved by six bells, are you?

CRATCHIT: I must be going home . . . (*He snuffs out his candle and puts on his hat.*) I hope you have a . . . very very lovely day tomorrow, sir . . .

SCROOGE: Hmmm. Oh, you'll be wanting the whole day tomorrow, I suppose?

CRATCHIT: If quite convenient, sir.

SCROOGE: It's not convenient, and it's not fair. If I was to stop half-a-crown for it, you'd think yourself ill-used, I'll be bound?

(CRATCHIT smiles faintly.)

CRATCHIT: I don't know, sir . . .

SCROOGE: And yet, you don't think me ill-used, when I pay a day's wages for no work . . .

CRATCHIT: It's only but once a year . . .

SCROOGE: A poor excuse for picking a man's pocket every 25th of December! But I suppose you must have the whole day. Be here all the earlier the next morning!

CRATCHIT: Oh, I will, sir. I will. I promise you. And, sir . . .

SCROOGE: Don't say it, Cratchit.

CRATCHIT: But let me wish you a . . .

SCROOGE: Don't say it, Cratchit. I warn you . . .

CRATCHIT: Sir!

SCROOGE: Cratchit!

(CRATCHIT opens the door.)

CRATCHIT: All right, then, sir . . . well . . . *(Suddenly)* Merry Christmas, Mr. Scrooge!

(And he runs out the door, shutting same behind him. SCROOGE moves to his desk; gathering his coat, hat, etc. A BOY appears at his window . . .)

BOY *(singing):* "Away in a manger . . ."

(SCROOGE seizes his ruler and whacks at the image of the BOY outside. The BOY leaves.)

SCROOGE: Bah! Humbug! Christmas! Bah! Humbug! *(He shuts out the light.)*

A note on the crossover, following Scene 2:
(SCROOGE will walk alone to his rooms from his offices. As he makes a long slow cross of the stage, the scenery should change. Christmas music will be heard, various people will cross by SCROOGE, often smiling happily.
There will be occasional pleasant greetings tossed at him.

(margin note) Metaphor: Christmas is a paid holiday. Do you think this was a law?

(margin note) Setting change

SCROOGE, *in contrast to all, will grump and mumble. He will snap at passing boys, as might a horrid old hound.*

In short, SCROOGE'S *sounds and movements will define him in contrast from all other people who cross the stage: he is the misanthrope, the malcontent, the miser. He is* SCROOGE.

This statement of SCROOGE'S *character, by contrast to all other characters, should seem comical to the audience.*

During SCROOGE'S *crossover to his rooms, snow should begin to fall. All passers-by will hold their faces to the sky, smiling. allowing snow to shower them lightly.* SCROOGE, *by contrast, will bat at the flakes with his walking-stick, as might an insomniac swat at a sleep-stopping, middle-of-the-night swarm of mosquitoes. He will comment on the blackness of the night, and, finally, reach his rooms and his encounter with the magical specter:* MARLEY, *his eternal mate.)*

SCENE 3

SCROOGE: No light at all . . . no moon . . . *that* is what is at the center of a Christmas Eve: dead black: void . . .

Brief soliloquy on feelings about Christmas

(SCROOGE *puts his key in the door's keyhole. He has reached his rooms now. The door knocker changes and is now* MARLEY'S *face. A musical sound; quickly: ghostly.* MARLEY'S *image is not at all angry, but looks at* SCROOGE *as did the old* MARLEY *look at* SCROOGE. *The hair is curiously stirred; eyes wide open, dead: absent of focus.* SCROOGE *stares wordlessly here. The face, before his very eyes, does deliquesce. It is a knocker again.* SCROOGE *opens the door and checks the back of same, probably for* MARLEY'S *pigtail. Seeing nothing but screws and nuts,* SCROOGE *refuses the memory.)*

Pooh, pooh!

(*The sound of the door closing resounds throughout the house as thunder. Every room echoes the sound.* SCROOGE *fastens the door and walks across the hall to the stairs, trimming his candle as he goes; and then he goes slowly up the staircase. He checks each*

---

deliquesce (del ih KWES) melt away

room: sitting room, bedroom, lumber-room. He looks under the sofa, under the table: nobody there. He fixes his evening gruel on the hob, changes his jacket. SCROOGE *sits near the tiny low-flamed fire, sipping his gruel. There are various pictures on the walls: all of them now show likenesses of* MARLEY. SCROOGE *blinks his eyes.)*

Bah! Humbug!

*(*SCROOGE *walks in a circle about the room. The pictures change back into their natural images. He sits down at the table in front of the fire. A bell hangs overhead. It begins to ring, of its own accord. Slowly, surely, begins the ringing of every bell in the house. They continue ringing for nearly half a minute.* SCROOGE *is stunned by the phenomenon. The bells cease their ringing all at once. Deep below* SCROOGE, *in the basement of the house, there is the sound of clanking, of some enormous chain being dragged across the floors; and now up the stairs. We hear doors flying open.)*

Bah still! Humbug still! This is not happening! I won't believe it!

*(*MARLEY'S GHOST *enters the room. He is horrible to look at: pigtail, vest, suit as usual, but he drags an enormous chain now, to which is fastened cash-boxes, keys, padlocks, ledgers, deeds, and heavy purses fashioned of steel. He is transparent.* MARLEY *stands opposite the stricken* SCROOGE.)*

How now! What do you want of me?
MARLEY: Much!
SCROOGE: Who are you?
MARLEY: Ask me who I *was.*
SCROOGE: Who *were* you then?
MARLEY: In life, I was your business partner: Jacob Marley.
SCROOGE: I see . . . can you sit down?
MARLEY: I can.
SCROOGE: Do it then.
MARLEY: I shall. *(*MARLEY *sits opposite* SCROOGE, *in the chair across the table, at the front of the fireplace.)* You don't believe in me.

---

gruel (GROOL) **on the hob** (HOB): a thin broth warming on a ledge at the back side of the fireplace

SCROOGE: I don't.

MARLEY: Why do you doubt your senses?

SCROOGE: Because every little thing affects them. A slight disorder of the stomach makes them cheat. You may be an undigested bit of beef, a blot of mustard, a crumb of cheese, a fragment of an underdone potato. There's more of gravy than of grave about you, whatever you are! *(There is a silence between them.* SCROOGE *is made nervous by it. He picks up a toothpick.)* Humbug! I tell you: humbug! *(*MARLEY *opens his mouth and screams a ghostly, fearful scream. The scream echoes about each room of the house. Bats fly, cats screech, lightning flashes.* SCROOGE *stands and walks backwards against the wall.* MARLEY *stands and screams again. This time, he takes his head and lifts it from his shoulders. His head continues to scream.* MARLEY's *face again appears on every picture in the room: all screaming.* SCROOGE, *on his knees before* MARLEY*)* Mercy! Dreadful apparition, mercy! Why, O! why do you trouble me so?

Metaphor. What does he mean?

Setting and mood change; rising action intensifies

MARLEY: Man of the worldly mind, do you believe in me, or not?

SCROOGE: I do. I must. But why do spirits such as you walk the earth? And why do they come to me?

MARLEY: It is required of every man that the spirit within him should walk abroad among his fellow-men, and travel far and wide; and if that spirit goes not forth in life, it is condemned to do so after death. *(*MARLEY *screams again; a tragic scream from his ghostly bones.)* I wear the chain I forged in life. I made it link by link, and yard by yard. Is its pattern strange to *you?* Or would you know, you, Scrooge, the weight and length of the strong coil you bear yourself? It was full as heavy and long as this, seven Christmas Eves ago. You have labored on it, since. It is a ponderous chain.

Symbolism: The chain is a symbol of what?

(Terrified that a chain will appear about his body, SCROOGE *spins and waves the unwanted chain away. None, of course, appears. Sees* MARLEY *watching him dance about the room.* MARLEY *watches* SCROOGE; *silently.)*

SCROOGE: Jacob. Old Jacob Marley, tell me more. Speak comfort to me, Jacob . . .

---

apparition (ap uh RISH un) ghost

MARLEY: I have none to give. Comfort comes from other regions, Ebenezer Scrooge, and is conveyed by other ministers, to other kinds of men. A very little more, is all that is permitted to me. I cannot rest, I cannot stay, I cannot linger anywhere . . . (*He moans again.*) my spirit never walked beyond our counting-house—mark me!—in life my spirit never roved beyond the narrow limits of our money-changing hole; and weary journeys lie before me!

SCROOGE: But you were always a good man of business, Jacob.

MARLEY (*screams word "business"; a flashpot explodes with him.*): BUSINESS!!! Mankind was my business; charity, mercy, forbearance, benevolence, were, all, my business. (SCROOGE *is quaking.*) Hear me, Ebenezer Scrooge! My time is nearly gone.

SCROOGE: I will, but don't be hard upon me. And don't be flowery, Jacob! Pray!

MARLEY: How is it that I appear before you in a shape that you can see, I may not tell. I have sat invisible beside you many and many a day. That is no light part of my penance. I am here tonight to warn you that you have yet a chance and hope of escaping my fate. A chance and hope of my procuring, Ebenezer.

SCROOGE: You were always a good friend to me. Thank'ee!

MARLEY: You will be haunted by Three Spirits.

SCROOGE: Would that be the chance and hope you mentioned, Jacob?

MARLEY: It is.

SCROOGE: I think I'd rather not.

MARLEY: Without their visits, you cannot hope to shun the path I tread. Expect the first one tomorrow, when the bell tolls one.

SCROOGE: Couldn't I take 'em all at once, and get it over, Jacob?

MARLEY: Expect the second on the next night at the same hour. The third upon the next night when the last stroke of twelve has ceased to vibrate. Look to see me no more. Others may, but you may not. And look that, for your own sake, you remember what has passed between us!

(MARLEY *places his head back upon his shoulders. He approaches the window and beckons to* SCROOGE *to watch. Outside the window, specters fly by, carrying money-boxes and chains. They make*

---

specters (SPEK turz) ghosts

a confused sound of lamentation. MARLEY, *after listening a moment, joins into their mournful dirge. He leans to the window and
floats out into the bleak, dark night. He is gone.)*

SCROOGE *(rushing to the window):* Jacob! No, Jacob! Don't leave
me! I'm frightened!

Indication of a dynamic character. Scrooge is starting to experience some change.

(He sees that MARLEY *has gone. He looks outside. He pulls the
shutter closed, so that the scene is blocked from his view. All
sound stops. After a pause, he re-opens the shutter and all is
quiet, as it should be on Christmas Eve. Carolers carol out of*

doors, in the distance. SCROOGE *closes the shutter and walks down the stairs. He examines the door by which* MARLEY *first entered.)*

No one here at all! Did I imagine all that? Humbug! *(He looks about the room.)* I did imagine it. It only happened in my foulest dream-mind, didn't it? An undigested bit of . . .

(Thunder and lightning in the room; suddenly)

Sorry! Sorry!

(There is silence again. The lights fade out.)

SCENE 4

(Christmas music, choral, "Hark the Herald Angels Sing," sung by an onstage choir of children, spotlighted, D.C. Above, SCROOGE *in his bed, dead to the world, asleep, in his darkened room. It should appear that the choir is singing somewhere outside of the house, of course, and a use of scrim is thus suggested. When the singing is ended, the choir should fade out of view and* MARLEY *should fade into view, in their place.)*

Another aside

MARLEY *(directly to audience):* From this point forth . . . I shall be quite visible to you, but invisible to him. *(Smiles)* He will feel my presence, nevertheless, for, unless my senses fail me completely, we are—you and I—witness to the changing of a miser: that one, my partner in life, in business, and in eternity: that one: SCROOGE. *(Moves to staircase, below* SCROOGE*)* See him now. He endeavors to pierce the darkness with his ferret eyes.[6] *(To audience)* See him, now. He listens for the hour.

(The bells toll. SCROOGE *is awakened and quakes as the hour approaches one o'clock, but the bells stop their sound at the hour of twelve.)*

SCROOGE *(astonished):* Midnight! Why this isn't possible. It was past two when I went to bed. An icicle must have gotten into

---

scrim (SKRIM) a light, semi-transparent curtain
[6]**ferret eyes:** A ferret is a small, weasel-like animal used for hunting rabbits; this expression means to look persistently, the way a ferret hunts.

the clock's works! I couldn't have slept through the whole day and far into another night. It isn't possible that anything has happened to the sun, and this is twelve at noon! *(He runs to window; unshutters same; it is night.)* Night, still. Quiet, normal for the season, cold. It is certainly not noon. I cannot in any way afford to lose my days. Securities come due, promissory notes, interest on investments: these are things that happen in the daylight! *(He returns to his bed.)* Was this a dream?

A soliloquy—Scrooge is speaking with no one present.

(MARLEY appears in his room. He speaks to the audience.)

MARLEY: You see? He does not, with faith, believe in me fully, even still! Whatever will it take to turn the faith of a miser from money to men?

SCROOGE: Another quarter and it'll be one and Marley's ghosty friends will come. *(Pauses; listens)* Where's the chime for one? *(Ding, dong)* A quarter past *(Repeats)* Half-past! *(Repeats)* A quarter to it! But where's the heavy bell of the hour one? This is a game in which I lose my senses! Perhaps, if I allowed myself another short doze . . .

MARLEY: Doze, Ebenezer, doze.

(A heavy bell thuds its one ring; dull and definitely one o'clock. There is a flash of light. SCROOGE sits up, in a sudden. A hand draws back the curtains by his bed. He sees it.)

SCROOGE: A hand! Who owns it! Hello!

(Ghostly music again, but of a new nature to the play. A strange figure stands before SCROOGE—like a child, yet at the same time like an old man: white hair, but unwrinkled skin, long, muscular arms, but delicate legs and feet. Wears white tunic; lustrous belt cinches waist. Branch of fresh green holly in its hand, but has its dress trimmed with fresh summer flowers. Clear jets of light spring from the crown of its head. Holds cap in hand. The Spirit is called PAST.)

Character description, using simile (. . . like . . .)

Are you the Spirit, sir, whose coming was foretold to me?

PAST: I am.

MARLEY: Does he take this to be a vision of his green grocer?

---

promissory notes (PROM ih sawr ee NOHTS): written promises to pay someone a certain sum of money

SCROOGE: Who, and what are you?

PAST: I am the Ghost of Christmas Past.

SCROOGE: Long past?

PAST: Your past.

SCROOGE: May I ask, please, sir, what business you have here with me?

PAST: Your welfare.

SCROOGE: Not to sound ungrateful, sir, and really, please do understand that I am plenty obliged for your concern, but, really, kind spirit, it would have done all the better for my welfare to have been left alone altogether, to have slept peacefully through this night.

PAST: Your reclamation, then. Take heed!

SCROOGE: My what?

PAST *(motioning to* SCROOGE *and taking his arm):* Rise! Fly with me!

(He leads SCROOGE *to the window.)*

More rising action

SCROOGE *(panicked):* Fly, but I am a mortal and cannot fly!

PAST *(pointing to his heart):* Bear but a touch of my hand *here* and you shall be upheld in more than this!

*(*SCROOGE *touches the* SPIRIT'S *heart and the lights dissolve into sparkly flickers. Lovely crystals of music are heard. The scene dissolves into another. Christmas music again)*

SCENE 5

*(*SCROOGE *and the* GHOST OF CHRISTMAS PAST *walk together across an open stage. In the background, we see a field that is open; covered by a soft, downy snow: a country road.)*

SCROOGE: Good Heaven! I was bred in this place. I was a boy here!

*(*SCROOGE *freezes, staring at the field beyond.* MARLEY'S *ghost appears beside him; takes* SCROOGE'S *face in his hands, and turns his face to the audience.)*

MARLEY: You see this Scrooge: stricken by feeling. Conscious of a thousand odors floating in the air, each one connected with a thousand thoughts, and hopes, and joys, and care long, long forgotten. *(Pause)* This one—this Scrooge—before your very eyes, returns to life, among the living. *(To audience, sternly)* You'd best pay your most careful attention. I would suggest rapt.

(There is a small flash and puff of smoke and MARLEY *is gone again.)*

PAST: Your lip is trembling, Mr. Scrooge. And what is that upon your cheek?

SCROOGE: Upon my cheek? Nothing . . . a blemish on the skin from the eating of overmuch grease . . . nothing . . . *(Suddenly)* Kind spirit of Christmas Past, lead me where you will, but *quickly!* To be stagnant in this place is, for me, *unbearable!*

PAST: You recollect the way?

SCROOGE: Remember it! I would know it blindfolded! My bridge, my church, my winding river! *(Staggers about, trying to see it all at once. He weeps again.)*

PAST: These are but shadows of things that have been. They have no consciousness of us.

(Four jocund travelers enter, singing a Christmas song in four-part harmony—"God Rest Ye Merry Gentlemen.")

SCROOGE: Listen! I know these men! I know them! I remember the beauty of their song!

PAST: But, why do you remember it so happily? It is Merry Christmas that they say to one another! What is Merry Christmas to you, Mr. Scrooge? Out upon Merry Christmas, right? What good has Merry Christmas ever done you, Mr. Scrooge? . . .

SCROOGE *(after a long pause):* None. No good. None . . . *(He bows his head.)*

PAST: Look, you, sir, a school ahead. The schoolroom is not quite deserted. A solitary child, neglected by his friends, is left there still.

*(*SCROOGE *falls to the ground; sobbing as he sees, and we see, a small boy, the young* SCROOGE, *sitting and weeping, bravely, alone at his desk: alone in a vast space, a void.)*

---

rapt (RAPT) giving complete attention, totally carried away by something

SCROOGE: I cannot look at him!

PAST: You must, Mr. Scrooge, you must.

Imagery

SCROOGE: It's me. *(Pauses; weeps)* Poor boy. He lived inside his head . . . alone . . . *(Pauses; weeps)* poor boy. *(Pauses; stops his weeping)* I wish . . . *(Dries his eyes on his cuff)* ah! It's too late!

PAST: What is the matter?

Scrooge continues to change—another example of dynamic character

SCROOGE: There was a boy singing a Christmas Carol outside my door last night. I should like to have given him something: that's all.

PAST *(smiles; waves his hand to* SCROOGE*):* Come. Let us see another Christmas.

(Lights out on little boy. A flash of light. A puff of smoke. Lights up on older boy)

SCROOGE: Look! Me, again! Older now! *(Realizes)* Oh, yes . . . still alone.

(The boy—a slightly older SCROOGE *—sits alone in a chair, reading. The door to the room opens and a young girl enters. She is much, much younger than this slightly older* SCROOGE. *She is, say, six, and he is, say, twelve. Elder* SCROOGE *and the* GHOST OF CHRISTMAS PAST *stand watching the scene, unseen.)*

FAN: Dear, dear brother, I have come to bring you home.

BOY: Home, little Fan?

Exposition, character clues. Does this give you some insight about Scrooge's childhood and home life? How did it help make him the man he became?

FAN: Yes! Home, for good and all! Father is so much kinder than he ever used to be, and home's like heaven! He spoke so gently to me one dear night when I was going to bed that I was not afraid to ask him once more if you might come home; and he said "yes" . . . you should; and sent me in a coach to bring you. And you're to be a man and are never to come back here, but first, we're to be together all the Christmas long, and have the merriest time in the world.

BOY: You are quite a woman, little Fan!

(Laughing; she drags at BOY, *causing him to stumble to the door with her. Suddenly we hear a mean and terrible voice in the hallway. Off. It is the* SCHOOLMASTER.*)*

SCHOOLMASTER: Bring down Master Scrooge's travel box at once! He is to travel!

FAN: Who is that, Ebenezer?

BOY: O! Quiet, Fan. It is the Schoolmaster, himself!

(The door bursts open and into the room bursts with it the SCHOOLMASTER.*)*

SCHOOLMASTER: Master Scrooge?

BOY: Oh, Schoolmaster, I'd like you to meet my little sister, Fan, sir . . .

(Two boys struggle on with SCROOGE'S *trunk.)*

FAN: Pleased, sir . . . *(She curtsies.)*

SCHOOLMASTER: You are to travel, Master Scrooge.

SCROOGE: Yes, sir, I know sir . . .

(All start to exit, but FAN *grabs the coattail of the mean old* SCHOOLMASTER.*)*

Schoolmaster is a flat, static character

BOY: Fan!

SCHOOLMASTER: What's this?

FAN: Pardon, sir, but I believe that you've forgotten to say your goodbye to my brother, Ebenezer, who stands still now awaiting it . . . *(She smiles, curtsies, lowers her eyes.)* pardon, sir.

SCHOOLMASTER *(amazed)*: I . . . uh . . . harumph . . . uhh . . . well, then . . . *(Outstretches hand)* Goodbye, Scrooge.

BOY: Uh, well, goodbye, Schoolmaster . . .

(Lights fade out on all but BOY *looking at* FAN; *and* SCROOGE *and* PAST *looking at them.)*

SCROOGE: Oh, my dear, dear little sister, Fan . . . how I loved her.

PAST: Always a delicate creature, whom a breath might have withered, but she had a large heart . . .

Imagery

SCROOGE: So she had.

PAST: She died a woman, and had, as I think, children.

SCROOGE: One child.

PAST: True. Your nephew.

SCROOGE: Yes.

PAST: Fine, then. We move on, Mr. Scrooge. That warehouse, there? Do you know it?

SCROOGE: Know it? Wasn't I apprenticed there?

PAST: We'll have a look.

"Your nephew" is Fred, who was in Scene 2. Character clue: Does this help explain the difference in disposition between Scrooge and his nephew?

---

apprenticed (uh PREN tist) receiving financial support and instruction in a trade in return for work

(They enter the warehouse. The lights crossfade with them, coming up on an old man in Welsh wig: FEZZIWIG.*)*

SCROOGE: Why, it's old Fezziwig! Bless his heart; it's Fezziwig, alive again!

*(*FEZZIWIG *sits behind a large, high desk, counting. He lays down his pen; looks at the clock: seven bells sound.)*

Quittin' time . . .

FEZZIWIG: Quittin' time . . . *(He takes off his waistcoat and laughs; calls off)* Yo ho, Ebenezer! Dick!

*(*DICK WILKINS *and* EBENEZER SCROOGE—*a young man version— enter the room.* DICK *and* EBENEZER *are* FEZZIWIG'S *apprentices.)*

SCROOGE: Dick Wilkins, to be sure! My fellow-'prentice! Bless my soul, yes. There he is. He was very much attached to me, was Dick. Poor Dick! Dear, dear!

FEZZIWIG: Yo ho, my boys. No more work tonight. Christmas Eve, Dick. Christmas, Ebenezer!

(They stand at attention in front of FEZZIWIG; *laughing)*

Hilli-ho! Clear away, and let's have lots of room here! Hilli-ho, Dick! Chirrup, Ebenezer!

(The young men clear the room, sweep the floor, straighten the pictures, trim the lamps, etc. The space is clear now. A fiddler enters, fiddling.)

Hi-ho, Matthew! Fiddle away . . . where are my daughters?

(The FIDDLER *plays. Three young daughters of* FEZZIWIG *enter followed by six young male suitors. They are dancing to the music. All employees come in: workers, clerks, housemaids, cousins, the baker, etc. All dance. Full number wanted here. Throughout the dance, food is brought into the feast. It is "eaten" in dance, by the dancers.* EBENEZER *dances with all three of the daughters, as does* DICK. *They compete for the daughters, happily. In the dance,* FEZZIWIG *dances with his daughters.* FEZZIWIG *dances with* DICK *and* EBENEZER. *The music changes:* MRS. FEZZIWIG *enters. She lovingly scolds her husband. They dance. She dances with* EBENEZER, *lifting him and throwing him about. She*

is enormously fat. When the dance is ended, they all dance off, floating away, as does the music. SCROOGE *and the* GHOST OF CHRIST-MAS PAST *stand alone now. The music is gone.)*

PAST: It was a small matter, that Fezziwig made those silly folks so full of gratitude.

SCROOGE: Small?

PAST: Shhh!

(Lights up on DICK *and* EBENEZER*)*

DICK: We are blessed, Ebenezer, truly, to have such a master as Mr. Fezziwig!

Irony: ghost means the opposite

Metaphor: Fezziwig is compared to a schoolteacher.

YOUNG SCROOGE: He is the best, best, the very and absolute best! If ever I own a firm of my own, I shall treat my apprentices with the same dignity and the same grace. We have learned a wonderful lesson from the master, Dick!

DICK: Ah, that's a fact, Ebenezer. That's a fact!

PAST: Was it not a small matter, really? He spent but a few pounds of his mortal money on your small party. Three or four pounds, perhaps. Is that so much that he deserves such praise as you and Dick so lavish now?

SCROOGE: It isn't that! It isn't that, Spirit. Fezziwig had the power to make us happy or unhappy; to make our service light or burdensome; a pleasure or a toil. The happiness he gave is quite as great as if it cost him a fortune.

PAST: What is the matter?

SCROOGE: Nothing particular.

PAST: Something, I think.

SCROOGE: No, no. I should like to be able to say a word or two to my clerk just now! That's all!

(EBENEZER enters the room and shuts down all the lamps. He stretches and yawns. The GHOST OF CHRISTMAS PAST turns to SCROOGE; all of a sudden.)

PAST: My time grows short! Quick!

Who do you think this character is? Why is she upset?

(In a flash of light, EBENEZER is gone, and in his place stands an OLDER SCROOGE, this one a man in the prime of his life. Beside him stands a young woman in a mourning dress. She is crying. She speaks to the man, with hostility.)

Imagery

WOMAN: It matters little . . . to you, very little. Another idol has displaced me.

MAN: What idol has displaced you?

WOMAN: A golden one.

MAN: This is an even-handed dealing of the world. There is nothing on which it is so hard as poverty; and there is nothing it professes to condemn which such severity as the pursuit of wealth!

Allegorical reference

WOMAN: You fear the world too much. Have I not seen your nobler aspirations fall off one by one, until the master-passion, Gain, engrosses you? Have I not?

---

pounds (POUNDZ) a common type of money used in Great Britain

SCROOGE: No!

MAN: What then? Even if I have grown so much wiser, what then? Have I changed towards you?

WOMAN: No . . .

MAN: Am I?

WOMAN: Our contract is an old one. It was made when we were both poor and content to be so. You *are* changed. When it was made, you were another man.

MAN: I was not another man: I was a boy.

WOMAN: Your own feeling tells you that you were not what you are. I am. That which promised happiness when we were one in heart is fraught with misery now that we are two . . .

SCROOGE: No!

WOMAN: How often and how keenly I have thought of this, I will not say. It is enough that I *have* thought of it, and can release you . . .

SCROOGE *(quietly):* Don't release me, madame . . .

MAN: Have I ever sought release?

WOMAN: In words, No. Never.

MAN: In what then?

WOMAN: In a changed nature; in an altered spirit. In everything that made my love of any worth or value in your sight. If this has never been between us, tell me, would you seek me out and try to win me now? Ah, no!

SCROOGE: Ah, yes!

MAN: You think not?

WOMAN: I would gladly think otherwise if I could, heaven knows! But if you were free today, tomorrow, yesterday, can even I believe that you would choose a dowerless girl[7]—you who in your very confidence with her weigh everything by Gain; or, choosing her, do I not know that your repentance and regret would surely follow? I do; and I release you. With a full heart, for the love of him you once were.

SCROOGE: Please, I . . . I . . .

MAN: Please, I . . . I . . .

WOMAN: Please. You may—the memory of what is past half makes me hope you will—have pain in this. A very, very

---

[7]**dowerless girl:** a girl without a dowery, the property or wealth a woman brought to her husband at marriage

brief time, and you will dismiss the memory of it, as an unprofitable dream, from which it happened well that you awoke. May you be happy in the life that you have chosen for yourself . . .

SCROOGE: No!

WOMAN: Yourself . . . alone . . .

SCROOGE: No!

WOMAN: Goodbye, Ebenezer . . .

SCROOGE: Don't let her go!

MAN: Goodbye.

SCROOGE: No!

(She exits. SCROOGE *goes to younger man: himself.)*

You fool! Mindless loon! You fool!

MAN *(to exited woman):* Fool. Mindless loon. Fool . . .

SCROOGE: Don't say that! Spirit, remove me from this place.

PAST: I have told you these were shadows of the things that have been. They are what they are. Do not blame me, Mr. Scrooge.

SCROOGE: Remove me! I cannot bear it!

(The faces of all who appeared in this scene are now projected for a moment around the stage: enormous, flimsy, silent.)

Leave me! Take me back! Haunt me no longer!

(There is a sudden flash of light: a flare. The GHOST OF CHRISTMAS PAST *is gone.* SCROOGE *is, for the moment, alone on-stage. His bed is turned down, across the stage. A small candle burns now in* SCROOGE'S *hand. There is a child's cap in his other hand. He slowly crosses the stage to his bed, to sleep.* MARLEY *appears behind* SCROOGE, *who continues his long, elderly cross to bed.* MARLEY *speaks directly to the audience.)*

MARLEY: Scrooge must sleep now. He must surrender to the irresistible drowsiness caused by the recognition of what was. *(Pauses)* The cap he carries is from ten lives past: his boyhood cap . . . donned atop a hopeful hairy head . . . askew, perhaps, or at a rakish angle. Doffed now in honor of regret.[8]

---

[8]**donned . . . regret:** To *don and doff a hat* means to put it on and take it off; askew means "crooked," and *at a rakish angle* means "having a dashing or jaunty look."

Perhaps even too heavy to carry in his present state of weak remorse . . .

(SCROOGE *drops the cap. He lies atop his bed. He sleeps. To audience*) He sleeps. For him, there's even more trouble ahead. (*Smiles*) For you? The playhouse tells me there's hot cider, as should be your anticipation for the specter Christmas Present and Future, for I promise you both. (*Smiles again*) So, I pray you hurry back to your seats refreshed and ready for a miser —to turn his coat of gray into a blazen Christmas holly-red.

(*A flash of lightning. A clap of thunder. Bats fly. Ghostly music.* MARLEY *is gone.*)

ACT II, SCENE 1

(*Lights. Choral music is sung. Curtain.* SCROOGE, *in bed, sleeping, in spotlight. We cannot yet see the interior of his room.* MARLEY, *opposite, in spotlight equal to* SCROOGE'S. MARLEY *laughs. He tosses his head in the air and a flame shoots from it, magically, into the air. There is a thunder clap, and then another; a lightning flash, and then another. Ghostly music plays under. Colors change.* MARLEY'S *spotlight has gone out and now reappears, with* MARLEY *in it, standing next to the bed and the sleeping* SCROOGE. MARLEY *addresses the audience directly.*)

MARLEY: Hear this snoring Scrooge! Sleeping to escape the nightmare that is his waking day. What shall I bring to him now? I'm afraid nothing would astonish Old Scrooge now. Not after what he's seen. Not a baby boy, not a rhinoceros, nor anything in between would astonish Ebenezer Scrooge just now. I can think of nothing . . . (*Suddenly*) that's it! nothing! (*He speaks confidently.*) I'll have the clock strike one and, when he awakes expecting my second messenger, there will be no one . . . nothing. Then I'll have the bell strike twelve. And then one again . . . and the nothing. Nothing . . . (*Laughs*) nothing will . . . astonish him. I think it will work.

(*The bell tolls one.* SCROOGE *leaps awake.*)

SCROOGE: One! One! This is it; time! (*Looks about the room*) Nothing!

(The bell tolls midnight.)

Midnight! How can this be? I'm sleeping backwards.

(One again)

Good heavens! One again! I'm sleeping back and forth! *(A pause.* SCROOGE *looks about.)* Nothing! Absolutely nothing!

(Suddenly, thunder and lightning. MARLEY *laughs and disappears. The room shakes and glows. There is suddenly springlike music.* SCROOGE *makes a run for the door.)*

MARLEY: Scrooge!
SCROOGE: What?
MARLEY: Stay you put!
SCROOGE: Just checking to see if anyone is in here.

(Lights and thunder again: more music. MARLEY *is of a sudden gone. In his place sits the* GHOST OF CHRISTMAS PRESENT—*to be called in the stage directions of the play,* PRESENT—*center of room. Heaped up on the floor, to form a kind of throne, are turkeys, geese, game, poultry, brawn, great joints of meat, suckling pigs, long wreaths of sausages, mince-pies, plum puddings, barrels of oysters, red hot chestnuts, cherry-cheeked apples, juicy oranges, luscious pears, immense twelfth cakes, and seething bowls of punch, that make the chamber dim with their delicious steam. Upon this throne sits* PRESENT, *glorious to see. He bears a torch, shaped as a Horn of Plenty.[9]* SCROOGE *hops out of the door, and then peeks back again into his bedroom.* PRESENT *calls to* SCROOGE.)*

PRESENT: Ebenezer Scrooge. Come in, come in! Come in and know me better!
SCROOGE: Hello. How should I call you?
PRESENT: I am the Ghost of Christmas Present. Look upon me.

*(*PRESENT *is wearing a simple green robe. The walls around the room are now covered in greenery, as well. The room seems to be a perfect grove now: leaves of holly, mistletoe and ivy reflect the stage lights. Suddenly, there is a mighty roar of flame in the*

---

[9]**horn of plenty:** a horn overflowing with fruits, flowers, and grain, standing for wealth and abundance

fireplace and now the hearth burns with a lavish, warming fire. There is an ancient scabbard girdling the GHOST'S *middle, but without sword. The sheath is gone to rust.)*

You have never seen the like of me before?

SCROOGE: Never.

PRESENT: You have never walked forth with younger members of my family; my elder brothers born on Christmases past.

SCROOGE: I don't think I have. I'm afraid I've not. Have you had many brothers, Spirit?

PRESENT: More than eighteen hundred.

SCROOGE: A tremendous family to provide for! *(PRESENT stands)* Spirit, conduct me where you will. I went forth last night on compulsion, and learnt a lesson which is working now. To-night, if you have aught to teach me, let me profit by it.

PRESENT: Touch my robe.

Another plot clue

(SCROOGE walks cautiously to PRESENT *and touches his robe. When he does, lightning flashes, thunder claps, music plays. Blackout)*

SCENE 2

(PROLOGUE; MARLEY *stands spotlit, L. He speaks directly to the audience.)*

MARLEY: My ghostly friend now leads my living partner through the city's streets.

(Lights up on SCROOGE *and* PRESENT*)*

See them there and hear the music people make when the weather is severe, as it is now.

(Winter music. Choral group behind scrim, sings. When the song is done and the stage is re-set, the lights will fade up on a row of shops, behind the singers. The choral group will hum the song they have just completed now and mill about the streets,[10] carrying their dinners to the bakers' shops and restaurants. They will, perhaps, sing about being poor at Christmastime, whatever.)

---

[10]**mill about the streets:** walk around aimlessly

PRESENT: These revelers, Mr. Scrooge, carry their own dinners to their jobs, where they will work to bake the meals the rich men and women of this city will eat as their Christmas dinners. Generous people these . . . to care for the others, so . . .

(PRESENT *walks among the choral group and a sparkling incense falls from his torch on to their baskets, as he pulls the covers off of the baskets. Some of the choral group become angry with each other.*)

MAN #1: Hey, you, watch where you're going.
MAN #2: Watch it yourself, mate!

(PRESENT *sprinkles them directly, they change.*)

MAN #1: I pray go in ahead of me. It's Christmas. You be first!
MAN #2: No, no, I must insist that YOU be first!
MAN #1: All right, I shall be, and gratefully so.
MAN #2: The pleasure is equally mine, for being able to watch you pass, smiling.
MAN #1: I would find it a shame to quarrel on Christmas Day . . .
MAN #2: As would I.
MAN #1: Merry Christmas then, friend!
MAN #2: And a Merry Christmas straight back to you!

(*Church bells toll. The choral group enter the buildings; the shops and restaurants; they exit the stage, shutting their doors closed behind them. All sound stops.* SCROOGE *and* PRESENT *are alone again.*)

SCROOGE: What is it you sprinkle from your torch?
PRESENT: Kindness.
SCROOGE: Do you sprinkle your kindness on any particular people or on all people?
PRESENT: To any person kindly given. And to the very poor most of all.
SCROOGE: Why to the very poor most?
PRESENT: Because the very poor need it most. Touch my heart . . . here, Mr. Scrooge. We have another journey.

---

incense (IN sens) any of various substances that produce a pleasant odor when burned

(SCROOGE *touches the* GHOST'S *heart and music plays, lights change color, lightning flashes, thunder claps. A choral group appears on the street, singing Christmas carols.*)

SCENE 3

(MARLEY *stands spotlit in front of a scrim on which is painted the exterior of* CRATCHIT'S *four-roomed house. There is a flash and a clap and* MARLEY *is gone. The lights shift color again, the scrim flies away, and we are in the interior of the* CRATCHIT *family home.* SCROOGE *is there, with the* SPIRIT (PRESENT), *watching* MRS. CRATCHIT *set the table, with the help of* BELINDA CRATCHIT *and* PETER CRATCHIT, *a baby, pokes a fork into the mashed potatoes on his highchair's tray. He also chews on his shirt collar.*)

SCROOGE: What is this place, Spirit?

PRESENT: This is the home of your employee, Mr. Scrooge. Don't you know it?

SCROOGE: Do you mean Cratchit, Spirit? Do you mean this is Cratchit's home?

PRESENT: None other.

SCROOGE: These children are his?

PRESENT: There are more to come presently.

SCROOGE: On his meager earnings! What foolishness!

PRESENT: Foolishness, is it?

SCROOGE: Wouldn't you say so? Fifteen shillings[11] a week's what he gets!

PRESENT: I would say that he gets the pleasure of his family, fifteen times a week times the number of hours a day! Wait, Mr. Scrooge. Wait, listen and watch. You might actually learn something . . .

MRS. CRATCHIT: What has ever got your precious father then? And your brother, Tiny Tim? And Martha warn't as late last Christmas by half an hour!

(MARTHA *opens the door, speaking to her mother as she does.*)

---

[11]**fifteen shillings:** a small amount of money for a week's work

MARTHA: Here's Martha, now, Mother! *(She laughs. The* CRATCHIT CHILDREN *squeal with delight.)*

BELINDA: It's Martha, Mother! Here's Martha!

PETER: Marthmama, Marthmama! Hullo!

BELINDA: Hurrah! Martha! Martha! There's such a enormous goose for us, Martha!

MRS. CRATCHIT: Why, bless your heart alive, my dear, how late you are!

MARTHA: We'd a great deal of work to finish up last night, and had to clear away this morning, Mother.

MRS. CRATCHIT: Well, never mind so long as you are come. Sit ye down before the fire, my dear, and have a warm, Lord bless ye!

BELINDA: No, no! There's Father coming. Hide, Martha, hide!

*(*MARTHA *giggles and hides herself.)*

MARTHA: Where? Here?

PETER: *Hide, hide!*

BELINDA: Not there! *THERE!*

*(*MARTHA *is hidden.* BOB CRATCHIT *enters, carrying* TINY TIM *atop his shoulder. He wears a threadbare and fringeless comforter hanging down in front of him.* TINY TIM *carries small crutches and his small legs are bound in an iron frame brace.)*

BOB AND TINY TIM: Merry Christmas.

BOB: Merry Christmas my love, Merry Christmas Peter, Merry Christmas Belinda. Why, where is Martha?

MRS. CRATCHIT: Not coming.

BOB: Not coming? Not coming upon Christmas Day?

MARTHA *(pokes head out):* Ohhh, poor Father. Don't be disappointed.

BOB: What's this?

MARTHA: 'Tis I!

BOB: Martha! *(They embrace.)*

TINY TIM: Martha! Martha!

MARTHA: Tiny Tim!

*(*TINY TIM *is placed in* MARTHA'S *arms.* BELINDA *and* PETER *rush him offstage.)*

BELINDA: Come, brother! You must come hear the pudding singing in the copper.

Personification

TINY TIM: The pudding? What flavor have we?

PETER: Plum! Plum!

TINY TIM: Oh, Mother! I love plum!

(The children exit the stage, giggling.)

MRS. CRATCHIT: And how did little Tim behave?

BOB: As good as gold, and even better. Somehow he gets thoughtful sitting by himself so much, and thinks the strangest things you ever heard. He told me, coming home, that he hoped people saw him in the church, because he was crippled, and it might be pleasant to them to remember upon Christmas Day, who made lame beggars walk and blind men see. *(Pauses)* He has the oddest ideas sometimes, but he seems all the while to be growing stronger and more hearty . . . one would never know.

Character clue about Tiny Tim

(Hears TIM'S crutch on floor outside door)

PETER: The goose has arrived to be eaten!

BELINDA: Oh, mama, mama, it's beautiful.

MARTHA: It's a perfect goose, Mother!

TINY TIM: To this Christmas goose, Mother and Father I say . . . *(Yells)* Hurray! Hurrah!

OTHER CHILDREN *(copying TIM):* Hurrah! Hurrah!

(The family sits round the table. BOB and MRS. CRATCHIT serve the trimmings, quickly. All sit; all bow heads; all pray.)

BOB: Thank you, dear Lord, for your many gifts . . . our dear children; our wonderful meal; our love for one another; and the warmth of our small fire—*(Looks up at all)* A merry Christmas to us, my dear. God bless us!

ALL *(except TIM):* Merry Christmas! God bless us!

TINY TIM *(in a short silence):* God bless us every one.

(All freeze. Spotlight on PRESENT and SCROOGE)

SCROOGE: Spirit, tell me if Tiny Tim will live.

PRESENT: I see a vacant seat . . . in the poor chimney corner, and a crutch without an owner, carefully preserved. If these shadows remain unaltered by the future, the child will die.

SCROOGE: No, no, kind Spirit! Say he will be spared!

PRESENT: If these shadows remain unaltered by the future, none other of my race will find him here. What then? If he be like to die, he had better do it, and decrease the surplus population.

(SCROOGE bows his head. We hear BOB's voice speak SCROOGE's name.)

BOB: Mr. Scrooge . . .

SCROOGE: Huh? What's that? Who calls?

BOB *(his glass raised in a toast):* I'll give you Mr. Scrooge, the Founder of the Feast!

SCROOGE: Me, Bob? You toast *me?*

PRESENT: Save your breath, Mr. Scrooge. You can't be seen or heard.

MRS. CRATCHIT: The founder of the Feast, indeed! I wish I had him here, that miser Scrooge. I'd give him a piece of my mind to feast upon, and I hope he'd have a good appetite for it!

BOB: My dear! Christmas Day!

MRS. CRATCHIT: It should be Christmas Day, I am sure, on which one drinks the health of such an odious, stingy, unfeeling man as Mr. Scrooge . . .

SCROOGE: Oh, Spirit, must I? . . .

MRS. CRATCHIT: You know he is, Robert! Nobody knows it better than you do, poor fellow!

BOB: This is Christmas Day, and I should like to drink to the health of the man who employs me and allows me to earn my living and our support and that man is Ebenezer Scrooge . . .

MRS. CRATCHIT: I'll drink to his health for your sake and the day's, but not for his sake . . . a Merry Christmas and a Happy New Year to you, Mr. Scrooge, wherever you may be this day!

SCROOGE: Just here, kind madam . . . out of sight, out of sight . . .

BOB: Thank you, my dear. Thank you.

SCROOGE: Thank *you,* Bob . . . and Mrs. Cratchit, too. No one else is toasting me . . . not now . . . not ever. Of that I am sure . . .

BOB: Children . . .

ALL: Merry Christmas to Mr. Scrooge.

BOB: I'll pay you sixpence, Tim, for my favorite song.

TINY TIM: Oh, Father, I'd so love to sing it, but not for pay. This Christmas goose—this feast—you and Mother, my brother and sisters close with me: that's my pay—

BOB: Martha, will you play the notes on the lute, for Tiny Tim's song.

BELINDA: May I sing, too, Father?

BOB: We'll all sing.

(They sing a song about a tiny child lost in the snow—probably from Wordsworth's poem. TIM sings the lead vocal; all chime in for the chorus. Their song fades under, as the GHOST OF CHRISTMAS PRESENT speaks.)

PRESENT: Mark my words, Ebenezer Scrooge. I do not present the Cratchits to you because they are a handsome, or brilliant family. They are not handsome. They are not brilliant. They are not well-dressed, or tasteful to the times. Their shoes are not even waterproofed by virtue of money or cleverness spent. So when the pavement is wet, so are the insides of their shoes and the tops of their toes. These are the Cratchits, Mr. Scrooge. They are not highly special. They are happy, grateful, pleased with one another, contented with the time and how it passes. They don't sing very well, do they? But, nonetheless, they do sing . . . *(Pauses)* think of that, Scrooge. Fifteen shillings a week and they do sing . . . hear their song until its end.

SCROOGE: I am listening.

(The chorus sings full volume now, until . . . the song ends here.)

Spirit, it must be time for us to take our leave. I feel in my heart that it is . . . that I must think on that which I have seen here . . .

PRESENT: Touch my robe again . . .

(SCROOGE touches PRESENT's robe. The lights fade out on the CRATCHITS, who sit, frozen, at the table. SCROOGE and PRESENT in a spotlight now. Thunder, lightning, smoke. They are gone.)

---

lute (LOOT) an old-fashioned stringed instrument like a guitar

SCENE 4

(MARLEY appears D.L. in single spotlight. A storm brews. Thunder and lightning. SCROOGE and PRESENT "fly" past, U. The storm continues, furiously, and now and again, SCROOGE and PRESENT will zip past in their travels. MARLEY will speak straight out to the audience.)

MARLEY: The Ghost of Christmas Present, my co-worker in this attempt to turn a miser, flies about now with that very miser, Scrooge, from street to street, and he points out partygoers on their way to Christmas parties. If one were to judge from the numbers of people on their way to friendly gatherings, one might think that no one was left at home to give anyone welcome . . . but that's not the case, is it? Every home is expecting company and . . . *(He laughs)* Scrooge is amazed.

(SCROOGE and PRESENT zip past again. The lights fade up around them. We are in the NEPHEW's home, in the living room, PRESENT and SCROOGE stand watching the NEPHEW: FRED and his WIFE, fixing the fire.)

SCROOGE: What is this place? We've moved from the mines!
PRESENT: You do not recognize them?
SCROOGE: It is my nephew! . . . and the one he married . . .

(MARLEY waves his hand and there is a lightning flash. He disappears.)

FRED: It strikes me as sooooo funny, to think of what he said . . . that Christmas was a humbug, as I live! He believed it!
WIFE: More shame for him, Fred!
FRED: Well, he's a comical old fellow, that's the truth.
WIFE: I have no patience with him.
FRED: Oh, I have! I am sorry for him; I couldn't be angry with him if I tried. Who suffers by his ill whims? Himself, always . . .
SCROOGE: It's me they talk of, isn't it, Spirit?
FRED: Here, wife, consider this. Uncle Scrooge takes it into his head to dislike us, and he won't come and dine with us. What's the consequence?
WIFE: Oh . . . you're sweet to say what I think you're about to say, too, Fred . . .

FRED: What's the consequence? He don't lose much of a dinner by it, I can tell you that!

WIFE: Ooooooo, Fred! Indeed, I think he loses a very good dinner . . . ask my sisters, or your bachelor friend, Topper . . . ask any of them. They'll tell you what old Scrooge, your uncle, missed: a dandy meal!

FRED: Well, that's something of a relief, wife. Glad to hear it! *(He hugs his wife. They laugh. They kiss.)* The truth is, he misses much yet. I mean to give him the same chance every year, whether he likes it or not, for I pity him. Nay, he is my only uncle and I feel for the old miser . . . but, I tell you, wife: I see my dear and perfect mother's face on his own wizened cheeks and brow: brother and sister they were, and I cannot erase that from each view of him I take . . .

WIFE: I understand what you say, Fred, and I am with you in your yearly asking. But he never will accept, you know. He never will.

FRED: Well, true, wife. Uncle may rail at Christmas till he dies. I think I shook him some with my visit yesterday . . . *(Laughing)* I refused to grow angry . . . *(Whoops)* It was HE who grew angry, wife! *(They both laugh now.)*

SCROOGE: What he says is true, Spirit . . .

FRED AND WIFE: Bah, humbug!

FRED *(embracing his wife):* There is much laughter in our marriage, wife. It pleases me. You please me . . .

WIFE: And you please me, Fred. You are a good man . . . *(They embrace)* Come now. We must have a look at the meal . . . our guests will soon arrive . . . my sisters, Topper . . .

FRED: A toast first . . . *(He hands her a glass.)* A toast to Uncle Scrooge . . . *(Fills their glasses)*

WIFE: A toast to him?

FRED: Uncle Scrooge has given us plenty of merriment, I am sure, and it would be ungrateful not to drink to his health. And I say . . . *Uncle Scrooge!*

WIFE *(laughing):* You're a proper loon,[12] Fred . . . and I'm a proper wife for you . . . *(She raises her glass.)* Uncle Scrooge! *(They drink. They embrace. They kiss.)*

---

[12] **a proper loon:** a silly person

SCROOGE: Spirit, please, make me visible! Make me audible! I want to talk with my nephew and my niece!

(Calls out to them. The lights that light the room and FRED *and wife fade out.* SCROOGE *and* PRESENT *are alone, spotlit.)*

PRESENT: These shadows are gone to you now, Mr. Scrooge. You may return to them later tonight in your dreams. *(Pauses)* My time grows short, Ebenezer Scrooge. Look you on me! Do you see how I've aged?

SCROOGE: Your hair has gone gray! Your skin, wrinkled! Are spirits' lives so short?

PRESENT: My stay upon this globe is very brief. It ends tonight.

SCROOGE: Tonight?

PRESENT: At midnight. The time is drawing near!

(Clock strikes 11:45.)

Hear those chimes? In a quarter hour, my life will have been spent! Look, Scrooge, man. Look you here.

(Two gnarled baby dolls are taken from PRESENT'S *skirts.)*

SCROOGE: Who are they?

PRESENT: They are Man's children, and they cling to me, appealing from their fathers. The boy is Ignorance; the girl is Want. Beware them both, and all of their degree, but most of all beware this boy, for I see that written on his brow which is doom, unless the writing be erased.

(He stretches out his arm. His voice is now amplified: loudly and oddly.)

SCROOGE: Have they no refuge or resource?

PRESENT: Are there no prisons? Are there no workhouses? *(Twelve chimes)* Are there no prisons? Are there no workhouses?

(A PHANTOM, *hooded, appears in dim light, D., opposite.)*

Are there no prisons? Are there no workhouses?

*(*PRESENT *begins to deliquesce.* SCROOGE *calls after him.)*

SCROOGE: Spirit, I'm frightened! Don't leave me! Spirit!

PRESENT: Prisons? Workhouses? Prisons? Workhouses . . .

(He is gone. SCROOGE *is alone now with the* PHANTOM, *who is, of course,* the GHOST OF CHRISTMAS FUTURE. *The* PHANTOM *is shrouded in black. Only its outstretched hand is visible from under his ghostly garment.)*

SCROOGE: Who are you, Phantom? Oh, yes, I think I know you! You are, are you not, the Spirit of Christmas Yet to Come? *(No reply)* And you are about to show me the shadows of the things that have not yet happened, but will happen in time before us. Is that not so, Spirit?

(The PHANTOM *allows* SCROOGE *a look at his face. No other reply wanted here. A nervous giggle here.)*

Oh, Ghost of the Future, I fear you more than any Specter I have seen! But, as I know that your purpose is to do me good and as I hope to live to be another man from what I was, I am prepared to bear you company.

(FUTURE *does not reply, but for a stiff arm, hand and finger set, pointing forward.*)

Lead on, then, lead on. The night is waning fast, and it is precious time to me. Lead on, Spirit!

(FUTURE *moves away from* SCROOGE *in the same rhythm and motion employed at its arrival.* SCROOGE *falls into the same pattern, a considerable space apart from the* SPIRIT. *In the space between them,* MARLEY *appears. He looks to* FUTURE *and then to* SCROOGE. *He claps his hands. Thunder and lightning. Three* BUSINESSMEN *appear, spotlighted singularly: One is D.L.; One is D.R.; One is U.C. Thus, six points of the stage should now be spotted in light.* MARLEY *will watch this scene from his position,* C. SCROOGE *and* FUTURE *are R. and L. of C.*)

FIRST BUSINESSMAN: Oh, no, I don't know much about it either way, I only know he's dead.

SECOND BUSINESSMAN: When did he die?

FIRST BUSINESSMAN: Last night, I believe.

SECOND BUSINESSMAN: Why, what was the matter with him? I thought he'd never die, really . . .

FIRST BUSINESSMAN *(yawning):* Goodness knows, goodness knows . . .

THIRD BUSINESSMAN: What has he done with his money?

SECOND BUSINESSMAN: I haven't heard. Have you?

FIRST BUSINESSMAN: Left it to his Company, perhaps. Money to money; you know the expression . . .

THIRD BUSINESSMAN: He hasn't left it to *me.* That's all I know . . .

FIRST BUSINESSMAN *(laughing):* Nor to me . . . (*Looks at* SECOND BUSINESSMAN) You, then? You got his money???

SECOND BUSINESSMAN *(laughing):* Me, Me, his money? Nooooo! (*They all laugh.*)

THIRD BUSINESSMAN: It's likely to be a cheap funeral, for upon my life, I don't know of a living soul who'd care to venture to it. Suppose we make up a party and volunteer?

SECOND BUSINESSMAN: I don't mind going if a lunch is provided, but I must be fed, if I make one.

FIRST BUSINESSMAN: Well, I am the most disinterested among you, for I never wear black gloves, and I never eat lunch. But I'll offer to go, if anybody else will. When I come to think of it, I'm not all sure that I wasn't his most particular friend; for we used to stop and speak whenever we met. Well, then . . . bye, bye!

SECOND BUSINESSMAN: Bye, bye . . .

THIRD BUSINESSMAN: Bye, bye . . .

(They glide offstage in three separate directions. Their lights follow them.)

SCROOGE: Spirit, why did you show me this? Why do you show me businessmen from my streets as they take the death of Jacob Marley? That is a thing past. You are *future!*

(JACOB MARLEY laughs a long, deep laugh. There is a thunder clap and lightning flash, and he is gone. SCROOGE faces FUTURE, alone on stage now. FUTURE wordlessly stretches out his arm-hand-and-finger-set, pointing into the distance, U. There, above them, Scoundrels "fly" by, half-dressed and slovenly. When this scene is passed, a woman enters the playing area. She is almost at once followed by a second woman: and then a man in faded black; and then, suddenly an old man, who smokes a pipe. The old man scares the other three. They laugh, anxious.)

FIRST WOMAN: Look here, old Joe, here's a chance! If we haven't all three met here without meaning it!

OLD JOE: You couldn't have met in a better place. Come into the parlor. You were made free of it long ago, you know; and the other two ain't strangers. *(He stands; shuts a door. Shrieking)* We're all suitable to our calling. We're well matched. Come into the parlor. Come into the parlor . . .

> Plot questions: What is the setting here? Who are these people and what are these people doing?

(They follow him D. SCROOGE and FUTURE are now in their midst, watching; silent. A truck comes in on which is set a small wall with fireplace and a screen of rags, etc. All props for the scene.)

Let me just rake this fire over a bit . . .

(He does. He trims his lamp with the stem of his pipe. The FIRST WOMAN throws a large bundle onto the floor. She sits beside it, crosslegged; defiantly.)

FIRST WOMAN: What odds then? What odds, Mrs. Dilber? Every person has a right to take care of themselves. HE always did!

MRS. DILBER: That's true indeed! No man more so!

FIRST WOMAN: Why, then, don't stand staring as if you was afraid, woman! Who's the wiser? We're not going to pick holes in each other's coats, I suppose?

MRS. DILBER: No, indeed! We should hope not!

FIRST WOMAN: Very well, then! That's enough. Who's the worse for the loss of a few things like these? Not a dead man, I suppose?

MRS. DILBER *(laughing):* No, indeed!

FIRST WOMAN: If he wanted to keep 'em after he was dead, the wicked old screw, why wasn't he natural in his lifetime? If he had been, he'd have had somebody to look after him when he was struck with Death, instead of lying gasping out his last there, alone by himself.

MRS. DILBER: It's the truest word that was ever spoke. It's a judgment on him.

FIRST WOMAN: I wish it were a heavier one, and it should have been, you may depend on it, if I could have laid my hands on anything else. Open that bundle, old Joe, and let me know the value of it. Speak out plain. I'm not afraid to be the first, nor afraid for them to see it. We knew pretty well that we were helping ourselves, before we met here, I believe. It's no sin. Open the bundle, Joe.

FIRST MAN: No, no, my dear! I won't think of letting you being the first to show what you've . . . earned . . . earned from this. I throw in mine. *(He takes a bundle from his shoulder, turns it upside down, and empties its contents out on to the floor.)* It's not very extensive, see . . . seals . . . a pencil case . . . sleeve buttons . . .

MRS. DILBER: Nice sleeve buttons, though . . .

FIRST MAN: Not bad, not bad . . . a brooch there . . .

OLD JOE: Not really valuable, I'm afraid . . .

FIRST MAN: How much, old Joe?

OLD JOE: *(writing on the wall with chalk)* A pitiful lot, really. Ten and six and not a sixpence more!

FIRST MAN: You're not serious!

OLD JOE: That's your account and I wouldn't give another sixpence if I was to be boiled for not doing it. Who's next?

MRS. DILBER: Me! *(Dumps out contents of her bundle)* Sheets, towels, silver spoons, silver sugar-tongs . . . some boots . . .

OLD JOE (*writing on wall*): I always give too much to the ladies. It's a weakness of mine and that's the way I ruin myself. Here's your total comin' up . . . two pounds-ten . . . if you asked me for another penny, and made it an open question, I'd repent of being so liberal and knock off half-a-crown.

FIRST WOMAN: And now do MY bundle, Joe.

OLD JOE (*kneeling to open knots on her bundle*): So many knots, madam . . . (*He drags out large curtains; dark*) What do you call this? Bed curtains!

FIRST WOMAN (*laughing*): Ah, yes, bed curtains!

OLD JOE: You don't mean to say you took 'em down, rings and all, with him lying there?

FIRST WOMAN: Yes, I did, why not?

OLD JOE: You were born to make your fortune and you'll certainly do it.

FIRST WOMAN: I certainly shan't hold my hand, when I can get anything in it by reaching it out, for the sake of such a man as he was, I promise you, Joe. Don't drop that lamp oil on those blankets, now!

OLD JOE: His blankets?

FIRST WOMAN: Whose else's do you think? He isn't likely to catch cold without 'em, I daresay.

OLD JOE: I hope that he didn't die of anything catching? Eh?

FIRST WOMAN: Don't you be afraid of that. I ain't so fond of his company that I'd loiter about him for such things if he did. Ah! You may look through that shirt till your eyes ache, but you won't find a hole in it, nor a threadbare place. It's the best he had, and a fine one, too. They'd have wasted it, if it hadn't been for me.

OLD JOE: What do you mean "They'd have wasted it?"

FIRST WOMAN: Putting it on him to be buried in, to be sure. Somebody was fool enough to do it, but I took it off again . . . (*She laughs, as do they all, nervously.*) If calico ain't good enough for such a purpose, it isn't good enough then for anything. It's quite as becoming to the body. He can't look uglier than he did in that one!

SCROOGE (*A low-pitched moan emits from his mouth; from the*

---

calico (KAL ih koh) a coarse and cheap cloth

bones): OOOOOOooooooOOOOOOooooooOOOOOOOOooooo OOOOOOooooooOO!

OLD JOE: One pound six for the lot. (*He produces a small flannel bag filled with money. He divvies it out. He continues to pass around the money as he speaks. All are laughing.*) That's the end of it, you see! He frightened every one away from him while he was alive, to profit us when he was dead! Hah ha ha!

ALL: HAHAHAHAhahahahahahah!

SCROOGE: OOOoooOOOoooOOOoooOOOoooOOoooOOooo OOOooo! (*He screams at them.*) Obscene demons! Why not market the corpse itself, and sell its trimmings??? (*Suddenly*) Oh, Spirit, I see it, I see it! This unhappy man—this stripped-bare corpse . . . could very well be my own. My life holds parallel! My life ends that way now!

(*SCROOGE backs into something in the dark behind his spotlight. SCROOGE looks at FUTURE, who points to the corpse. SCROOGE pulls back the blanket. The corpse is, of course, SCROOGE, who screams. He falls aside the bed; weeping.*)

Spirit, this is a fearful place. In leaving it, I shall not leave its lesson, trust me. Let us go!

(*FUTURE points to the corpse.*)

Spirit, let me see some tenderness connected with a death, or that dark chamber, which we just left now, Spirit, will be forever present to me.

(*FUTURE spreads his robes again. Thunder and lightning. Lights up, U., in the Cratchit home setting. MRS. CRATCHIT and her daughters, sewing.*)

TINY TIM'S VOICE (*off*): And He took a child and set him in the midst of them.

SCROOGE (*looking about the room; to FUTURE*): Huh? Who spoke? Who said that?

MRS. CRATCHIT (*puts down her sewing*): The color hurts my eyes. (*Rubs her eyes*) That's better. My eyes grow weak sewing by candlelight. I shouldn't want to show your father weak eyes when he comes home . . . not for the world. It must be near his time . . .

PETER (*in corner, reading. Looks up from book*): Past it, rather. But I think he's been walking a bit slower than usual these last few evenings, Mother.

MRS. CRATCHIT: I have known him walk with . . . *(Pauses)* I have known him walk with Tiny Tim upon his shoulder and very fast indeed.

PETER: So have I, Mother! Often!

DAUGHTER: So have I.

MRS. CRATCHIT: But he was very light to carry and his father loved him so, that it was not trouble—no trouble.

Plot question: What has happened to Tiny Tim?

(BOB, at door)

And there is your father at the door.

(BOB CRATCHIT enters. He wears a comforter. He is cold, forlorn.)

PETER: Father!

BOB: Hello, wife, children . . .

(The daughter weeps; turns away from CRATCHIT.)

Children! How good to see you all! And you, wife. And look at this sewing! I've no doubt, with all your industry, we'll have a quilt to set down upon our knees in church on Sunday!

MRS. CRATCHIT: You made the arrangements today, then, Robert, for the . . . service . . . to be on Sunday.

BOB: The funeral. Oh, well, yes, yes, I did. I wish you could have gone. It would have done you good to see how green a place it is. But you'll see it often, I promised him that I would walk there on Sunday, after the service. *(Suddenly)* My little, little child! My little child!

ALL CHILDREN *(hugging him)*: Oh, Father . . .

BOB *(he stands)*: Forgive me, I saw Mr. Scrooge's nephew, who you know I'd just met once before, and he was so wonderful to me, wife . . . he is the most pleasant-spoken gentleman I've ever met . . . he said "I am heartily sorry for it and heartily sorry for your good wife. If I can be of service to you in any way, here's where I live." And he gave me this card.

PETER: Let me see it!

BOB: And he looked me straight in the eye, wife, and said, meaningfully, "I pray you'll come to me, Mr. Cratchit, if you need some help. I pray you do." Now it wasn't for the sake of anything that he might be able to do for us, so much as for his kind way. It seemed as if he had known our Tiny Tim and felt with us.

MRS. CRATCHIT: I'm sure that he's a good soul.

Here, "situation" means a job.

BOB: You would be surer of it, my dear, if you saw and spoke to him. I shouldn't be at all surprised, if he got Peter a situation.

MRS. CRATCHIT: Only hear that, Peter!

MARTHA: And then, Peter will be keeping company with someone and setting up for himself!

PETER: Get along with you!

BOB: It's just as likely as not, one of these days, though there's plenty of time for that, my dear. But however and whenever we part from one another, I am sure we shall none of us forget poor Tiny Tim—shall we?—or this first parting that was among us?

ALL CHILDREN: Never, Father, never!

BOB: And when we recollect how patient and mild he was, we shall not quarrel easily among ourselves, and forget poor Tiny Tim in doing it.

ALL CHILDREN: No, Father, never!

LITTLE BOB: I am very happy, I am, I am, I am very happy.

(BOB *kisses his little son, as does* MRS. CRATCHIT, *as do the other children. The family is set now in one sculptural embrace. The lighting fades to a gentle pool of light, tight on them.*)

SCROOGE: Specter, something informs me that our parting moment is at hand. I know it, but I know not how I know it.

(FUTURE *points to the other side of the stage. Lights out on Cratchits.* FUTURE *moves slowly, gliding.* SCROOGE *follows.* FUTURE *points opposite.* FUTURE *leads* SCROOGE *to a wall and a tombstone. He points to the stone.*)

Am *I* that man those ghoulish parasites so gloated over? (*Pauses*) Before I draw nearer to that stone to which you point, answer me one question. Are these the shadows of things that will be, or the shadows of things that MAY be, only?

---

ghoulish parasites (GOOL ish PAR uh syts) the man and women who stole and divided Scrooge's goods after he died

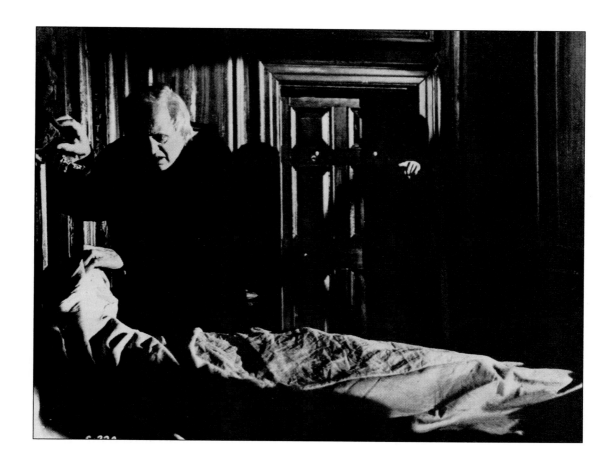

(FUTURE *points to the gravestone.* MARLEY *appears in light well U. He points to grave as well. Gravestone turns front and grows to ten feet high. Words upon it:* EBENEZER SCROOGE. *Much smoke billows now from the grave. Choral music here.* SCROOGE *stands looking up at gravestone.* FUTURE *does not at all reply in mortals' words, but points once more to the gravestone. The stone undulates and glows. Music plays, beckoning* SCROOGE. SCROOGE *reeling in terror)*

Oh, no. Spirit! Oh, no, no!

(FUTURE'S *finger still pointing)*

Spirit! Hear me! I am not the man I was. I will not be the man I would have been but for this intercourse. Why show me this, if I am past all hope?

(FUTURE *considers* SCROOGE'S *logic. His hand wavers.)*

Oh, Good Spirit, I see by your wavering hand that your good nature intercedes for me and pities me. Assure me that I yet may change these shadows that you have shown me by an altered life!

(FUTURE'S *hand trembles; pointing has stopped.*)

I will honor Christmas in my heart and try to keep it all the year. I will live in the Past, the Present, and the Future. The Spirits of all Three shall strive within me. I will not shut out the lessons that they teach. Oh, tell me that I may sponge away the writing that is upon this stone!

(SCROOGE *makes a desperate stab at grabbing* FUTURE'S *hand. He holds it firm for a moment, but* FUTURE, *stronger than* SCROOGE, *pulls away.* SCROOGE *is on his knees, praying.*)

Spirit, dear Spirit, I am praying before you. Give me a sign that all is possible. Give me a sign that all hope for me is not lost. Oh, Spirit, kind Spirit, I beseech thee: give me a sign . . .

(FUTURE *deliquesces, slowly, gently. The* PHANTOM'S *hood and robe drop gracefully to the ground in a small heap. Music in. There is nothing in them. They are mortal cloth. The Spirit is elsewhere.* SCROOGE *has his sign.* SCROOGE *is alone. Tableau. The lights fade to black.*)

SCENE 5

(*The end of it.* MARLEY, *spotlighted, opposite* SCROOGE, *in his bed, spotlighted.* MARLEY *speaks to audience, directly.*)

MARLEY (*he smiles at* SCROOGE): The firm of Scrooge and Marley is doubly blessed; two misers turned; one, alas, in Death, too late; but the other miser turned in Time's penultimate nick.[13] Look you on my friend, Ebenezer Scrooge . . .

SCROOGE (*scrambling out of bed; reeling in delight*): I will live in the Past, in the Present, and in the Future! The Spirits of all Three shall strive within me!

---

[13]**in Time's penultimate nick:** just at the last moment

MARLEY (*he points and moves closer to* SCROOGE'S *bed*): Yes, Ebenezer, the bedpost is your own. Believe it! Yes, Ebenezer, the room is your own. Believe it!

SCROOGE: Oh, Jacob Marley! Wherever you are, Jacob, know ye that I praise you for this! I praise you . . . and heaven . . . and Christmastime! (*Kneels facing away from* MARLEY) I say it to ye on my knees, old Jacob, on my knees! (*He touches his bed curtains.*) Not torn down. My bed curtains are not at all torn down! Rings and all, here they are! They are here: I am here: the shadows of things that would have been, may now be dispelled. They will be, Jacob! I know they will be! (*He chooses clothing for the day. He tries different pieces of clothing and settles, perhaps on a dress suit, plus a cape of the bed clothing: something of color.*) I am light as a feather. I am happy as an angel. I am as merry as a schoolboy. (*Yells out window and then out to audience*) Merry Christmas to everybody! Merry Christmas to everybody! A Happy New Year to all the world! Hallo here! Whoop! Whoop! Hallo! Hallo! I don't know what day of the month it is! I don't care! I don't know anything! I'm quite a baby! I don't care! I don't care a fig! I'd much rather be a baby than be an old wreck like me or Marley! (Sorry, Jacob, wherever ye be!) Hallo! Hallo there!

Similes

(*Church bells chime in Christmas Day. A small boy, named* ADAM *is seen now D.R., as a light fades up on him.*)

Hey, you boy! What's today? What day of the year is it?

ADAM: Today, sir? Why, it's Christmas Day!

SCROOGE: It's Christ's Day, is it? Whoop! Well, I haven't missed it after all, have I? The Spirits did all they did in one night. They can do anything they like, right? Of course they can! Of course they can!

ADAM: Excuse me, sir?

SCROOGE: Huh? Oh, yes, of course, what's your name, lad?

(SCROOGE *and* ADAM *will play their scene from their own spotlights.*)

ADAM: Adam, sir.

SCROOGE: Adam! What a fine, strong name! Do you know the poulterer's in the next street but one, at the corner?

ADAM: I certainly should hope I know him, sir!

SCROOGE: A remarkable boy! An intelligent boy! Do you know whether the poulterer's have sold the prize turkey that was hanging up there? I don't mean the little prize turkey, Adam, I mean the big one!

ADAM: What, do you mean the one they've got that's as big as me?

SCROOGE: I mean, the turkey the size of Adam: that's the bird!

ADAM: It's hanging there now, sir.

SCROOGE: It is? Go and buy it! No, no, I am absolutely in earnest. Go and buy it and tell 'em to bring it here, so that I may give them the directions to where I want it delivered, as a gift. Come back here with the man, Adam, and I'll give you a shilling. Come back here with him in less than five minutes, and I'll give you half-a-crown!

ADAM: Oh, my sir! Don't let my brother in on this.

(ADAM *runs offstage.* MARLEY *smiles.*)

MARLEY: An act of kindness is like the first green grape of summer: one leads to another and another and another. It would take a queer man indeed to not follow an act of kindness with an act of kindness. One simply whets the tongue for more . . . the taste of kindness is too too sweet. Gifts—goods—are lifeless. But the gift of goodness one feels in the giving is full of life. It . . . is . . . a . . . wonder.

(*Pauses; moves closer to* SCROOGE, *who is totally occupied with his dressing and arranging of his room and his day. He is making lists, etc.* MARLEY *reaches out to* SCROOGE.)

ADAM (*calling, off):* I'm here! I'm here!

(ADAM *runs on with a man, who carries an enormous turkey.*)

Here I am, sir. Three minutes flat! A world record! I've got the poultryman and he's got the poultry! (*He pants, out of breath.*) I have earned my prize, sir, if I live . . .

(*He holds his heart, playacting.* SCROOGE *goes to him and embraces him.*)

---

poulterer's (POHL tur urz) a British word for a store that sells chickens, turkeys, and geese

SCROOGE: You are truly a champion, Adam . . .

MAN: Here's the bird you ordered, sir. . .

SCROOGE: Oh, my, MY!!! Look at the size of that turkey, will you! He never could have stood upon his legs, that bird! He would have snapped them off in a minute, like sticks of sealing wax! Why you'll never be able to carry that bird to Camden-Town. I'll give you money for a cab . . .

Simile

MAN: Camden-Town's where it's goin', sir?

SCROOGE: Oh, I didn't tell you? Yes, I've written the precise address down just here on this . . . (*Hands paper to him*) Bob Cratchit's house. Now he's not to know who sends him this. Do you understand me? Not a word . . . (*Handing out money and chuckling*)

This continues the resolution: Scrooge is beginning to make amends.

MAN: I understand, sir, not a word.

SCROOGE: Good. There you go then . . . This is for the turkey . . . (*Chuckle*) and this is for the taxi. (*Chuckle*) . . . and this is for your world-record run, Adam . . .

ADAM: But I don't have change for that, sir.

SCROOGE: Then keep it, my lad. It's Christmas!

ADAM (*He kisses* SCROOGE'S *cheek, quickly.*): Thank you, sir. Merry, Merry Christmas! (*He runs off.*)

MAN: And you've given me a bit overmuch here, too, sir . . .

SCROOGE: Of course I have, sir. It's Christmas!

MAN: Oh, well, thanking you, sir. I'll have this bird to Mr. Cratchit and his family in no time, sir. Don't you worry none about that. Merry Christmas to you, sir, and a very happy New Year, too . . .

(*The man exits.* SCROOGE *walks in a large circle about the stage, which is now gently lit. A chorus sings Christmas music far in the distance. Bells chime as well, far in the distance. A gentleman enters and passes.* SCROOGE *is on the streets now.*)

SCROOGE: Merry Christmas, madam . . .

WOMAN: Merry Christmas, sir . . .

(*The* PORTLY BUSINESSMAN *from the first act enters.*)

SCROOGE: Merry Christmas, sir.

PORTLY MAN: Merry Christmas, sir.

SCROOGE: Oh, you! My dear sir! How do you do? I do hope that you succeeded yesterday! It was very kind of you. A Merry Christmas.

PORTLY MAN: Mr. Scrooge?

SCROOGE: Yes, Scrooge is my name though I'm afraid you may not find it very pleasant. Allow me to ask your pardon. And will you have the goodness to— *(He whispers into the man's ear.)*

Further resolution

PORTLY MAN: Lord Bless me! My dear Mr. Scrooge, are you *serious!?!*

SCROOGE: If you please. Not a farthing less. A great many back payments are included in it, I assure you. Will you do me that favor?

PORTLY MAN: My dear sir, I don't know what to say to such munifi—

SCROOGE *(cutting him off):* Don't say anything, please. Come and see me. Will you?

PORTLY MAN: I will! I will! Oh I will, Mr. Scrooge! It will be my pleasure!

SCROOGE: Thank'ee, I am much obliged to you. I thank you fifty times. Bless you!

(PORTLY MAN passes offstage, perhaps by moving backwards. SCROOGE now comes to the room of his NEPHEW and NIECE. He stops at the door, begins to knock on it, loses his courage, tries again, loses his courage again, tries again, fails again, and then backs off and runs at the door, causing a tremendous bump against it. The NEPHEW and NIECE are startled. SCROOGE, poking head into room)

NEPHEW: Why, bless my soul! Who's that?

NEPHEW AND NIECE *(together):* How now? Who goes?

SCROOGE: It's I. Your Uncle Scrooge.

NIECE: Dear heart alive!

Another instance of resolution, or the reversal of Scrooge's character.

SCROOGE: I have come to dinner. May I come in, Fred?

NEPHEW: *May you come in???!!!* With such pleasure for me you may, Uncle!!! What a treat!

NIECE: What a treat, Uncle Scrooge! Come in, come in!

---

farthing (FAHR *thing*) a small British coin

(They embrace a shocked and delighted SCROOGE. FRED *calls into the other room.)*

NEPHEW: Come in here, everybody, and meet my Uncle Scrooge! He's come for our Christmas party!

(Music in. Lighting here indicates that day has gone to night and gone to day again. It is early, early morning. SCROOGE *walks alone from the party, exhausted, to his offices, opposite side of the stage. He opens his offices. The offices are as they were at the start of the play.* SCROOGE *seats himself with his door wide open so that he can see into the tank, as he awaits* CRATCHIT, *who enters, head down, full of guilt.* CRATCHIT *starts writing almost before he sits.)*

SCROOGE: What do you mean by coming in here at this time of day, a full eighteen minutes late, Mr. Cratchit? Hallo, sir? Do you hear me?

Irony: Scrooge doesn't mean this

BOB: I am very sorry, sir. I *am* behind my time.

SCROOGE: You are? Yes, I certainly think you are. Step this way, sir, if you please . . .

BOB: It's only but once a year, sir . . . it shall not be repeated. I was making rather merry yesterday and into the night . . .

SCROOGE: Now, I'll tell you what, Cratchit. I am not going to stand this sort of thing any longer. And therefore . . .

(He stands and pokes his finger into BOB'S *chest.)*

I am . . . about . . . to . . . raise . . . your salary.

BOB: Oh, no, sir. I . . . *(Realizes)* what did you say, sir?

SCROOGE: A Merry Christmas, Bob . . . *(He claps* BOB'S *back.)* A merrier Christmas, Bob, my good fellow! than I have given you for many a year. I'll raise your salary and endeavor to assist your struggling family and we will discuss your affairs this very afternoon over a bowl of smoking bishop.[14] Bob! Make up the fires and buy another coal scuttle before you dot another i, Bob. It's too cold in this place! We need warmth and cheer, Bob Cratchit! Do you hear me? DO . . . YOU . . . HEAR . . . ME?

---

[14]**smoking bishop:** a hot, sweet, orange-flavored drink

(BOB CRATCHIT stands, smiles at SCROOGE. BOB CRATCHIT faints. Blackout. As the main lights black out, a spotlight appears on SCROOGE, C. Another on MARLEY. He talks directly to the audience.)

A final aside, providing more details about the resolution by tying up loose ends and answering remaining plot questions

MARLEY: Scrooge was better than his word. He did it all and infinitely more; and to Tiny Tim, who did NOT die, he was a second father. He became as good a friend, as good a master, as good a man, as the good old city knew, or any other good old city, town, or borough in the good old world. And it was always said of him that he knew how to keep Christmas well, if any man alive possessed the knowledge. *(Pauses)* May that be truly said of us, and all of us. And so, as Tiny Tim observed . . .

TINY TIM *(atop SCROOGE'S shoulder):* God Bless Us, Every One . . .

(Lights up on chorus, singing final Christmas Song. SCROOGE and MARLEY and all spirits and other characters of the play join in. When the song is over, the lights fade to black.)

Charles Dickens (1812–1870)

At the age of twenty-four, Dickens suddenly became famous for his book, *Pickwick Papers*, which was published in paper-bound weekly installments. Readers waited with anticipation to read each installment, making it an immediate success. He never stopped writing after this, and each of his books became more popular than the last.

The focus of Dickens's novels was on the injustices and hardships the poor had to endure. He had a profound influence in England, and through his writing, many wrongs were righted. He attacked the disgraceful working conditions in factories. He also brought attention to how children were treated in schools, the inadequacy of medical care for the poor, and the horrible conditions that existed in poorhouses.

Dickens was not unfamiliar with poverty. He grew up in a very poor family on the coast of England. When he was eleven, he was taken out of school to help support the family. At twelve, he went to work in a factory, and at thirteen he was sent to a school where the headmaster was very cruel. Much of this is recounted in the early chapters of his novel *David Copperfield*.

During his middle years, he continued to write about the virtues of kindness and courage and to attack social injustice. Dickens also enjoyed a rich personal life. He and his wife, Catherine Hogarth, lived in London where they raised ten children. Dickens also traveled to the United States where he was greeted by the leading authors of the day. His work was widely accepted in the United States, even though he strongly criticized slavery and the primitive living conditions of the American West.

Charles Dickens continues to be recognized for his superb writing and the effect he had in helping the less fortunate in English society.

Review the Selection

UNDERSTAND THE SELECTION

Recall

1. Why was Scrooge upset with Bob Cratchit in the second scene of Act I?

2. Who was Jacob Marley in life?

3. How many ghosts are characters in the play? Name them.

Infer

4. Did young Scrooge have any good qualities before he changed? What were they?

5. What is the significance of Scrooge having to touch the heart of the Spirit of Christmas Past?

6. Why did the Spirit of Christmas Present age so much while he was with Scrooge?

7. Describe how the Spirit of Christmas Future appeared to Scrooge.

Apply

8. Discuss the major theme of this drama. Do you agree? Explain.

9. Predict what might have happened if Scrooge had not had the visions.

10. Does it matter whether what happened to Scrooge existed only in his imagination? Why or why not?

Respond to Literature

Explain how Act 2, Scene 2 is representative of Victorian England.

WRITE ABOUT THE SELECTION

The time in which *A Christmas Carol* is set is the year 1843. Charles Dickens is known for being critical about much of Victorian-era society. This story contains many such criticisms.

Write a critique of the story, indicating the ways in which it can be seen as a critical commentary on the times and the society in which Dickens lived.

Prewriting Divide your worksheet into two columns, headed *Meanings* and *Examples*. Think about different scenes from the play, as well as what you have learned about the Victorian period. If you can see some significance in a certain scene in terms of the problems and conditions of that society, write a brief description of the scene in the *Example* column. Think of as many examples as you can. In the *Meanings* column, next to each example, explain the critical point you think Dickens is trying to make.

Writing Using your examples and their meanings, write your critique. Be sure to cite at least one example from the play for each critical point you mention.

Revising Add one more example—this one reflecting something positive about the society of the time. Again, state what the positive aspect is, and cite one or more examples from the text.

Proofreading Review your critique for correct punctuation. Also, make sure all your sentences are complete.

THINK ABOUT SETTING

Setting invokes the place, the time, and the general background against which the action in a literary work takes place. Sometimes a setting can be a major force in the events of the work. It can also play a role in determining the moods of different characters at different times.

1. How does the setting of one of the play's scenes enhance a feeling of longing, or sadness? Cite an example, and explain how the setting contributes to the mood.

2. How does the setting of *A Christmas Carol* help to bring out the central conflict?

3. The atmosphere of a setting can change even if the location does not. Describe how a particular setting changes from familiar to terrifying and the effect it has on Scrooge.

4. How do you think the setting, or world, in which Scrooge lives might look different to him at the end of the play from the way it looked at the beginning? Explain how the holidays are involved.

5. The same setting can look very different to different characters. Describe how Bob Cratchit's house might have appeared to the Cratchit family and how it might have appeared to Scrooge when he first saw it. Use your imagination.

DEVELOP YOUR VOCABULARY

Sometimes, the meaning of an unfamiliar word can be determined from the context in which it is used. **Context** refers to other words, phrases, and sentences that are around the unfamiliar word.

When you think you can figure out the meaning of a word from context clues, try substituting another word with a similar meaning in the same sentence. If the sentence still makes sense, you have probably figured out the correct meaning.

Try to determine the meaning of the following words in the play from context clues. Think of a word with a similar meaning that can be substituted for each one. Rewrite the sentences from the play using the substitute words. Does the sentence still make sense? If it does not, try another word. If it does, use the word from the play in an original sentence containing one or more context clues to indicate its meaning.

For example: Word: *comforter* (a long, woolen scarf). Sentence from play: Cratchit rubs his hands together, puts on a white *scarf,* and tries to heat his hands around a candle. New sentence: You will not get a sore throat no matter how cold it is if you remember to wear a *comforter.*

1. deliquesce
2. apparition
3. specters
4. scrim
5. lute
6. a proper loon
7. calico
8. ghoulish parasites
9. poulterer

Learn About

Portrait of Jean-François Gilibert, J.A.D. Ingres. The Granger Collection

READING FOCUS

Evaluate the Writer's Style Style is comprised of many elements, including word choice, tone, and sentence structure. In poetry, rhythm and rhyme also contribute greatly to style. To evaluate a writer's style, notice whether sentences are short or long, whether words evoke sensory images or merely define facts. Listen to a poem's rhythm and notice the music—and mood—it suggests. Finally, ask yourself what the writer's tone, or attitude, is toward the subject.

THEME

Theme is the central meaning of a work of literature. It is the main message that the writer is trying to get across. The theme usually involves ideas about life and the world we live in. It is an abstract notion or concept that is made real or concrete in the work.

Sometimes, the theme is very simple and straightforward. It is **stated** directly in one or more sentences. Sometimes the theme is brought out gradually, as the story progresses. Sometimes the theme is not stated at all. It is left for the reader to infer, based on all the other elements of the story. In a case such as this, the theme is **implied.**

Longer works, such as novels, plays, and lengthy poems, may have more than one theme. In some shorter works, the theme may be relatively unimportant or there may be no theme at all.

As you read "When I was one-and-twenty," keep the following in mind:
1. What is the central meaning or message of the poem?
2. Is it stated or implied?

WRITING CONNECTION

Think about independence as a theme. Write a brief paragraph that expresses your attitude toward the subject. You may want to narrow your theme to focus on the independence of a nation or of an individual.

When I was one-and-twenty

by A. E. Housman

When I was one-and-twenty
    I heard a wise man say,
"Give crowns and pounds and guineas
    But not your heart away;
5   Give pearls away and rubies
    But keep your fancy free."
But I was one-and-twenty,
    No use to talk to me.

When I was one-and-twenty
10   I heard him say again,
"The heart out of the bosom
    Was never given in vain;
'Tis paid with sighs a plenty
    And sold for endless rue."
15   And I am two-and-twenty,
    And oh, 'tis true, 'tis true.

---

crowns (KROUNZ) . . . **guineas** (GIN eez) denominations of money
fancy (FAN see) likings; imagination; whim
rue (ROO) sorrow; regret

Review the Selection

UNDERSTAND THE SELECTION

Recall

1. How old is the speaker at the beginning of the poem? At the end of it?

2. Whom does the poet quote?

3. What did the wise man tell the speaker not to give away?

Infer

4. How does the speaker feel at the end of the poem?

5. What did the wise man think about the relative value of wealth and independence? Which is worth more?

6. What did the speaker do with the wise man's advice?

7. In what person is the poem written— first, second, or third?

Apply

8. Restate the advice given by the wise man. Do you agree? Why or why not?

9. Describe how the speaker's feelings changed from the beginning to the end of the poem.

10. What, in your opinion, were the reasons for this change in feelings?

Respond to Literature

Do you think the speaker should have listened to the wise man? Explain.

WRITE ABOUT THE SELECTION

Think about what might lie ahead for the speaker in the poem during the next year of life. Will he or she still feel the same? Will something happen during this time to change his or her feelings again? How will they change? Write an additional four lines to the poem, describing how the speaker feels at twenty-three, and why.

Prewriting   To help gather your thoughts, try using a cause-and-effect chart. Divide the page into two columns, with *Cause* heading one column and *Effect* heading the other. Jot down ideas about what might happen to the speaker and why. Anything that answers the question "What?" goes in the *Effect* column. Anything that answers the question "Why?" goes under *Cause.* After you have written down all your ideas, fill in any blanks in your columns. Each effect must have a cause, and vice versa.

Writing   Now that you have decided what happens, write the additional four-line stanza, showing cause and effect.

Revising   Check the number of syllables in each line of your stanza. Do the lines contain the same, or almost the same, number of syllables? If not, rewrite the lines to make the syllable count uniform.

Proofreading   Check that each line of your poem begins with a capital letter and that you have used commas and quotation marks (if necessary) correctly.

THINK ABOUT THEME

The meaning, or theme, of a work can be based on lofty ideas or noble ideas, such as brotherhood or patriotism. Emotions, such as love or anger, can also provide the basis for a theme.

A theme can also describe a particular human dilemma or social concern. For example, the concept of brotherhood would be the basis for a specific theme concerning the civil rights movement.

1. Describe what you consider to be the theme of "When I was one-and-twenty."

2. What underlying ideas or concepts can you see as laying the groundwork for this meaning?

3. Would you say that the theme is one of general optimism or pessimism?

READING FOCUS

Evaluate the Writer's Style Briefly describe A. E. Housman's style in this poem. Give one example of each of the following elements: word choice, tone, rhythm, and rhyme.

DEVELOP YOUR VOCABULARY

An **adverb** is a word that usually modifies a verb. However, adverbs can also modify adjectives and other adverbs. An adverb describes manner, place, time, degree, or cause. In doing so, it tells how, where, when, how much, or how often.

Usually, adverbs end in *-ly*. When looking them up in the dictionary, it is often necessary to drop the *-ly* and look up the remaining word, which is usually an adjective. Almost any adjective can be made into an adverb by adding *-ly*.

Examples:

Question	Adjective	Adverb
How?	quiet	quietly
Where?	local	locally
When?	late	lately
How much?	tremendous	tremendously
How often?	frequent	frequently

Think of two adverbs that answer each of the above questions. Write down the question, the two adverbs, and their adjective forms. Use each adverb and adjective in a sentence.

Example:

How?	nicely (adv.)	She dresses nicely.
	nice (adj.)	She wore a nice dress.

Kilgerran Castle on the Twyvey, J. W. M. Turner. The National Trust/Art Resource

READING FOCUS

Paraphrase to Identify Theme The message, or theme, of a poem may be directly stated or it may be implied. In either case, you need to identify that message in order to fully understand the poem. Paraphrasing, or writing the ideas of the poem in your own words, may help you identify the theme. As you read "Dover Beach," write the central idea of each stanza in your own words. Ask yourself: What is the poet trying to say to me? What lesson or idea does he want to communicate? You can use the answers to these questions to determine the author's message.

SIMILE

Figurative language involves the use of words to express a meaning beyond the usual meaning of the words.

One form of figurative language is called simile. A **simile** is a figure of speech that compares two things that are basically different but are similar in one or more ways. Similes use the words *as* or *like* in drawing the comparison. An object which is "green as grass" or a person who "rides like the wind" is being described through simile.

Writers often use similes to enhance the reader's understanding of the experience they are trying to communicate. This form of figurative language can be more expressive than words that are used in more conventional ways. Poems are often rich in similes or other forms of figurative language.

As you read "Dover Beach," be aware of:

1. The things that are compared in similes.
2. How the use of simile helps express a thought or feeling.

WRITING CONNECTION

Write a poem about a pleasant experience you have had. Use similes in your poem.

DOVER BEACH

by Matthew Arnold

The sea is calm tonight.
The tide is full, the moon lies fair
Upon the straits;—on the French coast the light
Gleams and is gone; the cliffs of England stand,
5   Glimmering and vast, out in the tranquil bay.
Come to the window, sweet is the night air!
Only, from the long line of spray
Where the sea meets the moon-blanched land,
Listen! you hear the grating roar
10   Of pebbles which the waves draw back, and fling,
At their return, up the high strand,
Begin, and cease, and then again begin,
With tremulous cadence slow, and bring
The eternal note of sadness in.

---

straits (STRAYTS) Strait of Dover, between England and France
tranquil (TRANG kwil) calm; serene; free from emotional disturbance or agitation
moon-blanched (MOON blancht) made to look white or pale, by the moon
grating (GRAYT ing) grinding, rubbing against with a harsh, scraping sound
strand (STRAND) shore; land at the edge of a body of water
tremulous (TREM yuh lus) trembling; quivering
cadence (KAYD uns) flow of rhythm; beat of measured movement in marching or dancing
eternal (ih TUR nul) without beginning or end; existing through all time

Bay Scene in Moonlight, John Warwick Smith. Yale Center for British Art, Paul Mellon Collection

15   Sophocles long ago
Heard it on the Aegaean, and it brought
Into his mind the turbid ebb and flow
Of human misery; we
Find also in the sound a thought,
20   Hearing it by this distant northern sea.

The Sea of Faith
Was once, too, at the full, and round earth's shore
Lay like the folds of a bright girdle furled.
But now I only hear

Sophocles (SOF uh kleez) a Greek tragic dramatist (496-406 B.C.)
Aegaean (ih JEE un) an arm of the Mediterranean Sea, between Greece and Turkey
turbid (TUR bid) muddy, cloudy; dark, dense
folds (FOHLDZ) folded parts or layers
girdle (GUR dul) a belt or sash for the waist
furled (FURLD) rolled up tightly

25   Its melancholy, long, withdrawing roar,
     Retreating, to the breath
     Of the night wind down the vast edges drear
     And naked shingles of the world.

     Ah, love, let us be true
30   To one another! for the world, which seems
     To lie before us like a land of dreams,
     So various, so beautiful, so new,
     Hath really neither joy, nor love, nor light,
     Nor certitude, nor peace, nor help for pain;
35   And we are here as on a darkling plain
     Swept with confused alarms of struggle and flight,
     Where ignorant armies clash by night.

---

melancholy (MEL un kol ee) sad and depressed; gloomy
shingles (SHING gulz) beaches covered with large, coarse, waterworn gravel
darkling (DAHRK ling) in the dark

Review the Selection

UNDERSTAND THE SELECTION

Recall

1. Where is Dover Beach?

2. What great Greek dramatist does the poem mention?

3. Whom does the speaker address in the last stanza?

Infer

4. What sort of night is it? Cite specific images from the poem.

5. What feeling do you get from the last six lines of the first stanza?

6. What might the "Sea of Faith" be?

7. In the final stanza, what lies before the speaker and the speaker's love?

Apply

8. In the last stanza, the world is characterized in two ways. Describe both. Do you agree? Explain.

9. Cite the first example of simile in the final stanza. How did you recognize it as simile?

10. Cite the second example of simile in the final stanza. Describe what it means.

Respond to Literature

Is "Dover Beach" an example of Romanticism, Realism, or Naturalism? How would you characterize it?

WRITE ABOUT THE SELECTION

The beginning of this poem is very descriptive. Several images are employed by the poet, but similes are not used. Without being concerned about rhyme, write your own description of the scene described in the first stanza.

Prewriting An **analogy** is a comparison of two things that have some particular thing in common but are basically different. There are many things mentioned in the first stanza that can be compared to something else: sea, tide, moon, straits, cliffs, bay, waves. Think of comparisons for at least four of these items. Write down each item. As you think of something to compare waves to, for example, write it under *waves*. Write as many things as you can think of under as many headings as possible.

Writing Pick out the ones that appeal to you most—the ones that will give the reader a crisp, clear description. These words will make up the other half of your analogy. Rewrite the description using these analogies.

Revising Review your analogies. Revise at least two of them to paint an even clearer picture in the reader's mind.

Proofreading In similes, *like* is used as a preposition that begins a phrase. *As* is used to introduce an adverb clause. It introduces a clause that answers an adverb question. Check that you have used *like* and *as* correctly in your writing.

THINK ABOUT POETIC DEVICES

Simile is a form of figurative language that uses comparison. Another form of figurative language that uses comparison is metaphor. The difference between these two forms is that a metaphor does not directly or expressly compare and a simile does. You won't find the words *like* or *as* in a metaphor.

A **metaphor** uses an implied analogy, or comparison. It compares two different things. It focuses on a quality that is similar in the two items. The comparison enhances the reader's understanding or feeling.

1. There are many metaphors in "Dover Beach." In one, human misery is compared to the tide. Describe what this metaphor suggests to you.

2. The fourth stanza is filled with more images about water. In the first half, the speaker focuses on one aspect of the sea. In the second, he or she speaks about the opposite of this aspect. What are those two things?

3. What do the final lines tell you about the poet's view of life?

4. In the final stanza, how do the fifth and sixth lines reinforce the concept of "the eternal note of sadness"?

5. This poem contains both optimistic and pessimistic elements. Cite three examples of each, using words from the poem.

DEVELOP YOUR VOCABULARY

Imagery is concerned with description. Writers use adjectives to create pictures or images in the reader's mind. Adjectives are essential to producing vivid mental pictures.

The following adjectives appear in "Dover Beach." Some may not be familiar to you because they are not often used in modern writing. However, to appreciate the imagery in the poem, you must understand the meaning of these words.

First, write the definition of each word. Then, use each word in a descriptive sentence, employing simile. Remember that simile is a figure of speech in which two unlike things are compared. The comparison is usually introduced by the words *like* or *as*.

tranquil	eternal
moon-blanched	turbid
grating	melancholy
tremulous	darkling

READING FOCUS

Paraphrase to Identify Theme   As you read this poem, you put each stanza into your own words in order to help you identify theme. What is the theme of "Dover Beach"? Tell how paraphrasing helped you to identify this theme.

Learn About

Ciliege, Bartolomeo Bimbi. Art Resource

READING FOCUS

Evaluate the Writer's Purpose Writers usually have one of four main purposes for writing: to entertain, to inform, to describe, or to persuade. When reading informative writing, for example, you must read very carefully for facts. Remember, however, that writers may have another purpose, as well. As you read Lear's recipes, jot down words that provide clues to his purpose for writing.

TONE

Tone describes an author's attitude toward the subject or the characters in his or her work. An author's tone can be serious, humorous, sympathetic, mocking, and so forth. Some tones are harder to recognize than others because they are masked or disguised by another tone, such as humor. **Satire** hides a serious purpose under a funny or silly cover. **Irony** involves a character saying one thing and meaning the opposite.

Tone is often implied, not explicit. For example, satirical or ironic tone may not always be obvious. The reader must make inferences to understand them.

As you read "Three Recipes for Domestic Cookery," ask yourself:

1. Is there more to the author's tone than first meets the eye?
2. Is this tone directed toward the subject matter or the reader?

WRITING CONNECTION

Irony often involves a character deliberately saying the exact opposite of what he or she means. Imagine that you are a writer and want to use this kind of irony in a certain situation. Write a brief scene with two characters, one of whom is saying something in an ironic tone. Explain the character's reason for doing this.

Three Recipes for Domestic Cookery

by Edward Lear

1. To Make an Amblongus Pie

Take 4 pounds (say 4½ pounds) of fresh Amblongusses, and put them in a small pipkin.

Cover them with water and boil them for 8 hours incessantly, after which add 2 pints of new milk, and proceed to boil for 4 hours more.

When you have ascertained that the Amblongusses are quite soft, take them out and place them in a wide pan, taking care to shake them well previously.

Grate some nutmeg over the surface, and cover them carefully with powdered gingerbread, curry-powder, and a sufficient quantity of Cayenne pepper.

Remove the pan into the next room, and place it on the floor. Bring it back again, and let it simmer for three-quarters of an hour. Shake the pan violently till all the Amblongusses have become of a pale purple color.

Then, having prepared the paste, insert the whole carefully, adding at the same time a small pigeon, 2 slices of beef, 4 cauliflowers, and any number of oysters.

Watch patiently till the crust begins to rise, and add a pinch of salt from time to time.

Serve up in a clean dish, and throw the whole out of window as fast as possible.

---

pipkin (PIP kin) small earthenware pot
incessantly (in SES unt lee) without stopping
ascertained (as ur TAYND) found out with certainty

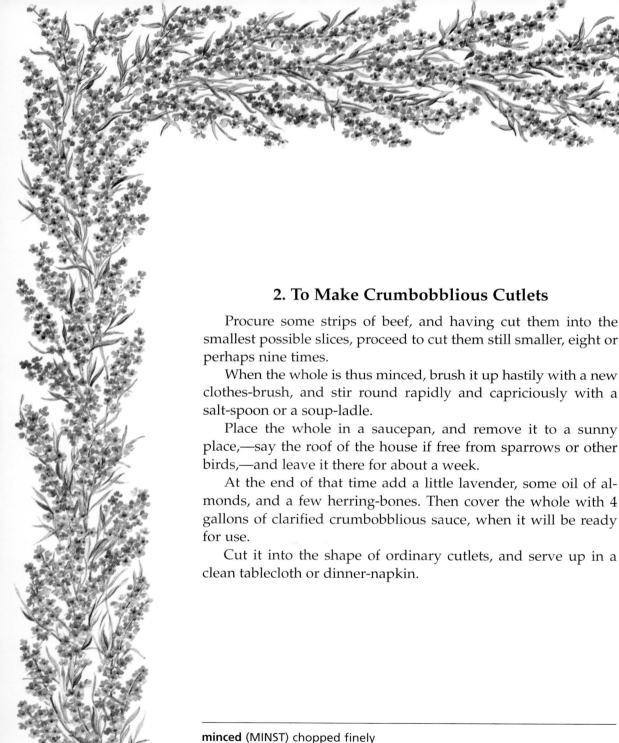

2. To Make Crumbobblious Cutlets

Procure some strips of beef, and having cut them into the smallest possible slices, proceed to cut them still smaller, eight or perhaps nine times.

When the whole is thus minced, brush it up hastily with a new clothes-brush, and stir round rapidly and capriciously with a salt-spoon or a soup-ladle.

Place the whole in a saucepan, and remove it to a sunny place,—say the roof of the house if free from sparrows or other birds,—and leave it there for about a week.

At the end of that time add a little lavender, some oil of almonds, and a few herring-bones. Then cover the whole with 4 gallons of clarified crumbobblious sauce, when it will be ready for use.

Cut it into the shape of ordinary cutlets, and serve up in a clean tablecloth or dinner-napkin.

---

minced (MINST) chopped finely
capriciously (kuh PRISH us lee) impulsively
lavender (LAV un dur) plant of the mint family
clarified (KLAR uh fyd) made free of impurities

3. To Make Gosky Patties

Take a Pig, three or four years of age, and tie him by the off-hind leg to a post. Place 5 pounds of currants, 3 of sugar, 2 pecks of peas, 18 roast chestnuts, a candle, and six bushels of turnips, within his reach. If he eats these, constantly provide him with more.

Then procure some cream, some slices of Cheshire cheese, four quires of foolscap paper, and a packet of black pins. Work the whole into a paste, and spread it out to dry on a sheet of clean brown waterproof linen.

When the paste is perfectly dry, but not before, proceed to beat the Pig violently, with the handle of a large broom. If he squeals, beat him again.

Visit the paste and beat the Pig alternately for some days, and ascertain if at the end of that period the whole is about to turn into Gosky Patties.

If it does not then, it never will; and in that case the Pig may be let loose, and the whole process may be considered as finished.

---

procure (proh KYUUR) obtain
quires (KWYRZ) a set of 24 sheets of paper
foolscap (FOOLZ kap) writing paper

Review the Selection

UNDERSTAND THE SELECTION

Recall

1. What is the main ingredient of an amblongus pie?

2. In what do you serve a crumbobblious cutlet?

3. What animal is involved in making Gosky Patties?

Infer

4. Why does the author use the phrase "8 hours incessantly"?

5. Could shaking cause food to turn purple? Explain your answer.

6. Why do you think the author includes herring bones in the second recipe?

7. What does the author assume the reader will hope regarding the final product in making Gosky Patties?

Apply

8. How do you think the seasoning for amblongus pie would taste?

9. Why do you think the author chose the names he gave these dishes?

10. Choose the line you think is the funniest.

Respond to Literature

What do you think prompted Lear to satirize recipes, or cookbooks, rather than something else?

WRITE ABOUT THE SELECTION

You have just read three "recipes." Suppose you were asked to contribute a recipe of your own to be included in Lear's cookbook. Where would you start?

Prewriting First, write down every thing humorous about food that comes to mind. Think in terms of Lear's three recipes and the things he includes in them—not always food we recognize. Think about quantities as well as ingredients. Organize your thoughts in a three-section outline.

I. Ingredients and quantities
II. Preparation and cooking
III. Serving

Writing Based on your outline, write out your recipe in paragraph form. Be sure to be specific about how much of each ingredient is used and the amount of time involved in the preparation and cooking. As with most recipes, you can use numbers and common abbreviations: for example, lb. instead of pound; tsp. instead of teaspoon.

Revising You have sampled your finished product. It tastes terrible. Add another paragraph describing what you do with your creation.

Proofreading Check your work for paragraph length. Do the paragraphs hold together? Do they follow the outline? If you need to break up or combine paragraphs for clarity, do so.

THINK ABOUT TONE

In the study of literature, a great deal is open to interpretation. Nowhere is this more evident than in the area of tone. Is a work simply humorous? Does it employ satire or irony? In some cases, perhaps only the author knew for sure. Even scholars can debate the meanings of certain works and never agree. The important thing is to be able to make a case for your opinion and defend it while remaining open to the ideas and interpretations of others.

1. What is the tone of "Three Recipes for Domestic Cookery"?

2. Do you see any elements of satire here? Explain your answer.

3. Do you see any elements of irony here? Explain your answer.

4. Do you see any worthwhile qualities in nonsense writing?

5. Briefly summarize, in your own words, your understanding of tone.

READING FOCUS

Evaluate the Writer's Purpose What do you think Edward Lear's purpose was in writing these recipes? List three words or phrases from each recipe that support your answer.

DEVELOP YOUR VOCABULARY

A suffix is a word part that is attached to the end of a word. It often changes a word's part of speech or its tense.

The suffix -ed can change a present tense verb into a past tense verb. For example: walk–walked.

The suffix -ly can change an adjective into an adverb. For example: nice–nicely.

The suffixes -ment and -er change a verb into a noun. For example: agree–agreement.

The suffixes -ish and -ful can change a noun into an adjective. For example: regret–regretful.

By adding suffixes to the following words, change their parts of speech according to the instructions. Then, use both forms of the word correctly in a sentence.

	Word	Part of Speech	Change to
1.	quick	adj.	adverb
2.	youth	noun	adj.
3.	joy	noun	adj.
4.	assign	verb	noun
5.	wait	verb	past tense
6.	contain	verb	noun
7.	entertain	verb	noun
8.	swim	verb	noun
9.	boy	noun	adj.
10.	slow	adj.	adverb

The Lady of Shalott, J.W. Waterhouse. The Granger Collection

READING FOCUS

Identify Mood   The mood of a literary piece is the general atmosphere the piece provides. The mood might be cheerful or sad, for example. A poet uses elements of style to establish moods. A poet's style may include rhyme scheme, rhythmic patterns, and choice of words or phrases. Listen to the rhyme and rhythm of Tennyson's poem. Notice the words he chooses. Then think about how they contribute to the poem's overall mood.

RHYTHM

Sometimes a song is said to have "good rhythm." Poems have rhythm, too. Along with rhyme, it is one of the reasons that listening to poetry is enjoyable.

Rhythm, in poetry, is the way in which accents fall in a particular number of syllables. The rhythm pattern is expressed in **feet** and **meter.** The basic rhythm unit is a **foot.** The number of feet in a line determines the meter.

The symbol for an unaccented syllable is ˘. The symbol for an accented syllable is ´. In a rhythm unit of an unaccented syllable (˘) followed by an accented (´) syllable, the foot would be marked ˘ ´. This type of foot is called **iambic.** If this same foot occurs five times in a line, the rhythm pattern is called **iambic pentameter** (penta meaning five). There are five ˘ ´ units in the line, or five iambic feet in the meter.

As you read the excerpt from "The Lady of Shalott," ask yourself:

1. Can you hear a definite rhythmic pattern as you read the poem?
2. Is the same rhythmic pattern used in every line?

WRITING CONNECTION

Write four lines of your own, using the rhythmic pattern of iambic pentameter.

from The Lady of Shalott

by Alfred, Lord Tennyson

On either side the river lie
Long fields of barley and of rye,
That clothe the wold[1] and meet the sky;
And through the field the road runs by
5   To many-towered Camelot;
And up and down the people go,
Gazing where the lilies blow[2]
Round an island there below,
      The island of Shalott.

10   Willows whiten, aspens quiver,
Little breezes dusk and shiver
Through the wave that runs forever
By the island in the river
      Flowing down to Camelot.
15   Four gray walls, and four gray towers,
Overlook a space of flowers,
And the silent isle embowers
      The Lady of Shalott.

There she weaves by night and day
20   A magic web with colors gay.
She has heard a whisper say,
A curse is on her if she stay
      To look down to Camelot.
She knows not what the curse may be,
25   And so she weaveth steadily,
And little other care hath she,
      The Lady of Shalott.

---

quiver (KWIV ur) to shake, tremble
dusk (DUSK) to make shadowy
embowers (em BOU urz) shelters, encloses
[1]**wold:** rolling plains
[2]**blow:** bloom

Review the Selection

UNDERSTAND THE SELECTION

Recall

1. What is on either side of the river?

2. What is in the river?

3. What is the name of the place to which the river flows?

Infer

4. How would you describe the scene that the poet is trying to paint?

5. Interpret the significance of Camelot.

6. How would you interpret the line "And the silent isle embowers"?

7. Who or what do you think the "Lady" is? Explain your answer.

Apply

8. Imagine you came upon a place like that described in the poem. Would you like to stay? Why or why not?

9. What do you think the "curse" is? Predict what might happen to the Lady.

10. In your opinion, why doesn't the Lady care about the curse?

Respond to Literature

Does the poem remind you of a place that has been affected by the Industrial Revolution? Explain your answer. What do you think was Tennyson's point in creating such a world in this poem?

WRITE ABOUT THE SELECTION

Two main elements of poetry are imagery and symbolism. The writer uses **imagery** to paint a mental picture for the reader. **Symbolism** is the use of one thing to represent something else.

Think about the imagery and symbolism in the poem. Then write a paragraph explaining your ideas about the meaning of the poem.

Prewriting Use two idea clusters to organize your thoughts. On the left side of your paper, write *Imagery.* On the right side, write *Symbolism.* Draw a circle around each. Think of examples of each in the poem. Write them down around the appropriate word. Circle them and draw lines connecting the circles. Next, picture the imagery in your mind and think about what the symbols mean to you. Write these ideas down around the appropriate image or symbol. Again, draw circles and lines to connect them.

Writing Write your paragraph about the meaning of the poem. Be sure to make references to the images and symbols in your clusters.

Revising Think of at least one more image or symbol. Add that to your cluster, then change your paragraph or expand it, depending on whether or not it has changed your thinking.

Proofreading Check over your spelling. Draw a circle around any misspelled word, then respell it correctly.

THINK ABOUT RHYTHM

There are several rhythm patterns. Each pattern is classified by the number of unaccented (˘) and accented (´) syllables in each foot and by the number of feet in the line, which is the meter. The following is a chart of the various types of feet:

Mark	Technical Name	Rhythm Category
˘ ´	iambic	rising
´ ˘	trochaic	falling
˘ ˘ ´	anapestic	rising
´ ˘ ˘	dactylic	falling

There are four basic types of meter. The most common type is called **classical.** This is simply a meter in which all the feet have the same pattern of accented and unaccented syllables.

1. Since *tri* means three, and *tetra* means four, and *hexa* means six, what do you call a meter with three feet? With four feet? With six feet?

2. Look at the chart above. There are two examples of rising rhythm. Which are they?

3. Again, looking at the chart, why do you think some rhythm is called "marching", and some "dancing"?

4. Iambic pentameter is marked ˘ ´ ˘ ´ ˘ ´ ˘ ´ ˘ ´. Based on the chart, how would you mark trochaic trimeter?

5. Look at "The Lady of Shalott." Write out the rhyme schemes for the first and last lines of the first stanza.

DEVELOP YOUR VOCABULARY

A **noun** is the name of a person, place or object. A **verb** is a word that expresses action or a state of being. Some words can be used as both nouns and verbs. *For example:* How many times a day do you *walk* down the *walk* from your home to the street? Here, "walk" is used first as a verb, then as a noun.

When a word can be either a noun or a verb, its part of speech depends on how it is used in a sentence.

In the second stanza of "The Lady of Shalott," there is an example of a word that is usually a noun, but is used in the verb form. What is the word? What do you think it means in its verb sense?

Think of five words that can be used either as a noun or a verb. List them. Then use each in two sentences—first as a noun, then as a verb.

READING FOCUS
Identify Mood Describe the style—rhythm, rhyme, word choice—of Tennyson's poem. What mood does it create?

Learn About

The Pink Dress, Frederic Bazille. The Granger Collection

READING FOCUS

Evaluate the Writer's Message The writer has a message to send in his or her writing. Often the reader needs to read a poem several times to understand the message. Think about whether the writer wants to teach you a lesson, for example, or merely share his or her comments about a topic. Remember that some poems state their message directly. Others make you think about the words of the poem and decide what message they imply.

RHYME

Rhyme, in poetry, is a regular recurrence of corresponding sounds. This means that the same or similar sounds occur at set intervals throughout the poem. Usually rhymes occur at the ends of lines.

As stated before, rhymes occur at regular intervals throughout a poem. The pattern that is established is known as the **rhyme scheme.** These schemes are identified in terms of letters used to designate the occurrence of the end rhymes. Rhyming words are represented by the same letter. For example, in a poem in which the ends of the first and third lines rhyme and the ends of the second and fourth lines rhyme, the scheme would be written *abab.* If the second and fourth lines rhyme, but the first and third do not, the scheme would be *abcb.*

As you read "How do I love thee?" and "Accuse me not" determine:
1. What sort of rhyme is being used: end or internal, masculine or feminine?
2. What is the rhyme scheme?

WRITING CONNECTION

Write a four-line stanza from a poem that you know. Show the rhyme scheme. Then make up your own four-line poem, following the same rhyme scheme.

How do I love thee?

by Elizabeth Barrett Browning

How do I love thee? Let me count the ways.
I love thee to the depth and breadth and height
My soul can reach, when feeling out of sight
For the ends of Being and ideal Grace.
5   I love thee to the level of everyday's
Most quiet need, by sun and candlelight.
I love thee freely, as men strive for Right;
I love thee purely, as they turn from Praise.
I love thee with the passion put to use
10   In my old griefs, and with my childhood's faith.
I love thee with a love I seemed to lose
With my lost saints,—I love thee with the breath,
Smiles, tears, of all my life!—and, if God choose,
I shall but love thee better after death.

Accuse me not

by Elizabeth Barrett Browning

Accuse me not, beseech thee, that I wear
Too calm and a sad face in front of thine;
For we two look two ways, and cannot shine
With the same sunlight on our brow and hair.

5   On me thou lookest with no doubting care,
As on a bee shut in a crystalline;
Since sorrow hath shut me safe in love's divine,
And to spread wing and fly in the outer air
Were most impossible failure, if I strove

10   To fail so. But I look on thee—on thee—
Beholding, besides love, the end of love,
Hearing oblivion beyond memory;
As one who sits and gazes from above,
Over the rivers to the bitter sea.

---

beseech (bee SEECH) ask earnestly
divine (dih VYN) mystical or heavenly state
beholding (bee HOHL ding) seeing
oblivion (oh BLIHV ee uhn) state of being completely forgotten
gazes (GAYZ uhz) looks intently

Elizabeth Barrett Browning (1806–1861)

Elizabeth Barrett Browning was the first-born of twelve children. She received no formal education, but a zest for knowledge, combined with her father's encouragement, enabled her to learn Latin and Greek. Elizabeth's childhood years were devoted to literature. Unfortunately, when she was fifteen she had a riding accident which injured her spine. It left her a semi-invalid, and after that she spent much of her time reading and writing.

Elizabeth Barrett Browning was married to Robert Browning, who was also a poet. They had become acquainted with each other's work upon publication. Then in 1844, Elizabeth mentioned him in one of her poems. This prompted Robert to write to her to express his respect for her work and to request a meeting.

Elizabeth secretly married Robert in 1846 and they left for Italy shortly thereafter. Her father never forgave her. However, with her marriage to Robert came new life. The couple entertained an array of American and British artists and writers in their Florence home, called Casa Guidi.

Sometime after their third anniversary, Elizabeth slipped a manuscript into Robert's pocket as he stood looking out the window. It was a beautiful book of sonnets she had written to him before they were married. He encouraged her to publish them. She suggested they call it "Sonnets from the Portuguese" to hide their true identities. Portuguese is a reference to a pet name Robert often called her. The sonnets became her best known work. Elizabeth and Robert had great happiness together, until her death in 1861.

Review the Selection

UNDERSTAND THE SELECTION

Recall

1. What does the speaker count in the poem "How do I love thee?"

2. When does the speaker expect to love best of all?

3. In "Accuse me not," to what does the poet compare herself that cannot fly?

Infer

4. Explain "by sun and candlelight" in "How do I love thee?"

5. What is the speaker referring to in "as they turn from Praise"?

6. What does the speaker in "Accuse me not" mean by "we two look two ways"?

7. What does the speaker mean by "the end of love"?

Apply

8. Would you say that the speaker is a religious person? Explain your answer.

9. How much do you think the speaker loves the person being addressed?

10. Imagine that you received a poem such as either of these from a loved one. What would your reaction be?

Respond to Literature

Are these poems examples of Victorian Romanticism or Realism? Explain.

WRITE ABOUT THE SELECTION

Imagine that you have just received one of these poems from a loved one, for whom you have the same feelings. You want to respond and express your feelings in the same manner, but do not know where or how to begin.

Prewriting Write a series of questions in which you ask yourself whether various comparisons are appropriate, and if so, to what degree. For example: "Do I love thee more than my favorite TV show?" Think of as many likely things as you can—things that would be meaningful to you and to the other person. Review these, and rank them from one to five—one being the most appropriate, five the least. Take all the top-ranked analogies and eliminate the rest; rank these on a scale of one to three. Continue this process of elimination until you are left with the single most appropriate analogy.

Writing You are down to one comparison which will be the basis of your poem. Write four lines of poetry, addressed to your loved one, explaining and expanding on this analogy.

Revising Rewrite the poem so that at least two of the four lines rhyme at the end.

Proofreading To make sure that you have at least two end rhymes, write down the rhyme scheme of your poem as it is now written. At least two of the four letters should be the same.

THINK ABOUT RHYME

Rhyme schemes depend on several things. One is the length of the stanza. Certain types of poetry have a standard number of lines. "How do I love thee?" and "Accuse me not" are sonnets; **sonnets** have fourteen lines.

Another type of structure is the pattern of rhyming in the poem. Some types of poetry have set rhyme schemes which the poet must follow with only slight variations. The Italian sonnet usually has a rhyme pattern of *abbaabba* in the first stanza and *cdecde* or *ccddee* in the second. The English (or Shakespearean) sonnet's rhyme scheme is commonly *abab cdcd efef gg*. Although most rhymes are end rhymes, some can occur within the same line, known as **internal rhyme.**

1. Using the lettering system, write out the rhyme scheme for "How do I love thee?" and "Accuse me not."

2. How many separate rhyming sounds are present in the poems? What is the basis for these?

3. Do these poems employ internal rhyme? If so, give an example.

4. How does internal rhyme differ from end rhyme? Can you find any examples of internal rhyme in "How do I love thee?"

5. Both poems are written as one stanza. If you were to separate them into two stanzas, between which lines would you make the separation? On what basis would you do this?

DEVELOP YOUR VOCABULARY

Verbs express action *(run)* or a state of being *(is)*. Verbs have different tenses that express time—past, present and future. Verbs have four principal forms or parts: **infinitive** (present); **past tense; past participle;** and **present participle.**

A dictionary will list all these parts, based on the infinitive (present). In cases where the past tense and past participle are the same, the word will only be listed once.

Look up the following infinitives in the dictionary, and list their remaining verb parts: past tense, past participle, present participle.

Example: To love *(infinitive)*—loved *(past tense),* have loved *(past participle),* is loving *(present participle).* Use each form of the verb in an original sentence.

1. count
2. have
3. go
4. run
5. lose
6. buy
7. ring
8. drive
9. catch
10. bring

READING FOCUS
Evaluate the Writer's Message What do you think Elizabeth Barrett Browning's message is in each of these poems?

From the complete illustrated works of Lewis Carroll, copyright 1982, reprinted by permission of Crown Publishers, a division of Random House Inc.; photo courtesy of The New York Public Library

Learn About

TONE

In literature, **tone** expresses the attitude of the author. This attitude could be toward the characters, the subject matter, or the reader. Tone may be serious or humorous, formal or informal.

It is important for the reader to recognize the author's tone. For example, something may seem funny or even silly on the surface. However, there may be more to it than that. It could be that the author is using humor or silliness for a serious purpose. This is sometimes a more effective way to make a meaningful point. If this is the case, the author is using **satire.**

Satirical literature uses humor in some form to disguise a critical statement about some condition of life. Although the meaning under the surface is critical, the author's motive is not necessarily negative.

As you read "The Walrus and the Carpenter," ask yourself:

1. Is there more to this than first meets the eye?
2. What is the author's real purpose?

WRITING CONNECTION

Think of an issue that is important to you. Write a satirical poem to make a statement about the issue.

READING FOCUS

Evaluate the Writer's Purpose Remember that writers may write for one of many reasons: to entertain, to comment or persuade, to inform, or to describe. Sometimes they also combine purposes. As you read Lewis Carroll's poem, ask yourself *why* he might have written it. Think about what his goal might have been. Use his tone, or attitude, about the poem's topic to help you decide.

The Walrus and the Carpenter

from

Through the Looking Glass

by Lewis Carroll

The sun was shining on the sea,
    Shining with all his might;
He did his very best to make
    The billows smooth and bright—
5   And this was odd, because it was
    The middle of the night.

The moon was shining sulkily,
    Because she thought the sun
Had got no business to be there
10   After the day was done—
"It's very rude of him," she said,
    "To come and spoil the fun!"

The sea was wet as wet could be,
    The sands were dry as dry.
15   You could not see a cloud, because
    No cloud was in the sky;
No birds were flying overhead—
    There were no birds to fly.

---

billows (BIL ohz) large waves of water
sulkily (SUL kuh lee) gloomily, resentfully

From the complete illustrated works of Lewis Carroll, copyright 1982, reprinted by permission of Crown Publishers, a division of Random House Inc.; photo courtesy of The New York Public Library

      The Walrus and the Carpenter
20   Were walking close at hand;
    They wept like anything to see
        Such quantities of sand.
     "If this were only cleared away,"
        They said, "it would be grand!"

25   "If seven maids with seven mops
        Swept it for half a year,
    Do you suppose," the Walrus said,
        "That they could get it clear?"
    "I doubt it," said the Carpenter,
30   And shed a bitter tear.

    "O Oysters, come and walk with us!"
        The Walrus did beseech.
    "A pleasant walk, a pleasant talk,
        Along the briny beach;
35   We cannot do with more than four,
        To give a hand to each."

---

oysters (OI sturz) a type of sea creature, which can be eaten, with a rough, hinged shell and
   which lives at the bottom of the sea
beseech (bih SEECH) to ask earnestly; beg
briny (BRY nee) very salty

The eldest Oyster looked at him,
    But never a word he said;
The eldest Oyster winked his eye,
40   And shook his heavy head—
Meaning to say he did not choose
    To leave the oyster-bed.

But four young Oysters hurried up,
    All eager for the treat;
45 Their coats were brushed, their faces washed,
    Their shoes were clean and neat—
And this was odd, because, you know,
    They hadn't any feet.

Four other Oysters followed them,
50   And yet another four;
And thick and fast they came at last,
    And more, and more, and more—
All hopping through the frothy waves,
    And scrambling to the shore.

From the complete illustrated works of Lewis Carroll, copyright 1982, reprinted by
permission of Crown Publishers, a division of Random House Inc.; photo courtesy of
The New York Public Library

---

frothy (FRAWTH ee) foamy

55 The Walrus and the Carpenter
      Walked on a mile or so,
And then they rested on a rock
      Conveniently low;
And all the little Oysters stood
60   And waited in a row.

"The time has come," the Walrus said,
      "To talk of many things:
Of shoes—and ships—and sealing-wax—
      Of cabbages—and kings—
65 And why the sea is boiling hot—
      And whether pigs have wings."

"But wait a bit," the Oysters cried,
      "Before we have our chat;
For some of us are out of breath,
70   And all of us are fat!"
"No hurry!" said the Carpenter.
      They thanked him much for that.

"A loaf of bread," the Walrus said,
      "Is what we chiefly need;
75 Pepper and vinegar besides
      Are very good indeed—
Now, if you're ready, Oysters dear,
      We can begin to feed."

"But not on us!" the Oysters cried,
80   Turning a little blue.
"After such kindness, that would be
      A dismal thing to do!"
"The night is fine," the Walrus said,
      "Do you admire the view?"

85 "It was so kind of you to come!
      And you are very nice!"
The Carpenter said nothing but
      "Cut us another slice.
I wish you were not quite so deaf—
90   I've had to ask you twice!"

From the complete illustrated works of Lewis Carroll, copyright 1982, reprinted by permission of Crown Publishers, a division of Random House Inc.; photo courtesy of The New York Public Library

"It seems a shame," the Walrus said,
    "To play them such a trick,
After we've brought them out so far,
    And made them trot so quick!"
95   The Carpenter said nothing but
    "The butter's spread too thick!"

"I weep for you," the Walrus said;
    "I deeply sympathize."
With sobs and tears he sorted out
100   Those of the largest size,
Holding his pocket-handkerchief
    Before his streaming eyes.

"O Oysters," said the Carpenter,
    "You've had a pleasant run!
105   Shall we be trotting home again?"
    But answer came there none—
And this was scarcely odd, because
    They'd eaten every one.

Review the Selection

UNDERSTAND THE SELECTION

Recall

1. What time of day was it?

2. Where were the Walrus and the Carpenter walking?

3. Whom did they invite to join them?

Infer

4. When did you first suspect that the poem's tone was not serious?

5. Why did they want the Oysters to come along?

6. Why do you think the eldest Oyster wouldn't go?

7. What did the Walrus do when the Oysters first became suspicious?

Apply

8. Part of what makes this poem funny is the impossible, contradictory information it presents. Which example of this do you think is funniest? Why?

9. Whom or what do you think the Oysters symbolize?

10. What would your opinion of this poem have been if you knew nothing about tone and satire?

Respond to Literature

Is it surprising that this was written during the Victorian period? Explain.

WRITE ABOUT THE SELECTION

Since satire uses humor to make a serious point, what do you think the point is in this case? The Walrus and the Carpenter would have to represent something, as would the Oysters. There may or may not be some significance to the setting.

Imagine you have been invited to give a lecture on Victorian literature. You have been asked to give your impressions about the author's underlying purpose.

Prewriting Make up a chart with three columns. The first column should be just wide enough to write down a number. Split the remaining space between columns two and three. Now reread the poem. Number each stanza and put the numbers in the first column. Take notes on the content of each stanza, and put them in the second column; use key words and phrases, not sentences. Use the third column to write down your impressions of the author's purpose, based on your notes, for each of the stanzas.

Writing Review the impressions you have written down in column three. You can now write your presentation to the class.

Revising Reread your presentation. Add remarks about your opinion of the author's purpose.

Proofreading Wherever you have added your own opinions, put them in parentheses ( ). Be sure you have used both opening and closing parentheses.

THINK ABOUT TONE

Another tone that an author may take is one of irony. **Situational irony** is a condition in which something is expected to happen or to be said, yet what actually does happen or is said turns out to be totally different.

For example, imagine that the biggest football game of the season is coming up. Your team is not favored to win, and, in addition, your star quarterback gets hurt. Despite all this, your team wins! That is situational irony. It is ironic because what was expected to happen, did not happen.

Verbal irony occurs when an author (or a character) does not mean what he or she says. Sometimes the intended meaning is the direct opposite of what is said.

1. What example of situational irony can you find in "The Walrus and the Carpenter"?

2. What is the author's attitude toward his characters?

3. Would you discuss tone in this poem in terms of subject or reader? Explain.

READING FOCUS
Evaluate the Writer's Purpose What do you think Carroll's overall purpose was in writing this poem? How does the tone he creates support this purpose?

DEVELOP YOUR VOCABULARY

Many words are simply a base word or a word root with a prefix attached to the beginning and/or a suffix attached to the end. Prefixes and suffixes are called **affixes.**

A **word root,** as opposed to a base word, is not a word. It is only part of a word. It becomes a word with the addition of a prefix or suffix. For example, *ept* is not a word—it is a word root. Add the prefix *in-,* and it becomes *inept. Inept* means "not suitable to the purpose; unfit." *Ept* comes from a Latin word meaning "suitable, fit." Since the prefix *in-* means "not," you can see where the definition of *inept* comes from.

Remove the prefixes and/or suffixes from each of the following words. What remains is a word root. If you do not know its meaning, look it up in the dictionary with its affixes. Then write what you think is the meaning of the word root and use each word, with its affixes, correctly in a sentence.

1. astronaut
2. dictation
3. fraternity
4. spectacle
5. phobic
6. extraterrestrial
7. fidelity

Study of Sky and Trees, Detail, John Constable. Art Resource

READING FOCUS

Evaluate the Writer's Style   A writer's style is reflected in his or her choice of words, mood, and tone. For example, a writer may use a clear point-by-point style to argue a political position or a great deal of description to convey a sense of place in a travelogue. As you read Charlotte Brontë's writing, think about her style. How does it suit the people and places she is writing about? Look at her choice of words and how it helps her bring the characters to life.

POINT OF VIEW

In literature, **point of view** indicates the way in which a story is presented. Basically, a story can be presented from either a first-person or third-person point of view. If the person telling the story is also one of the characters in that story, it is being told in the **first person.**

If the storyteller is someone who is not in the story, it is being told in the **third person.** Third person narrators can be of two types. The **limited** third person is restricted to the feelings, awareness, and thoughts of only one character— usually the main character.

On the other hand, an **omniscient,** or all-knowing, third person narrator has access to what is happening in the minds of all the characters. He or she is not restricted in terms of character or setting.

As you read this passage from *Jane Eyre,* think about the following:

1. From what point of view is the story told?
2. How does this affect the way in which you learn about the story?

WRITING CONNECTION

Briefly describe something happening around you now from both the first-person and the third-person points of view.

from

JANE EYRE

ADAPTED

by Charlotte Brontë

There was no possibility of taking a walk that day. We had been wandering in the leafless shrubbery an hour in the morning; but since dinner, the cold winter wind had brought with it clouds so somber, and a rain so penetrating, that further outdoor exercise was now out of the question.

I was glad of it. I never liked long walks, especially on chilly afternoons. It was dreadful to me to come home in the raw twilight, with nipped fingers and toes, and a heart saddened by the scoldings of Bessie, the nurse, and humbled by the consciousness of my physical inferiority to Eliza, John and Georgiana Reed.

Eliza, John and Georgiana were now clustered round their mama in the drawing room. She lay on a sofa by the fireside and with her darlings about her (for the time neither quarreling nor crying) looked perfectly happy. Me, she had excluded from the group. She said she regretted it was necessary to keep me at a distance, but that until she thought I was trying to be more sociable and childlike, with a more attractive and sprightly manner—something lighter, franker, more natural—she really must exclude me from privileges intended only for contented, happy little children.

"What does Bessie say I have done?" I asked.

"Jane, I don't like complainers or questioners; besides, there is something truly forbidding in a child talking to her elders in that manner. Be seated somewhere; and until you can speak pleasantly, remain silent."

A small breakfast room adjoined the drawing room. I slipped in there. It contained a bookcase; I chose a book, one full of pictures. I sat down on the window seat; gathering up my feet, I sat cross-legged, like a Turk. Having drawn the red moreen curtain nearly closed, I was almost hidden.

Folds of scarlet drapery were my view on the right; to the left were clear panes of glass, protecting, but not separating me from the drear November day. At intervals, while turning over the leaves of my book, I studied that winter afternoon. Afar, it offered a pale blank of mist and

---

forbidding (fur BID ing) shocking; terrible
moreen (muh REEN) a heavy wool or cotton fabric

cloud; near, a scene of wet lawn and storm-beat shrub, with ceaseless rain sweeping away wildly before long and lamentable blasts of wind.

I returned to my book, *Bewick's History of British Birds*. I cared little for the letterpress, generally speaking; and yet there were certain pages that, child as I was, I could not quite pass. They were those which tell of the haunts of seafowl: of "the solitary rocks and promontories" only inhabited by them; of the coast of Norway, studded with islands from the Lindeness, or Naze, to the North Cape.

Nor could I pass the illustration of the bleak shores of Lapland, Siberia, Spitzbergen, Nova Zembla, Iceland, Greenland,[1] with "the vast sweep of the Arctic Zone, and those forlorn regions of dreary space—that reservoir of frost and snow, where firm fields of ice, the accumulation of centuries of winters, glazed in Alpine heights above heights, surround the pole, and concenter the multiplied rigors of extreme cold."

About these death-white realms I formed an idea of my own: shadowy, like all the half-comprehended notions that float dim through children's brains, but strangely impressive. The words in these pages connected themselves with the pictures, and gave significance to the rock standing up alone in a sea of billow and spray; to the broken boat stranded on a desolate coast; to the cold and ghastly moon glancing through bars of cloud at a wreck just sinking.

I cannot tell what sentiment haunted the quiet solitary churchyard, with its inscribed headstone, its gate, its two trees, its low horizon, girdled by a broken wall, and its newly risen moon, signaling the hour of eventide.

The two ships becalmed on a torpid sea, I believed to be marine phantoms.

The fiend pinning down the thief's pack behind him, I passed over quickly: it was an object of terror.

So was the black, horned thing seated aloof on a rock, surveying a distant crowd surrounding a gallows.

Each picture told a story; mysterious often to my undeveloped understanding and young feelings, yet profoundly interesting—as interesting as the tales Bessie, the maid, sometimes narrated on winter evenings, when she was in a good humor. She would bring her ironing table to the nursery hearth, and allowed us to sit by it; and while she got up Mrs. Reed's lace frills and crimped her nightcap borders, fed our eager attention with passages of love and adventure taken from old fairy tales and older ballads.

---

letterpress (LET er pres) print; printed words
concenter (kun SEN tur) to come together at a common center point
girdled (GUR duld) surrounded; encircled
eventide (EE vun tyd) evening
becalmed (bih KAHMD) still; calm
torpid (TAWR pid) temporarily without motion
crimped (KRIMPT) pressed into narrow, regular folds
[1]**Lapland . . . Greenland:** countries and regions in the most northern parts of the world

At the Window, Hans Olaf Heyerdahl. Nasjonalgalleriet, Oslo, Norway/Bridgeman Art Library

With Bewick on my knee, I was then happy; happy at least in my way. I feared nothing but interruption, and that came too soon. The breakfast room door opened.

"Bah! Madame Mope!" cried the voice of John Reed. Then he paused: he found the room apparently empty.

"Where the dickens is she?" he continued. "Lizzy! Georgy!" calling to his sisters. "Jane is not here. Tell mama she has run out into the rain—bad animal!"

"It is well I drew the curtain," thought I, and I wished fervently that he might not discover my hiding place; nor would John Reed have found it out himself: he was not very bright, but Eliza just put her head in at the door, and said at once:

"She is in the window seat, to be sure, Jack."

And I came out immediately, for I trembled at the idea of being dragged out by Jack.

"What do you want?" I asked, with awkward diffidence.

"Say, 'What do you want, Master Reed?' " was the answer. "I want you to come here," and seating himself in an armchair, he gestured that I was to stand before him.

John Reed was a schoolboy of fourteen years old; four years older than I, for I was but ten. He was large and stout for his age, with a dingy and unwholesome skin; thick features in a wide face, heavy limbs and large hands and feet.

He gorged himself habitually at meals, which made him bilious, and gave him a dim eye and flabby cheeks. He ought to have been at school; but his mama had taken him home for a month or two, "on account of his delicate health."

Mr. Miles, the schoolmaster, said John would do very well if he had fewer cakes and sweets sent to him from home; but the mother's heart rejected an opinion so harsh, and she thought rather that John's sallowness was owing to overwork, and, perhaps, to homesickness.

John had not much affection for his mother and sisters, and a hatred of me. He bullied and punished me; not two or three times in the week, nor once or twice in the day, but continually. Every nerve I had feared him, and every morsel of flesh on my bones shrank when he came near. There were moments when I was bewildered by the terror he inspired, because I had no defense whatever against either his menaces or his punishment. The servants did not like to offend their young master by taking my side against him, and Mrs. Reed was blind and deaf on the subject; she never saw him strike or heard him abuse me, though he did both in her very presence; more frequently, however, behind her back.

Habitually obedient to John, I came up to his chair. He spent some three minutes in thrusting his tongue at me as far as he could. I knew he would soon strike,

---

bilious (BIL yus) bad-tempered; cross; nasty
sallowness (SAL oh nis) a sickly, pale-yellow complexion
habitually (huh BICH oo ul ee) by habit; regularly; customarily

Study of Sky and Trees, John Constable. Art Resource

and while dreading the blows, I mused on his disgusting and ugly appearance. I wonder if he read that notion in my face; for, all at once, without speaking, he struck suddenly and strongly. I tottered, and on regaining my balance moved back a step or two from his chair.

"That is for your impudence in answering mama before," said he, "and for your sneaking way of getting behind curtains and for the look you had in your eyes two minutes ago, you rat!"

Accustomed to John Reed's abuse, I never had an idea of replying to it; my concern was how to endure the blow which would certainly follow the insult.

"What were you doing behind the curtain?" he asked.

"I was reading."

"Show the book."

I returned to the window and fetched the book.

"You have no business to take our books; you are a dependent, mama says; you have no money; your father left you none; you ought to beg, and not to live here with gentlemen's children like us, and eat the same meals we do, and wear

---

tottered (TOT urd) staggered; was unsteady, as if about to fall

clothes at our mama's expense. Now, I'll teach you to rummage my bookshelves, for they *are* mine—all the house belongs to me, or will in a few years. Go and stand by the door, out of the way of the mirror and the windows."

I did so, not at first aware of his intention, but when I saw him lift the book and stand, about to throw it, I instinctively jumped aside with a cry of alarm. Not soon enough, however, the volume was flung, it hit me, and I fell, striking my head against the door and cutting it. The cut bled, the pain was sharp, but my terror was over.

"Wicked and cruel boy!" I said. "You are like a murderer, you are like a slave driver, you are like the Roman emperors!"

I had read Goldsmith's *History of Rome,* and had formed my opinion of Nero, Caligula, etc. Also I had made comparisons in silence, which I never intended to declare aloud.

"What! What!" he cried. "Did you say that to me? Did you hear her, Eliza and Georgiana? Won't I tell mama? but first . . . "

He ran headlong at me. I felt him grasp my hair and my shoulder, but he had made me desperate. I really saw in him a tyrant, a murderer. I felt a drop or two of blood from my head trickle down my neck, and felt the pain sharply. This made me unafraid, and I fought him fiercely. I don't very well know what I did with my hands, but he called me "rat! rat!" and bellowed out loud. Aid was near him: Eliza and Georgiana had run for Mrs. Reed, who had gone upstairs. She now came upon the scene, followed by Bessie and her maid Abbot. We were parted: I heard the words:

"Dear! dear! What a fury to fly at Master John!"

"Did ever anybody see such a picture of passion?"

Then Mrs. Reed commanded:

"Take her away to the red room, and lock her in there." Four hands were immediately laid upon me, and I was borne upstairs.

Nero, Caligula (NIR oh, cuh LIG yuh luh) Roman emperors
borne (BAWRN) carried

AUTHOR BIOGRAPHY
Charlotte Brontë (1818–1855)

Charlotte Brontë began her writing career at an early age, and by twelve, she was writing dramas, stories and critical reviews. Though her experiences in life were rather limited, her colorful, vivid imagination made up for what she lacked in experience, accomplishment, and age.

Her family moved to Haworth, Yorkshire, when she was four years old, and Brontë lived there for the rest of her life with her sisters, Emily and Anne and her brother, Branwell. Anne and Emily also wrote, and at one time the three sisters joined together to publish a poetry book using the names Currer, Ellis and Acton Bell to hide their true identities. By 1846, the sisters had each completed a novel.

Two themes run through Brontë's work, themes which she started to develop in her adolescence and which remained consistent throughout her adult writing; rival brothers and the orphan girl.

The orphan girl, alone in a hostile world and suffering from unrequited love, may have been based in part on Brontë's own experiences as a governess and of the unrequited love she had for a teacher at a boarding school she attended in Brussels. She began to develop the theme of the orphan girl in her adolescent stories and continued them into her adult novels, the most famous being *Jane Eyre,* which was published in 1847.

After *Jane Eyre,* she published *Shirley* in 1849 and *Villette* in 1853. *Villette* is considered by many to be Brontë's masterpiece and is also one of the great Victorian novels. It is also based on the story of an orphan girl who lives in Brussels and suffers from unrequited love.

Between 1848–49, Emily, Anne and Branwell died, leaving Charlotte alone. In 1854 she married and was happy for a very short time. A year later she died.

Painting of Ann, Emily and Charlotte Brontë, by their brother Branwell. National Portrait Gallery, London

Review the Selection

UNDERSTAND THE SELECTION

Recall

1. Why is Jane staying with the Reeds?

2. How old are Jane and John at the time of the story?

3. What violent act does John commit against Jane?

Infer

4. What seems to be Jane's favorite hobby? Discuss the reasons for this.

5. How does Jane feel toward John and why?

6. Why does Mrs. Reed treat Jane differently from the other children?

7. Whose hands carried Jane away at the end of the story? Explain why you think this.

Apply

8. What is your opinion of Jane? Was she a bad child? Did she deserve to be treated as she was? Explain.

9. Predict what will happen to Jane after she is carried from the room.

10. Imagine yourself in Jane's situation. How would you feel? Explain.

Respond to Literature

The author seems to be criticizing certain aspects of middle class Victorian society. What do you think they are?

WRITE ABOUT THE SELECTION

What you have read is an excerpt, or part of a much longer story. There is much that has not been presented here, in terms of the events that follow this passage.

The story is told from Jane Eyre's point of view. Each character in a story might think, feel, and react differently, and for different reasons. Pick another character in the story. Summarize the story from that character's point of view.

Prewriting Begin by making three columns. In the first, outline the main events in the story, using Roman numerals and capital letters to designate major and related minor topics. In the second column, record what Jane thought, felt, and experienced in relation to each event. Then select another character in the story. What do you think that character's perception of and reaction to these same events might be? Write your ideas about these in the third column.

Writing You have outlined the main events in the story and how they can be seen from two different points of view. You are now prepared to write your summary, as seen through the eyes of another character.

Revising If you wrote your summary in the first person, rewrite it in the limited third person, and vice versa.

Proofreading Review each of your summaries. Make sure that all punctuation marks are correctly placed.

THINK ABOUT POINT OF VIEW

A story can be presented from first- or third-person point of view. The **first-person point of view** is presented by the narrator, one of the characters in the story. The **third-person point of view** is someone outside the story. A third-person narrator might know everything about each character **(omniscient),** or he or she can be **limited** to that which is seen, known, and felt by just one character.

A story told through a limited third-person point of view has much in common with one told through the first-person point of view. In both cases, the reader only sees events through the eyes and mind of one character.

1. From what point of view is this excerpt from *Jane Eyre* written? How can you tell?

2. In what ways do you think the demands of the plot might determine whether an author presents a story in the first or third person?

3. Do you think your perception of Jane's situation might have been different if the story had been told from a different point of view? Explain.

READING FOCUS

Evaluate the Writer's Style   How does Brontë's use of words, mood, and tone help to convey the urgency of young Jane's experience?

DEVELOP YOUR VOCABULARY

Personal pronouns are words that can take the place of nouns—in this case, the names of persons. The form of the pronoun to be used depends on two factors, person and usage.

First person refers to the speaker; **second person** refers to the person being spoken to; **third person** refers to another person.

Examples: I am happy.
You are happy.
She is happy.

Usage indicates whether the pronoun is being used as a subject or an object in a sentence.

| | Subject | |
Person	*Singular*	*Plural*
First	I	we
Second	you	you
Third	he, she	they

| | Object | |
Person	*Singular*	*Plural*
First	me	us
Second	you	you
Third	him, her	them

Choose a paragraph from the *Jane Eyre* selection. Revise the paragraph so that it is written from the point of view of John Reed. Change only the proper names and pronouns accordingly.

Write About Literary Style

Select three works from this unit—one representing each of the following literary styles: Romanticism, Realism, and Naturalism. Explain why you consider each to be a good example of that style.

Prewriting Consider each selection you have studied in the unit in terms of subject and theme. Remember that **subject** is the specific thing that a work is about, whereas **theme** is the broader concept. Develop a matrix by making three columns titled Romanticism, Realism and Naturalism. List each work by subject and theme. Compare the work with each of the three categories and put an *X* in the column that is most appropriate.

Writing After you have filled in your matrix, study it and choose one selection to represent each category. You are now ready to write your discussion.

Revising Rethink your selections and change any of them that are not good examples. Explain why the works that you substitute are also representative of that particular literary style.

Proofreading Remember to underline titles of novels and other long works, and to place the titles of short stories, short plays, and poems in quotation marks.

Write About Dramatic Elements

The discussion of the elements of drama, Focus on Drama, consists of several main elements. These main elements are: plot, conflict/climax, character, setting, and dramatic technique.

Choose one of the dramas in this unit and find an example of each of these elements. State the element and how your example illustrates that element.

Prewriting Make a list of the possibilities of examples for the five elements. You will find that both dramas in the unit contain many examples of each element. Next to each element, write down examples that are a distinctive part of the work.

Writing You can now write your discussion of the elements of the drama you have chosen. Give reasons for your choices. Make certain you have chosen the best examples you could find of the elements.

Revising Scan the play for better examples of the five elements. If you find an example of an element that you think is more effective than the one you originally chose, substitute what you have found.

Proofreading Check that all sentences are complete thoughts and contain a subject and verb.

Vocabulary

Homophones, or **homonyms,** are words that sound the same. For this reason, these words can be confusing and sometimes present problems when writing. However, homophones are spelled differently and have different meanings. Usually, such words are also different parts of speech. Check the following homophones in the dictionary to determine their pronunciations and parts of speech. Use each homophone in a sentence, and state its part of speech.

hear	leak	read
here	leek	reed
grown	toe	steal
groan	tow	steel

There are many such words in the English language. Think of five other examples. Again, use each homophone in a sentence, and state its part of speech.

Grammar, Usage, and Mechanics

As you know, there are differences in format between a story and a play. Stories, written in narrative, or book form, are sometimes adapted as plays. Do you think plays can be adapted to narrative, or book form?

You know that the version of *A Christmas Carol* in this unit is an adaptation of a narrative. However, imagine that it was originally written as a play, and that you want to adapt it into a story.

Revise Scene 2 of Act 1, transforming it into narrative format, suitable for a novel. Remember that it is not enough to quote the characters—the reader can't see them, their reactions, or their emotions. You will have to describe such things as facial expressions, tone of voice, and movements. The emotions of the characters must now be shown through words, rather than actions.

SPEAKING AND LISTENING

Oral interpretation, or reading aloud with expression, is an important reading skill. Unfortunately, it is a reading skill that too few of us practice or take seriously. Two modern-day performers who do take it seriously are Hal Holbrook, who has become famous for his interpretation of Mark Twain, and Julie Harris, who has won acclaim for her portrayal of Emily Dickinson. If you were to ask them about reading aloud, they would probably try to convince you to make it a priority.

Reading aloud with expression requires some practice and some concentration. There are steps you can follow that will make the process both comfortable and successful for you.

1. Before you begin an oral interpretation, familiarize yourself with the selection and, more specifically, with the characters of the selection.

2. Decide which character you would like to portray and get to know him well. Think about how he might speak and look. Consider the type of voice he might have. Try to "hear" his voice as you read the dialogue.

3. Think about the mood of the selection. When you perform an oral interpretation, your speaking voice should suit the mood that is conveyed by the dialogue. Whether the scene is lighthearted and funny or sad and foreboding, your voice should help convey that idea.

4. When you feel comfortable with the mood of the selection and the scene you have chosen, practice reading it in character. Read it over several times until you are able to read it effortlessly.

5. Practice your oral interpretation in front of a friendly audience—a friend or a family member. This will help you feel more at ease. It will also give you an opportunity for some constructive criticism before you present it before a larger group.

For this assignment, choose a selection from this unit and consider which character you would like to portray. Then, choose a scene or a portion of dialogue from the selection to interpret in character. Follow the suggestions above to aid in your success. If the scene you choose requires another character, ask a classmate to join you. You can both have fun being someone else for awhile!

CRITICAL THINKING

Two of the most important elements of drama are character and conflict. The characters struggle through the conflict. They may change in the process, or they may not. The conflict serves to advance the plot and often to help express the theme. Early on in the drama, the major characters and their backgrounds are introduced. The conflict is then developed by one or more complications in the plot. The action rises as the conflict intensifies and it is then resolved.

Choose selections from the unit to discuss the differences and relationships between each of the following: protagonist and antagonist, static characters and dynamic characters, inner conflict and external conflict, climax and resolution.

EFFECTIVE STUDYING

Note Taking You can improve your studying and use your study time more efficiently by learning how to take good notes.

Here are some ways to take notes effectively:

1. Write down only important facts and main ideas as you read. By writing down key words and phrases, you develop an outline of what you are studying. The key words and phrases act as cues to help you recall the details of what you have studied.

2. Use your own words whenever you can. You will be better able to understand and remember what you have studied if you can restate or paraphrase what you have read.

Test Preparation

Organize your notes before you begin studying for a test. List the most important points as heads and place supporting notes beneath the correct head.

The Modern View

A dreamer is one who can only find his way by moonlight, and his punishment is that he sees the dawn before the rest of the world.

—Oscar Wilde

Impression Mist, Claude Monet. Three Lions/Superstock

1901 Rudyard Kipling's narrative of India, *Kim,* appears.

1906 Plays by George Bernard Shaw open in New York.

1914 Assassination of Archduke Ferdinand begins World War I.

1900	1905	1910	1915

1902 Boer War ends with British control of South Africa.

1912 Titanic hits iceberg; sinks with more than 1,500 people aboard.

1915 W. Somerset Maugham publishes *Of Human Bondage.*

The Modern View

Do you think that many of the ideas of previous times are out of place in today's world? If you do, you can understand the feelings of many English writers of the early years of the 20th century.

■ THE END OF VICTORIANISM

After Queen Victoria died in 1901, many people began to question the beliefs of the Victorian age. Must literary works always have a message? The Victorians thought so, but the new poets, novelists, and playwrights believed in "art for art's sake." The playwright Oscar Wilde was a leading spokesman for this point of view. His comedy, *The Importance of Being Earnest,* makes fun of Victorian seriousness.

■ THE EFFECTS OF WORLD WAR I

In 1914 Britain went to war with Germany. World War I was a devastating experience. By the time it ended, in 1918, almost an entire generation of young men had been killed. When you read Katherine Mansfield's "The Demon Lover," see if it helps you understand the horror and the loss of that time.

The war made people feel sad and disillusioned. They felt that many ideas of the past were no longer true. They searched for new ways to express themselves. Writers gave up romantic and sentimental themes. In every form of literature, they began to experiment. You will read poems by three writers who came from different backgrounds and used different techniques but who shared an interest in trying new ways of writing.

Dylan Thomas was a Welshman. He wrote "Do Not Go Gentle into That Good Night" for his dying father. T. S. Eliot was originally an American. "The Naming of Cats" is from a group of poems he wrote that became the basis of a hit musical play called "Cats." William Butler

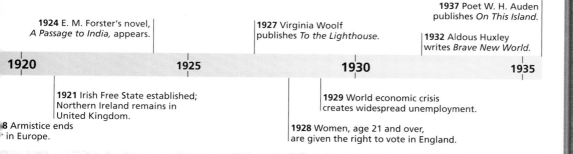

1924 E. M. Forster's novel, *A Passage to India,* appears.

1927 Virginia Woolf publishes *To the Lighthouse.*

1937 Poet W. H. Auden publishes *On This Island.*

1932 Aldous Huxley writes *Brave New World.*

1920   1925   1930   1935

1921 Irish Free State established; Northern Ireland remains in United Kingdom.

1929 World economic crisis creates widespread unemployment.

8 Armistice ends in Europe.

1928 Women, age 21 and over, are given the right to vote in England.

Yeats was Irish. See if you can spot the images he used in "The Wild Swans at Coole."

Do you enjoy humor with an ironic, or unexpected, twist? This was a favorite technique of the post-World War I period. You will read an example in the selection by George Bernard Shaw, a social reformer.

■ A NEW THEORY OF BEHAVIOR

Sigmund Freud was an Austrian psychiatrist whose theories had a great effect on writers of this period. Freud said that people never really forget anything, but that many of their memories are unconscious. You will read a story by Tagore that illustrates how the past can influence our reactions to the present.

Freud tried to bring unconscious memories to the surface by having his patients recount their dreams and also by using stream of consciousness, a technique in which patients were encouraged to say whatever came into their minds. Writers borrowed these devices. When you read George Orwell's "Shooting an Elephant," notice how the whole story could really be just a series of thoughts passing through the narrator's mind.

■ THE END OF EXPERIMENTATION

The 1930s brought renewed disillusionment to England and much of the rest of the world. The Great Depression left many people unemployed, and the rise of the Nazis in Germany and the Fascists in Italy brought the threat of another war. Writers became more concerned with the expression of ideas and emotions. They lost interest in the development of new techniques. However, the techniques they had pioneered earlier in the century still influence literature today.

As you read the selections in this unit, try to find elements that express the spirit of the period. Do the ideas still hold true today? Why?

TONE

The tone of a work of literature is set by the way in which the writer presents the work. The effectiveness of a work of literature—and its effect on the reader—depends partly on its tone.

Tone can range from serious, formal, or solemn to friendly, playful, or informal. It can be ironic, satirical, or condescending, depending on the writer's feelings, how the writer wants the audience to see the subject, and the effect the writer wants to create.

Tone is usually suggested throughout the work. By use of tone, a writer can invite the reader to laugh with him or her about a situation or indicate that the situation is no laughing matter. Tone can imply a writer's opinion of the subject by the particular words and manner of expression that the writer chooses.

As you read "The Wit and Wisdom of George Bernard Shaw," ask yourself:

1. What is Shaw's tone in each epigram?
2. How does Shaw intend the reader to react to each of them?

READING FOCUS

Paraphrase When you paraphrase, you retell the important main ideas and events of a literary work in your own words. In his epigrams or commentaries, George Bernard Shaw offers you summaries of life situations. As you read Shaw's epigrams, imagine the situations he summarizes. Think about the main ideas and key events each situation might include. Then paraphrase the epigrams in your own words.

WRITING CONNECTION

Write a sentence about something you did yesterday. Does it have a certain tone? Rewrite the sentence in three ways, using three different tones.

Wit and Wisdom of George Bernard Shaw

by George Bernard Shaw

On Conversation

I often quote myself. It adds spice to my conversation.

On Thinking

Few people think more than two or three times a year; I have made an intentional reputation for myself by thinking once or twice a week.

On Biography

When you read a biography, remember that the truth is never fit for publication.

On Children

Nothing offends children more than to play down to them. All the great children's books—*The Pilgrim's Progress, Robinson Crusoe, Grimm's Fairy Tales* and *Gulliver's Travels*—were written for adults.

On Contradiction

A man never tells you anything until you contradict him.

On Convalescence

I enjoy convalescence; it is the part that makes the illness worthwhile.

---

spice (SPYS) to add zest or piquancy; to make interesting
intentional (in TEN shuh nul) on purpose
offends (uh FENDZ) displeases

On Age

Old men are dangerous; it doesn't matter to them what is going to happen to the world.

On England and America

England and America are two countries separated by the same language.

On Hunting

When a man wants to murder a tiger, he calls it sport; when a tiger wants to murder him, he calls it ferocity.

On Music

There is nothing that soothes me more after a long and maddening course of piano recitals than to sit and have my teeth drilled by a fairly skilled hand.

The chief objection to playing wind instruments is that it prolongs the life of the player.

On Success

I dread success. To have succeeded is to have finished one's business on earth, like the male spider, who is killed by the female the moment he has succeeded in courtship.

On Punishment

The liar's punishment is not in the least that he is not believed, but that he cannot believe anyone else.

On Dreams

You see things; and you say "Why?" But I dream things that never were; and I say "Why not?"

George Bernard Shaw (1856–1950)

Shaw was born in Dublin into the genteel poverty of an extremely poor and unhappy home. He disliked school intensely and in later years referred to schools as prisons. Because of the misery of his home life, he turned to the world of books. He developed many interests, particularly music and art, which he maintained throughout life.

At twenty, Shaw moved to London where he began to write seriously. He became friends with Beatrice and Sidney Webb. The Webbs were part of the Fabian Society, an organization that was interested in socialism and social reform in England. Shaw devoted a great deal of his time writing pamphlets and speaking for them at least once a week for fifteen years. The Fabian Society was instrumental in furthering social advances in the early part of the 1900s in England.

During his lifetime, Shaw wrote about fifty plays, along with many essays that he would include at the beginning of his plays. He would share his feelings about a subject that the play suggested. He also wrote many books and pamphlets on art, music, and theater. He was an avid letter writer and was quick to offer his opinion on any subject.

Although the public sometimes found him strange, they also found him very interesting, and his thoughts and ideas were often quoted. From a lonely childhood a man emerged who was richly gifted and had a marvelous sense of humor, as well as a profound ability to bring important ideas to the stage.

Review the Selection

UNDERSTAND THE SELECTION

Recall

1. In the epigram, "On Thinking," how often does Shaw say he thinks?

2. What, according to Shaw, are the great children's books?

3. What does Shaw find soothing after attending piano recitals?

Infer

4. Why does Shaw say England and America are separated by the same language?

5. What is his opinion of the accuracy of biographies?

6. What two points of view are expressed in "On Hunting"?

7. Explain in your own words why "old men are dangerous."

Apply

8. Describe what you think Shaw's "intentional reputation" is.

9. In your opinion, is Shaw correct in his view on liars? Explain.

10. Based on these epigrams, what is your opinion of Shaw?

Respond to Literature

What are your reactions to Shaw's statements? Which apply to your life?

WRITE ABOUT THE SELECTION

In this collection of epigrams, Shaw tells you what he thinks about a wide variety of subjects. In some cases, he is deadly serious; in others, his tone is ironic. With which of his statements do you agree? Think about why you agree with these statements.

Prewriting   Select one of Shaw's statements or observations with which you agree. The statement that you select should be the one about which you feel most strongly. Define for yourself what the statement means to you. Next, list the reasons why you agree. Number them in order of importance.

Writing   Write a persuasive paragraph to convince your reader of the truth of the statement you have selected. Start off by defining what the statement means. Then, using your list of reasons, state your argument in the rest of the paragraph.

Revising   To make your argument more convincing, think of an example which illustrates the truth of the statement, and add it to your paragraph.

Proofreading   Use commas to set off parenthetical expressions. **Parenthetical expressions** are phrases or words not absolutely necessary to the sentence. For example: Shaw is, I think, essentially serious. If you've used a parenthetical expression in your paragraph, check to make sure the commas are placed correctly.

THINK ABOUT TONE

The tone of a work of literature expresses the writer's attitude toward the subject of the work. Tone can also express the writer's attitude toward his or her audience. The tone of a work is set by the writer's choice of words and phrasing.

Various tones can trigger various reactions in the reader. For example, the reader might feel on the verge of laughter, tenseness, or sympathy. The feeling the writer's tone creates in the reader is the mood. Most short works have one underlying mood throughout.

1. Name the basic underlying tone used by Shaw in these epigrams.

2. What does an ironic tone tell you?

3. What would you say Shaw's tone is in "On Music"?

4. How might "On Hunting" make you think differently about hunting?

5. How does Shaw's tone affect your reaction to "On Dreams"?

READING FOCUS

Paraphrase Choose one epigram and paraphrase it. Read your work to a classmate. See if your classmate can guess which epigram you paraphrased. Then, switch roles.

DEVELOP YOUR VOCABULARY

Synonyms are words that have the same, or nearly the same, meaning. They are words which can be substituted for each other. When you use a synonym in place of your original word, though, you may see that the synonym has given a slightly different meaning to the sentence.

For instance, compare these sentences:

It's cold outside.
It's chilly outside.
It's freezing outside.

Chilly and *freezing* are both synonyms for *cold*, yet each conveys a slightly different shade of meaning.

A dictionary or thesaurus is a good place to find synonyms. A dictionary lists synonyms for some words at the end of the word's definition. A **thesaurus** is a book in which synonyms and antonyms are usually arranged by subject. With a thesaurus, you can start with a very general word and find many words and phrases to express every shade of meaning associated with that word.

Review these words from the selection. Using a dictionary or thesaurus, find at least two synonyms for each word and write them next to the word. Then write an original sentence using the synonym you think most closely matches the original word.

1. spice
2. intentional
3. offends
4. contradict
5. convalescence
6. ferocity

CHARACTER

What makes a character in literature real to you? A writer must convince you that his or her characters are real people, even though they spring purely from the imagination. The way in which a character speaks and acts can help make him or her believable. If a character's speech and actions are consistent throughout a work and true to his or her personality, the character seems more like a real person.

Another factor that may help bring a character to life is a vivid description. This helps the reader form a mental picture of this imaginary person and can add to the reader's sense of realism.

A story, poem, or drama needs believable characters to be effective. One way to judge if a character is believable is by asking yourself how much you know about him or her. As you read *The Importance of Being Earnest,* ask yourself:

1. Which characters seem real?
2. How does Wilde create believable characters?

WRITING CONNECTION

How would a writer portray you if you were a character in a story? Write a brief description of yourself that is more than just physical.

READING FOCUS

Identify Cause and Effect A cause makes something happen. What happens is the effect. Identifying cause and effect links can help you track changes in characters, progression of events, and relationships between ideas. As you read Oscar Wilde's play, take notes on how the characters change and *what* causes them to change.

THE IMPORTANCE OF BEING EARNEST

ADAPTED   *by Oscar Wilde*

CHARACTERS

JACK WORTHING

LANE, *a manservant*

ALGERNON MONCRIEFF

LADY AUGUSTA BRACKNELL

GWENDOLEN FAIRFAX

MISS PRISM, *a governess*

CECILY CARDEW

DR. CHASUBLE, *a minister*

MERRIMAN, a butler

SCENE ONE

JACK: Half Moon Street, West, driver. Algernon Moncrieff's home. *(He arrives at* ALGERNON'S *home.)*

LANE *(announcing, in typical butler fashion)*: Mr. Ernest Worthing.

(Enter JACK. LANE *exits.)*

ALGERNON *(a young, pleasant man with brisk way of speaking)*: How are you, my dear Ernest? What brings you up to town?

JACK: Oh, pleasure, pleasure! What else should bring one anywhere?

ALGERNON: Where have you been since last Thursday?

JACK: In the country.

ALGERNON: What on earth do you do there?

JACK: When one is in town, one amuses oneself. When one is in the country, one amuses other people. It is excessively boring.

---

excessively (ik SES iv lee) too much

ALGERNON: And who are the people you amuse?

JACK (*airily*): Oh, neighbors, neighbors.

ALGERNON: Are they nice, your neighbors?

JACK: Perfectly horrible. Never speak to one of them.

ALGERNON: How immensely you must amuse them!

JACK: But why all these cups, Algy? Are you expecting someone to tea?

ALGERNON: Merely Aunt Augusta and Gwendolen.

JACK (*pleased*): How perfectly delightful!

ALGERNON: I'm afraid Aunt Augusta won't quite approve of your being here.

JACK: Oh? May I ask why?

ALGERNON: My dear fellow, the way you flirt with Gwendolen is perfectly disgraceful. It's almost as bad as the way Gwendolen flirts with you.

JACK: But I'm in love with Gwendolen. I've come up to town expressly to propose to her.

ALGERNON: I thought you had come up for pleasure. I call that business!

JACK: How utterly unromantic you are!

ALGERNON: I really don't see anything romantic in proposing. Oh, it's very romantic to be in love. But there's nothing romantic in a definite proposal. Besides, I don't give my consent.

JACK: Your consent?

ALGERNON: My dear fellow, Gwendolen is my first cousin. And before I allow you to marry her, you will have to clear up the whole question of Cecily. (*He rings bell.*)

JACK: Cecily? What do you mean, Algy, by Cecily? I don't know anyone of the name of Cecily.

LANE (*enters*): You rang, sir?

ALGERNON: Yes, Lane. Bring me the cigarette case Mr. Worthing left in the smoking room the last time he dined here.

LANE: Yes, sir.

JACK: Do you mean to say you have had my cigarette case all the time? I've been frantic over it. I was very nearly offering a reward.

ALGERNON: Well, I wish you would offer one. I happen to need cash!

JACK: There is no good offering a reward now that the thing has been found.

LANE: The cigarette case, sir. (ALGERNON *takes it at once.* LANE *exits.*)

ALGERNON: No matter if you should offer a reward, for I see now that I look at the inscription, that it isn't yours at all.

JACK: Of course it's mine.

ALGERNON: But this case is a present from someone named Cecily, and you said that you didn't know anyone of that name.

JACK: Well, if you want to know, Cecily happens to be my aunt.

ALGERNON: Then why does she call you her uncle? Here's the inscription: "From little Cecily, with her fondest love to her dear Uncle Jack." Besides, your name isn't Jack at all; it's Ernest.

JACK: It isn't Ernest; it's Jack.

ALGERNON: But your name has always been Ernest!

JACK: Well, my name is Ernest in town and Jack in the country, and the cigarette case was given to me in the country.

ALGERNON: Will you kindly explain yourself?

JACK: Give me my cigarette case first. Thank you. Now listen closely to what I am about to say. Old Mr. Thomas Cardew, who adopted me when I was a little boy, made me in his will guardian to his granddaughter, Miss Cecily Cardew. Cecily, who addresses me as her uncle, lives at my place in the country under the charge of her admirable governess, Miss Prism.

ALGERNON: Where is this place in the country?

JACK: That is nothing to you, dear boy. You are not going to be invited.

ALGERNON: Now go on. Why are you Ernest in town and Jack in the country?

JACK: In order to be a good guardian to Cecily, I must adopt a high moral tone regarding everything while I am in the country. This becomes rather boring at times, and so in order to get up to town, I have always pretended to have a younger brother by the name of Ernest, who lives in the Albany, and gets into the most dreadful scrapes. That, my dear Algy, is the whole truth pure and simple.

ALGERNON: The truth is rarely pure and never simple!

---

guardian (GAHRD ee un) a person who looks after the affairs of a minor
scrapes (SKRAYPS) predicaments

LANE (*enters to announce*): Lady Bracknell and Miss Fairfax. (*Turns and exits.*)

LADY BRACKNELL (*enters; a fatuous woman*): Good afternoon, dear Algernon. I hope you are behaving very well.

ALGERNON: I'm feeling very well, Aunt Augusta.

LADY BRACKNELL: That's not quite the same thing. Ah, Mr. Worthing, good afternoon.

ALGERNON: How are you today, Gwendolen?

GWENDOLEN (*a coy, almost too-sweet girl*): How do I look?

JACK: You're quite perfect, Miss Fairfax.

LADY BRACKNELL: While I think of it, Algernon, have you the music you promised to give me for my little musicale this evening?

ALGERNON: I've laid the music out on the piano. You can pick out those selections you prefer. If you'll kindly come into the next room for a moment . . .

LADY BRACKNELL: Thank you, Algernon. It is very thoughtful of you. I'm sure the program will be delightful. After all, you have such excellent taste. (*They exit.*)

JACK (*falteringly*): Charming day it has been, Miss Fairfax.

GWENDOLEN: Oh, oh yes.

JACK: I would like to take advantage of Lady Bracknell's absence . . .

GWENDOLEN: I would advise you to do so. Mamma has a way of coming back into a room so suddenly!

JACK (*nervously*): Miss Fairfax, ever since I met you, I have admired you more than any girl . . . I have ever met since . . . I met you.

GWENDOLEN: Yes, I am quite aware of that fact. And even before I met you, I must confess, I was far from indifferent to you. We live, as you know, in an age of ideals. My ideal has always been to love someone of the name of Ernest. There is something in that name that inspires confidence. The moment Algernon told me that he had a friend called Ernest, I knew that I was destined to love you.

JACK: But you don't really mean to say that you couldn't love me if my name wasn't Ernest? Supposing it were something else.

---

fatuous (FACH oo us) silly; foolish
musicale (myoo zih KAL) party featuring a musical program

GWENDOLEN: Like what?

JACK: Well . . . like Jack.

GWENDOLEN: Jack? No, there is very little music in the name of Jack, if any at all, indeed. It produces no vibrations. The only really safe name is Ernest.

JACK: Gwendolen, I must get christened at once—I mean, we must get married at once.

GWENDOLEN: But you haven't proposed to me yet.

JACK: Well, may I propose to you now?

GWENDOLEN: I think it would be an admirable opportunity. And I'll spare you any possible disappointment, Mr. Worthing. It's only fair to tell you that I am fully determined to accept you.

JACK: Gwendolen!

GWENDOLEN: Yes, Mr. Worthing? What have you to say to me?

JACK: Gwendolen, will you marry me?

GWENDOLEN: Of course I will, darling. Really, how long you took!

LADY BRACKNELL (*entering angrily*): Mr. Worthing! Rise, sir, from your knees. Such a position is most unbecoming.

GWENDOLEN: Mamma! I am engaged to Mr. Worthing.

LADY BRACKNELL: Well, in that event, sir, I have a few questions to put to you. Gwendolen, you will wait for me below in the carriage.

GWENDOLEN: Mamma!

LADY BRACKNELL: In the carriage, Gwendolen!

GWENDOLEN: Yes, Mamma. (*She exits.*)

LADY BRACKNELL: How old are you, Mr. Worthing?

JACK: Twenty-nine.

LADY BRACKNELL: A very good age to be married at. Now to your parents.

JACK: I have lost both my parents.

LADY BRACKNELL: Both? That seems like carelessness. Who was your father?

JACK: I'm afraid I really don't know. The fact is, Lady Bracknell, I was . . . well, found. In the cloakroom of a train station by a gentleman named Mr. Thomas Cardew. He gave me the name of Worthing because he happened to have a ticket to

---

christened (KRIS und) gave a name to; named

Worthing in his pocket. Yes, I was found, Lady Bracknell, in a large, black handbag.

LADY BRACKNELL *(indignant)*: I'm sure that you can hardly consider that a proper basis for recognition in society.

JACK: May I ask, then, what you would advise me to do?

LADY BRACKNELL: I would strongly urge you, sir, to try to acquire some relations as soon as possible. You can hardly imagine that I would allow my only daughter to marry into a cloakroom, and form an alliance with a parcel! Good morning, Mr. Worthing! *(She exits.)*

JACK *(calling out)*: It's all right, Algy. You can come in now.

ALGERNON: *(enters)* Didn't it go off all right, old boy? You don't mean to say that Gwendolen refused you!

JACK: Oh, Gwendolen is as right as a trivet. Her mother is unbearable.

ALGERNON: Did you tell Gwendolen the truth about Ernest?

JACK: My dear fellow, the truth isn't the sort of thing one tells a nice young lady like Gwendolen. I plan to get rid of Ernest by the end of the week; he shall die of a chill—in Paris.

LANE *(enters and announces)*: Miss Fairfax.

ALGERNON: Gwendolen, upon my word!

GWENDOLEN: Mamma has just told me all, Ernest. I may never meet you again in town. However, if you'll give me your country address . . .

JACK *(in a stage whisper)*: I don't want Algy to know, but it's the Manor House, Woolton, Hertfordshire.

GWENDOLEN: What is it again? I can't hear!

ALGERNON: He said he didn't want me to hear, but it's the Manor House, Woolton, Hertfordshire.

JACK *(outraged)*: Oh, bother, Algy! Come along, Gwendolen, I'll escort you to the door.

ALGERNON *(pleasantly)*: Good-bye, Cousin Gwendolen. Good-bye, Ernest. *(Calling off)* Oh, Lane. Tomorrow I'm going visiting— to Mr. Worthing's country home.

LANE: Yes, sir.

ALGERNON: I shall probably not be back till Monday. Pack my full dress and my summer suit. Oh, I hope tomorrow will be a

---

alliance (uh LY uns) union or joining

fine day, Lane.

LANE: It never is, sir. It never is!

SCENE TWO

Garden at the Manor House.

MISS PRISM *(a prim, proper voice, calling)*: Cecily! Cecily! Ah, so you're here in the garden. Put away that diary and come to your German lesson. You know your Uncle Jack put particular stress on your German lesson before he left town yesterday. I really don't see why you waste your time on a diary, when you could be spending it on your German lesson.

CECILY *(a sweet, but affected, girl)*: I keep a diary in order to enter the wonderful secrets of my life.

MISS PRISM: But memory is the diary that we all carry about with us.

CECILY: I believe it's memory that is responsible for those horrible three-volume novels everyone reads nowadays.

MISS PRISM: Do not speak slightly of the three-volume novel. I wrote one myself in earlier days. Alas, I lost the manuscript once, and so I was never able to finish it.

CECILY: That is a shame, Miss Prism. But look, I see dear Dr. Chasuble coming up through the garden.

MISS PRISM *(sighing)*: Ah, Dr. Chasuble. This is indeed a pleasure.

CHASUBLE : *(an elderly minister)* Has Mr. Worthing returned from town yet?

MISS PRISM: No, we don't expect him till Monday.

CHASUBLE: Well then, I'll be on my way. Would you care to walk a way with me, Miss Prism?

MISS PRISM *(sighing)*: Gladly. Now study your German, Cecily! *(They exit.)*

CECILY *(annoyed)*: Oh, horrid, horrid, horrid German!

MERRIMAN *(entering):* Excuse me, Miss Cardew. Mr. Ernest Worthing is calling.

CECILY *(delighted)*: Mr. Ernest Worthing! Uncle Jack's wicked brother! How exciting! Send him out, please, Merriman.

---

affected (uh FEK tid) artificial

ALGERNON (*enters*): You must be my little cousin Cecily, I'm sure!

CECILY: And you are Uncle Jack's brother, my cousin Ernest, my wicked cousin Ernest. I don't understand how you happen to be here. Uncle Jack won't be back till Monday afternoon.

ALGERNON: What a shame that I must leave, then, on Monday morning.

CECILY: It would be better if you could wait for him, I think. He is anxious to talk to you about emigrating. He said he's sending you to Australia. I shouldn't wonder that he does—you do look awfully pale.

ALGERNON: I expect it's because I'm so awfully hungry.

CECILY: How thoughtless of me! Won't you come in for tea?

ALGERNON: Thank you, cousin Cecily, you're the prettiest girl I ever saw.

CECILY: Miss Prism says that all good looks are a trap.

ALGERNON: They are a trap—one every sensible man wants to be caught in!

CECILY: Oh, I don't think I would care to catch a sensible man! I shouldn't know what to talk to him about! (*They pass into the house.* MISS PRISM *and* DR. CHASUBLE *return.*)

---

emigrating (EM ih grayt ing) leave one country to settle in another

JACK (enters): Ah, Miss Prism! Dr. Chasuble!

MISS PRISM: Mr. Worthing! Why, we didn't expect you back till Monday! But—are you in mourning?

JACK: My poor brother.

CHASUBLE: Still leading his shameful, wicked life?

JACK (mournfully): Alas, he is leading no life at all. He's dead—of a chill, in Paris.

CHASUBLE: My sympathies, sir. I shall mention this in Sunday's sermon.

JACK: Ah, that reminds me. I should like to be christened, Dr. Chasuble. This afternoon, if convenient.

CHASUBLE: But have you never been christened before?

JACK: I don't know. At any rate, I should like to be christened this afternoon. Will half-past-five do?

CECILY (entering): Uncle Jack! How nice to see you back. Who do you think is in the dining room? Your brother Ernest. He arrived half an hour ago. And what do you think? He has already proposed marriage to me. Of course, I have accepted him. And he's promised to be wicked no more, but to change his ways.

MISS PRISM: But Mr. Worthing's brother Ernest is dead, Cecily.

ALGERNON (enters): I am no such thing, Miss Prism. (With warmth) Dear brother Jack!

JACK (astonished): Algernon! (Catching himself) I mean, Ernest!

CHASUBLE: I think it is so touching to see this family reunion. Come, Cecily, Miss Prism; we shall leave them alone.

CECILY: Do forgive each other—please! (CECILY, MISS PRISM, and CHASUBLE exit.)

JACK: Algy, you young scoundrel. You must leave at once.

ALGERNON: Don't be silly, Jack. I'm engaged to Cecily, and I'm staying.

JACK (calling): Merriman, send for the dogcart. Mr. Ernest is leaving.

ALGERNON (calling): Never mind, Merriman. He's decided to stay after all.

JACK: He hasn't!

ALGERNON: He has.

---

scoundrel (SKOUN drul) rascal
dogcart (DAWG cahrt) small, open carriage

JACK: Oh, no he hasn't!

ALGERNON: Oh, yes he has!

JACK (*after a pause*): Ohhhhh, what's the use?

SCENE THREE

Manor House

MERRIMAN (*announcing*): Miss Gwendolen Fairfax.

CECILY: Pray let me introduce myself. I am Cecily Cardew.

GWENDOLEN: How do you do, Miss Cardew? I am Gwendolen Fairfax.

CECILY: How do you do?

GWENDOLEN: Are you on a visit here at Mr. Worthing's country home?

CECILY: Why no, I am Mr. Worthing's ward.

GWENDOLEN: His ward! He never told me that he had a ward. Though I must say, I'm not jealous. Ernest is so dependable!

CECILY: Oh, it is not Mr. Ernest Worthing who is my guardian. It is his elder brother—Jack. Oh no, Mr. Ernest is not my guardian—indeed, soon I shall be his. You see, Mr. Ernest and I are engaged.

GWENDOLEN (*with controlled coolness*): My darling Cecily, I think there must be some error. Mr. Ernest Worthing is engaged to me.

CECILY: My dearest Gwendolen, it is you who are mistaken. Ernest proposed to me just 15 minutes ago.

GWENDOLEN: It is certainly quite curious; he asked me to be his wife yesterday afternoon at 5:30. Therefore, I have the prior claim.

CECILY: I should say it was quite clear that he has changed his mind.

GWENDOLEN: But here he comes now. I'll ask him myself. Ernest, dear!

JACK (*enters*): Gwendolen, darling, this is a surprise.

CECILY: I knew there must be some mistake, Miss Fairfax. The gentleman whom you are now kissing is my dear guardian, Uncle Jack.

---

prior (PRY ur) earlier

GWENDOLEN (*horrified*): Jack!

CECILY: Here comes Ernest now.

ALGERNON (*enters*): Well, whom have we here?

CECILY: May I ask, Ernest, if you are engaged to this young lady?

ALGERNON: To what young lady? Good heavens, Gwendolen!

CECILY: Yes, Ernest, to good heavens, Gwendolen.

GWENDOLEN: I knew there was an error, Miss Cardew. The gentleman you now embrace is my cousin, Mr. Algernon Moncrieff.

CECILY (*horrified*): Algernon!

GWENDOLEN: Well, then, if *you* are not Ernest, and if *you* are not Ernest—who on earth *is* Ernest?

JACK (*slow and hesitatingly*): Gwendolen—Cecily—it is very painful for me to say this, but I'm afraid the truth is—that there is no Ernest!

MERRIMAN (*announces*): Lady Bracknell!

ALGERNON: Good lord, it's Aunt Augusta!

GWENDOLEN: Heavens, it's Mamma!

LADY BRACKNELL (*enters*): Mr. Worthing, why have you spirited off my daughter?

GWENDOLEN: He didn't spirit me off, Mamma. I came of my own free will. Mr. Worthing and I are engaged.

LADY BRACKNELL: You are no such thing. And Algernon, who is the girl around whose waist your left arm is twined?

JACK: Allow me to present my ward, Miss Cecily Cardew.

ALGERNON: Cecily and I are engaged.

LADY BRACKNELL: You are no such thing. There must be something strange in the air hereabouts. There seems to be a peculiar number of engagements!

MERRIMAN (*announcing*): Dr. Chasuble and Miss Prism.

CHASUBLE (*enters*): About the christenings, gentlemen . . .

GWENDOLEN AND CECILY: Christenings?

CHASUBLE: Yes, Mr. Jack Worthing is to be christened at 5:30; Mr. Ernest Worthing is to be christened—er, I don't know what—at 6:00.

GWENDOLEN: You were prepared to make this sacrifice for us?

CECILY: Darlings!

CHASUBLE: Well, about the christenings. Might they be postponed?

JACK: Whatever for?

CHASUBLE: Well, sir, the fact is—Miss Prism here and I have just become engaged!

LADY BRACKNELL: What's going on here? *(Suddenly shouting)* Miss Prism!

MISS PRISM: Lady Bracknell!!!

LADY BRACKNELL *(slowly and emphatically)*: Miss Prism, where is that baby?

ALL: What?

LADY BRACKNELL: Twenty-eight years ago, Miss Prism, you left Lord Bracknell's house in charge of a baby carriage containing a baby of the male sex. You never returned. A few weeks later, the police discovered the carriage standing by itself in a remote corner of Bayswater. It was empty, except for the unfinished manuscript of a dreadful novel. Miss Prism! Where is that baby?

MISS PRISM *(shamefully)*: I don't know, I admit it. I only wish I did. The plain facts are these. By mistake, I put the manuscript for a book I was writing into the carriage, and I put the baby into a large, black handbag that I had intended for the manuscript.

JACK *(urgently)*: Where did you deposit the handbag?

MISS PRISM: I left it in the cloakroom of one of the larger railway stations in London.

JACK: What railway station?

MISS PRISM *(crushed)*: Victoria. The Brighton Line.

JACK *(excitedly)*: Excuse me, for one moment! *(He exits.)*

LADY BRACKNELL: I need not tell you, Miss Prism, I suppose, of the weeks—nay, years of anguish your error has caused?

MISS PRISM *(sorrowful)*: I can imagine, Lady Bracknell. I can imagine!

LADY BRACKNELL: Can you?

JACK *(enters)*: Miss Prism. Is this the handbag? Examine it carefully before you speak! Is this the handbag?

MISS PRISM *(calmly)*: It seems to be mine. Yes, here are my initials on the clasp. Thank you so much for restoring it to me.

JACK: Miss Prism, more has been restored to you than the handbag. I am the baby that you placed in it.

---

anguish (ANG gwish) distress

LADY BRACKNELL: Mr. Worthing! Then you are the son of my dear dead sister, and therefore Algernon's elder brother.

JACK: Algy's elder brother! Then I have a brother after all. I always said I had a brother. Miss Prism, Dr. Chasuble, meet my unfortunate younger brother.

GWENDOLEN: My own! But what own are you? What is your real name, now that you have become someone else?

JACK: Good heavens! I almost forgot. Can you not love me but under that one name?

GWENDOLEN: Alas no. Cecily and I have both resolved to marry men by the name of Ernest.

LADY BRACKNELL: That's it. You were named after your father, Mr. Worthing; his name was General Ernest John Moncrieff!

JACK (*calmly*): I always told you my name was Ernest, didn't I, Gwendolen?

GWENDOLEN: Ernest, my own! I felt from the first you could have no other name.

JACK: Gwendolen, it is a terrible thing for a man to find out that all of his life he has been speaking nothing but the truth. Can you forgive me?

GWENDOLEN: I can. For I feel that you are sure to change.

ALGERNON: Do you forgive me too, Cecily?

CECILY: Yes, Algernon—if you promise to be rechristened Ernest tomorrow!

ALGERNON: I do, my love, I do. And now, may I kiss you?

CECILY: But of course!

LADY BRACKNELL (*taken aback*): My dear nephew, what has come over you?

ALGERNON: Why, Aunt Augusta, I've only just realized for the first time in my life, the vital importance of being earnest!

---

vital (VYT ul) of greatest importance

Review the Selection

UNDERSTAND THE SELECTION

Recall

1. What is the setting for Scene 1?

2. Where was Jack found as a baby?

3. Who is Cecily Cardew's fiancé?

Infer

4. In the first scene, what is the relationship between Jack and Algernon?

5. Are the characters upper class? Explain.

6. What is Lady Bracknell's attitude toward Jack?

7. Why does Jack find the country boring? Explain.

Apply

8. A play-on-words (a pun) is made in this drama. What are the two words involved?

9. Consider the words and attitude of Lady Bracknell. What is important to her?

10. Explain why Cecily and Gwendolyn both require that their fiances' names are Ernest.

Respond to Literature

How does Wilde satirize the Victorian virtue of earnestness?

WRITE ABOUT THE SELECTION

Sophisticated comedies such as *The Importance of Being Earnest* often arrive at their conclusions by way of an intricate sequence of events. The twists and turns of the plot may be hard to follow at certain times. Is the action of this play clear in your mind? Would you be able to describe this play to someone else? Write a summary of the play to give yourself a better understanding of what happens.

Prewriting Reread the play, writing down what you think are the major events. Since there are three scenes, make three chronological lists of the action in each. Use phrases, not sentences.

Writing Using your lists as a basis, write a summary of the play in your own words. Begin by telling your reader the title of the play and the name of its author. Then write a shortened version that tells of the major events in chronological order (as they happen).

Revising Reread your summary to see if it would make sense to someone who had not read the play. Add explanations of who the characters are, if necessary, to explain the major events.

Proofreading The preferred way to write a summary of a literary work is in the present tense. If you have not done so, change the verbs in your summary to the present tense throughout.

THINK ABOUT CHARACTER

A round character in a work of literature is one who has a fully-developed personality. This helps make the character seem like a real person even though he or she is imaginary. **Round characters** are multi-dimensional. In other words, they have depth and are more fully formed. One-dimensional characters are those in whom one personality trait, such as greed, wisdom, or stupidity, is dominant, and nothing else is included. A round character, on the other hand, is a complex collection of personality traits.

1. Which important character in *The Importance of Being Earnest* would you say is one-dimensional?

2. Why do you think the butler, the manservant, and the minister are not round characters?

3. How is Algernon first described?

4. In what way is Jack's character revealed to you in the first scene?

5. Which of the characters do you find real and believable?

READING FOCUS
Identify Cause and Effect   Which character do you think changes the most during the play? Which events cause that change?

DEVELOP YOUR VOCABULARY

A quick way to find out the meaning of an unfamiliar word is to look at its context. The **context** of a word is the other words that surround it. It may also help to read the sentences which come before and after the word. Look at an unfamiliar word and its context, then figure out what the word could mean. Substitute your guess for the word in the sentence.

Write the meaning of each of the following italicized words in your own words, using context clues to figure out their meanings. Then write an original sentence for each italicized word.

1. Young families are leaving their homes and *emigrating* from Australia.
2. For mutual protection, we must form an *alliance*.
3. "You've lost your wallet? How did you get into this *scrape?*"
4. Since she was an orphan, her older cousin became her *guardian*.
5. You could tell he was a *scoundrel* from his evil face and suspicious look.
6. The events of the *prior* week are now just a memory.
7. It is *vital* to use the *dogcart* to get to the train station since there is no other means of transportation.
8. The shipwrecked sailor gave a cry of *anguish*.
9. This 800-page novel is *excessively* lengthy.
10. Will you play your guitar at the *musicale?*

Learn About

SETTING

Setting is one of the four most important elements of fiction. **Setting** is the physical, and sometimes psychological, background against which the action of a literary work takes place.

Setting also consists of four major elements. The first is the actual **location** of the story's action. The location includes the actual geographical site—the country, the city, or the room of a house, for example. Setting can also include the climate or the weather.

The second element of setting involves the **lives** of the characters in the story—their occupations, their daily manner of living. The third element of setting is the time or **period** in which the events of the story take place. The fourth element of setting is the general **environment** in which the characters live and through which they move.

Setting shapes the characters and action of a story. It is important because it provides reference points which make the story more real.

1. What is the setting of "The Demon Lover"?
2. How does setting affect the characters and events?

WRITING CONNECTION

What setting are you in at the moment? Write a brief paragraph describing your actual location.

READING FOCUS

Make Inferences   Writers don't always tell you everything about characters and their relationships to one another. You can use clues provided by the writer to infer, or guess, how characters feel about one another and why they behave as they do. As you read the following story, keep track of the inferences you make about the characters.

THE DEMON LOVER

by Elizabeth Bowen

Towards the end of her day in London Mrs. Drover went round to her shut-up house to look for several things she wanted to take away. Some belonged to herself, some to her family, who were by now used to their country life. It was late August; it had been a steamy, showery day: at the moment the trees down the pavement glittered in an escape of humid yellow afternoon sun. Against the next batch of clouds, already piling up ink-dark, broken chimneys and parapets stood out. In her once familiar street, as in any unused channel, an unfamiliar queerness had silted up; a cat wove itself in and out of railings, but no human eye watched Mrs. Drover's return. Shifting some parcels under her arm, she slowly forced round her latchkey in an unwilling lock, then gave the door, which had warped, a push with her knee. Dead air came out to meet her as she went in.

The staircase window having been boarded up, no light came down into the hall. But one door, she could just see, stood ajar, so she went quickly through into the room and unshuttered the big window in there. Now, the prosaic woman, looking about her, was more perplexed than she knew by everything that she saw, by traces of her long former habit of life—the yellow smoke-stain up the white marble mantelpiece, the ring left by a vase on the top of the escritoire; the bruise in the wallpaper where, on the door being thrown open widely, the china handle had always hit the wall. The piano, having gone away to be stored, had left what looked like claw-marks on its part of the parquet. Though not much dust had seeped in, each object wore a film of another kind; and the only ventilation being the chimney, the whole drawing-room smelled of the cold hearth. Mrs. Drover put down her parcels on the escritoire and left the room to proceed upstairs; the things she wanted were in a bedroom chest.

She had been anxious to see how the house was—the part-time caretaker she

---

parapets (PAR uh pets) walls or railings on balcony, roof or bridge
prosaic (proh ZAY ik) matter-of-fact; dull
escritoire (ES krih twahr) writing desk or table
parquet (pahr KAY) flooring of inlaid woodwork in geometric form

An Interior, Sir William Rothenstein. The Fine Art Society, London, UK/Bridgeman Art Library

shared with some neighbors was away this week on his holiday, known to be not yet back. At the best of times he did not look in often, and she was never sure that she trusted him. There were some cracks in the structure, left by the last bombing, on which she was anxious to keep an eye. Not that one could do anything—

A shaft of refracted daylight now lay across the hall. She stopped dead and stared at the hall table—on this lay a letter addressed to her.

She thought first—then the caretaker *must* be back. All the same, who, seeing the house shuttered, would have dropped a letter in at the box? It was not a circular, it was not a bill. And the post office redirected, to the address in the country, everything for her that came through the post. The caretaker (even if he *were* back) did not know she was due in London today—her call here had been planned to be a surprise—so his negligence in the manner of this letter, leaving it to wait in the dusk and the dust, annoyed her. Annoyed, she picked up the letter, which bore no stamp. But it cannot be important, or they would know. . . She took the letter rapidly upstairs with her, without a stop to look at the writing till she reached what had been her bedroom, where she let in light. The room looked over the garden and other gardens: the sun had gone in; as the clouds sharpened and lowered, the trees and rank lawns seemed already to smoke with dark. Her reluctance to look again at the letter came from the fact that she felt intruded upon—and by someone contemptuous of her ways. However, in the tenseness preceding the fall of rain she read it: it was a few lines.

Dear Kathleen,

You will not have forgotten that today is our anniversary, and the day we said. The years have gone by at once slowly and fast. In view of the fact that nothing has changed, I shall rely upon you to keep your promise. I was sorry to see you leave London, but was satisfied that you would be back in time. You may expect me, therefore, at the hour arranged.

Until then . . . K.

Mrs. Drover looked for the date: it was today's. She dropped the letter on to the bed-springs, then picked it up to see the writing again—her lips, beneath the remains of lipstick, beginning to go white. She felt so much the change in her own face that she went to the mirror, polished a clear patch in it and looked at once urgently and stealthily in. She was confronted by a woman of forty-four, with eyes starting out under a hat-brim that had been rather carelessly pulled down. She had not put on any more powder since she left the shop where she ate her solitary tea. The pearls her husband had given her on their marriage hung loose round her now rather thinner throat, slipping in the V of the pink wool jumper her sister knitted last autumn as

---

circular (SUR kyuh lur) here, an advertisement or letter intended for mass distribution

they sat round the fire. Mrs. Drover's most normal expression was one of controlled worry, but of assent. Since the birth of the third of her little boys, attended by a quite serious illness, she had had an intermittent muscular flicker to the left of her mouth, but in spite of this she could always sustain a manner that was at once energetic and calm.

Turning from her own face as precipitately as she had gone to meet it, she went to the chest where the things were, unlocked it, threw up the lid and knelt to search. But as rain began to come crashing down she could not keep from looking over her shoulder at the stripped bed on which the letter lay. Behind the blanket of rain the clock of the church that still stood struck six—with rapidly heightening apprehension she counted each of the slow strokes. "The hour arranged. . . My God," she said, *"what* hour? How should I. . . ? After twenty-five years. . ."

The young girl talking to the solider in the garden had not ever completely seen his face. It was dark; they were saying goodbye under a tree. Now and then —for it felt, from not seeing him at this intense moment, as though she had never seen him at all—she verified his presence for these few moments longer by putting out a hand, which he each time pressed, without very much kindness, and painfully, on to one of the breast buttons of his uniform. That cut of the button on the palm of her hand was,

principally, what she was to carry away. This was so near the end of a leave from France that she could only wish him already gone. It was August 1916. Being not kissed, being drawn away from and looked at intimidated Kathleen till she imagined spectral glitters in the place of his eyes. Turning away and looking back up the lawn she saw, through branches of trees, the drawing-room window alight; she caught a breath for the moment when she could go running back there into the safe arms of her mother and sister, and cry: "What shall I do, what shall I do? He has gone."

Hearing her catch her breath, her fiancé said, without feeling: "Cold?"

"You're going away such a long way."

"Not as far as you think."

"I don't understand."

"You don't have to," he said. "You will. You know what we said."

"But that was—suppose you—I mean, suppose."

"I shall be with you," he said, "sooner or later. You won't forget that. You need do nothing but wait."

Only a little more than a minute later she was free to run up the silent lawn. Looking in through the window at her mother and sister, who did not for the moment perceive her, she already felt that unnatural promise drive down between her and the rest of all human kind. No other way of having given herself could have made her feel so apart, lost

---

precipitately (prih SIP uh tut lee) suddenly, abruptly
spectral (SPEK trul) ghostly; like a phantom

and foresworn. She could not have plighted a more sinister troth.

Kathleen behaved well when, some months later, her fiancé was reported missing, presumed killed. Her family not only supported her but were able to praise her courage without stint because they could not regret, as a husband for her, the man they knew almost nothing about. They hoped she would, in a year or two, console herself—and had it been only a question of consolation things might have gone much straighter ahead. But her trouble, behind just a little grief, was a complete dislocation from everything. She did not reject other lovers, for these failed to appear: for years she failed to attract men—and with the approach of her thirties she became natural enough to share her family's anxiousness on this score. She began to put herself out, to wonder; and at thirty-two she was very greatly relieved to find herself being courted by William Drover. She married him, and the two of them settled down in this quiet, arboreal part of Kensington; in this house the years piled up, her children were born and they all lived till they were driven out by the bombs of the next war. Her movements as Mrs. Drover were circumscribed, and she dismissed any idea that they were still watched.

As things were—dead or living the letter-writer sent her only a threat. Unable, for some minutes, to go on kneeling with her back exposed to the empty room, Mrs. Drover rose from the chest to sit on an upright chair whose back was firmly against the wall. The desuetude of her former bedroom, her married London home's whole air of being a cracked cup from which memory, with its reassuring power, had either evaporated or leaked away, made a crisis—and at just this crisis the letter-writer had, knowledgeably, struck. The hollowness of the house this evening canceled years on years of voices, habits and steps. Through the shut windows she only heard rain fall on the roofs around. To rally herself, she said she was in a mood—and, for two or three seconds shutting her eyes, told herself that she had imagined the letter. But she opened them—there it lay on the bed.

On the supernatural side of the letter's entrance she was not permitting her mind to dwell. Who, in London, knew she meant to call at the house today? Evidently, however, this had been known. The caretaker, *had* he come back, had had no cause to expect her: he would have taken the letter in his pocket, to forward it, at his own time, through the post. There was no other sign that the caretaker had been in—but, if not? Letters dropped in at doors of deserted houses do not fly or walk to tables in halls. They do not sit on the dust of empty tables with the air of certainty that

---

foresworn (fawr SWAWRN) having sworn falsely
troth (TRAWTH) betrothal; engagement
arboreal (ahr BAWR ee ul) wooded
circumscribed (SUR kum skrybd) limited; confined
desuetude (DES wih tood) disuse

they will be found. There is needed some human hand—but nobody but the caretaker had a key. Under circumstances she did not care to consider, a house can be entered without a key. It was possible that she was not alone now. She might be being waited for, downstairs. Waited for—until when? Until "the hour arranged." At least that was not six o'clock; six has struck.

She rose from the chair and went over and locked the door.

The thing was, to get out. To fly? No, not that: she had to catch her train. As a woman whose utter dependability was the keystone of her family life she was not willing to return to the country, to her husband, her little boys and her sister, without the objects she had come up to fetch. Resuming work at the chest she set about making up a number of parcels in a rapid, fumbling-decise way. These, with her shopping parcels, would be too much to carry; these meant a taxi—at the thought of the taxi her heart went up and her normal breathing resumed. I will ring up the taxi now; the taxi cannot come too soon; I shall hear the taxi out there running its engine, till I walk calmly down to it through the hall. I'll ring up—But no: the telephone is cut off . . . She tugged at a knot she had tied wrong.

The idea of flight. . . . He was never kind to me, not really. I don't remember him kind at all. Mother said he never considered me. He was set on me, that was what it was—not love. Not love, not meaning a person well. What did he do, to make me promise like that? I can't remember—But she found that she could.

She remembered with such dreadful acuteness that the twenty-five years since then dissolved like smoke and she instinctively looked for the weal left by the button on the palm of her hand. She remembered not only all that he said and did but the complete suspension of *her* existence during that August week. I was not myself—they all told me so at the time. She remembered—but with one white burning blank as where acid has dropped on a photograph: *under no conditions* could she remember his face.

So wherever he may be waiting, I shall not know him. You have no time to run from a face you do not expect.

The thing was to get to the taxi before any clock struck what could be the hour. She would slip down the street and round the side of the square to where the square gave on the main road. She would return in the taxi, safe, to her own door, and bring the solid driver into the house with her to pick up the parcels from room to room. The idea of the taxi driver made her decisive, bold; she unlocked her door, went to the top of the staircase and listened down.

She heard nothing—but while she was hearing nothing the *passé* air of the staircase was disturbed by a draft that traveled up to her face. It emanated from

weal (WEEL) a mark, line or ridge raised on the skin by a blow
passé (pa SAY) old; stale
emanated (EM uh nayt id) came forth; was emitted

The City Atlas, Sidney Starr

the basement; down there a door or window was being opened by someone who chose this moment to leave the house.

The rain had stopped; the pavements steamily shone as Mrs. Drover let herself out by inches from her own front door into the empty street. The unoccupied houses opposite continued to meet her look with their damaged stare. Making towards the thoroughfare and the taxi, she tried not to keep looking behind. Indeed, the silence was so intense—one of those creeks of London silence exaggerated this summer by the damage of war—that no tread could have gained on hers unheard. Where her street debouched on the square where people went on living, she grew conscious of, and checked, her unnatural pace. Across the open end of the square two buses impassively passed each other; women, a perambulator, cyclists, a man wheeling a barrow signalized, once again, the ordinary flow of life. At the square's most populous corner should be—and was—the short taxi rank. This evening, only one taxi—but this, although it presented its blank rump, appeared already to be alertly waiting for her. Indeed, without looking round the driver started his engine as she panted up from behind and put her hand on the door. As she did so, the clock struck seven. The taxi faced the main road, to make the trip back to her house it would have to turn—she had settled back on the seat and the taxi *had* turned before she, surprised by its knowing movement, recollected that she had not "said where." She leaned forward to scratch at the glass panel that divided the driver's head from her own.

The driver braked to what was almost a stop, turned round and slid the glass panel back. The jolt of this flung Mrs. Drover forward till her face was almost into the glass. Through the aperture driver and passenger, not six inches between them, remained for an eternity eye to eye. Mrs. Drover's mouth hung open for some seconds before she could issue her first scream. After that she continued to scream freely and to beat with her gloved hands on the glass all round as the taxi, accelerating without mercy, made off with her into the hinterland of deserted streets.

---

debouched (dih BOUCHT) emerged
perambulator (puh RAM byuh layt ur) baby carriage
hinterland (HIN tur land) an area far from cities and towns

Elizabeth Bowen (1899–1973)

What set Elizabeth Bowen apart from other writers of her day was that she chose to continue to write in the tradition of the 19th-century novel rather than to experiment as other writers were doing in the early 1900s. In so doing, she might have become a forgettable writer; however, she did not. She had a keen interest in contemporary life and combined her 19th-century techniques with lively and interesting contemporary characters.

Although she was born in Dublin, most of her novels and short stories take place in England among the upper class. Her characters are sophisticated people and she shows tremendous wit and insight in her observations. She started out writing short stories, and many of her later stories were inspired by World War II. Although she also wrote novels, she continued to write short stories throughout her career, and they were a necessary and important part of her work.

In both her novels and short stories she often addressed the issue of young women who are hurt by their surroundings. Her feminine point of view could have easily backfired if she had limited herself to domestic issues. However, she addressed a much broader range of subjects. In some of her best writing, she shares a woman's point of view of war, and the reader is able to share the consciousness of the character and how the war affected the woman's life.

Review the Selection

Recall

1. What is the time period in which the story takes place?

2. Where does the story take place?

3. During what time of the day is this story set?

Infer

4. Why is the Drover family living in the country?

5. Why can Mrs. Drover no longer remember the soldier's face?

6. Was the soldier killed in World War I? How do you know?

7. Who was the taxi driver?

Apply

8. What kind of feeling is evoked by the description of the weather?

9. Who do you think was in the house with Mrs. Drover?

10. What does the letter's fourth sentence imply?

Respond to Literature

Two World Wars play an important role in the story. How does World War I influence the story? What do you think the demon lover represents?

WRITE ABOUT THE SELECTION

"The Demon Lover" ends with Mrs. Drover screaming in horror as the taxi and its mysterious driver make off with her down deserted streets. Who is the taxi driver? Why is Mrs. Drover screaming? What was the promise she made 25 years ago? Where does the taxi go? Write an additional episode to "The Demon Lover" which answers these questions by telling what happens after the taxi drives off with Mrs. Drover.

Prewriting   The ending of "The Demon Lover" is ambiguous. Make a list, down the left-hand side of your page, of the questions you have about the story's ending—the events and the characters. On the right-hand side of the page, write possible answers across from each question.

Writing   Based on the answers to your list of questions and what you think happened after the conclusion of the story, write an additional episode to "The Demon Lover".

Revising   Add details about the setting in your episode to make it more real. What time of day was it? What was the weather like? If you think the taxi took Mrs. Drover somewhere, describe the place.

Proofreading   Be sure that each of your paragraphs has a single main idea and that all the other sentences relate to it.

THINK ABOUT SETTING

A work of literature is set in a time, in a place, and within the context of a specific society. The setting has an effect on both the characters and events of the story and the reader. Compare these two different settings: a sunny day in a green park; a stormy night in a haunted house. How does each make you feel? Part of a story's setting involves the details described, such as "boarded-up windows, dead air, a warped door, what look like claw marks on the floor."

1. Most of the action in the story takes place in what setting?

2. Name some of the first details which describe the weather.

3. What elements of the setting contribute to the mood of the story?

4. Which elements of the setting tell you when the story occurs?

5. Does the setting create a certain mood or feeling? Describe it.

READING FOCUS

Make Inferences What inferences can you make about Mrs. Drover's feelings for the two men in her life? What clues in the story helped you make these inferences?

DEVELOP YOUR VOCABULARY

At times in your reading, you may come across words which have been taken from another language. These words have been adapted into everyday use in English, or they describe something very specific for which there is no English equivalent.

There are several of these kinds of words in "The Demon Lover." For instance, *escritoire,* a table or desk for writing; and *parquet,* another word taken from the French language, which refers to a specific type of flooring.

Unless you are familiar with the language the word comes from, it may be difficult to figure out what the word means, even from its context. A dictionary lists "foreign" words which are used in everyday English, defines them, and tells you how to pronounce them. The dictionary also tells you which language the word comes from.

Some English-language words may be unfamiliar to you, but in common use in another English-speaking country. The word *perambulator* in this short story is the word the British use for "baby carriage," or "stroller."

Look up these three foreign words in a dictionary: *escritoire, parquet, perambulator.* Use them and seven other footnoted words in ten original sentences which demonstrate that you know their meanings.

FOCUS ON FICTION

*T*he short story shares many elements with that longer work of fiction, the novel. The four basic elements of the short story are plot, character, setting, and theme. These four elements are important parts of the novel as well. However, the short story differs from the novel in its treatment and use of these four elements. The difference is partly dictated by length. Other important elements of the short story include point of view, tone, and the use of symbolism, flashback, and other devices.

Plot   The series of events which occur in the short story makes up the plot. The plot has a beginning, middle, and end. Plot is the underlying element which transforms a series of events from random episodes into a unified whole. A sequence of episodes is changed into an arrangement based on cause and effect. The episodes become a pattern of events.

These relationships among events depend on **conflict**—the meeting of two opposing forces. The forces of opposition may be external and physical, or they may be internal and spiritual. It is the conflict which knits the events to one another.

Character   Although character is an element shared by short stories and longer fiction, it is treated differently in a short story. Generally, there are fewer characters because the story is shorter. For the same reason, the characters are revealed through a series of actions, usually under stress, rather than through lengthy narrative. Their reaction to the conflict informs us about them.

Setting   The setting is where the story occurs. Setting consists of the surroundings, or place, plus the time or period in which the story unfolds. Setting also consists of the objects found within the story and sometimes the weather, the society, or the social environment in which the characters live. Short stories usually have one setting, whereas novels may have many. That is, the events of a short story usually occur in one place.

Theme   The short story, unlike the longer novel, characteristically develops or presents only one central theme. The theme is the dominating idea of the short story—its underlying message. The theme of a short story may be **explicit,** or stated outright. It may be **implicit,** in which case you must figure it out for yourself.

Point of View, Tone, Flashback, and Symbolism   Short stories are generally told from a single point of view. Whether the narrator is the main character, a minor character, or the author, this point of view does not normally change. Likewise the writer's tone remains constant throughout the short story. Tone expresses the writer's attitude toward the subject of the story and toward the reader. Tone also can express the mood of the work.

Flashback is a device with which the writer presents scenes or incidents that occurred before the opening scene of the story. It is a way of introducing information or background. The flashback is presented in different ways; through the memory of a character, or through dreams or reveries.

The use of symbolism as a means of expression in a literary work is common to much of the literature in the modern period. Symbolism is the use of one object to represent or suggest another object, idea, or emotion. It is used to add richness and depth to the simple telling of a story.

As you read "The Cabuliwallah," consider the story's four basic elements. Ask yourself these questions:

1. What is the setting of the story? What are the details which establish the setting?
2. What objects or events in the story are symbolic?

THE CABULIWALLAH

by Sir Rabindranath Tagore

FOCUS ON FICTION
STUDY HINTS

My five years' old daughter Mini cannot live without chattering. I really believe that in all her life she has not wasted a minute in silence. Her mother is often vexed at this, and would stop her prattle, but I would not. To see Mini quiet is unnatural, and I cannot bear it long. And so my own talk with her is always lively.

The character of Mini is described; the point of view is established.

One morning, for instance, when I was in the midst of the seventeenth chapter of my new novel, my little Mini stole into the room, and putting her hand into mine, said: "Father! Ramdayal the door-keeper calls a crow a krow! He doesn't know anything, does he?"

Before I could explain to her the differences of language in this world, she was embarked on the full tide of another subject. "What do you think, Father? Bhola says there is an elephant in the clouds, blowing water out of his trunk, and that is why it rains!"

And then, darting off anew, while I sat still making ready some reply to this last, saying: "Father! what relation is Mother to you?"

"My dear little sister in the law!" I murmured involuntarily to myself, but with a grave face contrived to answer: "Go and play with Bhola, Mini! I am busy!"

The window of my room overlooks the road. The child had seated herself at my feet near my table, and was playing softly,

This sentence sets the scene.

Cabuliwallah (KAH buul ee wahl uh) a person from Cabul (also spelled Kabul)
prattle (PRAT ul) speak in a childish manner
contrived (kun TRYVD) managed

drumming on her knees. I was hard at work on my seventeenth chapter, where Protrap Singh, the hero, had just caught Kanchan-lata, the heroine, in his arms, and was about to escape with her by the third story window of the castle, when all of a sudden Mini left her play, and ran to the window, crying: "A Cabuliwal-lah! a Cabuliwallah!" Sure enough in the street below was a Cabuliwallah, passing slowly along. He wore the loose soiled clothing of his people, with a tall turban; there was a bag on his back, and he carried boxes of grapes in his hand.

This is a physical description of the Cabuliwallah.

I cannot tell what were my daughter's feelings at the sight of this man, but she began to call him loudly. "Ah!" I thought, "he will come in, and my seventeenth chapter will never be fin-ished!" At which exact moment the Cabuliwallah turned, and looked up at the child. When she saw this, overcome by terror, she fled to her mother's protection, and disappeared. She had a blind belief that inside the bag, which the big man carried, there were perhaps two or three other children like herself. The ped-dler meanwhile entered my doorway, and greeted me with a smiling face.

Here is another aspect of Mini's character.

So precarious was the position of my hero and my heroine, that my first impulse was to stop and buy something, since the man had been called. I made some small purchases, and a con-versation began about Abdurrahman, the Russians, the English, and the Frontier Policy.

As he was about to leave, he asked: "And where is the little girl, sir?"

And I, thinking that Mini must get rid of her false fear, had her brought out.

She stood by my chair, and looked at the Cabuliwallah and his bag. He offered her nuts and raisins, but she would not be tempted, and only clung the closer to me, with all her doubts increased.

This was their first meeting.

This is the first episode in the plot; questions are raised.

One morning, however, not many days later, as I was leaving the house, I was startled to find Mini, seated on a bench near the door, laughing and talking, with the great Cabuliwallah at her feet. In all her life, it appeared, my small daughter had never

---

turban (TUR bun) a headdress; a cap with a scarf wound round it

found so patient a listener, save her father. And already the corner of her little sari was stuffed with almonds and raisins, the gift of her visitor. "Why did you give her those?" I said, and taking out an eight-anna bit, I handed it to him. The man accepted the money without demur, and slipped it into his pocket.

What are the details of the setting here?

Alas, on my return an hour later, I found the unfortunate coin had made twice its own worth of trouble! For the Cabuliwallah had given it to Mini, and her mother catching sight of the bright round object, had pounced on the child with: "Where did you get that eight-anna bit?"

"The Cabuliwallah gave it me," said Mini cheerfully.

"The Cabuliwallah gave it to you!" cried her mother much shocked. "Oh, Mini! how could you take it from him?"

I, entering at the moment, saved her from impending disaster, and proceeded to make my own inquiries.

It was not the first or second time, I found, that the two had met. The Cabuliwallah had overcome the child's first terror by a judicious bribery of nuts and almonds, and the two were now great friends.

The two characters are developed further.

They had many quaint jokes, which afforded them much amusement. Seated in front of him, looking down on his gigantic frame in all her tiny dignity, Mini would ripple her face with laughter, and begin: "O Cabuliwallah! Cabuliwallah! what have you got in your bag?"

And he would reply, in the nasal accents of the mountaineer: "An elephant!" Not much cause for merriment, perhaps; but how they both enjoyed the witticism! And for me, this child's talk with a grown-up man had always in it something strangely fascinating.

Then the Cabuliwallah, not to be behindhand, would take his turn: "Well, little one, and when are you going to the father-in-law's house?"

Now most small Bengali maidens have heard long ago about

This episode foreshadows, or hints at, a development in the plot.

---

anna (AH nuh) a small copper coin of India
demur (dih MUR) to hesitate; hesitation
impending (im PEN ding) about to happen
judicious (joo DISH us) wise and careful
witticism (WIT uh siz um) a witty remark
behindhand (bih HYND hand) slow; late
Bengali (ben GAW lee) a native of Bengal, a province of India

the father-in-law's house; but we, being a little newfangled, had kept these things from our child, and Mini at this question must have been a trifle bewildered. But she would not show it, and with ready tact replied: "Are *you* going there?"

Amongst men of the Cabuliwallah's class, however, it is well known that the words *father-in-law's house* have a double meaning. It is a euphemism for *jail*, the place where we are well cared for, at no expense to ourselves. In this sense would the sturdy peddler take my daughter's question. "Ah," he would say, shaking his fist at an invisible policeman, "I will thrash my father-in-law!" Hearing this, and picturing the poor discomfited relative, Mini would go off into peals of laughter, in which her formidable friend would join.

These were autumn mornings, the very time of year when kings of old went forth to conquest; and I, never stirring from my little corner in Calcutta, would let my mind wander over the whole world. At the very name of another country, my heart would go out to it, and at the sight of a foreigner in the streets, I would fall to weaving a network of dreams—the mountains, the glens, and the forests of his distant home, with his cottage in its setting, and the free and independent life of far-away wilds. Perhaps the scenes of travel conjure themselves up before me, and pass and repass in my imagination all the more vividly, because I lead such a vegetable existence that a call to travel would fall upon me like a thunderbolt. In the presence of this Cabuliwallah, I was immediately transported to the foot of arid mountain peaks, with narrow little defiles twisting in and out amongst their towering heights. I could see the string of camels bearing the merchandise, and the company of turbanned merchants carrying some of their queer old firearms, and some of their spears, journeying downward towards the plains. I could see—but at some such point Mini's mother would intervene, imploring me to "beware of that man."

Mini's mother is unfortunately a very timid lady. Whenever she hears a noise in the street, or sees people coming towards the house, she always jumps to the conclusion that they are either

Tagore provides more clues to the setting.

What does this tell you about the setting and the characters?

Tagore describes a relatively minor character.

---

euphemism (YOO fuh miz um) a word or phrase substituted for another less expressive or direct but considered less offensive or distasteful
discomfited (dis KUM fit id) embarrassed

thieves, or drunkards, or snakes, or tigers, or malaria, or cockroaches, or caterpillars, or an English sailor. Even after all these years of experience, she is not able to overcome her terror. So she was full of doubts about the Cabuliwallah, and used to beg me to keep a watchful eye on him.

I tried to laugh her fear gently away, but then she would turn round on me seriously, and ask me solemn questions.

Were children never kidnapped?

Was it, then, not true that there was slavery in Cabul?

Was it so very absurd that this big man should be able to carry off a tiny child?

I urged that, though not impossible, it was highly improbable. But this was not enough, and her dread persisted. As it was indefinite, however, it did not seem right to forbid the man the house, and the intimacy went on unchecked.

Once a year in the middle of January Rahmun, the Cabuliwallah, was in the habit of returning to his country, and as the time approached he would be very busy, going from house to house collecting his debts. This year, however, he could always find time to come and see Mini. It would have seemed to an outsider that there was some conspiracy between the two, for when he could not come in the morning, he would appear in the evening.

Even to me it was a little startling now and then, in the corner of a dark room, suddenly to surprise this tall, loose-garmented, much bebagged man; but when Mini would run in smiling, with her, "O Cabuliwallah! Cabuliwallah!" and the two friends, so far apart in age, would subside into their old laughter and their old jokes, I felt reassured.

The setting is described in detail.

One morning, a few days before he had made up his mind to go, I was correcting my proof sheets in my study. It was chilly weather. Through the window the rays of the sun touched my feet, and the slight warmth was very welcome. It was almost eight o'clock, and the early pedestrians were returning home, with their heads covered. All at once, I heard an uproar in the street,

A turning point in the plot—what will this incident lead to?

and, looking out, saw Rahmun being led away bound between two policemen, and behind them a crowd of curious boys. There were bloodstains on the clothes of the Cabuliwallah, and one of

---

bebagged (bih BAGD) carrying many bags

the policemen carried a knife. Hurrying out, I stopped them, and inquired what it all meant. Partly from one, partly from another, I gathered that a certain neighbour had owed the peddler something for a Rampuri shawl, but had falsely denied having bought it, and that in the course of the quarrel, Rahmun had struck him. Now in the heat of his excitement, the prisoner began calling his enemy all sorts of names, when suddenly in a verandah of my house appeared my little Mini, with her usual exclamation: "O Cabuliwallah! Cabuliwallah!" Rahmun's face lighted up as he turned to her. He had no bag under his arm today, so she could not discuss the elephant with him. She at once therefore proceeded to the next question: "Are you going to the father-in-law's house?" Rahmun laughed and said: "Just where I am going, little one!" Then seeing that the reply did not amuse the child, he held up his fettered hands. "Ah," he said, "I would have thrashed that old father-in-law, but my hands are bound!"

> What does this house symbolize?

On a charge of murderous assault, Rahmun was sentenced to some years' imprisonment.

Time passed away, and he was not remembered. The accustomed work in the accustomed place was ours, and the thought of the once-free mountaineer spending his years in prison seldom or never occurred to us. Even my lighthearted Mini, I am ashamed to say, forgot her old friend. New companions filled her life. As she grew older, she spent more of her time with girls. So much time indeed did she spend with them that she came no more, as she used to do, to her father's room. I was scarcely on speaking terms with her.

> How has Mini changed?

Years had passed away. It was once more autumn and we had made arrangements for our Mini's marriage. It was to take place during the Puja Holidays. With Durga returning to Kailas, the light of our home also was to depart to her husband's house, and leave her father's in the shadow.

> Elements of the setting have changed. What are they?

The morning was bright. After the rains, there was a sense of ablution in the air, and the sun rays looked like pure gold. So bright were they that they gave a beautiful radiance even to the sordid brick walls of our Calcutta lanes. Since early dawn today the wedding pipes had been sounding, and at each beat my own

> What do these natural images symbolize?

---

fettered (FET urd) chained; shackled
ablution (uh BLOO shun) a cermonial washing or cleansing

heart throbbed. The wail of the tune, Bhairavi, seemed to intensify my pain at the approaching separation. My Mini was to be married tonight.

From early morning noise and bustle had pervaded the house. In the courtyard the canopy had to be slung on its bamboo poles; the chandeliers with their tinkling sound must be hung in each room and verandah. There was no end of hurry and excitement. I was sitting in my study, looking through the accounts, when someone entered, saluting respectfully, and stood before me. It was Rahmun the Cabuliwallah. At first I did not recognize him. He had no bag, nor the long hair, nor the same vigor that he used to have. But he smiled, and I knew him again.

"When did you come, Rahmun?" I asked him.

What has changed the Cabuliwallah?

"Last evening," he said, "I was released from jail."

The words struck harsh upon my ears. I had never before talked with one who had wounded his fellow, and my heart shrank within itself when I realized this, for I felt that the day would have been better-omened had he not turned up.

"There are ceremonies going on," I said, "and I am busy. Could you perhaps come another day?"

At once he turned to go; but as he reached the door he hesitated, and said: "May I not see the little one, sir, for a moment?" It was his belief that Mini was still the same. He had pictured her running to him as she used, calling "O Cabuliwallah! Cabuliwallah!" He had imagined too that they would laugh and talk together, just as of old. In fact, in memory of former days he had brought, carefully wrapped up in paper, a few almonds and raisins and grapes, obtained somehow from a countryman, for his own little fund was dispersed.

Elements of the setting are repeated.

I said again: "There is a ceremony in the house, and you will not be able to see any one today."

The man's face fell. He looked wistfully at me for a moment, said "Good morning," and went out.

I felt a little sorry, and would have called him back, but I found he was returning of his own accord. He came close up to me holding out his offerings and said: "I brought these few things, sir, for the little one. Will you give them to her?"

I took them and was going to pay him, but he caught my hand and said: "You are very kind, sir! Keep me in your recollection. Do not offer me money!—You have a little girl; I too have one like her in my own home. I think of her, and bring fruits to your child—not to make a profit for myself."

Saying this, he put his hand inside his big loose robe, and brought out a small and dirty piece of paper. With great care he unfolded this, and smoothed it out with both hands on my table. It bore the impression of a little hand. Not a photograph. Not a drawing. The impression of an ink-smeared hand laid flat on the paper. This touch of his own little daughter had been always on his heart, as he had come year after year to Calcutta to sell his wares in the streets.

What does this paper symbolize?

Tears came to my eyes. I forgot that he was a poor Cabuli fruit seller, while I was—but no, what was I more than he? He also was a father.

The symbolism is explained and the theme is made clearer.

That impression of the hand of his little *Parbati* in her distant mountain home reminded me of my own little Mini.

I sent for Mini immediately from the inner apartment. Many difficulties were raised, but I would not listen. Clad in the red silk of her wedding day, with the sandal paste on her forehead, and adorned as a young bride, Mini came, and stood bashfully before me.

The Cabuliwallah looked a little staggered at the apparition. He could not revive their old friendship. At last he smiled and said: "Little one, are you going to your father-in-law's house?"

The previous incidents lead up to this moment of truth in the plot.

But Mini now understood the meaning of the word "father-in-law," and she could not reply to him as of old. She flushed up at the question, and stood before him with her bride-like face turned down.

I remembered the day when the Cabuliwallah and my Mini had first met, and I felt sad. When she had gone, Rahmun heaved a deep sigh, and sat down on the floor. The idea had suddenly come to him that his daughter too must have grown in this long time, and that he would have to make friends with her anew. Assuredly he would not find her as he used to know her. And besides, what might not have happened to her in these eight years?

The marriage pipes sounded, and the mild autumn sun streamed round us. But Rahmun sat in the little Calcutta lane, and saw before him the barren mountains of Afghanistan.

What does the reaction of the narrator tell you about his character?

I took out a bank note and gave it to him, saying: "Go back to your own daughter, Rahmun, in your own country, and may the happiness of your meeting bring good fortune to my child!"

Having made this present, I had to curtail some of the festivities. I could not have the electric lights I had intended, nor the military band, and the ladies of the house were despondent at it.

Think about the theme; consider the symbolism of a wedding and a father's reunion with his daughter.

But to me the wedding feast was all the brighter for the thought that in a distant land a long-lost father met again with his only child.

Parbati (pahr BAH tee) a woman's name

Sir Rabindranath Tagore (1861–1941)

Sir Rabindranath Tagore (1861–1941) was a man of many talents who came from a wealthy, intellectual family in the Bengal region of India. Showing promise at an early age, he gave his first public poetry reading at age 14, at a Bengali cultural and nationalistic festival, for which he was widely acclaimed. He had eleven older brothers and sisters, among them a musician, a writer/philosopher and Bengal's first woman novelist.

He was discovered for the Western world in 1912 on a trip to London by W.B. Yeats and Ezra Pound. Tagore won the Nobel Prize for Literature in 1913. He founded an open university and a model village in India and was knighted by the British crown in 1913, but resigned his knighthood six years later to protest a massacre of Indians demonstrating against British Rule.

Review the Selection

UNDERSTAND THE SELECTION

Recall

1. Where is this short story set?

2. What is the narrator's occupation?

3. How old is Mini when the story begins?

Infer

4. Where do you think Mini learned to be afraid of the Cabuliwallah?

5. How does the Cabuliwallah become Mini's friend?

6. What is Cabul?

7. Why doesn't Mini's father mind the Cabuliwallah in his house?

Apply

8. Of whom does Mini remind the Cabuliwallah?

9. Describe the Cabuliwallah's character.

10. What is your reaction to this story? What emotions did it cause?

Respond to Literature

When the Cabuliwallah returns from prison, an event is about to take place involving Mini. He thinks she is still a child although many years have passed. What is the event? How does Mini's father feel about it? What reaction does it cause in the Cabuliwallah?

WRITE ABOUT THE SELECTION

What is your opinion of this short story? What could you say about the story that would make someone else want to read it? Recommendations and reviews of literary works are based on opinion. Your opinion of the work is a result of whether or not you thought the elements are successfully combined to create a good story.

Prewriting   List the four basic elements of the short story down the left side of your paper. These elements are setting, character, plot, and theme. On the basis of these essentials and your reading of the story, list the reasons you think each element is successful and effective, or not. Write your reasons on the right side of the page across from the element you have listed.

Writing   Write a paragraph which reviews this short story. Begin by stating your opinion of the work, then cite the reasons you have listed.

Revising   An effective way to illustrate your opinion is to give examples from the work. Add appropriate quotes from the story which support your opinion.

Proofreading   The title of this story and one of its characters are the same. When you refer to the title of a short story, use quotation marks around the title. Do not use quotations marks around the name of the character.

THINK ABOUT THEME

The **theme** of a work of literature is its underlying idea or message. The author usually tries to communicate the theme (often without stating it directly) in order to convey a strong belief about life or humanity. Sometimes the theme is a moral, or a prescription for how to live life. At other times it is only an idea or emotion.

Novels often have several interrelated themes that wind throughout the work. Short stories normally develop only one theme. This is the overriding message of the story. It can usually be summed up in one sentence.

1. What is the narrator's underlying feeling toward his daughter, Mini?

2. How does Cabuliwallah feel toward Mini?

3. How does she feel toward him?

4. How are the feelings the two men have for their daughters similar?

5. What is the theme of this story?

DEVELOP YOUR VOCABULARY

The pronunciation of an unfamiliar word may be just as mysterious as its meaning when you first come across it.

In foreign languages, some letters are pronounced very differently than they are in English. This can make it more difficult to figure out the meaning and pronunciation of an unfamiliar word you encounter. For instance, the *j* in the Spanish name *José* is pronounced like an *h*. The *j* in the Indian name *Punjab* (a province of India) is pronounced like the *j* in *jam*.

The place to look for a word's proper pronunciation is in a dictionary. Some books include pronunciations and definitions at the bottom of a page or in a glossary at the end of a work.

Each of these words is from the selection. Look them up in a dictionary. Rewrite the words using the diacritical marks and accents that are listed after each word. For example: Cabuliwallah (KAH buul ee wahl uh)

1. prattle
2. contrived
3. turban
4. demur
5. impending
6. judicious
7. witticism
8. Bengali (or Bengal)
9. euphemism
10. discomfited
11. fettered

If a word is not listed in the past tense form in a dictionary, write the present tense form that you find. For example: *discomfit* instead of *discomfited*.

Learn About

IMAGERY

An author's use of imagery helps the reader go through a sensory experience. Imagery can appeal to any of the senses. The writer's words carry the sight, sound, smell, taste, or touch of something that he or she is trying to communicate to the reader.

Poetry is often full of imagery. The power of the images helps make a poem effective. In essence, the poet is trying to convey a sensory experience he or she has had to the reader.

Vision is often considered to be the most powerful of the five senses. For this reason, most imagery is visual. Writers try to make the reader "see" what they are describing.

The writer's use of imagery in a literary work enriches its meaning for the reader. Imagery can reveal deeper levels of meaning to ordinary things as it appeals to our senses.

As you read "The Wild Swans at Coole," ask yourself:
1. What kind of imagery is used?
2. What does Yeats describe in the poem?

WRITING CONNECTION

Choose four objects that you can see at the moment. For each object, write an example of imagery that conveys what it looks like.

READING FOCUS

Summarize When you summarize, you retell the main ideas and important events of a piece of writing. As you read Yeats's poem, ask yourself after each stanza: What important events does the poet describe? What is the main idea of the stanza? Write a sentence or two that answers these questions to summarize Yeats's poems.

THE WILD SWANS AT COOLE

by William Butler Yeats

The trees are in their autumn beauty,
The woodland paths are dry,
Under the October twilight the water
Mirrors a still sky;
5   Upon the brimming water among the stones
Are nine-and-fifty swans.

The nineteenth autumn has come upon me
Since I first made my count;
I saw, before I had well finished,
10   All suddenly mount
And scatter wheeling in great broken rings
Upon their clamorous wings.

I have looked upon those brilliant creatures,
And now my heart is sore.
15   All's changed since I, hearing at twilight,
The first time on this shore,
The bell-beat of their wings above my head,
Trod with a lighter tread.

Unwearied still, lover by lover,
20   They paddle in the cold
Companionable streams or climb the air;
Their hearts have not grown old;

---

clamorous (KLAM ur us) noisy; loud and confused
companionable (kum PAN yun uh bul) sociable

Passion or conquest, wander where they will,
Attend upon them still.

25   But now they drift on the still water,
     Mysterious, beautiful;
     Among what rushes will they build,
     By what lake's edge or pool
     Delight men's eyes when I awake some day
30   To find they have flown away?

Wall mural, Tiffany Studios. The Metropolitan Museum of Art, Gift of Lillian Nassau, 1976, and Gift of Mr. L. Groves Geer, 1978

William Butler Yeats (1865–1939)

As a young boy, Yeats' father read and discussed poetry with him. His father urged him to write certain kinds of poetry and for many years was his most helpful critic. Despite, or perhaps because of, the attention and influence of his father, Yeats said that his childhood was very painful.

Yeats was born in Dublin, but the family later moved to London where Yeats was educated at home by his father. However, the family moved back to Dublin in 1880, and Yeats attended Erasmus High School. Afterward he attended the Metropolitan School of Art where he studied painting. In 1886 he decided to be a writer and left school.

Yeats moved to London where he met other literary figures of the day, and his first book of poetry was published in 1889. That same year he met Maud Gonne, an Irish nationalist and actress. Though she did not feel the same way about him, she was his lifelong love and influenced much of his poetry. Through her he became more interested in the literary history of Ireland. He learned more about Ireland's myths, legends, and folk-tales. During this time he helped to start the Irish Literary Society and helped to make plans for an Irish national theater. The theater opened in 1899 and was very successful.

In 1904 the company bought the Abbey Theater in Dublin, and for the next ten years Yeats was involved in the theater and contributed a number of important plays. The Abbey Theater enjoyed tremendous success for many years.

Yeats was well-known in Dublin for his honest, if not always popular, opinions. Throughout his life he continued to take a serious interest in Irish life, not only writing poems and prose, but retelling Irish myths and legends and giving radio broadcasts. He also organized the Irish Academy of Letters. He moved to the south of France in 1938 when his health failed. He died a year later.

Review the Selection

UNDERSTAND THE SELECTION

Recall

1. In what season is the poem set?

2. How many swans are there?

3. How did the speaker feel when he or she first saw the swans?

Infer

4. How long ago did the speaker first count the swans?

5. How does the speaker feel about the swans?

6. What has changed since the speaker first saw the swans?

7. Why does the speaker envy them?

Apply

8. How does the poem make you feel?

9. How do the swans "climb the air"?

10. Explain what the speaker expects the swans to do.

Respond to Literature

"The nineteenth autumn" which Yeats refers to is the year 1916. Bearing in mind the world events of that year, as they affected England and Europe, what do you think Yeats means when he says that "all's changed"? Based on the emotions he expresses in the poem, how does Yeats feel about it?

WRITE ABOUT THE SELECTION

Think about a bird or an animal that you have seen. What did it look like? How did it make you feel? Write a poem about it. Try to communicate what your experience was like.

Prewriting   Make a list of your impressions of the bird or animal. Include how it looked or sounded and how it made you feel. Create a vivid image in your readers' minds. For instance, if a particular color comes to mind when you think of the bird or animal, be sure your words give a clear impression of that color. If it reminded you of something, add that to your list as well. Try to write down everything you can remember about the experience.

Writing   Use your list to write a poem about the bird or animal. Try to express the experience accurately. Ask yourself how it made you feel. Does your poem capture that feeling for the reader?

Revising   Read your poem carefully. Does it merely report an experience, or does it communicate it to the reader in a fresh, interesting, or vivid way? Rewrite any lines that you think are dull.

Proofreading   Each line of your poem should express a complete thought. If a line is too long for the page, it should be indented when it continues. Be sure that you start each line with a capital letter. Do not use a capital for the continuation of a line, although this poem does.

THINK ABOUT IMAGERY

Onomatopoeia is the use of words that sound like what they are describing. Poets sometimes combine words to create a sound they want to evoke. This helps convey the sound they are describing.

Think about how Yeats communicates his experience of the swans. Does he merely use adjectives to describe them? Look through the poem to find images that appeal to the sense of hearing.

1. Find two images that appeal to the sense of hearing. What sounds do they describe?

2. Have you ever heard the sounds these images describe? Are they effective in helping you to imagine or recall these sounds?

3. Can you find an example of onomatopoeia in the poem? Which words actually mirror the sound they describe?

READING FOCUS

Summarize Write a paragraph that summarizes "The Wild Swans at Coole." Use the sentences that you wrote about each stanza as an outline to help you summarize the entire poem.

DEVELOP YOUR VOCABULARY

What is the difference between the word *complete* and the word *incomplete? In-* is the negative prefix which turns the word *complete* into its opposite, *incomplete*. A **prefix** is one or more letters added to the beginning of a word or word root to change its meaning or make a new word. A negative prefix acts like the word *not*.

Frequently-used negative prefixes include *un-, dis-, il-, in-, im-* and *non-*. These prefixes change the words from their positive forms into negative forms.

Find the words with negative prefixes in the following sentences. After each sentence, rewrite the words in the *positive* form—without the negative prefix. Check the dictionary definition of each word with a negative prefix that you find in the sentences to be sure of its meaning.

1. Rain seems unlikely today, even though it is cloudy.
2. The inability to read or write is defined as illiteracy.
3. He was in a great discomfort from a headache, which he had had all day long.
4. The fox disappeared into the woods.
5. Unfortunately, his reaction is immature.
6. It is unlike her to be tardy.
7. The parrot can talk, but it talks nonsense.
8. Inattention will not be permitted in class.

Learn About

POETIC RHYTHM

Just as the rhythm in a song is expressed by its beat, the rhythm in a poem is expressed by the pattern of stressed and unstressed syllables and the recurrence of specific sounds. **Rhythm** in poetry is a recognizable pattern that is established by a combination of accents and the number of syllables. This pattern is pleasing to hear and heightens the emotional response to the poem.

A **rising rhythm** begins with unstressed syllables and ends with stressed syllables. A **falling rhythm** begins with stressed syllables and ends with unstressed syllables.

A **marching rhythm** has a pattern of one stressed and one unstressed syllable. A **dancing rhythm** has a pattern of one stressed and two unstressed syllables.

As you read "Do Not Go Gentle into That Good Night," ask yourself:
1. Which lines, if any, have a marching rhythm?
2. Which lines, if any, have a dancing rhythm?

WRITING CONNECTION

Write five words whose first syllable is accented and five more whose final syllable is accented.

READING FOCUS

Identify Cause and Effect A cause is an event or idea that makes something happen. The thing that happens is the effect or result.

As you read the following poem, keep notes on index cards of events. Think about how the events are related. Later you can label each event as a cause or an effect.

Do Not Go Gentle into That Good Night

by Dylan Thomas

Do not go gentle into that good night,
Old age should burn and rave at close of day;
Rage, rage against the dying of the light.

Though wise men at their end know dark is right,
5   Because their words had forked no lightning they
Do not go gentle into that good night.

Good men, the last wave by, crying how bright
Their frail deeds might have danced in a green bay,
Rage, rage against the dying of the light.

10   Wild men who caught and sang the sun in flight,
And learn, too late, they grieved it on its way,
Do not go gentle into that good night.

Grave men, near death, who see with blinding sight
Blind eyes could blaze like meteors and be gay,
15   Rage, rage against the dying of the light.

And you, my father, there on the sad height,
Curse, bless, me now with your fierce tears, I pray.
Do not go gentle into that good night.
Rage, rage against the dying of the light.

---

rave (RAYV) to rage, talk wildly
meteors (MEE tee urz) shooting stars

Review the Selection

UNDERSTAND THE SELECTION

Recall

1. What does the poem tell us to rage against?

2. What types of men does the poem mention?

3. When should old age burn and rage?

Infer

4. Do you think the poem is addressed to a specific person? If so, to whom?

5. Explain what "their words had forked no lightning" means.

6. What do you think is "the sad height" Thomas's father is on?

7. What does the poem refer to? What are all its images of?

Apply

8. Imagine you are the poet writing this poem. What are your emotions?

9. What is another way you could say "Do not go gentle into that good night"?

10. What is your opinion of the poem?

Respond to Literature

Each stanza of the poem contains at least one image that reveals Thomas's subject. What is his subject? Describe the imagery that expresses it.

WRITE ABOUT THE SELECTION

This poem urges you toward a course of action. It tells you to "rage, rage against the dying of the light" and commands that you "do not go gentle into that good night." It tells you that wise men and wild men "do not go gentle. . ." and good men and grave men "rage, rage. . ."

Stanzas two through four illustrate this declaration with vivid, expressive imagery. Although reducing imagery and poetry to prose may rob it of its unique beauty, it can help you to better understand the poet's meaning and his or her method of expressing that meaning. Rewriting the poem in your own words—paraphrasing—is one way of analyzing a poem.

Prewriting Reread the poem. Make notes on each stanza by writing down key words and phrases in your own words which are clues to the meaning of the lines and images.

Writing Using your notes as a basis, paraphrase by writing six one- or two-sentence paragraphs, one for each stanza, explaining the meaning of each in your own words.

Revising To augment your explanations, include quotations from the poem.

Proofreading When you use part of a literary work in your writing, remember that it must be enclosed in quotation marks. Check your paragraphs to make sure that you have punctuated the quotations correctly.

THINK ABOUT RHYTHM

Rhythm in poetry is established by the pattern of stressed and unstressed syllables plus the number of syllables in a line. The rhythmic pattern of a poem is called **meter**, and it is one way in which poetry is classified and analyzed.

The rhythmic unit in a line of poetry is called a **foot.** For example, one standard foot in poetry is known as **iambic** and consists of an unstressed syllable followed by a stressed syllable:

> ah chóo!
> for lórn
> oh, yeáh!

Each of these is an iambic foot. The number of feet in a line describes the meter of a poem.

1. Name an example of an iambic foot in the poem.

2. What are the stressed and unstressed syllables in the first stanza of this poem?

3. What kind of rhythm is this, dancing, or marching?

READING FOCUS
Identify Cause and Effect Use your index cards to choose one cause-and-effect relationship in the poem. Write a paragraph that explains this relationship.

DEVELOP YOUR VOCABULARY

A **root** is a word or word part which is used as a base to create other words. Prefixes and suffixes are added to roots to form other words with different meanings. A **prefix** is a syllable, or group of syllables which is added to the beginning of the root. A **suffix** is a syllable, or group of syllables added to the end of the root to create another word. Both prefixes and suffixes can be added to a root. More than one of each may also be added.

Take the word *affirm,* for instance. Add the prefix *re-,* meaning *again,* and you have *reaffirm,* which means "affirm again." Add the suffix *-ation,* which is used to form nouns from verbs, and you have *affirmation,* which means "a confirmation or ratification."

Find the root in each of the words below. Use the root to figure out the meaning of the word, and write your definition next to it. Check your definitions in the dictionary.

1. addition
2. artistic
3. changeable
4. classification
5. immortal
6. maladjustment
7. mistrust
8. playful
9. recollection
10. television

Wall painted with many Buddhas, detail, Indian.
Giraudon/Art Resource

READING FOCUS

Recognize Sequence of Events The sequence of events is the order in which events occur. This can also be called time order. Recognizing sequence helps you keep story events clear in your mind. It also helps you see any cause-and-effect links between events. As you read, think about which event happens first, second, third, and so on. Number the events on a note pad to keep them organized in your mind.

NARRATION

Narration, simply stated, is the telling of a story. In fiction or nonfiction, it is the recounting of an event or a series of events. Narration usually contains a considerable amount of description. The narrator is the person telling the story.

There are two basic forms of narration. The first is called **simple narrative.** In this, the story is told mainly in chronological order. The second form of narrative is **narrative with plot.** The emphasis in this form of narration falls on causes and the relationships among the events.

Narration and description often go hand-in-hand in fiction and nonfiction. Narration depends on description to enrich the story with images, to add color and uniqueness to the setting, to the people or characters, to their environment, and to the plot.

As you read "Shooting an Elephant," ask yourself the following questions:
1. How does the author describe the story's setting?
2. How does he describe the feelings of the narrator?

WRITING CONNECTION

Think of the things that happened in your life yesterday. Write a short narrative of those events.

SHOOTING AN ELEPHANT

by George Orwell

In Moulmein, in Lower Burma, I was hated by large numbers of people—the only time in my life that I have been important enough for this to happen to me. I was subdivisional police officer of the town, and in an aimless, petty kind of way anti-European feeling was very bitter. No one had the guts to raise a riot, but if a European woman went through the bazaars alone somebody would probably spit betel juice over her dress. As a police officer I was an obvious target and was baited whenever it seemed safe to do so. When a nimble Burman tripped me up on the football field and the referee (another Burman) looked the other way, the crowd yelled with hideous laughter. This happened more than once. In the end the sneering yellow faces of young men that met me everywhere, the insults hooted after me when I was at a safe distance, got badly on my nerves. The young Buddhist priests were the worst of all. There were several thousands of them in the town and none of them seemed to have anything to do except stand on street corners and jeer at Europeans.

All this was perplexing and upsetting. For at that time I had already made up my mind that imperialism was an evil thing and the sooner I chucked up my job and got out of it the better. Theoretically—and secretly, of course—I was all for the Burmese and all against their oppressors, the British. As for the job I was doing, I hated it more bitterly than I can perhaps make clear. In a job like that you see the dirty work of the Empire at close quarters. The wretched prisoners huddling in the stinking cages of the lockups, the grey, cowed faces of the long-term convicts, the scarred buttocks of the men who had been flogged with bamboos—all these oppressed me with an intolerable sense of guilt. But I could

---

betel juice (BEET ul joos) juice produced by chewing the betel nut
imperialism (im PIR ee uhl iz um) the policy and practice of forming and
   maintaining an empire by controlling other countries or colonies

get nothing into perspective. I was young and ill-educated and I had had to think out my problems in the utter silence that is imposed on every Englishman in the East. I did not even know that the British Empire is dying, still less did I know that it is a great deal better than the younger empires that are going to supplant it. All I knew was that I was stuck between my hatred of the empire I served and my rage against the evil-spirited little beasts who tried to make my job impossible. With one part of my mind I thought of the British Raj as an unbreakable tyranny, as something clamped down, in *saecula saeculorum*,[1] upon the will of prostrate peoples; with another part I thought that the greatest joy in the world would be to drive a bayonet into a Buddhist priest's guts. Feelings like these are the normal byproducts of imperialism; ask any Anglo-Indian official, if you can catch him off duty.

One day something happened which in a roundabout way was enlightening. It was a tiny incident in itself, but it gave me a better glimpse than I had had before of the real nature of imperialism— the real motives for which despotic governments act. Early one morning the sub-inspector at a police station the other end of the town rang me up on the phone and said that an elephant was ravaging the bazaar. Would I please come and do something about it? I did not know what I could do, but I wanted to see what was happening and I got on to a pony and started out. I took my rifle, an old .44 Winchester and much too small to kill an elephant, but I thought the noise might be useful *in terrorem*.[2] Various Burmans stopped me on the way and told me about the elephant's doings. It was not, of course, a wild elephant, but a tame one which had gone "must." It had been chained up as tame elephants always are when their attack of "must" is due, but on the previous night it had broken its chain and escaped. Its mahout, the only person who could manage it when it was in that state, had set out in pursuit, but he had taken the wrong direction and was now twelve hours' journey away, and in the morning the elephant had suddenly reappeared in the town. The Burmese population had no weapons and were quite helpless against it. It had already destroyed somebody's bamboo hut, killed a cow and raided some fruit stalls and devoured the stock; also it had met the municipal rubbish van and, when the driver jumped out and took to

Raj (RAHJ) rule; government authority
prostrate (PROS trayt) lying flat on the ground
despotic (dih SPOT ik) tyrannical
must (MUST) the state of dangerous frenzy in an animal
mahout (muh HOUT) an elephant driver or keeper
[1]**saecula saeculorum:** forever and ever
[2]**in terrorem:** Latin for terror

his heels, had turned the van over and inflicted violence upon it.

The Burmese sub-inspector and some Indian constables were waiting for me in the quarter where the elephant had been seen. It was a very poor quarter, a labyrinth of squalid bamboo huts, thatched with palm-leaf, winding all over a steep hillside. I remember that it was a cloudy, stuffy morning at the beginning of the rains. We began questioning the people as to where the elephant had gone and, as usual, failed to get any definite information. That is invariably the case in the East; a story always sounds clear enough at a distance, but the nearer you get to the scene of events the vaguer it becomes. Some of the people said that the elephant had gone in one direction, some said that he had gone in another, some professed not even to have heard of any elephant. I had almost made up my mind that the whole story was a pack of lies, when we heard yells a little distance away. There was a loud, scandalized cry of "Go away, child! Go away this instant!" and an old woman with a switch in her hand came round the corner of a

labyrinth (LAB uh rinth) maze

hut, violently shooing away a crowd of naked children. Some more women followed, clicking their tongues and exclaiming; evidently there was something that the children ought not to have seen. I rounded the hut and saw a man's dead body sprawling in the mud. He was an Indian, a black Dravidian coolie, almost naked, and he could not have been dead many minutes. The people said that the elephant had come suddenly upon him round the corner of the hut, caught him with its trunk, put its foot on his back and ground him into the earth. This was the rainy season and the ground was soft, and his face had scored a trench a foot deep and a couple of yards long. He was lying on his belly with arms crucified and head sharply twisted to one side. His face was coated with mud, the eyes wide open, the teeth bared and grinning with an expression of unendurable agony. (Never tell me, by the way, that the dead look peaceful. Most of the corpses I have seen looked devilish.) The friction of the great beast's foot had stripped the skin from his back as neatly as one skins a rabbit. As soon as I saw the dead man I sent an orderly to a friend's house nearby to borrow an elephant rifle. I had already sent back the pony, not wanting it to go mad with fright and throw me if it smelled the elephant.

The orderly came back in a few minutes with a rifle and five cartridges, and meanwhile some Burmans had arrived and told us that the elephant was in the paddy fields below, only a few hundred yards away. As I started forward, practically the whole population of the quarter flocked out of their houses and followed me. They had seen the rifle and were all shouting excitedly that I was going to shoot the elephant. They had not shown much interest in the elephant when he was merely ravaging their homes, but it was different now that he was going to be shot. It was a bit of fun to them, as it would be to an English crowd; besides, they wanted the meat. It made me vaguely uneasy. I had no intention of shooting the elephant—I had merely sent for the rifle to defend myself if necessary —and it is always unnerving to have a crowd following you. I marched down the hill, looking and feeling a fool, with the rifle over my shoulder and an ever-growing army of people jostling at my heels. At the bottom, when you got away from the huts, there was a metaled road and beyond that a miry waste of paddy fields a thousand yards across, not yet ploughed but soggy from the first rains and dotted with coarse grass. The elephant was standing eight yards from the road, his left side towards us. He took not the slightest notice of the crowd's approach. He was tearing up bunches of grass, beating them against his knees to clean them and stuffing them into his mouth.

I had halted on the road. As soon as I saw the elephant I knew with perfect certainty that I ought not to shoot him. It

---

Dravidian (druh VID ee un) a group of intermixed races in India
metaled (MET uld) paved

is a serious matter to shoot a working elephant—it is comparable to destroying a huge and costly piece of machinery—and obviously one ought not to do it if it can possibly be avoided. And at that distance, peacefully eating, the elephant looked no more dangerous than a cow. I thought then and I think now that his attack of "must" was already passing off; in which case he would merely wander harmlessly about until the mahout came back and caught him. Moreover, I did not in the least want to shoot him. I decided that I would watch him for a little while to make sure that he did not turn savage again, and then go home.

But at that moment I glanced round at the crowd that had followed me. It was an immense crowd, two thousand at the least and growing every minute. It blocked the road for a long distance on either side. I looked at the sea of yellow faces above the garish clothes—faces all happy and excited over this bit of fun, all certain that the elephant was going to be shot. They were watching me as they would watch a conjurer about to perform a trick. They did not like me, but with the magical rifle in my hands I was momentarily worth watching. And suddenly I realized that I should have to shoot the elephant after all. The people expected it of me and I had got to do it; I could feel their two thousand wills pressing me forward, irresistibly. And it was at this moment, as I stood there with the rifle in my hands, that I first grasped the hollowness, the futility of the white man's dominion

in the East. Here was I, the white man with his gun, standing in front of the unarmed native crowd—seemingly the leading actor of the piece; but in reality I was only an absurd puppet pushed to and fro by the will of those yellow faces behind. I perceived in this moment that when the white man turns tyrant it is his own freedom that he destroys. He becomes a sort of hollow, posing dummy, the conventionalized figure of a sahib. For it is the condition of his rule that he shall spend his life in trying to impress the "natives," and so in every crisis he has got to do what the "natives" expect of him. He wears a mask, and his face grows to fit it. I had got to shoot the elephant. I had committed myself to doing it when I sent for the rifle. A sahib has got to act like a sahib; he has got to appear resolute, to know his own mind and do definite things. To come all that way, rifle in hand, with two thousand people marching at my heels, and then to trail feebly away, having done nothing—no, that was impossible. The crowd would laugh at me. And my whole life, every white man's life in the East, was one long struggle not to be laughed at.

But I did not want to shoot the elephant. I watched him beating his bunch of grass against his knees, with that preoccupied grandmotherly air that elephants have. It seemed to me that it would be murder to shoot him. At that age I was not squeamish about killing animals, but I had never shot an elephant

---

sahib (SAH ib) formerly, a title used in colonial India when speaking of or to a European

and never wanted to. (Somehow it always seems worse to kill a *large* animal.) Besides, there was the beast's owner to be considered. Alive, the elephant was worth at least a hundred pounds; dead, he would only be worth the value of his tusks—five pounds, possibly. But I had got to act quickly. I turned to some experienced-looking Burmans who had been there when we arrived, and asked them how the elephant had been behaving. They all said the same time: he took no notice of you if you left him alone, but he might charge if you went too close to him.

It was perfectly clear to me what I ought to do. I ought to walk up to within, say, twenty-five yards of the elephant and test his behavior. If he charged, I could shoot; if he took no notice of me, it would be safe to leave him until the mahout came back. But also I knew that I was going to do no such thing. I was a poor shot with a rifle and the ground was soft mud into which one should sink at every step. If the elephant charged and I missed him, I should have about as much chance as a toad under a steamroller. But even then I was not thinking particularly of my own skin, only of the watchful yellow faces behind. For at that moment, with the crowd watching me, I was not afraid in the ordinary sense, as I would have been if I had been alone. A white man mustn't be frightened in front of "natives"; and so, in general, he isn't frightened. The sole thought in my mind

was that if anything went wrong those two thousand Burmans would see me pursued, caught, trampled on, and reduced to a grinning corpse like that Indian up the hill. And if that happened it was quite probable that some of them would laugh. That would never do. There was only one alternative. I shoved the cartridges into the magazine and lay down on the road to get a better aim.

The crowd grew very still, and a deep, low, happy sigh, as of people who see the theatre curtain go up at last, breathed from innumerable throats. They were going to have their bit of fun after all. The rifle was a beautiful German thing with cross-hair sights. I did not then know that in shooting an elephant one should shoot to cut an imaginary bar running from ear-hole to ear-hole. I ought, therefore, as the elephant was sideways on, to have aimed straight at his ear-hole; actually I aimed several inches in front of this, thinking the brain would be further forward.

When I pulled the trigger I did not hear the bang or feel the kick—one never does when a shot goes home—but I heard the devilish roar of glee that went up from the crowd. In that instant, in too short a time, one would have thought, even for the bullet to get there, a mysterious, terrible change had come over the elephant. He neither stirred nor fell, but every line of his body had altered. He looked suddenly stricken, shrunken, immensely old, as though the frightful

magazine (mag uh ZEEN) space in a rifle that holds cartridges

impact of the bullet had paralyzed him without knocking him down. At last, after what seemed a long time—it might have been five seconds, I dare say—he sagged flabbily to his knees. His mouth slobbered. An enormous senility seemed to have settled upon him. One could have imagined him thousands of years old. I fired again into the same spot. At the second shot he did not collapse but climbed with desperate slowness to his feet and stood weakly upright, with legs sagging and head drooping. I fired a third time. That was the shot that did for him. You could see the agony of it jolt his whole body and knock the last remnant of strength from his legs. But in falling he seemed for a moment to rise, for as his hind legs collapsed beneath him he seemed to tower upwards like a huge rock toppling, his trunk reaching skyward like a tree. He trumpeted, for the first and only time. And then down he came, his belly towards me, with a crash that seemed to shake the ground even where I lay.

I got up. The Burmans were already racing past me across the mud. It was obvious that the elephant would never rise again, but he was not dead. He was breathing very rhythmically with long rattling gasps, his great mound of a side painfully rising and falling. His mouth was wide open—I could see far down into caverns of pale pink throat. I waited a long time for him to die, but his breathing did not weaken. Finally I fired my two remaining shots into the spot where I thought his heart must be. The thick blood welled out of him like red velvet, but still he did not die. His body did not even jerk when the shots hit him, the tortured breathing continued without a pause. He was dying, very slowly and in great agony, but in some world remote from me where not even a bullet could damage him further. I felt that I had got to put an end to that dreadful noise. It seemed dreadful to see the great beast lying there, powerless to move and yet powerless to die, and not even to be able to finish him. I sent back for my small rifle and poured shot after shot into his heart and down his throat. They seemed to make no impression. The tortured gasps continued as steadily as the ticking of a clock.

In the end I could not stand it any longer and went away. I heard later that it took him half an hour to die. Burmans were bringing dahs and baskets even before I left, and I was told they had stripped his body almost to the bones by the afternoon.

Afterwards, of course, there were endless discussions about the shooting of the elephant. The owner was furious, but he was only an Indian and could do nothing. Besides, legally I had done the right thing, for a mad elephant has to be killed, like a mad dog, if its owner fails to control it. Among the Europeans opinion was divided. The older men said I was right, the younger men said it was a

---

dahs (DAHZ) large knives

damn shame to shoot an elephant for killing a coolie, because an elephant was worth more than any damn Coringhee coolie. And afterwards I was very glad that the coolie had been killed; it put me legally in the right and it gave me a sufficient pretext for shooting the elephant. I often wondered whether any of the others grasped that I had done it solely to avoid looking a fool.

Review the Selection

UNDERSTAND THE SELECTION

Recall

1. In what country is the story set?

2. What is the narrator's occupation?

3. What is the size of the crowd that gathers to watch the narrator shoot the elephant?

Infer

4. Why do the Burmese hate the British?

5. Why does this upset the narrator?

6. Why is the narrator unafraid of the elephant?

7. What is the narrator's sole reason for shooting the elephant?

Apply

8. Do you think the narrator has ever shot an elephant before? Explain.

9. Explain why the younger European men's reaction to the shooting could be called racist.

10. Predict what might have happened to the narrator if he had not shot the elephant.

Respond to Literature

The narrator of this story describes two forces which eventually caused the British Empire to grant Burma its independence. Describe those two forces.

WRITE ABOUT THE SELECTION

One way to diagram and follow the sequence of events in a narrative is to construct a timeline. Being able to see the sequence of events recorded on a timeline can give you an insight into how the story is constructed and help you understand it. You may be able to discover cause-and-effect relationships within the narration which are not immediately apparent.

Prewriting   Reread the story and make a list of all the important events you find. Draw a line across a piece of paper. Divide it into three equal lengths, and label them *beginning, middle* and *end.* Write these words underneath the line in the appropriate place. Above the line, write each of the important events you have identified in the order that they occur.

Writing   Using your timeline as a basis, write a short summary of the narration which shows how the events flow.

Revising   Certain events in the story cause certain other events to happen as you will see in your timeline. Add to your paragraph a description of a cause-and-effect relationship you see in the story.

Proofreading   Remember that **proper nouns**—the names of places or people— are always capitalized. For instance, the name of the country in which "Shooting an Elephant" takes place is *Burma,* not *burma.*

THINK ABOUT NARRATION

Narration in nonfiction is the telling of a story. When you read a work of literature, think about who is telling you the story. Think about who the narrator is. The narrator tells the story from his or her point of view, and that obviously affects how the story is told, and what is told. A native of the Burmese town who observed these events might tell this story very differently from the way Orwell, a British police officer, tells it.

1. Who is the main character of this story?

2. Define the point of view of the narrator in this selection.

3. What makes the narrator's position in the society in which the story is set unusual?

4. What, in your opinion, is the purpose of this story?

READING FOCUS

Recognize Sequence of Events Are the events told in chronological order? What kind of running monologue of the narrator accompanies the events? Use your notes to write a paragraph that summarizes the events in one part of the story in the correct order.

DEVELOP YOUR VOCABULARY

In some literary works, especially those which are set in a foreign land, you may come across words you have never seen before. In writing about a foreign land and its people, a writer may use words that are unique to that country to add color and authenticity. Sometimes a writer will use a foreign word because there is no equivalent English word.

One way to get an immediate understanding of the foreign word is to guess its meaning based on context clues. The **context** is other words and sentences which surround the unfamiliar word. The writer may include some explanation of the foreign word within the sentence, as in this example from "Shooting an Elephant": "It was not, of course, a wild elephant, but a tame one which had gone 'must.'" From this sentence, you can guess that the approximate meaning of *going must* is *going wild.*

Another writer might have explained the word by writing, "The usually tame elephant had gone must, or temporarily crazy." The meaning of the foreign word is spelled out in the sentence.

Review the dictionary definitions of these words from "Shooting an Elephant." Use each word in a sentence.

1. imperialism
2. Raj
3. prostrate
4. despotic
5. mahout
6. labyrinth
7. metaled
8. sahib
9. magazine
10. dahs

Learn About

RHYME

Rhyme consists of the repetition of accented sounds in words. The accented sounds are similar or identical to each other. In a **perfect rhyme,** the accented vowels and consonants sound alike, but each is preceded by a different consonant. For example, *fame* and *same.* The *-ame* sounds are identical, but the preceding sounds are different.

Internal rhyme refers to the position of the rhymed syllables in a line of poetry. Thus, **internal rhyme** occurs within a single line—after the beginning and before the closing syllables. An example in internal rhyme is found in this line of a familiar nursery rhyme: "Mary, Mary, quite contrary." The other positions of rhyme are **end rhyme,** which occurs at the end of a line, and **beginning rhyme,** which occurs in the first syllable or syllables.

As you read "The Naming of Cats," ask yourself:

1. Does Eliot use internal, end, or beginning rhyme, or some combination of these rhyme positions?
2. Which rhymes unify the poem?

WRITING CONNECTION

Write the first five perfect rhymes you can think of.

READING FOCUS

Understand Symbolism A symbol represents itself, and at the same time it represents an idea other than itself. Symbols in poetry help readers to understand the central idea of a poem. As you read "The Naming of Cats" list symbols and what you think they represent.

The Naming of Cats

by T. S. Eliot

The Naming of Cats is a difficult matter,
    It isn't just one of your holiday games;
You may think at first I'm as mad as a hatter
When I tell you, a cat must have THREE DIFFERENT NAMES.
5   First of all, there's the name that the family use daily,
    Such as Peter, Augustus, Alonzo or James,
Such as Victor or Jonathan, George or Bill Bailey—
    All of them sensible everyday names.
There are fancier names if you think they sound sweeter,
10   Some for the gentlemen, some for the dames:
Such as Plato, Admetus, Electra, Demeter—
    But all of them sensible everyday names.
But I tell you, a cat needs a name that's particular,
    A name that's peculiar, and more dignified,
15   Else how can he keep up his tail perpendicular,
    Or spread out his whiskers, or cherish his pride?
Of names of this kind, I can give you a quorum,
    Such as Munkustrap, Quaxo, or Coricopat,
Such as Bombalurina, or else Jellylorum—
20   Names that never belong to more than one cat.
But above and beyond there's still one name left over,
    And that is the name that you never will guess;
The name that no human research can discover—
    But THE CAT HIMSELF KNOWS, and will never confess.
25   When you notice a cat in profound meditation,
    The reason, I tell you, is always the same:
His mind is engaged in a rapt contemplation
    Of the thought, of the thought, of the thought of his name:
      His ineffable effable
30   Effanineffable
Deep and inscrutable singular Name.

---

perpendicular (pur pun DIK yuh lur) straight up and down
quorum (KWAWR um) a select group
rapt (RAPT) completely absorbed or engrossed
ineffable (in EF uh bul) too awesome to be spoken of
inscrutable (in SKROOT uh bul) mysterious; enigmatic

Review the Selection

UNDERSTAND THE SELECTION

Recall

1. What is the poem about?

2. How many names does a cat have?

3. What are four examples of "sensible everyday names"?

Infer

4. What kind of name makes a cat proud? Why?

5. Why would you think the poet is "as mad as a hatter?"

6. Why might humans never discover a cat's third name?

7. Why are names like Peter, James, or George "family" names?

Apply

8. How would you characterize names like Munkustrap or Quaxo?

9. What do you think inspired Eliot to write this poem?

10. What is your opinion of "The Naming of Cats?" Did you ever wonder about the thoughts of a cat?

Respond to Literature

Although Eliot's tone can be read as humorous, there is a deeper, more serious theme which underlies this poem. What do you think it is?

WRITE ABOUT THE SELECTION

Poems, like other forms of literature, are told from a certain point of view. The narrator in "The Naming of Cats" is a human being. Suppose you wanted to describe the naming of cats from a cat's point of view. How would a cat feel about the necessity of three names? If a cat were to write about the same subject, would it reveal its third name?

Prewriting   Assume that you are a cat, and that you have three names. You are asked to explain why cats must have three names and which ones they prefer. Make up three cat names. Beside each, list when, how and why it is used. Who gave you the names? What do they mean, and which do you prefer?

Writing   Based on your prewriting, write a paragraph about cats' names from a cat's point of view. Describe how you feel about each name. Reveal the mysterious third name, if you think a cat would. If not, explain your cat-reasons for keeping the name a secret. Provide answers to the questions in prewriting.

Revising   Since you are writing from the point of view of a cat, you will use the first-person point of view. Add a description of your cat-self.

Proofreading   The first-person point of view uses the words *I, me, my,* and *mine.* Make sure your paragraph is told consistently from the first-person point of view.

THINK ABOUT RHYME

Internal rhyme is rhyme that occurs within a line of poetry. The other types of rhyme are **beginning** and **end rhyme**.

True rhymes are based on the similar sounds of accented syllables. Therefore, *trying* and *lying* are true rhymes. *Trying* and *saying* are not, because the similar sound is in the unaccented syllables.

When the rhyme sound is the final accented syllable or the only syllable, it is called **masculine**. If the rhyme sound is an accented syllable followed by an unaccented syllable, it is called **feminine**. *Names/games* is a masculine rhyme; *fighting/lighting* is a feminine rhyme.

1. Name two examples of internal and end rhyme in "The Naming of Cats."

2. What makes "particular/perpendicular" a feminine rhyme?

3. How would you describe the rhymes "dignified/pride"?

READING FOCUS

Understand Symbolism Write three sentences that tell what you think each level of the cats' names symbolizes.

DEVELOP YOUR VOCABULARY

Words that have the same or almost the same meaning are called **synonyms**. Some words have many synonyms. For example, *happy, joyous,* and *ecstatic* are synonyms, but you can see that each word expresses a different degree of the same feeling.

Antonyms have opposite meanings. For example: *simple/complex; plain/fancy; easy/difficult* are antonyms.

In many cases, the dictionary will list synonyms and an antonym for entry words. A **thesaurus** is a comprehensive listing of synonyms and antonyms that is usually arranged according to subject. It is very helpful when you are seeking a certain word to express your meaning exactly.

Using a dictionary or a thesaurus, find a synonym and an antonym for each of these words from the selection:

1. perpendicular
2. rapt
3. ineffable
4. inscrutable

UNIT 5 *Review*

Write About the Literary Period

The literature of a certain period is directly affected by the significant events of that time. The reactions of writers and poets to their time are expressed in the authors' work and writing technique. The modern period (1901–1939) was a time of turbulent change in Britain. The First World War effectively put an end to what was a stable, civilized society in which ideas of values and morality were assumed to be constant. The economic depression that followed the war continued the turmoil. How do these selections express the spirit and change of this modern period?

Prewriting   Reread the opening selection to refresh your memory about this period. Make a list of the themes that you have identified in the selections. Also list any ideas or emotions expressed in the selections that you think are important. Then list what you think are the significant events, trends, and changes within the modern period.

Writing   Based on the relationships you have identified in your lists, discuss the themes, ideas, and emotions in those selections which characterize this period.

Revising   Cite specific examples from the selections to illustrate the points you make in your written discussion.

Proofreading   Check your work to make sure that you have punctuated the sentences correctly.

Write About Genre

You have read and written about a variety of literary genres in this unit—epigrams, drama, poetry, short stories, and nonfiction. You have also discussed specific literary elements which are found in various genres.

Which literary elements are shared among the different genres? Which elements are unique to a genre, or found only in that genre? Write about the elements of literature by comparing and contrasting them as they appear in different genres.

Prewriting   Write these headings across the top of your paper: setting, character, tone, theme, plot, point of view, imagery, narration, rhythm, and rhyme. Under each heading, write the literary genres in which the element is found.

Writing   Based upon your lists, identify the elements that are shared by different genres and those that are specific to one. Then compare and contrast the use of different elements.

Revising   Use words that are specific in your discussion to make sure your meaning is clear and exact. Do not use general words or slang words, such as *stuff*, a *bunch of, you know,* and *thing.*

Proofreading   Use an apostrophe and the letter s to form the possessive of any singular or plural noun that does not end in s. For example: this *poem's* theme; *literature's* variety.

BUILD LANGUAGE SKILLS

Vocabulary

It is not uncommon to encounter words in the English Language that are unfamiliar to you. When this happens, how can you figure out the meaning of an unfamiliar word? One way is to take it apart. Separate the word root or root word from prefixes and suffixes and see what you have left. Remember that prefixes are added to the beginning of a word root, and suffixes are added to the end of a word root. It is important to pay attention to the prefixes and suffixes, too, because they are added to a word to alter its meaning. Look at the following example.

> *Example:* indefensible
> **prefix:** in- (meaning *not*)
> **suffix:** -ible (meaning *capable of*)
> **root:** defens(e)

If you know the meanings of these parts of the word, you can figure out that *indefensible* means "cannot be defended or protected." It is always a good idea to check the word's meaning in a dictionary to be certain of it.

Separate these words into prefix, root, and suffix. Then write what you think each word means. Compare the definition that you have come up with to the dictionary definition.

1. adjustment	6. unreasonable
2. inability	7. nonperfor-
3. nonconformity	mance
4. inalienable	8. illogically
5. dehumanize	9. inaccessible

Grammar, Usage, and Mechanics

The use of the correct punctuation marks is essential if you want the reader to understand your work. End sentences with periods, question marks, or exclamation points depending upon the nature of the sentence. Use commas before *and* or *but* to separate the two main clauses of a compound sentence. Use commas to set off parenthetical expressions and phrases.

Add punctuation marks so that these sentences from the selections are correctly punctuated.

1. She stood by my chair and looked at the Cabuliwallah and his bag

2. I was subdivisional police officer of the town and in an aimless petty kind of way anti-European feeling was very bitter

3. It made me vaguely uneasy

4. The staircase window having been boarded up no light came down into the hall

5. Kathleen behaved well when some months later her fiancé was reported missing presumed killed

6. The two of them settled down in this quiet arboreal part of Kensington

7. What hour How should I . . .

8. I would have thrashed that old father-in-law but my hands are bound

9. Were children never kidnapped

SPEAKING AND LISTENING

In this assignment you will be working in groups of four or five. In previous lessons you have been asked to choose one particular selection from a unit and concentrate on it alone. For this assignment, you will have to skim through and possibly reread several of the selections. However, since you will be working in a group, you can divide the labors.

Your goal at the end of this assignment is to present a talk to other groups. Each person in your group will be expected to participate. The subject of your group talk will be "Figurative Language." Follow these steps as you prepare to complete your assignment.

1. Meet with four or five of your classmates and discuss the various aspects of figurative language—metaphor, simile, personification, and hyperbole. Be sure all members of your group can define or give examples of each figure of speech.

2. As a group, or individually (whichever your group decides), skim the selections to find examples of each type of figurative language.

3. Have one person in the group act as recorder to take notes while others peruse the selections. The recorder can jot down page numbers where the example can be found or write the example itself. Discuss how you will organize the notekeeping so all group members have access to the information accumulated.

4. Once you have uncovered several examples of each type of figurative language, divide them among the group members for presentation. Decide the order of speaking. Individual members should then prepare a brief talk.

5. When you present your portion of the talk, you can tell the audience what literary term you are responsible for, or, for some excitement, you can give your examples and let them guess.

6. After all groups have made their presentations, take a couple of minutes and invent some of your own examples of simile, metaphor, hyperbole, and personification. Have a contest and decide which group created the most novel example.

It is as simple as that to prepare a talk—especially when you have group support. Set to your task and try to limit your group presentation to four minutes.

CRITICAL THINKING

Theme   Most works of literature have an underlying theme. Whether it is poetry, drama, a short story, or a novel, the writer has often created the work with a basic idea—or a message—in mind. The theme is the central idea of a work. In poetry, fiction, and drama the theme is the abstract concept which is expressed through the characters, the action, and the images in the work.

Recognizing the theme of a work of literature will add to your appreciation of it. The dialogue in fiction and drama, and the voice of the speaker in a poem are made more meaningful. The actions and the reactions of the characters and the pattern of events take on more significance in light of the theme. Deeper levels and shades of meaning in the images are apparent when you can refer to the theme, or central idea.

Consider the themes of a poem and a short story in this unit, and answer the following questions.

1. What is the theme of the poem? Does the writer discuss or state the theme within the work? What is your reaction to the theme?
2. Describe the theme of the short story. How is it expressed in the work? Give two specific examples.

EFFECTIVE STUDYING

Techniques for Effective Studying   Literature is a form of art, and the study of literature should be approached in a different way from the study of biology, math, or other subject areas. Studying literature offers you a chance to experience the pleasure of reading. This pleasure can be enhanced by a better understanding of the work through your understanding of the elements of literature. It is just as important to learn techniques for studying effectively. Here are several:

1. Plan your study time so that you can make it as effective, efficient, and enjoyable as possible. Set aside a large block of time each day to study.

2. Turn studying into an active process. Take notes. Review what you study.

3. Find a good place to study. Your study area should be quiet, well-lighted, and as free from distractions as possible. Have all your supplies, reference works, textbooks, and other study materials at hand.

Test Preparation

One way to make studying more effective is to take notes. When you read a passage on a standardized test, you can use this technique to remember important ideas and supporting details. This will help you comprehend the passage better.

The Contemporary Perspective

Listen, I shall have to whisper it
into your heart directly: we are all
supernatural/every day
we rise new creatures/cannot be predicted
—Elaine Feinstein

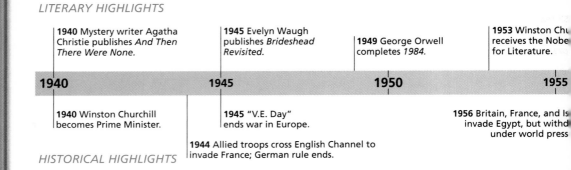

LITERARY HIGHLIGHTS

1940 Mystery writer Agatha Christie publishes *And Then There Were None.*

1945 Evelyn Waugh publishes *Brideshead Revisited.*

1949 George Orwell completes *1984.*

1953 Winston Chu receives the Nobe for Literature.

1940   1945   1950   1955

1940 Winston Churchill becomes Prime Minister.

1945 "V.E. Day" ends war in Europe.

1956 Britain, France, and Is invade Egypt, but withd under world press

1944 Allied troops cross English Channel to invade France; German rule ends.

HISTORICAL HIGHLIGHTS

The Contemporary Perspective

Think about your own writing. Does it change according to your mood? When you are happy, do you choose more cheerful subjects than you do when you are sad?

Professional writers are affected by the mood around them, too. Just before World War II, England was a gloomy place. In 1939, many people were out of work. Even for those people lucky enough to have jobs, salaries were low and health services were poor. Everybody was worried that another war was coming. The British had suffered terrible losses in World War I, and they dreaded another clash with Germany.

The writing of the time showed these concerns. Some older writers continued to write about love and heroism and other traditional subjects, but younger writers began to speak out against social injustices. These writers liked to examine people's thoughts, feelings, and ambitions.

■ WORLD WAR II AND AFTER

The British fought bravely in World War II, but it was a terrible time for them. London was bombed repeatedly. Many of the survivors of the German blitz lost their homes.

In May 1945, when the war in Europe ended, England was ready for a change. British voters elected the Labour Party. The new government took control of many industries and introduced a national health program. More jobs opened up, and wages rose. For a time, the British people felt optimistic about the future. However, in 1951, the people voted the Labour Party out of office.

The British writers of this period reacted to what was happening in the world around them. Their writings dealt with social and political issues.

57 Ted Hughes's
ok of poetry, *The*
wk and the Rain,
pears.

1962 Doris Lessing's novel
The Golden Notebook is published.

1963 John LeCarré's *The Spy Who*
Came in From the Cold appears.

1960	1965	1970	1975

1961 South Africa
leaves the
Commonwealth.

1965 Celebrations mark 700th
anniversary of British Parliament.

1977 *Concorde*, supersonic
aircraft, begins service between
New York and London.

They observed how people tried to fit into society. This interest in psychology was reflected in their writing.

Perhaps you have heard of the novel *Lord of the Flies*. Its author, William Golding, worried about violence and dictatorship. In this unit, you will meet other authors who are also concerned with the problems of the world.

Philip Larkin believed that people should write only about things that they feel deeply. Ted Hughes, England's poet laureate from 1984 until his death in 1998, wrote poems about the struggles of survival. Doris Lessing is famous for her examination of the roles of women in modern society. See if you agree with her conclusions.

How would you feel if the rules you had grown up with suddenly changed? The group of writers that emerged in the period after World War II include many from the colonies that were once ruled by England but are now independent. R. K. Narayan and Ved Mehta were born in India. In their works, both these writers try to reconcile the British traditions of their youth with the demands made on them by India today.

■ TOWARD THE FUTURE

Now is a time of consolidation for many British writers. They try to combine their vision of a new and better world with the vision of writers of the past.

As you read the excerpt from *West With the Night*, think about Beryl Markham's courage and ability. In *Face to Face*, observe Ved Mehta's determination and perseverance. Do you think Markham's courage and Mehta's determination are typical of the characteristics that helped England during World War II?

AUTOBIOGRAPHY

An **autobiography** is an account of a person's life written by that person himself or herself. The person may choose to tell about an important event from his or her life or to tell the whole life story up to the time when it is written. Autobiographies are almost always written in the first-person *I*.

Reading an autobiography can be interesting and enlightening because it gives you a first-hand report of what another person does, feels, and thinks. You may read about someone who led an exemplary life and find that you are trying to follow in that person's footsteps. Knowing that the story is true encourages you to remember important information from it, information that may be useful to you, now and in the future.

As you read *West With the Night,* ask yourself:

1. How do you know this is an autobiography?
2. Did the writer tell about an event from her life or all of it?

WRITING CONNECTION

Think about an event in your life that you feel might be interesting, informative, or amusing to other people. Write a paragraph about the event using the first-person *I*.

READING FOCUS

Use Prior Knowledge   When you read an autobiography, it is helpful to try to recall or learn something about the setting or the events described by the author. Having background knowledge about the topic, the setting, and related events puts the autobiography in the context of its time. Before you read the following autobiography, jot down what you already know about aviation and women pilots in the 1930s.

from
WEST WITH THE NIGHT

ADAPTED

by Beryl Markham

You can live a lifetime and, at the end of it, know more about other people than you know about yourself. You learn to watch other people, but you never watch yourself because you strive against loneliness. If you read a book, or shuffle a deck of cards, or care for a dog, you are avoiding yourself. The abhorrence of loneliness is as natural as wanting to live at all. If it were otherwise, people would never have bothered to make an alphabet, nor to have fashioned words out of what were only animal sounds, nor to have crossed continents—each person to see what the other looked like.

Being alone in an aeroplane for even so short a time as a night and a day, irrevocably alone, with nothing to observe but your instruments and your own hands in semi-darkness, nothing to contemplate but the size of your small courage, nothing to wonder about but the beliefs, the faces, and the hopes rooted in your mind—such an experience can be as startling as the first awareness of a stranger walking by your side at night. You are the stranger.

It is dark already and I am over the south of Ireland. There are the lights of Cork and the lights are wet; they are drenched in Irish rain, and I am above them and dry. I am above them and the plane roars in a sobbing world, but it imparts no sadness to me. I feel the security of solitude, the exhilaration of escape. So long as I can see the lights and imagine the people walking under them, I feel selfishly triumphant, as if I have escaped care and left even the small sorrow of rain in other hands.

It is a little over an hour now since I left Abingdon. England, Wales, and the Irish Sea are behind me like so much time used up. On a long flight distance and time are the same. But there had been a moment when Time stopped—and Distance too. It was the moment I lifted the blue-and-silver Gull from the aerodrome. It was the moment the photographers aimed their cameras. It was the moment I felt the craft refuse its burden and strain toward the earth in

---

abhorrence (ab HAWR uns) a feeling of disgust or hatred
irrevocably (ih REV uh kuh blee) in a way that cannot be changed
exhilaration (ig zil uh RAY shun) a feeling of great happiness

sullen rebellion, only to listen at last to the persuasion of stick and elevators, the argument of blueprints that said she *had* to fly because the figures proved it.

So she had flown, and once airborne, she had said, "There: I have lifted the weight. Now, where are we bound?"—and the question had frightened me.

"We are bound for a place thirty-six hundred miles from here—two thousand miles of it unbroken ocean. Most of the way it will be night. We are flying west with the night."

So there behind me is Cork; and ahead of me is Berehaven Lighthouse. It is the last light, standing on the last land. I watch it, counting the frequency of its flashes—so many to the minute. Then I pass it and fly out to sea.

The fear is gone now—not overcome nor reasoned away. It is gone because something else has taken its place; the confidence and the trust, the inner belief in the security of land underfoot—now this faith is transferred to my plane, because the land has disappeared and there is no other real thing to fix faith upon. Flight is but momentary escape from the permanent custody of earth.

Rain continues to fall, and outside the cabin it is totally dark. My altimeter says that the Atlantic is two thousand feet below me, my Sperry Artificial Horizon says that I am flying level. I judge my drift at three degrees more than my weather chart suggests, and fly accordingly. I am flying blind. A beam to follow would help. So would a radio—but then, so would clear weather. The voice of the man at the Air Ministry had not promised storm.

I feel the wind rising and the rain falls hard. The smell of petrol in the cabin is so strong and the roar of the plane so loud that my senses are almost deadened. Gradually it becomes unthinkable that existence was ever otherwise.

At ten o'clock p.m. I am flying along the Great Circle Course for Harbour Grace, Newfoundland, into a forty-mile headwind at a speed of one hundred and thirty miles an hour. Because of the weather, I cannot be sure of how many more hours I have to fly, but I think it must be between sixteen and eighteen.

At ten-thirty I am still flying on the large cabin tank of petrol, hoping to use it up and put an end to the liquid swirl that has rocked the plane since my take-off. The tank has no scale, but written on its side is the assurance: "This tank is good for four hours."

There is nothing unclear about such a guaranty. I believe it, but at twenty-five minutes to eleven, my motor coughs and dies, and the Gull is powerless above the sea.

I realize that the heavy low sound of the plane has been, until this moment, complete and comforting silence. It is the actual silence following the last splutter of the engine that stuns me. I can't feel any fear; I can't feel anything. I can only observe with a kind of stupid

---

sullen (SUL un) full of resentment
altimeter (al TIM uh tur) an instrument that determines how high something is, as an airplane

disinterest that my hands are violently active and know that, while they move, I am being hypnotized by the needle of my altimeter.

I suppose that the denial of natural impulse is what is meant by "keeping calm," but impulse has reason in it. If it is night and you are sitting in an aeroplane with a stalled motor, and there are two thousand feet between you and the sea, nothing can be more reasonable than the impulse to pull back your stick in the hope of adding to that two thousand, if only by a little. The thought, the knowledge, the law that tells you that your hope lies not in this, but in a contrary act —the act of directing your powerless craft toward the water—seems a terrifying abandonment, not only of reason, but of sanity. Your mind and your heart reject it. It is your hands—your stranger's hands—that follow with unfeeling precision the letter of the law.

I sit there and watch my hands push forward on the stick and feel the Gull respond and begin its dive to the sea. Of course it is a simple thing; surely the cabin tank has run dry too soon. I need only to turn another petcock . . .

But it is dark in the cabin. It is easy to see the luminous dial of the altimeter and to note that my height is now eleven hundred feet, but it is not easy to see a petcock that is somewhere near the floor of the plane. A hand reached blindly and reappears with an electric torch, and fingers, moving with effortful steadiness, find the petcock and turn it; and I wait.

At three hundred feet the motor is still dead, and I am aware that the needle of my altimeter seems to whirl like the spoke of a spindle winding up the remaining distance between the plane and the water. There is some lightning, but the quick flash only serves to emphasize the darkness. How high can waves reach —twenty feet, perhaps? Thirty?

It is impossible to avoid the thought that this is the end of my flight, but my reactions are not normal; the various incidents of my entire life do not run through my mind like a motion-picture film gone mad. I only feel that all this has happened before—and it has. It has all happened a hundred times in my mind, in my sleep, so that now I am not really caught in terror; I recognize a familiar scene, a familiar story with its climax dulled by too much telling.

I do not know how close to the waves I am when the motor explodes to life again. But the sound is almost meaningless. I see my hand easing back on the stick, and I feel the Gull climb up into the storm, and I see the altimeter whirl like a spindle again, paying out the distance between myself and the sea.

The storm is strong. It is comforting. It is like a friend shaking me and saying, "Wake up! You were only dreaming."

But soon I am thinking. By simple calculation I find that my motor has been silent for perhaps an instant more than thirty seconds.

---

petcock (PET kok) a small valve or faucet used in draining fluid or releasing air
luminous (LOO muh nus) giving off light

I ought to thank God—and I do, though indirectly. I thank Geoffrey de Havilland who designed the indomitable Gipsy,[1] and who, after all, must have been designed by God in the first place.

A lighted ship—the daybreak—some steep cliffs standing in the sea. The meaning of these will never change for pilots. If one day an ocean can be flown within an hour, if planes can be built that so master time, the sight of land will be no less welcome to the pilots of those fantastic crafts. They will have cheated laws that the cunning of science has taught them how to cheat, and they will feel guilt and be eager for the sanctuary of the soil.

I saw the ship and the daybreak, and then I saw the cliffs of Newfoundland wound in ribbons of fog. I felt the joy I had so long imagined, and I felt the happy guilt of having gotten the better of the stern authority of the weather and the sea. But mine was a minor triumph; my swift Gull was not so swift as to have escaped unnoticed. The night and the storm had caught her and we had flown blind for nineteen hours.

I was tired now, and cold. Ice began to film the glass of the cabin windows and the fog played a magician's game with the land. But the land was there. I could not see it, but I had seen it. I could not afford to believe that it was any land but the land I wanted. I could not afford to believe that my navigation was at fault, because there was no time for doubt.

South to Cape Race, west to Sydney on Cape Breton Island. With my protractor, my map, and my compass, I set my new course, humming the ditty that Tom had taught me: "Variation West—magnetic best. Variation East—magnetic least." A silly rhyme, but it served to soothe, for the moment, two warring poles—the magnetic and the true. I flew south and found the lighthouse of Cape Race sticking out from the fog like a warning finger. I circled twice and went on over the Gulf of Saint Lawrence.

After a while there would be New Brunswick, and then Maine—and then New York. I could anticipate. I could almost say, "Well, if you stay awake, you'll find it's only a matter of time now"—but there was no question of staying awake. I was tired and I had not moved an inch since that uncertain moment at Abingdon when the Gull had elected to rise with her load and fly, but I could not have closed my eyes. I could sit there in the cabin, walled in glass and petrol tanks, and be grateful for the sun and the light, and the fact that I could see the water under me. They were almost the last waves I had to pass. Four hundred miles of water, but then the land again—Cape Breton. I would stop at Sydney to refuel and go on. It was easy now.

Success breeds confidence. But who

---

indomitable (in DOM ih tuh bul) not capable of being overcome
sanctuary (SANGK choo er ee) a place where one can find safety
[1]**Gipsy:** Beryl made her first solo flight in June 1931 in a Gipsy Moth. She liked this type of plane and respected the man who designed it.

has a right to confidence except the Gods? I had a following wind, my last tank of petrol was more than three-quarters full, and the world was as bright to me as if it were a new world, never touched. If I had been wiser, I might have known that such moments are, like innocence, short-lived. My engine began to shudder before I saw the land. It died, it spluttered, it started again and limped along. It coughed and spat black exhaust toward the sea.

There are words for everything. There was a word for this—airlock, I thought. This had to be an airlock because there was petrol enough. I thought I might clear it by turning on and turning off all the empty tanks, and so I did that. The handles of the petcocks were sharp little pins of metal, and when I had opened and closed them a dozen times, I saw that my hands were bleeding and that the blood was dropping on my maps and on my clothes, but the effort wasn't any good. I coasted along on a sick and halting engine. The oil pressure and the oil temperature gauges were normal, the magnetos working, and yet I lost altitude slowly while the realization of failure seeped into my heart. If I made the land, I should have been the first to fly the North Atlantic from England, but from my point of view, from a pilot's point of view, a forced landing was failure because New York was my goal. If only I could land and then take off, I would make it still . . . if only, if only . . .

The engine cuts again, and then catches, and each time it spurts to life I climb as high as I can get, and then it splutters and stops and I glide once more toward the water, to rise again and descend again, like a hunting sea bird.

I find the land. Visibility is perfect now and I see land forty or fifty miles ahead. If I am on my course, that will be Cape Breton. Minute after minute goes by. The minutes almost materialize; they pass before my eyes like links in a long slow-moving chain, and each time the engine cuts, I see a broken link in the chain and catch my breath until it passes.

The land is under me. I snatch my map and stare at it to confirm my whereabouts. I am, even at my present crippled speed, only twelve minutes from Sydney Airport, where I can land for repairs and then go on.

The engine cuts once more and I begin to glide, but now I am not worried; she will start again, as she has done, and I will gain altitude and fly into Sydney.

But she doesn't start. This time she's dead as death; the Gull settles earthward and it isn't any earth I know. It is black earth stuck with boulders and I hang above it, on hope and on a motionless propeller. Only I cannot hang above it long. The earth hurries to meet me. I bank, turn, and sideslip to dodge the boulders, my wheels touch, and I feel them go under something. The nose of the plane is engulfed in mud, and I go forward striking my head on the glass of

---

visibility (viz uh BIL uh tee) the distance over which it is possible to see things without the use of instruments

the cabin front, hearing it shatter, feeling blood pour over my face.

I stumble out of the plane and sink to my knees in muck and stand there foolishly staring, not at the lifeless land, but at my watch.

Twenty-one hours and twenty-five minutes.

Atlantic flight. Abingdon, England, to a nameless swamp—nonstop.

A Cape Breton Islander found me—a fisherman trudging over the bog saw the Gull with her tail in the air and her nose buried, and then he saw me floundering in the embracing soil of his native land. I had been wandering for an hour and the black mud had got up to my waist and the blood from the cut in my head had met the mud halfway.

From a distance, the fisherman directed me with his arms and with shouts toward the firm places in the bog, and for another hour I walked on them and came toward him like a citizen of Hades blinded by the sun, but it wasn't the sun; I hadn't slept for forty hours.

He took me to his hut on the edge of the coast and I found that built upon the rocks there was a little cubicle that houses an ancient telephone—put there in case of shipwrecks.

I telephoned to Sydney Airport to say that I was safe and to prevent a needless search being made. On the following morning I did step out of a plane at Floyd Bennett Field and there was a crowd of people still waiting there to greet me. The plane I stepped from, however, was not the Gull, and for days while I was in New York I kept thinking about that and wishing over and over again that it had been the Gull, until the wish lost its significance, and time moved on, overcoming many things it met on the way.

Hades (HAY deez) in Greek myths, the home of the dead, beneath the earth

Beryl Markham (1902–1986)

Beryl Markham was a remarkable woman who accomplished a number of impressive feats in her lifetime. At the age of four, she moved with her father from England to British East Africa where her life began to take an unconventional course.

As a child she learned how to use a spear and spent her days hunting or riding horses. When she was seventeen, a severe drought hit East Africa, wiping out her father's farm. Her father decided to move to Peru where he could make a living training horses. Markham remained in Africa, determined to obtain her own horse trainer's license. It was hard work, but at the age of eighteen she was the first woman in Africa to be granted this license.

Successful at horse training, she turned to flying. She met Tom Black, one of the great early fliers, who had a big impact on Markham's life. He taught her to fly, and eighteen months later she had earned a commercial pilot's license.

Even though this life was full of adventure and excitement, Markham decided that she wanted to return to England. She did return there in March 1936. Then in September of that same year she made headlines by becoming the first person ever to fly the Atlantic solo the hard way—against the head winds.

Beryl Markham published her book *West With the Night* in 1942. It is both her personal memoirs and a record of her historic flight based on her logbooks and other notes and papers. The book was not successful when it was released, but it was more successful when it was reissued in 1983. After her transatlantic flight, she returned to Africa where she lived in Kenya for the rest of her life.

Review the Selection

UNDERSTAND THE SELECTION

Recall

1. For what reason was this an especially important flight for Markham?

2. When did she do most of her flying?

3. Where did Markham land?

Infer

4. How do you think Markham felt after the Gull's lift-off at Abingdon?

5. Why did Markham feel nothing when the Gull stalled?

6. Do you think she experienced the time in which the Gull stalled as longer or shorter than it actually was?

7. Why do you think Markham believed that the feeling pilots get upon seeing land will never change?

Apply

8. How do you think Markham felt when she finally landed safely?

9. Choose a line from the story that best illustrates how Markham felt about flying.

10. Predict what you think Markham did following this flight.

Respond to Literature

Markham was obviously a skilled pilot. What other things did you learn or infer about her character?

WRITE ABOUT THE SELECTION

Beryl Markham recalled vividly her experience of her first flight across the Atlantic Ocean. It was probably likely that she kept a journal in which she wrote about her feelings and thoughts either during or after the flight. Suppose you are a skilled pilot who is on a solo flight across the Atlantic Ocean. It is the first time anyone has attempted to make this flight. How do you feel? What is the weather like? What are your thoughts as you fly through the dark night?

Prewriting Freewrite for a few minutes to explore what you want to include in your journal entry. Jot down notes about how you felt and what your thoughts were as you sat in that plane alone, hour after endless hour. What did you hear? What did you see?

Writing Look over your notes and then write a journal entry about your flight. Be sure that you include your thoughts, feelings, and some observations about the flight.

Revising When you revise, check to see if you have included specific details about the airplane you are flying. If you have not, be sure to include them when you revise.

Proofreading Reread your journal entry to check for errors. Be sure that you have written complete sentences and that they end with periods, question marks, or exclamation points.

THINK ABOUT AUTOBIOGRAPHY

An **autobiography** is the true story of a person's life or experiences written by the person himself or herself. It may tell the story of a person's whole life up to the time the book is written or may instead concentrate on some important event in that person's life. In *West With the Night,* Beryl Markham tells how she made an incredible achievement in aviation history. She shares her personal feelings and thoughts about the experience. While you may never be a pilot or make aviation history, reading about her experience can give you insight into the risks someone was willing to take to fulfill a dream.

1. How do you know *West with the Night* is an autobiography?

2. In which person did Markham write her story?

3. Why do you think Markham chose to write about this event from her life?

4. What important information did you learn from reading this selection?

5. Is there wisdom to be gained from thinking about Markham's achievement?

READING FOCUS

Use Prior Knowledge What prior knowledge helped you appreciate Markham's autobiography?

DEVELOP YOUR VOCABULARY

A **synonym** is a word that has a meaning that is similar or the same as the meaning of another word. For example, *triumphant* means almost the same thing as *victorious.* Other words that have similar meanings are *proud, elated,* and *joyful.* Knowing synonyms can make your writing more interesting and enjoyable.

shining	freezing
observable	resentful
happiness	unconquerable

Choose a word from the list above that is a synonym for each italicized word in the paragraph below. Then write an original sentence using each new word.

Tara's *sullen,* gloomy mood immediately changed to total *exhilaration* when she saw the boat sailing toward her. Because of the morning fog, nothing had been *visible.* Now the fog lifted, and there was a boat! Tara's *indomitable* spirit had kept her alive through the night as she clung to her overturned boat. The sight of the *luminous* fish lighting up the sea had kept up her hope. Then the morning fog had taken hope away. Now her elation grew as her rescuers pulled her from the *frigid* water.

Focus ON NONFICTION

*N*onfiction is literature that deals with factual material or events. The people written about in nonfiction are real. Autobiographies, biographies, essays, and informational articles are some of the different types of nonfiction writing.

In an **autobiography,** the writer gives a personal account of his or her own life. In a **biography,** the story of one person's life is written by another person. Autobiographies and biographies usually narrate the events in a person's life in time order. In biographies, the author may interview the biographical subject and also gather information from other sources.

An **essay** is a short piece of writing in which the writer shares his or her point of view about a certain subject. In informational articles, factual material about a specific subject is presented. **Informational articles** appear in newspapers and magazines and in reference books, such as encyclopedias, almanacs, and atlases.

There are several elements that writers concern themselves with when they write. Examining some of these elements will allow you to have a better appreciation of nonfiction writing.

The Forms of Nonfiction   Nonfiction is broken down into four kinds of writing. The four kinds of writing are **exposition, persuasion** (or argumentation), **description,** and **narration.**

Exposition is writing that explains something or gives you information about a topic. Writers use a number of different methods in exposition. In one method, writers use definition, writing that explains the meaning of a term, such as *liberty*. Another method writers use is classification. In classification, writers group ideas or things according to their similarities or differences. Animals and plants are assigned to specific groups according to a scientific system of classification. Still another method of exposition that writers use is comparison and contrast. This is writing that explains how something is like or unlike something else. Writing that shows the similarities and differences between two kinds of rock music is an example of comparison and contrast. Finally, writers might use analysis, a method that examines how different parts of something fit together to make a whole. Explaining the parts of a stereo system is an example of analysis.

Persuasion (or argumentation) is writing that attempts to convince you of something by showing that a statement is true or false. Speeches in which candidates for election try to prove that their ideas are right are examples of argumentation.

Description is writing that helps you to form a clear mental picture of something. In order to help you form the picture, writers use specific details, such as shapes, sizes, tastes, sounds, and textures. An article in a magazine about a formal dinner party at the White House would be full of description.

Narration is writing that tells of an event or a series of events. Nonfiction narration is concerned with when events take place. Frequently, writers use a combination of the different kinds of nonfiction writing in one piece as a way to share information and ideas.

Organization of Nonfiction   There are three parts to most nonfiction writing. The **introduction** tells you the main idea of what the piece is about. It may also give background material or state a problem. The **body** of the work develops the main idea through details that support the main idea. Finally, in the **conclusion,** the work is ended. The conclusion may restate or summarize the author's main ideas, it may answer a question raised in the work, or it may urge the reader to future action.

As you read *Face to Face,* pay close attention to the ideas and feelings conveyed by Ved Mehta about himself and the other people in the work. Ask yourself:

1. Which forms of nonfiction does Ved Mehta use?

2. What event or events in the work interest you the most?

from

FACE to FACE

ADAPTED

by Ved Mehta

It was seven in the morning, and I was awakened by brother Om, who was leaning over my bed looking through the frosty window. Soon my sisters joined him in searching the sky for the balloon which would indicate safe skating.

"I guess the ice didn't freeze last night," Umi said in a disappointed voice.

"There!" brother Om shouted, and there were exclamations of pleasure as they caught sight of the signal.

They left my room, the partitioned-off end of our sun porch. Brother Om could not find his ice-skate shoes, so I got up to help him. The house was bitterly cold, and some icy air came in through the cracks around the window. At last all paraphernalia were collected and everyone dressed in heavy coats and left the house.

Almost every day now the weather was clear and cold enough to freeze the ice, and my sisters and brother Om spent three hours in the morning, three in the evening ice skating. I alone could not take part in this treat of the Simla hill station. At first they took me to the rink, and I stood at the edge listening to the blaring music and shouts of the skaters. But I had put a stop to that. I preferred staying home to standing alone at the edge with now and then someone skating up to talk to me.

I stood for a while now, shivering at the open door, listening to the voices fade as they hurried up the hill toward the ice-skating

---

paraphernalia (par uh fur NAYL yuh) one's personal belongings

rink. Finally I shut the door and returned to bed—the only place where I could keep warm—but I could not go to sleep again. With everyone gone and Mother and Ashok not up yet, the house seemed dreary indeed.

I tried to pick up my Braille book to read, but my fingers were stiff with cold and I gave up. For almost two hours I lay there, thinking what school to write next.

Mehta reveals that he is blind, what his goal —the main idea—is, and how he attempts to achieve it.

I had missed several schools on the list, most of them in the southern part of the United States. As I had not even heard the names of the states they were located in, I felt no particular desire to go there. I wanted to go to Boston, New York, Chicago or San Francisco. For me, that was the United States. Nevertheless I decided to try them all.

I wrote a letter to Arkansas School for the Blind, presenting my meager qualifications as impressively as I could.

The introduction ends and the body of the autobiography begins.

---

dreary (DRIR ee) gloomy; dismal
meager (MEE gur) lacking in quantity

SIMLA.

31ST JANUARY, 1949

TO

THE MANAGER

ARKANSAS SCHOOL FOR THE BLIND,

LITTLE ROCK,

ARK.

DEAR SIR,

Mehta includes a letter that he wrote years before.

Unfortunately I am a Blind boy of nearly 15 years of age. I beg to state that I would like to come over to America for my further studies, I know the following subjects.

English.

Mathematics.

I can read Braille and can write Braille and I know sighted Typing with touch system. I know contraction and abrivations. I have colified from the following Instituation.:—

1. Dadar Blind School fr the Blind
2. Emerson Instituation for the Blind.
   Lahore Pakistan.
3. St. Dunstan's for the War Blinded. Dehra dun.
   India.

Mehta reveals important autobiographical information about his schooling.

I have been studying in Dadar Blind School Bombay for nearly four years. I learnt Braille reading and Writing and English. I was sent there by my father when I was only five and a Half. I got Blind when I was Four Years old, I lost eyesight with Manigitis. I studied in Emerson Instituation for the Blind Lahore for one year, whereXXI learnt only AXXMathematics. And little bit of my Country Language. Then I was sent over to St. Dunstan's for the War Blinded. As this Instituation was only ment for War Blind Soldiers then even as I was Civilian I had to come across many difficulties before I could get myself admitted in St.Dunstan's. I was taken there as a extra ordinary case. I stayed there for only one year but I must CX confess that I made very good progress in St. Dunstan's. I stayed in St. Dunstan's Hostel for eight months and rest with my relation. I am herewith enclosing a copy of a Certificate from St. Dunstan's from which I think that you will be able to judge that what is my position at present. St. Dunstan's is the biggest Instituation going in India. And there is no more scope in India for my studies as I have gained from St. Dunstan's

You find out how much he values education and supporting details about his goal.

what they could teach me. However, I shall feel obliged if you could send me your Application Form & Particulars. Anyhow I would like to possess your form & Particulars even if you do not think or if such question arises that with which you would like to know some information. As this matter has been already been extremely delayed I won't like the matter to be more delayed. I am very sure that you will help me in this matter. I am typing this letter myself. The typing and Braille gr 2 was taught me in st. Dunstan's My Father won't mind spending any thing as far I can be admitted in your School. I would like to completeX your full course. I am herewith enclosing a Picture of mine I hope you will appreciate it. Do you have university Examination?

I do hope to get a reply in affirmative.

An early reply is requested.

Thanking you.

Yours faithfully,

s/o DR. A. R. MEHTA,

DEPUTY DIECTOR OF HEALTH SERVICES,

ERNESTON, (UPPER FLAT),

SIMLA,   AST,

EAST PUNJAB.

(INDIA).

Mehta tells you that he is writing about this event many years later.

I wrote the letter with no expectation that this school would respond more favorably than any other. Then, in the last week of February, I received a letter from them, and as usual took it to sister Nimi to read.

Mehta tells you something very important about himself.

FEBRUARY 16, 1949

MR. V. P. MEHTA

c/o DR. A. R. MEHTA

DEPUTY DIRECTOR OF HEALTH SERVICES

ERNESTON,

SIMLA—E.

EAST PUNJAB, INDIA

DEAR MR. MEHTA:

I have your letter of January 31, in which you state you would like to attend the Arkansas School for the Blind.

He finds out that he is closer to his goal.

In reply, I will say that we shall be happy to have you if details can be arranged. By this I mean, entrance into the United States, which I presume can be arranged on a student basis, financial details, length of time you will want to stay, course, or courses you will want to pursue and perhaps other details.

The usual fee charged for out of state pupils is $600.00 per

---

pursue (pur SOO) to devote oneself to, as by studying

school year of nine months. I am not sure that $600.00 would be the fee charged you, but certainly no more than that.

We offer an academic course which prepares you for University entrance. This consists of the usual courses offered in most American public schools. In addition we offer broad courses in music, many vocations and athletics.

I am not enclosing an application form, but will send one later if you are still interested. We are sending you a Braille copy of the *Arkansas Braille News* so that you may read for yourself something of our educational program here.

May we hear from you again, if you are still interested in our school.

Sincerely yours,
J. M. WOOLLY, SUPERINTENDENT

I was ecstatic. I could scarcely believe sister Nimi's voice. *They would be happy to have me.*

She read it fast and then reread it. There was no doubt of its contents. Had it not been that every letter before this had refused me, perhaps I would have run to my mother and cried jubilantly that finally I was going to America, and asked her blessings. But disappointment after disappointment had made me wary.

"Tell me something about the school," she said.

"I don't know anything about it." There was a pause, a pause long enough to sober me.

"I think you better keep this letter and show it only to Daddyji," she said in an expressionless voice.

So it was that in the evening, before handing the letter to my father, I told him, "I know absolutely nothing about the school." Heretofore I had not taken any letter to him that was not written by a great and famous school like Perkins, or Worcester College, or a printing house like the National Institute. All my other correspondence with less known schools I had considered too unimportant to trouble him with. The contents of those letters, which indeed varied little from one to the next, remained between sister Nimi and myself.

Mehta chooses words that convey a certain tone.

---

ecstatic (ek STAT ik) in a state of great joy
jubilantly (JOO buh lunt lee) in a way that shows great joy
wary (WAIR ee) cautious, as from suspicion

"That's encouraging, all right," he began. He said it with perfect composure, with no sign of any particular feelings.

I sensed the same hesitations that I had imagined he would feel at sending me to a school ten thousand miles away which, for all we knew, might be no more than two classrooms.

"Anyway, I shall follow this lead through and write to Mr. Woolly, but I warn you in advance not to bank too much on this."

What is the tone of the selection at this point?

For three more weeks, a childish but quiet hope lingered on, and I fancied, sometimes, that maybe all was not over. As March came and passed, however, and then April, I resolved to forget about it completely, for no word had come from Mr. Woolly, nor indeed had the *Arkansas Braille News* arrived.

He learns that his hard work and persistence have paid off.

Then finally in April, I received the *Braille News*. I started reading it more as a chore than with any great expectation; but as I read on and learned of their social-adjustment program which made blind people independent, able to go about the streets themselves, and read something about their curriculum, my hope was aroused, though it was a cautious hope, for I did not wish to be disappointed again. I waited in a somewhat expectant mood until the middle of May, when my father brought home a letter informing him that I was admitted at Arkansas School for the Blind.

"Are you going to send me there?"

"That depends. Anyway, this letter can be used to get you a visa and dollars. After you are once in the United States, if you find that Arkansas School is not suited to you, you can always change."

I could tell by his warm voice, in spite of its caution that I might never really attend Arkansas School, that he was happy for me. Yet I felt a certain remorse, for I was going to America over the protest of all educational authorities, and against the opinion of all my relatives. Suppose I had been wrong all this time and I were to fail, what then? Would I be able to bear the disappointment?

Such was the inconsistency of my reaction that I could see nothing but utter disaster ahead. Perhaps I had waited so long it

---

composure (kum POH zhur) control over one's feelings
remorse (rih MAWRS) a feeling of guilt

seemed an anticlimax. I wanted to discuss these anxieties with someone, someone who could understand all my different feelings. My father was the one person who had seen what my struggle meant to me. He told me that he had decided to take his accumulated leave before retirement and journey with me as far as Britain. He had some special business there, and perhaps he would go as far as America if dollars could be obtained. I felt very much relieved. During the long sea voyage I would be able to discuss my fears with him and seek his guidance.

Even though Mehta is fearful, the importance of furthering his education takes priority. He gives you a hint about the theme.

One day, when all the arrangements for my father and me to sail together for England had been made, passports and visas secured, Father returned home to say that his leave had been canceled. He had been promoted to Deputy Director General of Health Services in the Federal Government and had been asked to stay on for another year, because he was "indispensable."

He said, "My first duty is to the nation, then to my family." He added in the same breath, however, "It isn't all altruism. If you are going to America, I must continue earning. If you can wait another year, I will take you. Otherwise you will have to go alone. It is all up to you."

"I will go alone now," I returned, and for all my eagerness, the word "alone" shocked me.

His goal continues to come first. You learn more about how much he values education.

My father's new job required a move to New Delhi, so the preparations for my departure were interrupted while we packed our meager belongings.

The body of the story ends.

I did not really feel I was going until three days before my flight, when I had an interview with Pandit Nehru. I was the first blind boy, it seemed, who had ever left home to go to America. Panditji therefore wanted to see me.

The conclusion begins. Mehta tells you something very important about himself.

It was a hot and sultry August day in New Delhi, and I felt uncomfortable in my new long pants and oversized coat. My interview with Pandit Nehru was still a few minutes away, and to pass the time we rode around the streets, which were unusually quiet for India.

We finally pulled into the house of the Prime Minister of new

---

indispensable (in dih SPEN suh bul) essential; absolutely required
altruism (AL troo iz um) unselfish concern for the welfare of others
Panditji (PUN dit jee) a beloved wise man
sultry (SUL tree) hot and humid

from Face to Face ■ **493**

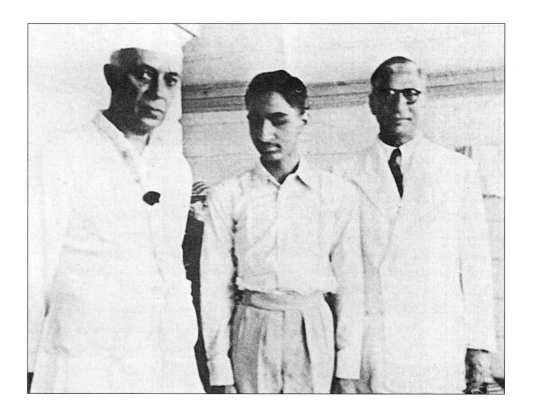

free India. I took my father's large hand, and with brother Om carrying my typewriter, the *Arkansas Braille News* and his camera, we went in.

"Do you think, Daddyji, that Pandit Nehru will ever remember this visit?"

"I think he will," he said, but I wondered. I was one fifteen-year-old boy out of a mass of three hundred and fifty million people to whom Panditji was both servant and lord.

Just then Panditji walked in. His step seemed to me gentle but firm, just as I had imagined it. Instantaneously all three of us stood up. Father, putting his arm around my waist, said, "This is my blind son, of whom I spoke to you, Panditji," and after brother Om was presented, we all sat down.

Many a time I had heard the voice of the Prime Minister over the radio, or listened to his dramatic political speeches in a public square packed so tight with people that it was hard to breathe or move one's elbows. Now I was sitting at his right hand in his own house. I wanted to tell him that I loved him as I did my father, that during the cruel days of partition I had really believed in him and that I would even give up going to America for him if he wanted me to, but all this seemed to me like baby talk, compared to his few carefully chosen words of encouragement.

He dictated a few sentences which he then read aloud and signed. Before I had read even a paragraph from the *Arkansas Braille News,* he interrupted, "Why Arkansas?"

"That is the only place in America which would have me," I said. He did not pursue the question, and asked me how I had lost my sight.

"With meningitis," I replied, "when I was three and a half years old."

After a slight pause, Panditji recalled, "I was almost your age when I went to England. That was a long while ago."

All of a sudden I felt closer to him.

"My elder son," Father proposed, "would like to take your picture, Panditji, if you will allow it." And with this we all rose together and went to the veranda. With the two clicks of the camera, the interview was over. While Panditji gave me his blessing, brother Om collected our things.

We got into the car and made our way home. For the rest of the day, I would be the center of interest, and the interview with Panditji, brief though it was, the topic of conversation.

---

meningitis (men in JYT is) inflammation of the membranes that cover the brain and spinal cord

Review the Selection

UNDERSTAND THE SELECTION

Recall

1. What was the goal of Ved Mehta?

2. What did he do to achieve his goal?

3. To which school did Mehta apply and why?

Infer

4. Why do you think Mehta's father sent him to school at such an early age?

5. Why do you think Mehta revealed so much information in his letter?

6. Describe how Mehta felt when he learned that he had been accepted at the school.

7. Explain why the meeting with Nehru was so important to Mehta.

Apply

8. If you were J. M. Woolly, why would you want Ved Mehta to attend your school?

9. What action did Mehta take to achieve his goals?

10. Predict what will happen to Mehta when he attends the school.

Respond to Literature

Mehta grew up in a British Colony and remembers the separation from England. How did this affect his writing?

WRITE ABOUT THE SELECTION

Suppose you work for the *Arkansas Braille News.* The editor has suggested that you write an article about Ved Mehta for the paper. You set up an interview and talk with him for several hours. First of all, ask him about himself and his family. How old is he? What are his father and mother like? Does he have any brothers and sisters? Next, ask him about his trip to Arkansas. How did he get there? When did he leave India? Did the trip take long? When did he arrive in America? Finally, ask why it was so important to him to come to the Arkansas School for the Blind. Now you have completed your interview, and it is time to write your story.

Prewriting On a separate sheet of paper write the six questions that should be answered in a good news story. These questions are *who, what, when, where, why,* and *how.* Then jot down some notes from your interview to answer these questions about Mehta.

Writing Use the notes you made in prewriting to write the newspaper article in which you tell about Mehta and how he came to the school.

Revising When you revise, make sure that you have answered all the newspaper questions.

Proofreading Reread your newspaper article to check for errors, especially errors in punctuation.

THINK ABOUT NONFICTION

One form of nonfiction writing is autobiography. An **autobiography** is the story of a person's life as written by the person himself or herself.

In the selection from *Face to Face,* Ved Mehta tells about his admission to the Arkansas School for the Blind.

By using elements of nonfiction writing, however, Mehta is able to tell more than the simple story of his admission. He is able to reveal many things about himself and the people he encountered.

The elements of nonfiction Mehta includes are his choice of words, the point of view he uses, and the tone of his writing.

1. How do you know this is nonfiction?

2. What did Mehta tell you about himself in the introduction?

3. List several sensory words that Mehta used in the introduction.

4. Which point of view does Mehta use?

5. What is the tone of this story and why did Mehta use this tone?

DEVELOP YOUR VOCABULARY

An **antonym** is a word that has a meaning that is opposite or almost opposite to the meaning of another word. For example, *ecstatic* means "in a state of great joy." Words with an opposite or nearly opposite meaning are *gloomy, sullen, melancholy,* or *sad.*

rash	unnecessary
plentiful	cheerful
cool	joylessly

Choose a word from the above list that is an antonym for each italicized word in the paragraph below. Then write an original sentence using each word.

The *sultry* day made Jennifer feel *dreary.* The rain had fallen for hours, and she was afraid about the river flooding. If it overflowed, it would rush through her cabin and damage her *meager* belongings, which were *indispensable* to her. As she looked out the window once again, she saw a change of color in the sky. Although she was *wary* about believing there was really a change in the weather, she went outside to check. *Jubilantly* she shouted, "Hurray, the storm is over."

THEME

The central or most important idea of a piece of literature is called the **theme.** In order to discover and understand the theme of a literary work, you must think about who the characters are, what they say and do, and what happens to them.

Throughout the history of literature some great themes have evolved. One that has appeared in many different cultures is the idea that love can bring peace of mind to someone who is troubled. The "someone" who is troubled in "Old Man of the Temple" is a spirit who has been restlessly seeking happiness for hundreds of years.

The idea that the truth is hard to accept is another theme that has been explored by many writers. In "Like the Sun," the leading character finds it is sometimes harder to tell the truth than to accept it.

As you read these stories, ask yourself:
1. What do the main characters want?
2. Is what they want worthwhile?

WRITING CONNECTION

Make a list of what you think are some of the timeless themes about which authors have written. Then tell which theme you would like to write a story about and why.

READING FOCUS

Identify Facts and Opinions   You can analyze information in your reading to identify facts and opinions. To identify opinions, look for signal words. These words—*believe, think, should, suppose,* and so on—tell you that an opinion is coming. Then look for clues to facts. These would be names, dates, times, actions, and so on that can be proved or disproved.

OLD MAN OF THE TEMPLE

by R. K. Narayan

The Talkative Man said:

It was some years ago that this happened. I don't know if you can make anything of it. If you do, I shall be glad to hear what you have to say; but personally I don't understand it at all. It has always mystified me. Perhaps the driver was drunk; perhaps he wasn't.

I had engaged a taxi for going to Kumbum, which, as you may already know, is fifty miles from Malgudi. I went there one morning and it was past nine in the evening when I finished my business and started back for the town. Doss, the driver, was a young fellow of about twenty-five. He had often brought his car for me and I liked him. He was a well-behaved, obedient fellow, with a capacity to sit and wait at the wheel, which is really a rare quality in a taxi driver. He drove the car smoothly, seldom swore at passers-by, and exhibited perfect judgment, good sense, and sobriety; and so I preferred him to any other driver whenever I had to go out on business.

It was about eleven when we passed the village Koopal, which is on the way down. It was the dark half of the month and the surrounding country was swallowed up in the night. The village street was deserted. Everyone had gone to sleep; hardly any light was to be seen. The stars overhead sparkled brightly. Sitting in the back seat and listening to the continuous noise of the running wheels, I was half lulled into a drowse.

All of a sudden Doss swerved the car and shouted: "You old fool! Do you want to kill yourself?"

I was shaken out of my drowse and asked: "What is the matter?"

Doss stopped the car and said, "You see that old fellow, sir. He is trying to kill himself. I can't understand what he is up to."

I looked in the direction he pointed and asked, "Which old man?"
"There, there. He is coming towards us again. As soon as I saw him open that temple door and come out I had a feeling, somehow, that I must keep an eye on him."

I took out my torch, got down, and walked about, but could see no one.

There was an old temple on the roadside. It was utterly in ruins; most portions of it were mere mounds of old brick; the walls were awry; the doors were shut to the main doorway, and brambles and thickets grew over and covered them. It was difficult to guess with the aid of the torch alone what temple it was and to what period it belonged.

"The doors are shut and sealed and don't look as if they had been opened for centuries now," I cried.

"No, sir," Doss said coming nearer. "I saw the old man open the doors and come out. He is standing there; shall we ask him to open them again if you want to go in and see?"

I said to Doss, "Let us be going. We are wasting our time here."

We went back to the car. Doss sat in his seat, pressed the self-starter, and asked without turning his head, "Are you permitting this fellow to come with us, sir? He says he will get down at the next milestone."

"Which fellow?" I asked.

Doss indicated the space next to him.

"What is the matter with you, Doss? Have you had a drop of drink or something?"

"I have never tasted any drink in my life, sir," he said, and added, "Get down, old boy. Master says he can't take you."

"Are you talking to yourself?"

"After all, I think we needn't care for these unknown fellows on the road," he said.

"Doss," I pleaded. "Do you feel confident you can drive? If you feel dizzy don't drive."

"Thank you, sir," said Doss. "I would rather not start the car now. I am feeling a little out of sorts." I looked at him anxiously. He closed his eyes, his breathing became heavy and noisy, and gradually his head sank.

"Doss, Doss," I cried desperately. I got down, walked to the front seat, opened the door, and shook him vigorously. He opened his eyes, assumed a hunched-up position, and rubbed his eyes with his hands, which trembled like an old man's.

"Do you feel better?" I asked.

"Better! Better! Hi! Hi!" he said in a thin, piping voice.

"What has happened to your voice? You sound like someone else," I said.

"Nothing. My voice is as good as it was. When a man is eighty he is bound to feel a few changes coming on."

"You aren't eighty, surely," I said.

"Not a day less," he said. "Is nobody going to move this vehicle? If not, there is no sense in sitting here all day. I will get down and go back to my temple."

"I don't know how to drive," I said. "And unless you do it, I don't see how it can move."

"Me!" exclaimed Doss. "These new

---

awry (uh RY) not straight; twisted or crooked
milestone (MYL stohn) a stone or other kind of marker set up to indicate the distance in miles
 to or from a certain place
vigorously (VIG ur us lee) with great force

chariots! God knows what they are drawn by, I never understand, though I could handle a pair of bullocks in my time. May I ask a question?"

"Go on," I said.

"Where is everybody?"

"Who?"

"Lots of people I knew are not to be seen at all. All sorts of new fellows everywhere, and nobody seems to care. Not a soul comes near the temple. All sorts of people go about but not one who cares to stop and talk. Why doesn't the king ever come this way? He used to go this way at least once a year before."

"Which king?" I asked.

"Let me go, you idiot," said Doss, edging towards the door on which I was leaning. "You don't seem to know anything." He pushed me aside, and got down from the car. He stooped as if he had a big hump on his back, and hobbled along towards the temple. I followed him, hardly knowing what to do. He turned and snarled at me: "Go away, leave me alone. I have had enough of you."

"What has come over you, Doss?" I asked.

"Who is Doss, anyway? Doss, Doss, Doss. What an absurd name! Call me by my name or leave me alone. Don't follow me calling 'Doss, Doss.' "

"What is your name?" I asked.

"Krishna Battar, and if you mention my name people will know for a hundred miles around. I built a temple where there was only a cactus field before. I dug the earth, burnt every brick, and put them one upon another, all single-handed. And on the day the temple held up its tower over the surrounding country, what a crowd gathered! The king sent his chief minister . . ."

"Who was the king?"

"Where do you come from?" he asked.

"I belong to these parts certainly, but as far as I know there has been only a collector at the head of the district. I have never heard of any king."

"Hi! Hi! Hi!" he cackled, and his voice rang through the gloomy silent village. "Fancy never knowing the king! He will behead you if he hears it."

"What is his name?" I asked.

This tickled him so much that he sat down on the ground, literally unable to stand the joke any more. He laughed and coughed uncontrollably.

"I am sorry to admit," I said, "that my parents have brought me up in such utter ignorance of worldly affairs that I don't know even my king. But won't you enlighten me? What is his name?"

"Vishnu Varma, the emperor of emperors . . ."

I cast my mind up and down the range of my historical knowledge but there was no one by that name. Perhaps a local chief of pre-British days, I thought.

---

bullocks (BUUL uks) young bulls; steers
snarled (SNAHRLD) spoke in an angry, harsh way
enlighten (en LYT un) to give knowledge or information

"What a king! He often visited my temple or sent his minister for the Annual Festival of the temple. But now nobody cares."

"People are becoming less godly nowadays," I said. There was silence for a moment. An idea occurred to me, I can't say why. "Listen to me," I said. "You ought not to be here any more."

"What do you mean?" he asked, drawing himself up, proudly.

"Don't feel hurt; I say you shouldn't be here any more because you are dead."

"Dead! Dead!" he said. "Don't talk nonsense. How can I be dead when you see me before you now? If I am dead how can I be saying this and that?"

"I don't know all that," I said. I argued and pointed out that according to his own story he was more than five hundred years old, and didn't he know that man's longevity was only a hundred? He constantly interrupted me, but considered deeply what I said.

He said: "It is like this . . . I was coming through the jungle one night after visiting my sister in the next village. I had on me some money and gold ornaments. A gang of robbers set upon me. I gave them as good a fight as any man could, but they were too many for me. They beat me down and knifed me; they took away all that I had on me and left thinking they had killed me. But soon I got up

and tried to follow them. They were gone. And I returned to the temple and have been here since . . ."

I told him, "Krishna Battar, you are dead, absolutely dead. You must try and go away from here."

"What is to happen to the temple?" he asked.

"Others will look after it."

"Where am I to go? Where am I to go?"

"Have you no one who cares for you?" I asked.

"None except my wife. I loved her very much."

"You can go to her."

"Oh, no. She died four years ago . . ."

Four years! It was very puzzling. "Do you say four years back from now?" I asked.

"Yes, four years ago from now." He was clearly without any sense of time.

So I asked, "Was she alive when you were attacked by thieves?"

"Certainly not. If she had been alive she would never have allowed me to go through the jungle after nightfall. She took very good care of me."

"See here," I said. "It is imperative you should go away from here. If she comes and calls you, will you go?"

"How can she when I tell you that she is dead?"

I thought for a moment. Presently I

---

longevity (lon JEV uh tee) the greatest length of time a person can live
imperative (im PER uh tiv) absolutely necessary; essential

found myself saying, "Think of her, and only of her, for a while and see what happens. What was her name?"

"Seetha, a wonderful girl . . ."

"Come on, think of her." He remained in deep thought for a while. He suddenly screamed, "Seetha is coming! Am I dreaming or what? I will go with her . . ." He stood up, very erect; he appeared to have lost all the humps and twists he had on his body. He drew himself up, made a dash forward, and fell down in a heap.

Doss lay on the rough ground. The only sign of life in him was his faint breathing. I shook him and called him. He would not open his eyes. I walked across and knocked on the door of the first cottage. I banged on the door violently.

Someone moaned inside, "Ah, it is come!"

Someone else whispered, "You just cover your ears and sleep. It will knock for a while and go away." I banged on the door and shouted who I was and where I came from.

I walked back to the car and sounded the horn. Then the door opened, and a whole family crowded out with lamps. "We thought it was the usual knocking and we wouldn't have opened if you hadn't spoken."

"When was this knocking first heard?" I asked.

"We can't say," said one. "The first time I heard it was when my grandfather was living; he used to say he had even seen it once or twice. It doesn't harm anyone, as far as I know. The only thing it does is bother the bullock carts passing the temple and knock on the doors at night . . ."

I said as a venture, "It is unlikely you will be troubled any more."

It proved correct. When I passed that way again months later I was told that the bullocks passing the temple after dusk never shied now and no knocking on the doors was heard at night. So I felt that the old fellow had really gone away with his good wife.

LIKE THE SUN

by R. K. Narayan

Truth, Sekhar reflected, is like the sun. I suppose no human being can ever look it straight in the face without blinking or being dazed. He realized that, morning till night, the essence of human relationships consisted in tempering truth so that it might not shock. This day he set apart as a unique day—at least one day in the year we must give and take absolute Truth whatever may happen. Otherwise life is not worth living. The day ahead seemed to him full of possibilities. He told no one of his experiment. It was a quiet resolve, a secret pact between him and eternity.

The very first test came while his wife served him his morning meal. He showed hesitation over a tidbit, which she had thought was her culinary masterpiece. She asked, "Why, isn't it good?" At other times he would have said, considering her feelings in the matter, "I feel full-up, that's all." But today he said, "It isn't good. I'm unable to swallow it." He saw her wince and said to himself, Can't be helped. Truth is like the sun.

His next trial was in the common room when one of his colleagues came up and said, "Did you hear of the death of so and so? Don't you think it a pity?" "No," Sekhar answered. "He was such a fine man—" the other began. But Sekhar cut him short with: "Far from it. He always struck me as a mean and selfish brute."

During the last period when he was teaching geography for Third Form A, Sekhar received a note from the head-master: "Please see me before you go home." Sekhar said to himself: It must be about these horrible test papers. A hundred papers in the boys' scrawls; he

---

wince (WINTS) to shrink or draw back, as in pain or distress

had shirked this work for weeks, feeling all the time as if a sword were hanging over his head.

The bell rang and the boys burst out of the class.

Sekhar paused for a moment outside the headmaster's room to button up his coat; that was another subject the headmaster always sermonized about.

He stepped in with a very polite "Good evening, sir."

The headmaster looked up at him in a very friendly manner and asked, "Are you free this evening?"

Sekhar replied, "Just some outing which I have promised the children at home—"

"Well, you can take them out another day. Come home with me now."

"Oh . . . yes, sir, certainly . . ." And then he added timidly, "Anything special, sir?"

"Yes," replied the headmaster, smiling to himself . . . "You didn't know my weakness for music?"

"Oh, yes, sir. . ."

"I've been learning and practicing secretly, and now I want you to hear me this evening. I've engaged a drummer and a violinist to accompany me—this is the first time I'm doing it full-dress and I want your opinion. I know it will be valuable."

Sekhar's taste in music was well

---

shirked (SHURKT) avoided or neglected a task or duty

known. He was one of the most dreaded music critics in the town. But he never anticipated his musical inclinations would lead him to this trial. . . . "Rather a surprise for you, isn't it?" asked the headmaster. "I've spent a fortune on it behind closed doors. . . ." They started for the headmaster's house. "God hasn't given me a child, but at least let him not deny me the consolation of music," the headmaster said, pathetically, as they walked. He incessantly chattered about music: how he began one day out of sheer boredom; how his teacher at first laughed at him, and then gave him hope; how his ambition in life was to forget himself in music.

At home the headmaster proved very ingratiating. He sat Sekhar on a red silk carpet, set before him several dishes of delicacies, and fussed over him as if he were a son-in-law of the house. He even said, "Well, you must listen with a free mind. Don't worry about these test papers." He added half humorously, "I will give you a week's time."

"Make it ten days, sir," Sekhar pleaded.

"All right, granted," the headmaster said generously. Sekhar felt really relieved now—he would attack them at the rate of ten a day and get rid of the nuisance.

The headmaster lighted incense sticks. "Just to create the right atmosphere," he explained. A drummer and a violinist, already seated on a Rangoon mat, were waiting for him. The headmaster sat down between them like a professional at a concert, cleared his throat, and began an alapana, and paused to ask, "Isn't it good Kalyani?" Sekhar pretended not to have heard the question. The headmaster went on to sing a full song composed by Thyagaraja and followed it with two more. All the time the headmaster was singing, Sekhar went on commenting within himself, "He croaks like a dozen frogs. He is bellowing like a buffalo. Now he sounds like loose window shutters in a storm."

The incense sticks burnt low. Sekhar's head throbbed with the medley of sounds that had assailed his ear-drums for a couple of hours now. He felt half stupefied. The headmaster had gone nearly hoarse, when he paused to ask, "Shall I go on?" Sekhar replied, "Please don't, sir, I think this will do. . . ." The headmaster looked stunned. His face was beaded with perspiration. Sekhar felt the greatest pity for him. But he felt he could not help it. No judge delivering a sentence felt more pained and helpless. Sekhar noticed that the headmaster's wife peeped in from the kitchen, with eager curiosity. The drummer and the violinist put away their burdens with an air of

---

inclinations (in cluh NAY shunz) preferences
consolation (kon suh LAY shun) comfort; relief
ingratiating (in GRAY shee ayt ing) charming; agreeable
assailed (uh SAYLD) had a forceful, unpleasant effect on

relief. The headmaster removed his spectacles, mopped his brow, and asked, "Now, come out with your opinion."

"Can't I give it tomorrow, sir?" Sekhar asked tentatively.

"No. I want it immediately—your frank opinion. Was it good?"

"No, sir . . ." Sekhar replied.

"Oh! . . . Is there any use continuing my lessons?"

"Absolutely none, sir . . ." Sekhar said with his voice trembling. He felt very unhappy that he could not speak more soothingly. Truth, he reflected, required as much strength to give as to receive.

All the way home he felt worried. He felt that his official life was not going to be smooth sailing hereafter. There were questions of increment and confirmation and so on, all depending upon the headmaster's goodwill. All kinds of worries seemed to be in store for him. . . . Did not Harischandra lose his throne, wife, child, because he would speak nothing less than the absolute Truth whatever happened?

At home his wife served him with a sullen face. He knew she was still angry with him for his remark of the morning. Two casualties for today, Sekhar said to himself. If I practice it for a week, I don't think I shall have a single friend left.

He received a call from the headmaster in his classroom next day. He went up apprehensively.

"Your suggestion was useful. I have paid off the music master. No one would tell me the truth about my music all these days. Why such antics at my age! Thank you. By the way, what about those test papers?"

"You gave me ten days, sir, for correcting them."

"Oh, I've reconsidered it. I must positively have them here tomorrow. . . ." A hundred papers in a day! That meant all night's sitting up! "Give me a couple of days, sir . . ."

"No. I must have them tomorrow morning. And remember, every paper must be thoroughly scrutinized."

"Yes, sir," Sekhar said, feeling that sitting up all night with a hundred test papers was a small price to pay for the luxury of practicing Truth.

---

scrutinized (SCROOT un yzd) examined very carefully

Review the Selection

UNDERSTAND THE SELECTION

Recall

1. From whose point of view is the "Old Man of the Temple" told?

2. From where did the spirit make his appearance and through whom?

3. For what reason did Sekhar resolve to tell the truth for a day?

Infer

4. When did the spirit enter Doss's body?

5. Do you think that Doss recovered after the spirit left his body?

6. Explain why Sekhar believed that it took strength to tell the truth.

7. Why do you think Sekhar believed it was important to tell the truth?

Apply

8. Do you, like the narrator, believe that the spirit will never return? Explain.

9. Predict Sekhar's future behavior.

10. Do you agree that people must soften the truth to have good human relations? Explain.

Respond to Literature

Explain how "Like the Sun" is a good example of the contemporary British writers' interest in psychology.

WRITE ABOUT THE SELECTION

At the conclusion of "Old Man of the Temple," the narrator of the story returns to the temple to find out if the spirit had returned. It had not. The narrator had helped the spirit find peace of mind by reuniting him with his wife, his long-lost love. Only then was the spirit able to go to his eternal peace. Stories about spirits, or ghosts, are universal. Write a story in which you tell about a ghost who is searching for something, finds it, and then goes to his or her eternal peace.

Prewriting   Freewrite for a few minutes about who the ghost is and for what he or she might be searching. It could be a friend, a lost love, or money owed to the ghost. It could be the truth about a question that has mystified the ghost, or the answer to an unresolved problem.

Writing   Use your freewriting as a basis for your story. Have you thought about the people the ghost will meet? Describe them as vividly as you do the ghost.

Revising   When you revise, make sure you have included details about the setting in which your story takes place. Make it eerie in a way that is appropriate for a ghost story. Conclude your story with a few lines about the ghost finding eternal peace and happiness.

Proofreading   Read over your story to check for errors. Make sure that you have put commas where they belong.

THINK ABOUT THEME

Understanding the great themes in literature can help you develop a greater appreciation of the things you read. In the "Old Man of the Temple," R. K. Narayan used the universal theme that love can bring peace of mind to tell a wonderful, timeless ghost story. With the help of "The Talkative Man," a spirit who has been woefully adrift for hundreds of years is able to finally find eternal happiness.

In "Old Man of the Temple," you must figure out the theme of the story. In "Like the Sun," however, Narayan states the theme immediately: Truth, like the sun, is hard to face. Interestingly, the story makes it plain that sometimes it is just as difficult to speak the truth as to face it.

1. What did the spirit want in "Old Man of the Temple"?

2. How did "The Talkative Man" help the spirit resolve his problem?

3. What did Sekhar decide to do for one day?

4. What problems did he encounter?

5. What are the outcomes of "Old Man of the Temple" and "Like the Sun"?

READING FOCUS

Identify Facts and Opinions   Choose a passage from either story. Identify each statement as either a fact or an opinion. Tell how you decided.

DEVELOP YOUR VOCABULARY

Vivid verbs give you a lively picture of the way a character acts in a story. For example, there are many ways to move from one place to another. You can *skip, waddle, run, jog, leap* or *crawl*. Each of these words has a precise definition that describes a particular way of moving.

Use a dictionary to find the meaning of each italicized vivid verb in the following sentences. Then write an original sentence using that verb.

1. Jess *hobbled* back to the dugout after being hit with the baseball.

2. Melissa *stooped* down to look for shells as she walked along the beach.

3. Stars *sparkle* with particular brilliance in August.

4. "I bet you don't know where I hid your present," *exclaimed* Molly.

Each of the following verbs describes a way of communicating. Use a dictionary to find the exact definition of each word. Then write an original sentence using that word.

jabber	snarl
bellow	chortle
cackle	croak

Learn About

FIGURATIVE LANGUAGE

One of the things that makes a poem beautiful, exciting, or meaningful is figurative language. Specific examples of figurative language are called figures of speech. Some of the most important and commonly used figures of speech are simile, metaphor, hyperbole, and personification.

A **simile** compares two things using the words *like* or *as*. *I'm happy as a clam* is a simile. A **metaphor** compares two things without using extra words. *Big gas-guzzling cars were dinosaurs by the 1980s* is an example of a metaphor. **Hyperbole** is exaggeration. *That kitten eats like a horse!* is an example of hyperbole. In **personification,** nonhuman subjects are given human qualities. *The sea is angry tonight* is personification. **Imagery** is the use of vivid language to paint clear word pictures. *Your hands are ice cold* is an example of imagery.

As you read "Hawk Roosting," ask yourself:

1. Which kind of figurative language did Hughes use?
2. Did the hawk seem human to you?

WRITING CONNECTION

Think about an animal with characteristics like those of an angry person. Write a list of phrases to describe it.

READING FOCUS

Identify the Speaker   The speaker of a poem is the voice or perspective from which the work is told. The speaker is not necessarily the poet; it may be a character created by the poet.

As you read "Hawk Roosting," identify who is narrating the poem, and try to determine his or her perspective on the situation of the poem. This will give you insight into the meaning of the poem.

Hawk Roosting

by Ted Hughes

I sit in the top of the wood, my eyes closed.
Inaction, no falsifying dream
Between my hooked head and hooked feet:
Or in sleep rehearse perfect kills and eat.

5   The convenience of the high trees!
The air's buoyancy and the sun's ray
Are of advantage to me;
And the earth's face upward for my inspection.

My feet are locked upon the rough bark.
10   It took the whole of Creation
To produce my foot, my each feather:
Now I hold Creation in my foot

Or fly up, and revolve it all slowly—
I kill where I please because it is all mine.
15   There is no sophistry in my body:
My manners are tearing off heads—

The allotment of death.
For the one path of my flight is direct
Through the bones of the living
20   No arguments assert my right:

The sun is behind me.
Nothing has changed since I began.
My eye has permitted no change.
I am going to keep things like this.

---

roosting (ROOST ing) sitting or resting on a perch
inaction (in AK shun) the absence of action or motion; stillness
buoyancy (BOI un see) the ability to float or rise in the air
sophistry (SOF is tree) reasoning that seems sound but is actually false or misleading
allotment (uh LOT munt) something that is distributed
assert (uh SURT) to defend; uphold; maintain

Review the Selection

UNDERSTAND THE SELECTION

Recall

1. Who is the "I" that is speaking in "Hawk Roosting"?

2. What is the hawk doing?

3. How does the hawk describe its head and feet?

Infer

4. Why do you think the hawk refers to the "convenience" of the high trees?

5. Do you think a hawk feels guilty about killing its prey? Give a reason for your answer.

6. Why were the sun's rays an advantage to the hawk?

7. Explain in your own words what the speaker of the poem is trying to say.

Apply

8. If you were the speaker, how would you like your life? Explain your answer.

9. Predict what the hawk will do tomorrow, and the day after, and so on.

10. Choose a line that illustrates that the hawk liked what it was doing.

Respond to Literature

Think about "Hawk Roosting." In what way might a nation be compared to a hawk?

WRITE ABOUT THE SELECTION

Reread "Hawk Roosting." Do you feel that Ted Hughes has written an interesting poem? Did you like it, or did you find it a little strange? Think about the subject matter of the poem for a few minutes. Do you believe that Hughes was writing only about a hawk? Or was he really writing about something more? If you believe he was writing about something more, what was it? Think of yourself as a literary critic for your school magazine. Your assignment is to write a review of "Hawk Roosting."

Prewriting   Freewrite for a few minutes about what pictures the poem creates in your mind, and what you think the poet was trying to say. Ask yourself: Is the poem well written? How do you feel about the length of the poem? Was it long enough, or was it too short to convey what Hughes wanted to say? Has Hughes used figurative language successfully?

Writing   Write your review of "Hawk Roosting." Be sure to include terms such as figurative language, personification, and imagery in your review.

Revising   When you revise make sure you have explained the way in which Hughes used personification and imagery.

Proofreading   Reread your criticism to look for errors in spelling. Check your sentences to see that each ends with a period, question mark, or exclamation point.

THINK ABOUT POETIC DEVICES

Writers use figurative language to give their writing strength, freshness of expression, and vivid pictorial effect. Different types of figurative language are called figures of speech. Four figures of speech that are often found in good writing are **simile, metaphor, hyperbole,** and **personification.**

In "Hawk Roosting," Ted Hughes powerfully writes about the thoughts and feelings of a hawk. He makes us understand that hawks don't question their ability or their right to kill. Theirs is inherent behavior that has been the same since the beginning of their existence.

1. Which kind of figurative language does Hughes use?

2. Explain how Hughes uses personification.

3. Give some examples of the words Hughes uses to create vivid images.

4. Do you think that Hughes's use of personification works to the benefit of the poem? Explain your answers.

5. Do you think the hawk was a good choice of bird for Hughes to have made to convey the particular message and feelings of the poem?

READING FOCUS

Identify the Speaker Who is the speaker of "Hawk Roosting"? What is the speaker's perspective on the situation presented in the poem?

DEVELOP YOUR VOCABULARY

A **homograph** is a word that has the same spelling as another or others but has a different meaning and a different origin and, sometimes, a different pronunciation. For example, *school* can be a place for learning or a large group of fish.

Each of the italicized words in the following sentences is a homograph. Write a definition of each homograph as it is used in the sentence in which it appears. Use a dictionary to help you. Then, from the dictionary, choose one of the other words that is spelled the same as the word you have defined. Use that word in an original sentence.

1. The peddler *hawks* his books every day near the park.

2. He cried *tears* of joy when he saw his sister after twenty years.

3. Melissa wished the dog's *bark* was not so loud; it distracted her.

4. Working in the *mine* for thirty years had taught him a lot about the earth.

CONFLICT

Plot is the story line or series of events in a work of literature. One of the principal components of a good plot is conflict. **Conflict** contributes to the dramatic action of a plot. It is often the element of a story that is most important in the creation of excitement and suspense.

Conflict develops when two opposite forces meet. There are four kinds of conflict that can occur in a story. Conflict can take place between two people or two groups of people. It can occur within a single person, an internal conflict. Conflict can occur between people and things. Finally, it can occur between people and nature. Many plots contain two or more kinds of conflict.

All of us face conflicts in our lives. We have conflicts with friends and family members. We have conflicts at school.

As you read "A Mild Attack of Locusts," ask yourself:

1. Is there one or more than one conflict in the story?
2. What kinds of conflicts are there?

WRITING CONNECTION

Suppose that you have decided to write the screenplay for a new movie. Decide which kind of conflict will be in your plot. Write a paragraph explaining why you chose that kind of conflict.

READING FOCUS

Recognize Fictional Details Writers often use details to make their stories seem more realistic. These details may be actual facts that you could verify or they may be fictional details that only someone in the story could verify. For example, the description of a farm as being 3000 acres includes the fact of its size though the farm is fictional. As you read, ask yourself whether information contains actual facts or fictional details.

A Mild Attack
of Locusts

by Doris Lessing

The rains that year were good; they were coming nicely just as the crops needed them—or so Margaret gathered when the men said they were not too bad. She never had an opinion of her own on matters like the weather, because even to know about what seems a simple thing like the weather needs experience. Which Margaret had not got. The men were Richard her husband, and old Stephen, Richard's father, a farmer from way back; and these two might argue for hours whether the rains were ruinous or just ordinarily exasperating. Margaret

---

exasperating (ig ZAS puh rayt ing) very irritating or annoying

had been on the farm three years. She still did not understand how they did not go bankrupt altogether, when the men never had a good word for the weather, or the soil, or the Government. But she was getting to learn the language. Farmers' language. And they neither went bankrupt nor got very rich. They jogged along doing comfortably.

Their crop was maize. Their farm was three thousand acres on the ridges that rise up toward the Zambesi escarpment— high, dry windswept country, cold and dusty in winter, but now, in the wet season, steamy with the heat rising in wet soft waves off miles of green foliage. Beautiful it was, with the sky blue and brilliant halls of air, and the bright green folds and hollows of country beneath, and the mountains lying sharp and bare twenty miles off across the rivers. The sky made her eyes ache; she was not used to it. One does not look so much at the sky in the city she came from. So that evening when Richard said: "The Government is sending out warnings that locusts are expected, coming down from the breeding grounds up North," her instinct was to look about her at the trees. Insects—swarms of them—horrible! But Richard and the old man had raised their eyes and were looking up over the mountain. "We haven't had locusts in seven years," they said. "They go in cycles, locusts do." And then: "There goes our crop for this season!"

But they went on with the work of the farm just as usual until one day they were coming up the road to the homestead for the midday break, when old Stephen stopped, raised his finger and pointed: "Look, look, there they are!"

Out ran Margaret to join them, looking at the hills. Out came the servants from the kitchen. They all stood and gazed. Over the rocky levels of the mountain was a streak of rust-colored air. Locusts. There they came.

At once Richard shouted at the cookboy. Old Stephen yelled at the houseboy. The cookboy ran to beat the old plowshare hanging from a tree branch, which was used to summon the laborers at moments of crisis. The houseboy ran off to the store to collect tin cans, any old bit of metal. The farm was ringing with the clamor of the gong; and they could see the laborers come pouring out of the compound, pointing at the hills and shouting excitedly. Soon they had all come up to the house, and Richard and old Stephen were giving them orders— Hurry, hurry, hurry.

And off they ran again, the two white men with them, and in a few minutes Margaret could see the smoke of fires rising from all around the farmlands. Piles of wood and grass had been prepared there. There were seven patches of bared soil, yellow and oxblood color and pink,

---

maize (mayz) corn
Zambesi escarpment (zam BEE zee ih SKAHRP munt) steep cliffs along the Zambesi River in southern Africa
plowshare (PLOU shair) the cutting blade of a plow

where the new mealies were just show-ing, making a film of bright green; and around each drifted up thick clouds of smoke. They were throwing wet leaves on to the fires now, to make it acrid and black. Margaret was watching the hills. Now there was a long, low cloud advanc-ing, rust-color still, swelling forward and out as she looked. The telephone was ringing. Neighbors—quick, quick, there come the locusts. Old Smith had had his crop eaten to the ground. Quick, get your fires started. For of course, while every farmer hoped the locusts would overlook his farm and go on to the next, it was only fair to warn each other; one must play fair. Everywhere, fifty miles over the countryside, the smoke was rising from myriads of fires. Margaret answered the telephone calls, and between calls she stood watching the locusts. The air was darkening. A strange darkness, for the sun was blazing—it was like the dark-ness of a veld fire, when the air gets thick with smoke. The sunlight comes down distorted, a thick, hot orange. Op-pressive it was, too, with the heaviness of a storm. The locusts were coming fast. Now half the sky was darkened. Behind the reddish veils in front, which were the

---

mealies (MEEL eez) ears of corn
acrid (AK rid) sharp, bitter, or irritating to the smell or taste
myriads (MIR ee udz) very large numbers

advance guards of the swarm, the main swarm showed in dense black cloud, reaching almost to the sun itself.

Margaret was wondering what she could do to help. She did not know. Then up came old Stephen from the lands. "We're finished, Margaret, finished! Those beggars can eat every leaf and blade off the farm in half an hour! And it is only early afternoon—if we can make enough smoke, make enough noise till the sun goes down, they'll settle somewhere else perhaps. . . ." And then: "Get the kettle going. It's thirsty work, this."

So Margaret went to the kitchen, and stoked up the fire, and boiled the water. Now, on the tin roof of the kitchen she could hear the thuds and bangs of falling locusts, or a scratching slither as one skidded down. Here were the first of them. From down on the lands came the beating and banging and clanging of a hundred gasoline cans and bits of metal. Stephen impatiently waited while one gasoline can was filled with tea, hot, sweet and orange-colored, and the other with water. In the meantime, he told Margaret about how twenty years back he was eaten out, made bankrupt, by the locust armies. And then, still talking, he hoisted up the gasoline cans, one in each hand, by the wood pieces set cornerwise across each, and jogged off down to the road to the thirsty laborers. By now the locusts were falling like hail on to the roof of the kitchen. It sounded like a heavy storm. Margaret looked out and saw the air dark with a criss-cross of the insects, and she set her teeth and ran out into it—what the men could do, she could. Overhead the air was thick, locusts everywhere. The locusts were flopping against her, and she brushed them off, heavy red-brown creatures, looking at her with their beady old-men's eyes while they clung with hard, serrated legs. She held her breath with disgust and ran through into the house. There it was even more like being in a heavy storm. The iron roof was reverberating, and the clamor of iron from the lands was like thunder. Looking out, all the trees were queer and still, clotted with insects, their boughs weighed to the ground. The earth seemed to be moving, locusts crawling everywhere, she could not see the lands at all, so thick was the swarm. Towards the mountains it was like looking into driving rain—even as she watched, the sun was blotted out with a fresh onrush of them. It was a half-night, a perverted blackness. Then came a sharp crack from the bush—a branch had snapped off. Then another. A tree down the slope leaned over and settled heavily to the ground. Through the hail of insects a man came running. More tea, more water was needed. She supplied them. She kept the fires stoked and filled cans with liquid, and then it was four in the afternoon, and the locusts had been pouring across overhead for a couple of hours. Up came old Stephen again, crunching locusts underfoot with every step, locusts

---

serrated (SER ayt id) having notches like the teeth of a saw along the edge
reverberating (rih VUR buh rayt ing) echoing

clinging all over him; he was cursing and swearing, banging with his old hat at the air. At the doorway he stopped briefly, hastily pulling at the clinging insects and throwing them off, then he plunged into the locust-free living-room.

"All the crops finished. Nothing left," he said.

But the gongs were still beating, the men still shouting, and Margaret asked "Why do you go on with it, then?"

"The main swarm isn't settling. They are heavy with eggs. They are looking for a place to settle and lay. If we can stop the main body settling on our farm, that's everything. If they get a chance to lay their eggs, we are going to have everything eaten flat with hoppers later on." He picked up a stray locust off his shirt and split it down with his thumbnail—it was clotted inside with eggs. "Imagine that multiplied by millions. You ever seen a hopper swarm on the march? Well, you're lucky."

Margaret thought an adult swarm was bad enough. Outside now the light on the earth was a pale, thin yellow, clotted with moving shadows; the clouds of moving insects thickened and lightened like driving rain. Old Stephen said, "They've got the wind behind them, that's something."

"Is it very bad?" said Margaret fearfully, and the old man said emphatically: "We're finished. This swarm may pass over, but once they've started, they'll be coming down from the North now one after another. And then there are the hoppers—it might go on for two or three years."

Margaret sat down helplessly, and thought: Well, if it's the end, it's the end. What now? We'll all three have to go back to town. . . . But at this, she took a quick look at Stephen, the old man who had farmed forty years in this country, been bankrupt twice, and she knew nothing would make him go and become a clerk in the city. Yet her heart ached for him, he looked so tired, the worry lines deep from nose to mouth. Poor old man. . . . He had lifted up a locust that had got itself somehow into his pocket, holding it in the air by one leg. "You've got the strength of a steel-spring in those legs of yours," he was telling the locust, good-humoredly. Then, although he had been fighting locusts, squashing locusts, yelling at locusts, sweeping them in great mounds into the fires to burn for the last three hours, nevertheless he took this one to the door and carefully threw it out to join its fellows, as if he would rather not harm a hair of its head. This comforted Margaret; all at once she felt irrationally cheered. She remembered it was not the first time in the last three years the man had announced their final and irremediable ruin.

"Get me a drink, lass," he then said, and she set the bottle of whisky by him.

In the meantime, out in the pelting

---

hoppers (HOP urz) baby locusts
irrationally (ih RASH uh nul ee) not reasonable; senseless; absurd
irremediable (ir ih MEE dee uh bul) impossible to correct or remedy

storm of insects, her husband was banging the gong, feeding the fires with leaves, the insects clinging to him all over —she shuddered. "How can you bear to let them touch you?" she asked. He looked at her, disapproving. She felt suitably humble—just as she had when he had first taken a good look at her city self, hair waved and golden, nails red and pointed. Now she was a proper farmer's wife, in sensible shoes and a solid skirt. She might even get to letting locusts settle on her—in time.

Having tossed back a whisky or two, old Stephen went back into the battle, wading now through glistening brown waves of locusts.

Five o'clock. The sun would set in an hour. Then the swarm would settle. It was as thick overhead as ever. The trees were ragged mounds of glistening brown.

Margaret began to cry. It was all so hopeless—if it wasn't a bad season, it was locusts; if it wasn't locusts, it was army-worms or veld fires. Always something. The rustling of the locust armies was like a big forest in the storm; their settling on the roof was like the beating of the rain; the ground was invisible in a sleek, brown, surging tide—it was like being drowned in locusts, submerged by the loathsome brown flood. It seemed as if the roof might sink in under the weight of them, as if the door might give in under their pressure and these rooms fill with them—and it was getting so dark . . . she looked up. The air was thinner; gaps of blue showed in the dark, moving clouds. The blue spaces were cold and thin—the sun must be setting.

---

army-worms (AHR mee WURMZ) the larvae of certain moths that travel in large groups, ruining crops and grass

Through the fog of insects she saw figures approach. First old Stephen, marching bravely along, then her husband, drawn and haggard with weariness. Behind them the servants. All were crawling all over with insects. The sound of the gongs had stopped. She could hear nothing but the ceaseless rustle of a myriad wings.

The two men slapped off the insects and came in.

"Well," said Richard, kissing her on the cheek, "the main swarm has gone over."

"For the Lord's sake," said Margaret angrily, still half-crying, "what's here is bad enough, isn't it?" For although the evening air was no longer black and thick, but a clear blue, with a pattern of insects whizzing this way and that across it, everything else—trees, buildings, bushes, earth, was gone under the moving brown masses.

"If it doesn't rain in the night and keep them here—if it doesn't rain and weight them down with water, they'll be off in the morning at sunrise."

"We're bound to have some hoppers. But not the main swarm—that's something."

Margaret roused herself, wiped her eyes, pretended she had not been crying, and fetched them some supper, for the servants were too exhausted to move. She sent them down to the compound to rest.

She served the supper and sat listening.

There is not one maize plant left, she heard. Not one. The men would get the planters out the moment the locusts had gone. They must start all over again.

But what's the use of that, Margaret wondered, if the whole farm was going to be crawling with hoppers? But she listened while they discussed the new government pamphlet that said how to defeat the hoppers. You must have men out all the time, moving over the farm to watch for movement in the grass. When you find a patch of hoppers, small lively black things, like crickets, then you dig trenches around the patch or spray them with poison from pumps supplied by the Government. The Government wanted them to cooperate in a world plan for eliminating this plague forever. You should attack locusts at the source. Hoppers, in short. The men were talking as if they were planning a war, and Margaret listened, amazed.

In the night it was quiet; no sign of the settled armies outside, except sometimes a branch snapped, or a tree could be heard crashing down.

Margaret slept badly in the bed beside Richard, who was sleeping like the dead, exhausted with the afternoon's fight. In the morning she woke to yellow sunshine lying across the bed—clear sunshine, with an occasional blotch of shadow moving over it. She went to the window. Old Stephen was ahead of her. There he stood outside, gazing down over the bush. And she gazed, astounded

---

haggard (HAG urd) looking exhausted, as from worry, sleeplessness, or illness

—and entranced, much against her will. For it looked as if every tree, every bush, all the earth, were lit with pale flames. The locusts were fanning their wings to free them of the night dews. There was a shimmer of red-tinged gold light everywhere.

She went out to join the old man, stepping carefully among the insects, They stood and watched. Overhead the sky was blue, blue and clear.

"Pretty," said old Stephen, with satisfaction.

Well, thought Margaret, we may be ruined, we may be bankrupt, but not everyone has seen an army of locusts fanning their wings at dawn.

Over the slopes, in the distance, a faint red smear showed in the sky, thickened and spread. "There they go," said old Stephen. "There goes the main army, off south."

And now from the trees, from the earth all round them, the locusts were taking wing. They were like small aircraft, maneuvering for the take-off, trying their wings to see if they were dry enough. Off they went. A reddish-brown steam was rising off the miles of bush, off the lands, the earth. Again the sunlight darkened.

And as the clotted branches lifted, the weight on them lightening, there was nothing but the black spines of branches, trees. No green left, nothing. All morning they watched, the three of them, as the brown crust thinned and broke and dissolved, flying up to mass with the main army, now a brownish-red smear in the southern sky. The lands which had been filmed with green, the new tender mealie plants, were stark and bare. All the trees stripped. A devastated landscape. No green, no green anywhere.

By midday the reddish cloud had gone. Only an occasional locust flopped down. On the ground were the corpses and the wounded. The African laborers were sweeping these up with branches and collecting them in tins.

"Ever eaten sun-dried locust?" asked old Stephen. "That time twenty years ago, when I went broke, I lived on mealie meal and dried locusts for three months. They aren't bad at all—rather like smoked fish, if you come to think of it."

But Margaret preferred not even to think of it.

After the midday meal the men went off to the lands. Everything was to be replanted. With a bit of luck another swarm would not come traveling down just this way. But they hoped it would rain very soon, to spring some new grass, because the cattle would die otherwise—there was not a blade of grass left on the farm. As for Margaret, she was trying to get used to the idea of three or four years of locusts. Locusts were going to be like bad weather, from now on, always imminent. She felt like a survivor after war—if this devastated and mangled countryside was not ruin, well, what then was ruin?

But the men ate their supper with good appetites.

"It could have been worse," was what they said. "It could be much worse."

Doris Lessing (1919–   )

Doris Lessing grew up in southern Rhodesia. She once said that being reared outside of England was the best thing that could have happened to her. She had experiences in Rhodesia that a middle-class girl in England could never have had. She described the setting of her upbringing in the first two volumes of *Children of Violence.* These books represent her greatest literary achievement. They describe a woman's struggle against political and racial issues.

One of her strongest themes is that of a person's relationship to and breaking away from society. Her hope is to focus public attention on the problems of the world as a call to action. Although Lessing explores the catastrophes of the human race, much of her work still suggests that she believes in the potential of human beings. She directly addresses what causes the problems of the world and examines what can be done to change things. She has spent a lifetime speaking and writing about her political concerns, the changing role of women in the world, and her fear of nuclear disaster.

In the selection you have read, which is set on a farm in the bush country of Rhodesia, the reader is reminded of the hope of living, not the defeat of living. Think about how this selection reflects Lessing's themes of home and harmony in the world.

Review the Selection

Recall

1. Where did this story take place?

2. What were the farmers' concerns when they heard the warning about locusts?

3. What did the farmers do to prepare for the attack by the locusts?

Infer

4. What do you think Margaret meant by "Farmer's language"?

5. Describe how the horizon looked as the locusts headed toward the farm.

6. What did Margaret learn about farmers from the locust attack?

7. What was seen in the midst of the devastation the locusts brought?

Apply

8. Would you like to meet Stephen? Why?

9. After all she had been through, do you think Margaret will stay on the farm? Why or why not?

10. Describe what the farmland might have looked like after the attack.

Respond to Literature

What signs suggest the characters in Lessing's story wanted self-government?

Near the conclusion of the story, Stephen and Margaret watched the locusts ready themselves for flight. Stephen remarked how pretty they were. Then all morning they watched as the locusts flew off to the south, leaving a devastated landscape behind them.

Think about a natural event, such as a hurricane, which you might find very beautiful but which has the potential for devastation. What does it look like? Might others see the same beauty that you see? Write a descriptive paragraph in which you tell how the natural event looked to you.

Prewriting   Freewrite for a few minutes about what kind of natural disaster might produce moments of incredible beauty. Think about what it would look like, what colors you would see, what sounds you might hear.

Writing   Use your freewriting as the basis for a descriptive paragraph in which you tell how a natural occurrence of nature that had the potential for disaster still looked beautiful to you.

Revising   Be sure to use vivid sensory words to describe what you saw. If you have not used such words, include them in your revision.

Proofreading   Reread your descriptive paragraph to check for errors. Make sure that you have followed all the rules for capitalization.

THINK ABOUT CONFLICT

Conflict is one of the elements of the plot of a story. Think about your favorite short stories and novels. Remember the best plays and movies you've seen. Most likely, each of them contained one or more conflicts. Some of them were **external,** centered on the opposition between two people or two groups of people. Others were based on **internal** conflicts and the personal problem of a single man or woman.

In "A Mild Attack of Locusts," the conflict is revealed very early in the story. It is external. Then as the story unfolds, you get an inkling of a possible inner conflict in the leading character.

This story works wonderfully to show how conflict makes a story more interesting by including both external and internal conflicts.

1. Which kind of conflict does Lessing use first in this story?

2. What are the two forces in the conflict?

3. What is Margaret's inner conflict?

4. As a result of Margaret's inner conflict, do you think she might at some future time have an external conflict with another character in the story? Why?

5. Are the conflicts in this story resolved?

READING FOCUS

Recognize Fictional Details Explain the difference between a fact and a fictional detail, using one example of each from the story.

DEVELOP YOUR VOCABULARY

Words can have several meanings in English. **Context clues** can help you figure out the meaning of an unfamiliar word. In a sentence, the context of a word is made up of the other words that surround it.

Example: The situation was *exasperating;* I found it very irritating.

By looking at the context of the word *exasperating,* you can figure out that it means "very irritating."

Read the following sentences. Use context clues to help you figure out the meaning of each italicized word. Then use the word in an original sentence.

1. The old man's face was *haggard;* he looked exhausted from worrying about the nearby brush fires.

2. After the fire, the air was *acrid;* it reminded me of the harsh, bitter smell of burning rubber.

3. The damage to the nearby forest was *irremediable;* it could never be corrected.

Les Nymphéas, detail, Claude Monet. L'Orangerie, Paris

READING FOCUS

Evaluate the Writer's Purpose Writers will use facts and opinions differently depending on their purpose for writing. Their purpose may be to inform, to entertain, to persuade, or to describe. Evaluate the writing purpose first. Then you can consider how facts and opinions are used to support that purpose. For example, think about how opinions would support a poem about a personal experience. Consider how facts would enhance a poem's description by making it more realistic.

IMAGERY

Words that appeal to the five senses are often used by poets to create images in a reader's mind. All of these images in any literary work are called its **imagery**. For example, a poet might write:

Sparkling stars guide me to evening delights.

The words "sparkling stars" appeal to your sense of sight. The imagery helps you to share the experience of the speaker.

As you read the poems that follow, ask yourself:

1. Which sensory words help you to appreciate the poem's meaning?
2. What sensory reactions did the poets' imagery create in your mind?

WRITING CONNECTION

On a piece of paper, write the names of the five senses: *sight, hearing, smell, taste* and *touch.* Under each sense list several words or phrases that might create an image appropriate to the sense. For example, under *taste* you could write "sweet." Under *hearing* you could write "screechy."

Then write three sentences in which you use several of the words or phrases from your list.

This Is a Photograph of Me

by Margaret Atwood

It was taken some time ago.
At first it seems to be
a smeared
print: blurred lines and gray flecks
5   blended with the paper;

then, as you scan
it, you see in the left-hand corner
a thing that is like a branch: part of a tree
(balsam or spruce) emerging
10   and, to the right, halfway up
what ought to be a gentle
slope, a small frame house.

In the background there is a lake,
and beyond that, some low hills.

15   (The photograph was taken
the day after I drowned.

I am in the lake, in the center
of the picture, just under the surface.

---

smeared (SMIRD) soiled or blurred, as with grease or dirt
scan (SKAN) to look at closely

It is difficult to say where
20 precisely, or to say
how large or small I am:
the effect of water
on light is a distortion

but if you look long enough,
25 eventually
you will be able to see me.)

---

precisely (prih SYS lee) definitely; exactly
eventually (ee VEN choo ul ee) in the end; finally

COMING

by Philip Larkin

On longer evenings,
Light, chill and yellow,
Bathes the serene
Foreheads of houses.
5   A thrush sings,
Laurel-surrounded
In the deep bare garden,
Its fresh-peeled voice
Astonishing the brickwork.
10   It will be spring soon,
It will be spring soon—
And I, whose childhood
Is a forgotten boredom,
Feel like a child
15   Who comes on a scene
Of adult reconciling,
And can understand nothing
But the unusual laughter,
And starts to be happy.

Love After Love

by Derek Walcott

The time will come
When, with elation
You will greet yourself arriving
At your own door, in your own mirror
And each will smile at the other's welcome,

and say, sit here. Eat.
You will love again the stranger who was your self.
Give wine. Give bread. Give back your heart
To itself, to the stranger who has loved you

all your life, whom you ignored
for another, who knows you by heart.
Take down the love letters from the bookshelf.

the photographs, the desperate notes,
Peel your own image from the mirror.
Sit. Feast on your life.

---

elation (ee LAY shuhn) high spirits; joy
greet (GREET) welcome by speaking to in a friendly way
desperate (DEHS puhr uht) showing recklessness caused by despair
image (IHM ihj) likeness

In Front of the Mirror, Konstantin N. Istomin. Tretyakov Gallery, Moscow, Russia/Scala/Art Resource, NY

Review the Selection

UNDERSTAND THE SELECTION

Recall

1. Who is the speaker in "This Is a Photograph of Me"?

2. In "Coming" what are the two signs of spring that the speaker mentions?

3. What advice does Derek Walcott give in "Love After Love"?

Infer

4. What does "You will love again the stranger who was your self" mean?

5. What kind of childhood do you think the speaker in "Coming" had?

6. Interpret what Atwood was saying in "This Is a Photograph of Me."

7. Why does the child in "Coming" not understand seeing adults reconciling?

Apply

8. How are the coming of spring and the ending of an argument alike?

9. How might you be able to see the speaker in "This Is a Photograph of Me" if you look long enough?

10. What will happen to natural beauty in the future, considering many people's lack of concern for the environment?

Respond to Literature
Explain how one poem reflects the feelings of contemporary British writers.

WRITE ABOUT THE SELECTION

Margaret Atwood uses many sensory words in her poem "This Is a Photograph of Me." At first they describe the photograph itself. Words like *smeared print*, *blurred lines*, and *gray flecks* produce such vivid images in our minds that it almost seems as if we are holding the photograph in our hands. Then Atwood goes on to describe the scene that the photograph recorded. She speaks of the "branch of a tree (balsam or spruce)," "a gentle slope," "a small frame house."

Only after all these details are set down does Atwood mention the central event of the poem—a drowning. She never tells who the drowned person was or gives a description of the person. That is your assignment. Write a paragraph about the drowning and the person who drowned. Let your readers know who the "Me" in the photograph really was.

Prewriting Jot down words to describe the "Me" in the photograph. Make the person really visible in your imagination.

Writing Use the prewriting notes to write your paragraph. One vital thing you must decide is whether the drowning was an accident or suicide.

Revising When you revise, make sure you have included specific details and sensory images.

Proofreading Check for errors in spelling, punctuation, and grammar.

THINK ABOUT IMAGERY

Through a poet's choice of words, he or she is able to create a strong picture in the reader's mind. For example, Atwood chooses to use the image of a photograph to share her feelings. People can immediately identify with a photograph. To further emphasize her point visually, Atwood also uses certain words such as *smeared, blurred,* and *distortion.* These sensory words contribute greatly to the imagery of Atwood's poem. They create vivid images that help the reader to focus his or her attention and to experience the depth of the feelings Atwood wants to share.

1. To which senses did Larkin appeal most in "Coming"?

2. What picture did Atwood's choice of words create in your mind?

3. Describe the photograph in "This Is a Photograph of Me."

4. What personification does Larkin use in describing evening light?

5. What is the image Walcott uses in the first verse and returns to again in the last verse?

READING FOCUS

Evaluate the Writer's Purpose   Explain each poet's purpose for writing. Provide one example from each poem that shows its purpose.

DEVELOP YOUR VOCABULARY

A **syllable** is a word or part of a word that is pronounced with a single or uninterrupted sound of the voice. *Help,* for example, is a word that has one syllable. *Helpless* has two syllables; *helplessly* has three. It is important to know how to divide words into syllables. When you are writing and need to split a word at the end of a line, you should split it only between syllables.

Division into syllables can help you spell and pronounce words too. For example, when you divide a long word into syllables, you make shorter parts out of it. Short word parts are easy to spell and to pronounce.

Divide each of the following words into syllables. If you do not know how to divide some of them, look them up in your dictionary. Then use each word in an original sentence.

1. halfway
2. question
3. pleasure
4. unintended
5. emerging
6. background
7. difficult
8. photograph
9. distortion
10. neighboring

WRITING APPLICATIONS

Write About the Literary Period

In the Period Discussion at the beginning of this unit, you learned about the contemporary trends of British writing. Suppose that you could interview one of the writers in this unit. The purpose of the interview would be to find out how the historical period in which the writer grew up influenced her or his writing. Which writer would you choose? What questions would you ask the writer? Your task now is to prepare a short interview with the writer of your choice.

Prewriting   Before you begin to write, review the work of the writer you will interview. Make sure to examine how the selection reflects the contemporary writing trends in England. Jot down some notes as you review the work to help you write your interview questions.

Writing   Use your notes as the basis for your interview. Be sure to include questions about when and where the writer grew up. Find out what schools the writer attended and whether he or she has done any work other than writing.

Revising   As you revise, be sure that you have asked specific questions about the selection and what influenced the writer to write it. If you have not, include them in your revision.

Proofreading   Reread your interview to check for errors. Be sure to use periods, question marks, or exclamation points at the end of sentences.

Write About Genre

In this unit, you have learned what the different elements of nonfiction are. Now you can use what you learned to write a paper about one of the nonfiction pieces in the unit. With the help of a list of the elements of nonfiction, discuss how they helped you to enjoy the selection about which you have chosen to write.

Prewriting   Review the elements of nonfiction. Remember, there are four forms of nonfiction writing: exposition, persuasion (or argumentation), description, and narration. The methods used in writing exposition are: definition, classification, comparison and contrast, and analysis. Most nonfiction has three parts: an introduction, a body, and a conclusion. Now, put the name of the selection you have chosen to write about at the top of a piece of paper. Then list the elements of nonfiction that are used in the selection.

Writing   Using your list, write a paper in which you tell how your knowledge of nonfiction increased your appreciation of it. Be sure to include specific examples.

Revising   When you revise, make sure that you have included all the different elements of nonfiction in your selection. If you have not, include them when you revise.

Proofreading   Read over your paper to check for errors. Make sure that you have spelled the words correctly. Capitalize all proper nouns.

Vocabulary

Sometimes you can look at an unfamiliar word in a sentence and figure out what it means by looking at the words that are before and after it. These words that give hints about a new word's meaning are called **context clues.**

Of course, context clues do not always help you to understand unfamiliar words. Read the following sentence. "The chariots in the movie were great!" The context does not provide enough information about the word *chariots* for you to figure out what it means.

Read the following sentences or parts of sentences. If the context clues help you to define the italicized words, define them without looking at a dictionary. If they do not help, consult your dictionary.

1. ". . . the thing that struck me first about him was the extraordinary *candor* of his eyes. They were large and round and honest."

2. "She kept the fires *stoked,* and filled cans of liquids. . . ."

3. "So very sorry, *grieved,* distressed, afflicted, pained. . . ."

4. "I thank Geoffrey de Havilland who designed the *indomitable* Gipsy. . . ."

Grammar, Usage, and Mechanics

When you are writing a **direct quotation** —the exact words of a person—surround the words with quotation marks. Phrases that introduce a quotation should be followed by a comma. Example: Sam shouted to her dentist, "You're hurting me!" Phrases that interrupt a quotation should be surrounded by commas. Example: "If we leave early," I said, "our host may be annoyed." If a concluding phrase follows a quotation, use a comma, question mark, or exclamation point at the end of the quotation but before the final quotation mark. Example: "Are you feeling better?" Kim asked.

An **indirect quotation** is not the exact words of a person or a character but a restatement of the words. Quotation marks are not used to surround indirect quotations. Example: Marie said that she got a promotion in her job.

Correct the following errors in punctuation by changing or adding quotation marks, periods, commas, question marks, and exclamation points.

1. Counselor, the judge remarked your client's remarks were out of order

2. Kim asked "if I wanted to go out?"

3. "Do you have five bucks to lend me! Jack asked, or are you as broke as I am."

4. The angry driver shouted to the car ahead, You're blocking traffic?

SPEAKING AND LISTENING

Have you ever tried to convince your parents that you should be able to stay out beyond your normal curfew? Have you ever had a discussion with a friend about why one book was better than another? If you have, then you have taken part in an informal debate. The idea behind a debate is to convince the listener that your side of an argument is the correct one. To do this you must present your statements, support them with evidence and reasoning, and prove them in a clear and effective manner.

For this assignment, you will be asked to participate in a debate. To prepare for the experience, read the following guidelines.

1. Make all your arguments direct and informal; informal discussion, which persuades the listeners and brings them to your point of view, is the perfect debating style.

2. Don't try to prove more than is necessary. The less you try to prove, the better your chances are of getting your case across. Say as little as possible about side issues. Focus on giving strong support to your main points.

3. Use methods to hold your listeners' interest. Use plenty of comparisons or illustrations to make your arguments concrete and specific.

4. Use fair methods to weaken your opponents' arguments. Point out errors or contradictions in their arguments. If they give inadequate evidence, point that out, too. Take the offensive in the debate, but remember always to be courteous.

5. Listen carefully to your opponents' arguments. See if they make any statements that you can use to support your own ideas.

6. Before any debate, you should always practice giving your arguments. If possible, have your teacher listen to you. Ask for criticism; your teacher's suggestions will be helpful. Try new techniques of speaking and different methods of presentation to improve your skill.

Now, apply the suggestions above to gain experience in debating. As a class, select a topic for your debate. Choose one that requires you to refer to one or several of the selections you have read. Concentrate on ideas presented in this unit. Then, using those ideas, determine how your debate will be organized. Perhaps you will debate one-on-one. Perhaps the class will choose several topics for debate and divide into debating groups. Whatever you decide, prepare well and you may be successful.

CRITICAL THINKING

Cause and Effect One of the ways to enjoy reading literature more is to understand the cause-and-effect relationships in a story. The **cause** is an event or idea that makes something happen. The thing that happens is the **effect,** or result.

We all know that life is not so simple that every situation can be reduced to the action of a single cause resulting in a single effect. There can be, and there usually are, a number of effects for every cause. And there are several causes for every effect. For example, suppose you have a friend named Anna. Anna has just won an important race. What caused Anna to win the race? Anna's determination caused her to win the race. That much is true, but, in fact, more than determination caused Anna to win the race. She practiced hard, ate the right foods, took good care of her health, and had a positive attitude about running a good race. These causes were all responsible for the effect: Anna's winning of the race.

In this unit, there are several stories with good examples of cause-and-effect relationships. Choose one of the selections, and answer the following questions.

1. What is an important cause in this story? What are its effects? Are they positive or negative?

2. Are there effects in the story that have more than one cause or which seem to have no cause at all? Explain what they are.

EFFECTIVE STUDYING

Using References Books or online resources are excellent references for information about a wide variety of subjects. Knowing which types of references to use is an important skill.

A **dictionary** is a book of alphabetized words which gives each word's spelling, its pronunciation, its meaning or meanings, and often its origin.

An **encyclopedia** is a book or set of books in which information on a wide variety of subjects is given. The listings in encyclopedias are usually in alphabetical order.

An **atlas** is primarily a collection of maps. Atlases contain other information, however, such as statistics and descriptive information about cities, countries, geographical features, and resources.

Almanacs are published once a year. They contain information and statistics on current events.

Explain which type of reference you would use to find the following:

1. the origin of the word *pleasure*

2. the four states that meet at a place called Four Corners

3. how many games the Red Sox won in their regular season in 1985

4. the origin of the game of baseball

Test Preparation

Reference materials are useful in checking information you are unsure of. Be sure you are using the correct information when studying for a test.

GLOSSARY

PRONUNCIATION KEY

Accent is the stress given to some words or syllables in speech. In this book, accent is indicated by upper-case letters. One-syllable words are always shown as accented. Thus, the pronunciation of *hand* is (HAND). In words of more than one syllable, the accented syllable is printed in uppercase letters. The other syllable or syllables are printed in lowercase letters. Thus, the pronunciation of *handbag* is (HAND bag).

Letter(s) in text words	Letter(s) used in respelling	Sample words	Phonetic respelling	Letter(s) in text words	Letter(s) used in respelling	Sample words	Phonetic respelling
a	a	bandit	(BAN dit)	i	uh	possible	(POS uh bul)
a	ay	makeup	(MAYK up)	o	o	bottle	(BOT ul)
a	air	daring	(DAIR ing)	o	u	gallon	(GAL un)
a	ah	dart	(DAHRT)	o	oh	open	(OH pun)
a	uh	about	(uh BOUT)	o	aw	horn	(HAWRN)
a	aw	ball	(BAWL)	o	oo	move	(MOOV)
e	e	denim	(DEN im)	oo	uu	football	(FUUT bawl)
e	eh	ingest	(in JEHST)	oo	oo	pool	(POOL)
e	ih	delight	(dih LYT)	oi	oi	point	(POINT)
e	u	darken	(DAHR kun)	ou	ou	output	(OUT put)
e	ee	he	(HEE)	u	u	upshot	(UP shot)
i	i	mitten	(MIT un)	u	uh	support	(suh PAWRT)
i	ih	gravity	(GRAV ih tee)	u	oo	ruler	(ROO lur)
i	y	idle	(YD ul)	y	i	rhythm	(RITH um)
i	eye	idea	(eye DEE uh)	y	ee	lazy	(LAY zee)
i	ee	medium	(MEE dee um)	y	y	thyme	(TYM)

A

abhorrence (ab HAWR uns) a feeling of disgust or hatred *p. 475*

ablution (uh BLOO shun) a ceremonial washing or cleansing *p. 433*

abroad (uh BRAWD) (as used here) about; spread around *p. 86*

acrid (AK rid) sharp, bitter, or irritating to the smell or taste *p. 519*

adder (AD ur) a small, poisonous snake *p. 24*

adulteries (uh DUL tuh reez) impure; not genuine substances *p. 125*

Aegaean (ih JEE un) arm of the Mediterranean Sea, between Greece and Turkey *p. 342*

affected (uh FEK tid) artificial *p. 403*

affliction (uh FLIK shun) something that causes great pain or distress *p. 9*

alack (uh LAK) alas; oh my *p. 79*

alliance (uh LY uns) union or joining *p. 402*

allotment (uh LOT munt) something that is distributed *p. 513*

altimeter (al TIM uh tur) an instrument that determines how high something is, as an airplane *p. 476*

altruism (AL troo iz um) unselfish concern for the welfare of others *p. 493*

amorous (AM ur us) in love *p. 123*

amorously (AM ur us lee) as if in love *p. 96*

anemone (uh NEM uh nee) a flower of the buttercup family known for its bright medium-sized blooms; sometimes called "wind flower" *p. 231*

anguish (ANG gwish) distress *p. 408*

anna (AH nuh) a small copper coin of India *p. 429*

apothecary (uh POTH uh ker ee) a person who prepares and sells drugs and medicines *p. 16*

apparition (ap uh RISH un) phantom; spirit; ghost *pp. 84, 291*

apprenticed (uh PREN tist) receiving financial support and instruction in a trade in return for work *p. 299*

arboreal (ahr BAWR ee ul) wooded *p. 417*

army-worms (AHR mee WURMZ) the larvae of certain moths that travel in large groups, ruining crops and grass *p. 522*

ascertained (as ur TAYND) found out with certainty *p. 347*

aside (uh SYD) an actor's words heard by the audience but supposedly not heard by certain other actors *p. 148*

aspire (us SPYR) ascend; soar *p. 195*

assailed (uh SAYLD) had a forceful, unpleasant effect on *p. 507*

assay (uh SAY) *(archaic)* attempt *p. 117*

assert (uh SURT) to defend; uphold, maintain *p. 513*

attire (uh TYR) clothing *p. 75*

awry (uh RY) not straight; twisted or crooked *p. 500*

B

balm (BAHM) soothing ointment *p. 80*

bard (BAHRD) poet or singer who composes heroic or epic verse *p. 240*

baser (BAYS ur) of relatively little value *p. 117*

bebagged (bih BAGD) carrying many bags *p. 432*

becalmed (bih KAHMD) still; calm *p. 372*

beguile (bih GYL) to mislead; deceive *p. 77*

behindhand (bih HYND hand) slow; late *p. 429*

beholding (bee HOHL ding) seeing *p. 358*

Bengali (ben GAW lee) a native of Bengal, a province of India *p. 429*

beseech (bih SEECH) to ask earnestly *pp. 358, 364*

beset (bih SET) surround; bothered, troubled *pp. 96, 161*

betel juice (BEE tul joos) juice produced by chewing the betel nut *p. 451*

bilious (BIL yus) bad-tempered; cross; nasty *p. 374*

billows (BIL ohs) large waves of water *p. 363*

birch (BURCH) any of a family of small deciduous trees and shrubs characterized by their peeling bark *p. 231*

blanching (BLANCH ing) turning white *p. 82*

blood-boltered (BLUD BOHL turd) (as used here) with blood matting his hair *p. 84*

bootless (BOOT lis) futile *p. 108*

borne (BAWRN) carried *p. 376*

brandished (BRAN disht) waved or shook in a menacing or exultant way *p. 30*

briny (BRY nee) very salty *p. 364*

brood (BROOD) a group of a particular kind of people or an outward expression of sorrow; wail *p. 6*

bullocks (BUUL uks) young bulls; steers *p. 501*

buoyancy (BOI un see) the ability to float or rise in the air *p. 513*

C

Cabuliwallah (KAH buul ee wahl uh) a person from Cabul (also spelled Kabul) *p. 427*

caldron (KAWL drun) large open kettle or boiler *p. 83*

calico (KAL ih koh) a coarse and cheap cloth *p. 321*

capriciously (kuh PRISH us lee) impulsively *p. 348*

career (kuh RIR) speed *p. 63*

chalice (CHAL is) a cup; goblet *p. 78*

chaste (CHAYST) pure in thought and act; virtuous *p. 123*

Christendom (KRIS un dum) those parts of the world where most of the inhabitants practice the Christian faith *p. 26*

christened (KRIS und) gave a name to; named *p. 401*

circular (SUR kyuh lur) here, an advertisement or letter intended for mass distribution *p. 415*

circumscribed (SUR kum skrybd) limited; confined *p. 417*

clamorous (KLAM ur us) noisy; loud and confused *p. 441*

clarified (KLAR uh fyd) made free of impurities *p. 348*

coincidence (koh IN suh duns) two unrelated events accidentally occurring at the same time *p. 259*

comforter (KUM fur tur) a long, woolen scarf *p. 282*

commends (kuh MENDZ) puts in one's hands; entrusts *p. 78*

companionable (kum PAN yun uh bul) sociable *p. 441*

compassion (kum PASH un) sympathy *p. 102*

composure (kum POH zhur) control over one's feelings *p. 492*

concenter (kun SEN tur) to come together at a common center point *p. 372*

conclusion (kun KLOO zhun) judgment; guess based on available facts *p. 259*

confound (kun FOUND) confuse; bewilder *p. 80*

conjecture (kun JEK chur) guess; inference; supposition *p. 226*

consolation (kon suh LAY shun) comfort; relief *p. 507*

consumptive (kun SUMP tiv) afflicted with tuberculosis, a serious lung disease *p. 139*

contemptuous (kun TEMP choo us) feeling or expressing hate *p. 217*

contrived (kun TRYVD) managed *p. 427*

cowering (KOU ur ing) crouching fearfully, shrinking from *p. 187*

crimped (KRIMPT) pressed into narrow, regular folds *p. 372*

croaked (KROHKT) made a deep, harsh sound *p. 212*

crowns (KROUNZ) denominations of British money *p. 337*

D

dahs (DAHZ) large knives *p. 458*

damasked (DAM uskt) varied in appearance *p. 111*

darkling (DAHRK ling) in the dark *p. 343*

date (DAYT) ending *p. 95*

debouched (dih BOUCHT) emerged *p. 420*

deceive (dih SEEV) prove false *p. 63*

deliquesce (del ih KWES) melt away *p. 289*

demesne (dih MAYN) realm *p. 240*

demur (dih MUR) to hesitate; hesitation *p. 429*

desperate (DEHS puhr uht) showing recklessness caused by despair *p. 532*

despotic (des POT ik) tyrannical *p. 452*

desuetude (DES wih tood) disuse *p. 427*

diplomatic (dip luh MAT ik) concerning relationships between countries; also skillful in handling people's feelings *p. 273*

discomfited (dis KUM fit id) embarrassed *p. 431*

dismounted (dis MOUNT id) got off a horse *p. 23*

dispatch (dih SPACH) official message *p. 255*

dispersed (dih SPURST) caused to spread widely; evaporated *p. 212*

divine (duh VYN) mystical or heavenly state; priest or other clergyman *pp. 86, 358*

dogcart (DOG cahrt) small, open carriage *p. 405*

doom (DOOM) Judgment Day *p. 110*

doth (DUTH) *(archaic)* does *p. 64*

drafts (DRAFTS) drinks *p. 201*

Dravidian (druh VID ee un) a group of intermixed races in India *p. 454*

dreary (DRIR ee) gloomy; dismal *p. 487*

dun (DUN) dull, grayish brown *p. 111*

dusk (DUSK) to make shadowy *p. 353*

E

ecstatic (ek STAT ik) in a state of great joy *p. 491*

edelweiss (AYD ul vys) a small perennial herb with tiny white flowers that grows high in the Alps *p. 211*

eek (EEK) *(archaic)* also *p. 117*

elation (ee LAY shun) high spirits; joy *p. 532*

emanated (EM uh nayt id) came forth; was emitted *p. 418*

embassy (EM buh see) a country's official headquarters in another country *p. 258*

embowers (em BOU urz) shelters, encloses *p. 353*

emigrating (EM ih grayt ing) leaving one country to settle in another *p. 404*

endueth (en DOO ith) endoweth *p. 63*

enlighten (en LYT un) to give knowledge or information *p. 501*

ensuing (en SOO ing) taking place afterward or as a result *p. 188*

entrails (EN truhlz) internal parts of a body; intestines *p. 83*

entreat (en TREET) plead with to persuade; beg *p. 103*

ere (AIR) *(archaic)* before; sooner than *pp. 64, 74*

escritoire (ES krih twahr) writing desk or table *p. 413*

euphemism (YOO fuh miz um) a word or phrase substituted for another less expressive or direct but considered less offensive or distasteful *p. 431*

eventide (EE vun tyd) evening *p. 372*

eventually (ee VEN choo ul ee) in the end; finally *p. 530*

exact (ig ZAKT) demand *p. 64*

exasperating (ig ZAS puh rayt ing) very irritating or annoying *p. 517*

excessively (ik SES iv lee) too much *p. 395*

exeunt (EK see unt) they go offstage (a plural of exit) *p. 144*

exhilaration (ig zil uh RAY shun) a feeling of great happiness *p. 475*

F

fancies (FAN seez) ideas; notions; thoughts *p. 15*

fancy (FAN see) love; likings; imagination; whim *pp. 95, 337*

farthing (FAHR *th*ing) a small British coin *p. 330*

fatuous (FACH oo us) silly; foolish *p. 399*

fealty (FEE ul tee) *(archaic or poetic)* fidelity; loyalty *p. 240*

fettered (FET urd) chained; shackled *p. 433*

fiendish (FEEN dish) inhumanly wicked or cruel *p. 16*

florin (FLAWR in) any of certain gold or silver coins used in a number of European countries *p. 13*

folds (FOHLDZ) folded parts or layers *p. 342*

foliage (FOH lee ij) leaves of one or more plants *p. 188*

foolscap (FOOLZ kap) writing paper *p. 349*

forbidding (fur BID ing) shocking; terrible *p. 371*

foresworn (fawr SWAWRN) having sworn falsely *p. 417*

frenzy (FREN zee) wild excitement *p. 76*

frothy (FRAWTH ee) foamy *p. 365*

furled (FURLD) rolled up tightly *p. 342*

furze (FURZ) an evergreen shrub with dark-green spines and yellow flowers *p. 231*

G

gall (GAWL) bitterness *p. 95*

gang aft agley (GANG AFT uh GLEE) go often astray *p. 189*

garnet (GAHR nit) kind of red gem *p. 160*

gazes (GAYZ uhz) looks intently *p. 358*

gild (GILD) (as used here) cover with blood *p. 80*

girdle (GUR dul) a belt or sash for the waist *p. 342*

girdled (GUR duld) surrounded; encircled *p. 372*

go (GOH) walk *p. 111*

grating (GRAYT ing) grinding, rubbing against with a harsh, scraping sound *p. 341*

greet (GREET) welcome by speaking in a friendly way *p. 532*

gruel (GROOL) **on the hob** (HOB) a thin broth warming on a ledge at the back side of the fireplace *p. 290*

guardian (GAHRD ee un) a person who looks after the affairs of a minor *p. 398*

guile (GYL) slyness; cunning *p. 38*

guineas (GIN eez) denominations of British money *p. 337*

H

habitually (huh BICH oo uh lee) by habit; regularly; customarily *p. 374*

Hades (HAY deez) in Greek myths, the home of the dead, beneath the earth *p. 480*

haggard (HAG urd) looking exhausted, as from worry, sleeplessness, or illness *p. 523*

harness (HAHR nis) (as used here) armor *p. 87*

harper (HAHR pur) person who plays the harp *p. 38*

hasting (HAYST ing) *(archaic)* moving swiftly *p. 63*

hath (HATH) *(archaic)* have *p. 73*

hawthorn (HAW thawrn) any of a group of spiny shrubs or small trees of the rose family with glossy leaves, white or pink fragrant flowers, and small red fruits *p. 231*

heath (HEETH) area of open wasteland *p. 74*

heathen (HEE *th*un) a person who didn't worship the God of the Bible *p. 9*

hinterland (HIN tur land) an area far from cities and towns *p. 420*

hoppers (HOP urz) baby locusts *p. 521*

host (HOHST) great number *p. 237*

Humbug (HUM bug) Nonsense! *p. 282*

hurlyburly (HUR lee BUR lee) uproar; confusion; (as used here) the battle *p. 74*

hypocrisy (hih POK ruh see) pretending to be what one is not, or to feel what one does not feel *p. 154*

I

image (IHM ihj) likeness *p. 532*

impediments (im PED uh munts) hindrances; obstacles; (as used here) reasons why a marriage should not be allowed to take place *p. 110*

impending (im PEN ding) about to happen *p. 429*

imperative (im PER uh tiv) absolutely necessary; essential *p. 502*

imperialism (im PIR ee uhl iz um) the policy and practice of forming and maintaining an empire by controlling other countries or colonies *p. 451*

impression (im PRESH un) copy made by pressure on some sort of mold to show shape *p. 270*

impudence (IM pyuh duns) rudeness; disregard of others *p. 174*

inaction (in AK shun) the absence of action or motion; stillness *p. 513*

incense (IN sens) any of various substances that produce a pleasant odor when burned *p. 308*

incessantly (in SES unt lee) without stopping *p. 347*

inclinations (in cluh NAY shunz) preferences *p. 507*

inclined (in KLYND) to have a particular disposition; having a tendency *p. 199*

inconstancy (in KON stun see) unsteadiness in affection or loyalties *p. 123*

indispensable (in dis SPEN suh bul) essential; absolutely required *p. 493*

indomitable (in DOM ih tuh bul) not capable of being overcome *p. 478*

ineffable (in EF·uh bul) too awesome to be spoken of *p. 463*

infirmity (in FUR muh tee) weakness; disease *p. 83*

ingratiating (in GRAY shee ayt ing) charming; agreeable *p. 507*

inscrutable (in SKROOT uh bul) mysterious; enigmatic *p. 463*

intentional (in TEN shuh nul) on purpose *p. 389*

irrationally (ih RASH uh nul ee) not reasonable; senseless; absurd *p. 521*

irremediable (ir ih MEE dee uh bul) impossible to correct or remedy *p. 521*

irrevocably (ih REV uh kuh blee) in a way that cannot be changed *p. 475*

J

jocund (JOK und) joyous; jolly *p. 237*

jubilantly (JOO buh lunt lee) in a way that shows great joy *p. 491*

judicious (joo DISH us) wise and careful *p. 429*

K

keening (KEEN ing) wailing for the dead *p. 31*

ken (KEN) range of vision; view *p. 240*

kirtle (KUR tul) *(archaic)* skirt *p. 93*

knell (NEL) warning bell *p. 79*

L

labyrinth (LAB uh rinth) maze *p. 453*

languish (LANG gwish) to lose vigor; become weak *p. 123*

lavender (LAV un dur) plant of the mint family *p. 348*

lea (LEE) meadow *p. 38*

letterpress (LET er pres) print; printed words *p. 372*

levity (LEV ih tee) lightness of mind, conduct or speech; lack of seriousness *p. 179*

liege (LEEJ) a lord or sovereign *p. 27*

loam (LOHM) rich soil *p. 189*

loath (LOHTH) unwilling; reluctant *pp. 96, 187*

longevity (lon JEV uh tee) the greatest length of time a person can live *p. 502*

lot (LOT) fate *p. 63*

luminous (LOO muh nus) giving off light *p. 477*

lute (LOOT) an old-fashioned stringed instrument like a guitar *p. 313*

M

madrigals (MAD rih gulz) songs with parts for several voices *p. 93*

magazine (mag uh ZEEN) space in a rifle that holds cartridges *p. 457*

mahout (muh HOUT) an elephant driver or keeper *p. 452*

maize (MAYZ) corn *p. 518*

mead (MEED) meadow *p. 193*

meager (MEE gur) lacking in quantity *p. 487*

mealies (MEEL eez) ears of corn *p. 519*

melancholy (MEL un kol ee) sad and depressed, gloomy *p. 343*

meningitis (men in JYT is) inflammation of the membranes that cover the brain and spinal cord *p. 495*

metaled (MET uld) paved *p. 454*

meteors (MEET ee urz) shooting stars *p. 447*

Michaelmas (MIK ul mus) the feast of the archangel Michael, celebrated on September 29 *p. 224*

milestone (MYL stohn) a stone or other kind of marker set up to indicate the distance in miles to or from a certain place *p. 500*

minced (MINST) chopped finely *p. 348*

mire (MYR) an area of wet, soggy ground *p. 26*

mirth (MURTH) joyfulness; merriment *p. 35*

miscellany (MIS uh lay nee) a collection of writings on various subjects; separate writings collected in one volume *p. 232*

misshapen (mis SHAY pun) not correctly shaped *p. 215*

moon-blanched (MOON blancht) made to look white or pale, by the moon *p. 341*

moors (MOORZ) an area of open, rolling wasteland *p. 6*

moreen (muh REEN) a heavy wool or cotton fabric *p. 371*

muse (MYOOZ) think; ponder *p. 162*

musicale (myoo zih KAL) party featuring a musical program *p. 399*

musings (MYOO zingz) ponderings; meditations *p. 226*

must (MUST) the state of dangerous frenzy in an animal *p. 452*

myriads (MIR ee udz) very large numbers *p. 519*

N

nectar (NEK tur) in mythology, the life-giving drink of the gods *p. 163*

newt (NOOT) salamander; small lizard-like creature *p. 83*

O

oblivion (oh BLIHV ee uhn) state of being completely forgotten *p. 358*

obsessed (ub SEST) dominated; completely ruled in thought and feeling *p. 76*

offends (uh FENDZ) displeases *p. 389*

on's (AHNZ) of his *p. 86*

ow'st (OHST) ownest *p. 107*

oysters (OI sturz) a type of sea creature, which can be eaten, with a rough, hinged shell and which lives at the bottom of the sea *p. 364*

P

Panditji (PUN dit jee) a beloved wise man *p. 493*

parable (PAR uh bul) short story with a moral lesson *p. 101*

parapets (PAR uh pets) walls or railings on balcony, roof or bridge *p. 413*

paraphernalia (par uh fur NAYL yuh) one's personal belongings *p. 486*

parquet (pahr KAY) flooring of inlaid woodwork in geometric form *p. 413*

passé (pa SAY) old; stale *p. 418*

pedestal (PED us tul) base of a statue *p. 238*

pensive (PEN siv) deeply thoughtful *p. 237*

perambulator (puh RAM byuh lay tur) baby carriage *p. 420*

perpendicular (pur pun DIK yuh lur) straight up and down *p. 463*

petcock (PET kok) a small valve or faucet used in draining fluid or releasing air *p. 477*

petty (PET ee) small or slow *p. 87*

Philomel (FIL uh mel) the nightingale *p. 95*

pile wort (PYL wurt) a plant of the crowfoot family with a grainlike, underground stem; sometimes referred to as the lesser celandine *p. 231*

pillage (PIL ij) robbery by force *p. 13*

pilot (PY lut) (as used here) any guide or leader *p. 75*

pipkin (PIP kin) small earthenware pot *p. 347*

plowshare (PLOU shair) the cutting blade of a plow *pp. 189, 518*

polecat (POHL kat) a European animal somewhat like a weasel *p. 16*

posies (POH zeez) flowers *pp. 93, 95*

post (POHST) (archaic) travel quickly; hasten *p. 64*

poulterer's (POL tur urz) a British word for a store that sells chickens, turkeys, and geese *p. 328*

pounds (POUNDZ) a common type of money used in Great Britain *p. 302*

prattle (PRAT ul) speak in a childish manner *p. 427*

precipitately (prih SIP uh tut lee) suddenly, abruptly *p. 416*

precisely (prih SYS lee) definitely; exactly *p. 530*

press (PRES) a crowd; throng *p. 26*

prior (PRY ur) earlier *p. 406*

procure (proh KYUUR) obtain *p. 349*

prodigal (PROD ih gul) recklessly wasteful *p. 101*

promissory notes (PROM ih sawr ee NOHTS) written promises to pay someone a certain sum of money *p. 295*

prosaic (proh ZAY ik) matter-of-fact; dull *p. 413*

prostrate (PROS trayt) lying flat on the ground *p. 452*

prove (PROOV) (archaic) experience *pp. 93, 96*

prow (PROU) the forward part of a ship or boat; bow *p. 9*

pursue (pur SOO) to devote oneself to, as by studying *p. 490*

Q

quires (KWYRZ) a set of 24 sheets of paper *p. 349*

quiver (KWIV ur) to shake, tremble *p. 353*

quod (KWOHD) (archaic) said *p. 117*

quorum (KWAWR um) a select group *p. 463*

R

rabble (RAB ul) common people; the masses *p. 88*

Raj (RAHJ) rule; government authority *p. 452*

rapt (RAPT) giving complete attention, totally carried away by something; completely absorbed or engrossed *pp. 297, 463*

rave (RAYV) to rage, talk wildly *p. 447*

ravelled (RAV uld) frayed *p. 80*

reeks (REEKS) emanates; comes out *p. 111*

remorse (rih MAWRS) a feeling of guilt *p. 492*

reserved (rih ZURVD) quiet and formal in manner *p. 141*

retinue (RET un oo) group of servants of an important person *p. 85*

reverberating (rih VUR buh rayt ing) echoing *p. 520*

rioters (RY ut urz) people who lead a noisy, uncontrolled life *p. 13*

roosting (ROOST ing) sitting or resting on a perch *p. 513*

roundelay (ROUN duh lay) a short song in which a phrase or line is continually repeated *p. 35*

rue (ROO) sorrow; regret *p. 337*

S

sahib (SAH ib) formerly, a title used in colonial India when speaking of or to a European *p. 455*

sallowness (SAL oh nis) a sickly, pale-yellow complexion *p. 374*

samite (SAM ut) a heavy silk fabric sometimes containing gold and silver threads *p. 30*

sanctuary (SANGK choo er ee) a place where one can find safety *p. 478*

scan (SKAN) to look at closely *p. 529*

scepter (SEP tur) a decorated rod or staff held by rulers as a sign of authority *p. 81*

scoundrel (SKOUN drul) rascal *p. 405*

scrapes (SKRAYPS) predicaments *p. 398*

scrim (SKRIM) a light, semi-transparent curtain *p. 294*

scrutinized (SCROOT un yzd) examined very carefully *p. 509*

sear (SIR) to burn the surface of *p. 84*

Sea Wolves (SEE WUULVZ) pirates *p. 22*

secretary (SEK ruh ter ee) high government official in charge of a particular department *p. 253*

seething (SEE*TH* ing) very angry *p. 85*

semblance (SEM bluns) outward appearance *p. 63*

sensible (SEN suh bul) (as used here) able to be sensed; perceptible *p. 79*

serene (suh REEN) calm; (in this selection) clean air *p. 240*

serrated (SER ayt id) having notches like the teeth of a saw along the edge *p. 520*

shingles (SHING gulz) beaches covered with large, coarse, waterworn gravel *p. 343*

shirked (SHURKT) avoided or neglected a task or duty *p. 506*

shoal (SHOHL) piece of rising ground forming a shallow place in a river, sea, etc. *p. 78*

sickle (SIK ul) crescent-shaped tool for cutting grain *p. 110*

sleave (SLEEV) tangle of threads *p. 80*

sloe (SLOH) kind of small black fruit *p. 157*

smeared (SMIRD) soiled or blurred, as with grease or dirt *p. 529*

snarled (SNAHRLD) spoke in an angry, harsh way *p. 501*

solemnized (SOL um nyzd) honored or remembered *p. 281*

sophistry (SOF is tree) reasoning that seems sound but is actually false or misleading *p. 513*

spawned (SPAWND) born or produced *p. 6*

specters (SPEK turz) ghosts *p. 292*

spectral (SPEK trul) ghostly; like a phantom *p. 416*

spice (SPYS) to add zest or piquancy; to make interesting *p. 389*

sprightly (SPRYT lee) lively; joyful *p. 237*

squander (SKWAHN dur) to spend foolishly or wastefully *p. 103*

squire (SKWYR) country gentleman *p. 137*

squires (SKWYRZ) a knight's attendants *p. 22*

state (STAYT) dignity *p. 121*

stile (STYL) one or more steps used to climb over a fence *p. 13*

still (STIL) always *p. 63*

straits (STRAYTS) Strait of Dover, between England and France *p. 341*

strand (STRAND) beach; shore; land at the edge of a body of water *pp. 117, 341*

suitor (SOOT ur) man who courts a woman *p. 137*

sulkily (SULK ul ee) gloomily, resentfully *p. 363*

sullen (SUL un) full of resentment *p. 476*

sultry (SUL tree) hot and humid *p. 493*

surmise (sur MYZ) a thought or idea based on scanty evidence *p. 240*

swain (SWAYN) *(archaic)* boy; youth *p. 94*

swine (SWYN) pigs *p. 101*

T

tact (TAKT) wise kindness *p. 267*

tamper (TAM pur) to interfere with *p. 187*

tane (TAYN) taken *p. 36*

tarry (TAR ee) *(archaic)* wait *p. 69*

Tartar (TAHR tur) member of old eastern European tribe *p. 83*

thane (THAYN) rank of high noble in Scotland *p. 75*

torpid (TAWR pid) temporarily without motion *p. 372*

tottered (TOT urd) staggered; was unsteady, as if about to fall *p. 375*

tranquil (TRANG kwil) calm; serene; free from emotional disturbance or agitation *p. 341*

transgress (trans GRES) break *p. 103*

transpires (tran SPYRZ) breathes out *p. 122*

troth (TRAWTH) betrothal; engagement *p. 417*

trunkless (TRUNK lis) without the torso, or main part of the body *p. 238*

tumult (TOO mult) commotion; noisy activity *p. 226*

tumultuous (tuu MUL choo us) disorderly; noisy *p. 81*

turban (TUR bun) a headdress; a cap with a scarf wound round it *p. 428*

turbid (TUR bid) muddy, cloudy; dark, dense *p. 342*

U

unlineal (un LIN ee ul) (as used here) not in direct line of descent from the king *p. 81*

usurper (yoo SURP ur) a person who takes power by force or without right *p. 21*

V

vales (VAYLZ) small valleys *pp. 193, 237*

valet (VAL it) personal servant who takes care of a man's clothing *p. 255*

vellum (VEL um) a fine kind of parchment made from the skin of certain animals *p. 24*

verily (VER uh lee) truly; certainly *p. 232*

vermin (VUR mun) various small animals that cause harm or destruction *p. 16*

vigorously (VIG ur us lee) with great force *p. 500*

visage (VIZ ij) face *p. 238*

visibility (viz uh BIL uh tee) the distance over which it is possible to see things without the use of instruments *p. 479*

vital (VYT ul) of greatest importance *p. 409*

W

wanton (WAHN tun) luxurious; lavish *p. 95*

war-hosts (WAWR HOHSTS) armies *p. 21*

wary (WAIR ee) cautious, as from suspicion *p. 491*

weal (WEEL) a mark, line or ridge raised on the skin by a blow *p. 418*

wince (WINTS) to shrink or draw back, as in pain or distress *p. 505*

withal (*with* AWL) with it all *p. 80*

witness (WIT nis) (as used here) evidence; proof of guilt *p. 80*

witticism (WIT uh siz um) a witty remark *p. 429*

wrack (RAK) wreck; destroy *p. 87*

wrenched (RENCHT) pulled or jerked violently *p. 81*

Z

Zambesi escarpment (zam BEE zee ih SKAHRP munt) steep cliffs along the Zambesi River in southern Africa

INDEX OF TITLES AND AUTHORS

INDEX OF SKILLS

Index of Fine Art

ACKNOWLEDGMENTS

Unit 1: *Beowulf* translated by Burton Raffel. Copyright © 1963 by Burton Raffel. Published by New American Library. "The Last Battle," from *The Road to Camlann* by Rosemary Sutcliff, copyright © 1981 by Rosemary Sutcliff. Used by permission of Dutton Children's Books, a division of Penguin Putnam Inc. for US & P.I. David Higham Assoc for Canada & Open UK . "From The Book of St. Albans" from *English Hawking and Hunting in the Boke of St. Albans* by Rachel Hands. Copyright © 1975 Oxford University Press. **Unit 2:** "Sonnet 75" from *The Poetical Works of Edmund Spenser* by Edmund Spenser. First published in 1912 and reprinted in 1916, 1921, 1924, 1926, 1929, 1932, 1935, 1937, 1940, 1942, 1947, 1948, 1950, 1952, 1957, 1959 and 1960. "Counsel to Girls" from *Poems of Robert Herrick* by Robert Herrick. Copyright © 1967 by Winfield Townley Scott. "The Passionate Shepherd To His Love" from *Marlowe's Poems* by Christopher Marlowe. Edited by R.H. Case. Reed books. "The Parable of the Prodigal Son" from *The Bible.* **Unit 3:** From "She Stoops To Conquer" by Oliver Goldsmith. Copyright © 1958 by Barron's Educational Series, Inc. Reprinted by permission of Barron's Educational Series, Inc. **Unit 4:** "The Walrus and the Carpenter" from *The Annotated Alice* by Lewis Carroll. Copyright © 1960 by Martin Gardner. Used by permission of Woods End. **Unit 5:** "Shooting an Elephant" from *An Age Like This.* Edited by Sonia Orwell and Ian Angus. Copyright © 1968 by Sonia Brownell Orwell. Published by Harcourt Brace & Company. "The Naming of Cats" from *Old Possum's Book of Practical Cats* by T.S. Eliot. Copyright 1939 by T.S. Eliot. Copyright renewed 1967 by Esme Valerie Eliot. Published by Harcourt Brace & Company for US rights. Faber & Faber for world excluding US. "Do Not Go Gentle Into That Good Night" by Dylan Thomas, from *The Poems of Dylan Thomas,* copyright © 1952 by Dylan Thomas. Reprinted by permission of New Directions Publishing Corp. "The Demon Lover" from *Collected Stories by Elizabeth Bowen.* Copyright © 1946 and renewed 1974 by Elizabeth Bowen. Reprinted by permission of Alfred A. Knopf, a Division of Random House Inc. "The Importance of Being Earnest" by Oscar Wilde. Reprinted by permission from *The Big Book of Comedies,* edited by Sylvia E. Kamerman. Copyright © 1989, 1997 by Plays, Inc. This play is for reading purposes only; for permission to produce, write to Plays, Inc., 120 Boylston St., Boston, MA 02116 "The Cabuliwallah" from *The Hungry Stones and Other Stories* by Rabindranath Tagore. Used by permission of Visva-Bharati **Unit 6:** "Hawk Roosting" from *New Selected Poems* by Ted Hughes. Copyright © 1982 by Ted Hughes. Faber and Faber Limited. "Love After Love" from *Sea Grapes* by Derek Walcott. World rights excluding US from Jonathan Clowes. US rights Farrar, Strauss & Giroux. Excerpt from "West With the Night" from *West with the Night* by Beryl Markham. Copyright © 1942, 1983 by Beryl Markham. Reprinted by permission of North Point Press, a division of Farrar, Straus and Giroux, LLC. British rights from Laurence Pollinger. "A Mild Attack of Locusts" reprinted in the United States with permission of Simon & Schuster from *African Stories* by Doris Lessing. Jonathan Clowes rest of the world. Copyright © 1951, 1953, 1954, 1957, 1958, 1962, 1963, 1964, 1965, 1972, 1981 by Doris Lessing. "Like the Sun" and "The Old Man of the Temple" from *Under the Banyan Tree* by R.K. Narayan, copyright © 1985 by R.K. Narayan. Used by permission of Viking Penguin, a division of Penguin Putnam Inc. for US, Canada & Open. Wallace Literary Agency for rest of World. "from Anniversary" from *The Magic Apple Tree* by Elaine Feinstein. Copyright © Elaine Feinstein 1971. Published by Hutchinson & Co. LTD. "Coming" from *Philip Larkin Collected Poems* by Philip Larkin. Copyright 1988, 1989 by the

Estate of Philip Larkin. Published by Marvell Press. "This Is a Photograph of Me" *The Circle Game.* Copyright © 1966 by Margaret Atwood. Reprinted by permission of House of Anansi Press Limited. From *Face to Face,* Atlantic-Little, Brown (New York) 1957, Collins (London) 1958, copyright © Ved Mehta 1957.

ART CREDITS

Illustrations

Unit 1: p. 34: Copie; pp. 49, 50: Linda Draper; **Unit 2:** pp. 100, 102, 103: Ira M. Korman; **Unit 3:** pp. 136, 139, 142, 150, 155, 159, 162, 177, 181: James Watling; p. 166: Tovert Pasternak; pp. 186, 188: Robert Stone; pp. 210, 213, 217, 218: David Palladini; p. 239: Robert A. Parker; **Unit 4:** pp. 278, 285, 293, 301, 316: Donna Day; pp. 348, 349: Jeni Bassett; **Unit 5:** pp. 426, 430, 434: Sandra Speidel; **Unit 6:** p. 503: Jean and Hou-Sien Tseng; p. 508: Michael Garland.

Photographs

Unit 1: p. 4: Paul Almasy/Corbis; p. 17: The Bridgeman Art Library; p. 51: Art Resource; **Unit 2:** p. 65: The Granger Collection; pp. 72, 77, 82: Vandam, Billy Rose Theatre Collection/The New York Public Library, Astor, Lenox and Tilden Foundation; p. 89: The Granger Collection; p. 97: Corbis Bettmann; **Unit 3:** p. 198: Klaus Rose/Okapia/Photo Researchers Inc.; p. 219: The Granger Collection; p. 236: Vincent Dellaperuto/Globe Photos; p. 241: Topham/The Image Works; **Unit 4:** pp. 252, 257, 262, 269, 278, 285, 293, 301, 316, 325: The Museum of Modern Art/Film Stills Archive; p. 333: The Granger Collection; p. 357: KJ Historical/The Stock Market; p. 359: The Granger Collection; **Unit 5:** p. 388: Topham/The Image Works; p. 391: Corbis Bettmann; pp. 394, 397, 400, 404: Museum of Modern Art/Film Stills Archive; p. 421: The Granger Collection; p. 437: Archive Photos; pp. 440, 446: Photo Researchers, Inc.; p. 443: The Granger Collection; p. 453: Holton/Photo Researchers, Inc.; p. 459: Stone; p. 462: Lester Lefkowitz/The Stock Market; **Unit 6:** p. 474: Image Works; p. 481: The Granger Collection; pp. 487, 489, 494: W.W. Norton Inc.; p. 506: Stone; p. 512: Stan Osolinski/The Stock Market; p. 516: M. Hamblin/Animals Animals Earth Scenes; p. 517: MacDuff Everton/Image Bank; pp. 519, 522: Photo Researchers, Inc.; p. 525: Miriam Berkley; p. 530: The Museum of Modern Art/Film Stills Archive.